Programming Microsoft Dynamics™ NAV 2015

Sharpen your skills and increase your productivity when programming Microsoft Dynamics NAV 2015

David Studebaker

Christopher Studebaker

BIRMINGHAM - MUMBAI

Programming Microsoft Dynamics™ NAV 2015

First published: July 2015

Production reference: 1240715

Published by Packt Publishing Ltd.
Livery Place
35 Livery Street
Birmingham B3 2PB, UK.

ISBN 978-1-78439-420-2

www.packtpub.com

Credits

Authors
David Studebaker

Christopher Studebaker

Reviewers
Mark Brummel

Danilo Capuano

Stefano Demiliani

Commissioning Editor
Taron Pereira

Acquisition Editors
Purav Motiwalla

Sam Wood

Content Development Editor
Neeshma Ramakrishnan

Technical Editors
Utkarsha S. Kadam

Mohita Vyas

Copy Editors
Tani Kothari

Kausambhi Majumdar

Alpha Singh

Project Coordinator
Shweta H Birwatkar

Proofreader
Safis Editing

Indexer
Rekha Nair

Graphics
Abhinash Sahu

Production Coordinator
Melwyn Dsa

Cover Work
Melwyn Dsa

Foreword

Like many other enthusiasts in the NAV community, David ran a family business with his wife, Karen. Their son, Christopher, got his start in NAV by working in the family business. This is the kind of business that made NAV more successful than any other product in the ERP mid-market.

For many years, David has been a key influencer on the new versions of Dynamics NAV and has helped us evolve our developer Help. Based on this work, David wrote his first book on Dynamics NAV in 2007 about how to develop in "classic" NAV.

In 2009, he wrote his second book to help close the gap between the Classic client and the new world of the RoleTailored client and RDLC reporting. Overnight, the book proved to be extremely helpful to the greater community to cross the chasm from the "old" world to the "new" world.

Since then, David and his coauthor and, son Chris, also a NAV expert, have twice rewritten and extended these books to include new versions of Dynamics NAV. Reading the latest book reminds me of how far Dynamics NAV has evolved, both as a product since the first version came out in 1987 and as a thriving community with Karen and David as pioneers and later Chris as a key contributor to books like these.

Michael Nielsen

Director of Engineering,
Dynamics NAV at Microsoft

About the Authors

David Studebaker is the Chief Technical Officer and a cofounder of Liberty Grove Software with his partner, Karen Studebaker. David has had a wide range of development, consulting, sales and management roles throughout his career. He has been a partner or owner and manager of several software development businesses while always maintaining a significant role as a business application developer.

David started programming in 1962. He has been developing in C/AL since 1996. David has been an active participant in each step of computing technology from the first solid state mainframes to today's technology, from binary assembly language coding to today's C/AL. David's special achievements include his role as co-developer of the first production multiprogrammed SPOOLing system in 1967. He has worked on a diverse set of software applications including manufacturing, distribution, retail, engineering, and others.

David has a BS in mechanical engineering from Purdue University and an MBA from the University of Chicago. He has been writing for publications since he was an undergraduate and has had numerous magazine and reference books published. Prior to coauthoring this book, David was the author of *Programming Microsoft Dynamics NAV* (for the Classic Client), *Programming Microsoft Dynamics NAV 2009* (for the Role Tailored Client), and *Programming Microsoft Dynamics NAV 2013*. He has been a member of the Association for Computing Machinery since 1963 and was a founding officer of two local chapters of the ACM.

Acknowledgments

This book would not have been possible without my coauthor (and son), Christopher Studebaker. I'm very lucky to get to work with such a smart, knowledgeable son, who is also my good friend.

I especially want to thank my partner in life and at work, Karen Studebaker, for her unflagging support, patience, love, and encouragement in all ways. The first 50 years we have been together have been great; I'm looking forward to the next 50.

One of my life's principle treasures has been the enthusiastic support and love of my children, Christopher and Rebecca, of whom I am very proud. Both are successful, thoughtful, high quality professionals, and managers. More importantly, they each place the highest value to their roles as parents and spouses (here, I say "hi" to my special grandchildren, Cole, Alec, and CeCe, and my terrific in-law children, Elizabeth and Frederick).

Special thanks are due to Michael Nielsen of Microsoft for his wholehearted support of this and the previous three Programming NAV books. Many thanks to Mark Brummel, who knows more about NAV than almost anyone (except maybe Michael) and generously shares his knowledge. I also wish to thank all the people at Microsoft and Packt as well as our technical reviewers who assisted us a great deal with their contributions and advice.

Much of what I know about NAV was gained while working with excellent teams of associates at Studebaker Technology and Liberty Grove Software. All my life, I have benefitted from the help of many friends, mentors, and associates. Life would be very poor without all these kind and generous folks.

May you enjoy using this book even a fraction as much as I enjoyed working on it with Chris.

Christopher Studebaker is an NAV developer/implementer and has 15 years' experience in designing, developing, implementing, and selling in the NAV and SQL Server environments. He has specialized in retail, manufacturing, job shop, and distribution implementations, mostly in high user count and high data volume applications. Chris has worked on many NAV implementations with integrations to external databases and third-party add-on products. Some special applications include high-volume order entry, pick-to-light systems, procurement analysis, and web frontends.

Chris acts in a consulting and training role for customers and for peer NAV professionals. He provides training both in informal and classroom situations, often developing custom course material to support courses tailored to specific student group needs. Courses have included various NAV functional and development areas.

Before becoming a certified NAV developer, Chris was a certified environmental consultant working with manufacturing facilities to meet national and state regulations. His duties included regulatory reporting, data analysis, project management, and subcontractor oversight. His accomplishments include obtaining several safety certifications and managing projects for hazardous material management and abatement.

Chris is an expert at NAV installation, configuration, and development. He has been working with SQL in both NAV and other Microsoft applications for over a decade. He has a bachelor of science degree from Northern Illinois University and has done graduate work at Denmark Technical University. Chris was the coauthor of the Packt Publishing book *Programming Microsoft Dynamics 2013*.

First and foremost, I would like to thank my parents, David and Karen Studebaker, for giving me the opportunity to start in the NAV world and allowing me the room to grow on my own. Of course, I could not have participated in this book if it weren't for my wife, Beth. Having worked within the NAV community for the past decade, I have worked with many wonderful people, most notably, my parents (of course), Betty Cronin, Kathy Nohr, Tommy Madsen, Susanne Priess, David Podjasek, Joy Bensur , Diane Beck, Chris Pashby, and Anthony Fairclough. Without them, I would not have been the NAV professional I am today.

About the Reviewers

Mark Brummel is a freelance all-round Microsoft Dynamics NAV specialist focused on helping end users of the product.

His passion is evangelizing and documenting the "NAV way". This is a combination of architectural principles and design best practices formalized in a workshop called Master Class for Microsoft Dynamics NAV Application Architecture and Design Patterns. The methodology helps in creating solutions that are easy to upgrade, recognizable for users, and maintainable outside the ecosystem of their creators. All three elements apply to the original Navision product that shipped in 1995 and are extracted, updated, and documented in this methodology.

In 2015, his new book, *Learning Dynamics NAV Patterns*, will be published, which is a book about his methodology. He also organizes hands-on workshops together with a group of MVPs and MCTs all across the globe.

Before starting freelancing in 2006, he started in 1997 as an end user and worked 8 years for NAV partners after that. Designing and maintaining add-on systems was his specialization. Some of these add-on systems exceed the standard product when it comes to size and complexity. Coaching colleagues and troubleshooting complex problems are his passions and part of his day-to-day work.

Many end users of Microsoft Dynamics NAV struggle with questions about how to upgrade their two-tier solution to a three-tier solution. Mark can help you answer these questions and plot a roadmap to the future, retaining the investment in the solution.

When Microsoft introduced the three-tier architecture in 2009, it was meant to be a major shift for experienced NAV developers and consultants. Mark has trained most of them in the Netherlands and Belgium.

To be able to share knowledge in an efficient and global way, Mark wrote the book *Dynamics NAV 2009 Application Design* and *Dynamics NAV 2013 Application Design*, which is often referred to as the NAV Bible. Its content is applicable to newer and older versions of the product too.

In 2010, he started a think tank called Partner Ready Software together with four other Dynamics NAV experts. Partner Ready Software brings fresh ideas of designing applications in NAV and creates awareness about applying design patterns while creating repeatable solutions.

Mark is an associate in the Liberty Grove Software network, a member of the NAVUG advisory board, and a cofounder of the Dutch Dynamics Community.

A special project and performance tuning of the Dynamics NAV product on SQL Server. As a unique specialist, he has done groundbreaking research in improving the performance of Dynamics NAV on SQL Server.

On the site, `http://nav-skills.com/`, Mark maintains a blog. This blog contains a wide range of articles about both Microsoft Dynamics NAV and SQL Server products. He is also a frequent speaker at Microsoft events and publishes articles on Pulse for LinkedIn.

Since 2006, Mark has been rewarded by Microsoft with the Most Valuable Professional award for his contribution to online and offline communities. He has received the award 10 times.

Mark is a father of four, is married, and lives in a small town in the Netherlands.

Danilo Capuano is a senior software engineer with over 10 years of industry experience. He lives in Naples, Italy, where he earned a degree in computer science. He currently works as a consultant for Microsoft Dynamics NAV and Microsoft Dynamics CRM at a Microsoft Gold Partner company, where he also completed the MCTS certification.

He is already a reviewer of several books on Microsoft Dynamics NAV.

You can contact him on his home page at `http://www.capuanodanilo.com/`

You can also contact him via Twitter at `@capuanodanilo`.

Stefano Demiliani is a Microsoft Certified Solution Developer (MCSD), MCAD, MCTS on Microsoft Dynamics NAV, MCTS on Sharepoint, MCTS on SQL Server, and a long-time expert on other Microsoft-related technologies.

He has a master's degree in computer engineering from Politecnico of Turin.

He works as a senior project manager and solution developer for EID (http://www.eid.it/), a company of the Navlab group (http://www.navlab.it/), one of the biggest Microsoft Dynamics group in Italy (where he's also the Chief Technical Officer). His main activity is the architecture and development of enterprise solutions based on the entire stack of Microsoft technologies (Microsoft Dynamics NAV, Microsoft Sharepoint, and Azure and .NET applications in general), and he's often focused on engineering distributed service-based applications.

He works as a full-time NAV consultant (15+ years of international NAV projects), and he is available for architecture solutions based on Microsoft's ERP and for NAV database tuning and optimization (performance and locking management). He's the author of several different Microsoft Certified NAV add-ons.

He has written many articles and blogs on different Microsoft-related topics, and he's frequently involved in consulting and teaching. He has worked with Packt Publishing in the past for many Microsoft Dynamics NAV-related books.

You can get more details and keep in touch with him by reaching http://www.demiliani.com/ or via Twitter (@demiliani).

www.PacktPub.com

Support files, eBooks, discount offers, and more

For support files and downloads related to your book, please visit www.PacktPub.com.

Did you know that Packt offers eBook versions of every book published, with PDF and ePub files available? You can upgrade to the eBook version at www.PacktPub.com and as a print book customer, you are entitled to a discount on the eBook copy. Get in touch with us at service@packtpub.com for more details.

At www.PacktPub.com, you can also read a collection of free technical articles, sign up for a range of free newsletters and receive exclusive discounts and offers on Packt books and eBooks.

https://www2.packtpub.com/books/subscription/packtlib

Do you need instant solutions to your IT questions? PacktLib is Packt's online digital book library. Here, you can search, access, and read Packt's entire library of books.

Why subscribe?

- Fully searchable across every book published by Packt
- Copy and paste, print, and bookmark content
- On demand and accessible via a web browser

Free access for Packt account holders

If you have an account with Packt at www.PacktPub.com, you can use this to access PacktLib today and view 9 entirely free books. Simply use your login credentials for immediate access.

Instant updates on new Packt books

Get notified! Find out when new books are published by following @PacktEnterprise on Twitter or the *Packt Enterprise* Facebook page.

Table of Contents

Preface   **xiii**

Chapter 1: An Introduction to NAV 2015   **1**

  NAV 2015 – an ERP system   **2**

    Financial Management   4

    Manufacturing   4

    Supply Chain Management   5

    Business Intelligence and reporting   6

    Relationship Management   7

    Human Resource management   8

    Project Management   8

  Significant changes in NAV 2015   **8**

    Application changes   9

    Client enhancements   9

    Development tools   9

    Other areas   10

  A developer's overview of NAV 2015   **10**

    NAV object types   11

    The C/SIDE integrated development environment   11

    Object Designer tool icons   12

    The C/AL programming language   13

    NAV object and system elements   14

    NAV functional terminology   18

    User interface   19

  Hands-on development in NAV 2015   **21**

    The NAV 2015 development exercise scenario   21

    Getting started with application design   22

    Application tables   22

      Designing a simple table   23

      Creating a simple table   24

Pages   27
  Standard elements of pages   27
  List pages   28
  Card pages   28
  Document pages   29
  Journal/Worksheet pages   31
Creating a List page   31
Creating a Card page   35
Creating some sample data   40
Creating a List Report   41
Other NAV object types   49
  Codeunits   49
  Queries   50
  MenuSuites   50
  XMLports   50
Development backups and documentation   51
Summary   **52**
Review questions   **52**
Chapter 2: Tables   **57**
An overview of tables   **58**
Components of a table   59
Naming a table   60
Table numbering   61
Table properties   61
Table triggers   64
Keys   67
SumIndexFields   70
Field Groups   71
Enhancing our sample application   **75**
Creating and modifying tables   75
Assigning a Table Relation property   80
Assigning an InitValue property   83
Adding a few activity-tracking tables   84
New tables for our WDTU project   85
New list pages for our WDTU project   88
Keys, SumIndexFields, and table relations in our examples   88
  Secondary keys and SumIndexFields   88
  Table relations   90
Modifying a standard table   92
Version list documentation   93

Types of tables   **95**

  Fully Modifiable tables   95

    Master   96
    Journal   97
    Template   98
    Ledger   99
    Reference tables   101
    Register   103
    Posted Document   104
    Setup   106
    Temporary   107

  Content modifiable tables   108

    System   108

  Read-only tables   109

    Virtual   110

Summary   **111**

Review questions   **112**

Chapter 3: Data Types and Fields   **115**

Basic definitions   **116**

Fields   **116**

  Field properties   117
  Field triggers   124
  Data structure examples   125
  Field numbering   125
  Field and Variable naming   126

Data types   **127**

  Fundamental data types   127

    Numeric data   128
    String data   129
    Date/Time data   130

  Complex data types   131

    Data structure   132
    Objects   132
    Automation   132
    Input/Output   133
    DateFormula   133
    References and other data types   140

  Data type usage   141

FieldClass property options   **142**

  FieldClass – Normal   143
  FieldClass – FlowField   143
  FieldClass – FlowFilter   146
  FlowFields and a FlowFilter for our application   149

Filtering   **154**
     Experimenting with filters   155
     Accessing filter controls   162
       Development Environment filter access   162
       Role Tailored Client filter access   163
Summary   **165**
Review questions   **165**
Chapter 4: Pages – The Interactive Interface   **169**
     Page design and structure overview   **170**
       Page design guidelines   171
       The NAV 2015 page structure   172
     Types of pages   **175**
       Role Center page   175
       List page   177
       Card page   178
       Document page   178
         FastTab   179
       ListPlus page   180
       Worksheet (Journal) page   181
       ConfirmationDialog page   181
       StandardDialog page   182
       NavigatePage   182
         Navigate page 344   183
       Special pages   183
         Request page   184
         Departments page   184
       Page parts   185
         FactBox Area   186
       Charts   187
         Chart part   187
       Page names   188
     Page Designer   **189**
       New Page Wizard   190
     Page components   **194**
       Page Triggers   195
       Page properties   196
       Page Preview tool   199
       Inheritance   201
     WDTU Page Enhancement – part 1   **202**
     Page controls   **206**
       Control types   209
         Container controls   209

Group controls	209
Field controls	213
Page Part controls	**216**
Page control triggers	218
Bound and Unbound Pages	**219**
WDTU Page Enhancement – part 2	**219**
Page Actions	**222**
Page Action Types and Subtypes	224
Action Groups	225
Action properties	225
Navigation Pane Button actions	228
Actions Summary	229
Learning more	**230**
UX (User Experience) Guidelines	230
Creative plagiarism and patterns	230
Experimenting on our own	231
Experimentation	231
Summary	**234**
Review questions	**234**
Chapter 5: Queries and Reports	**237**
Queries	**238**
Building a simple Query object	239
Query and Query component properties	244
Query properties	244
The DataItem properties	245
Column properties	246
Reports	**247**
What is a report?	248
Four NAV report designers	249
NAV report types	252
Report types summarized	256
Report naming	256
Report components – overview	**257**
Report structure	257
Report data overview	258
Report Layout overview	259
Report data flow	**260**
Report components – detail	**263**
C/SIDE Report properties	263
SQL Server Report Builder – Report properties	265
Report triggers	267
Request Page Properties	268

Request page triggers 268
DataItem properties 269
DataItem triggers 271
Creating a Report in NAV 2015 **272**
Learn by experimentation 272
Report building – phase 1 273
Report building – phase 2 276
Report building – phase 3 280
Modifying an existing report with Report Designer or Word 285
Runtime rendering 290
Inheritance 290
Interactive report capabilities 290
Interactive sorting 291
Interactive visible/not visible 292
Request page 293
Add a Request Page option 294
Processing-Only reports 297
Creative report plagiarism and patterns 297
Summary **298**
Review questions **298**
Chapter 6: Introduction to C/SIDE and C/AL **301**
Understanding C/SIDE **302**
Object Designer 302
Starting a new object 304
Query Designer 306
XMLport Designer 307
MenuSuite Designer 308
Object Designer Navigation 311
Importing objects 314
Text objects 318
Some useful practices 318
Some C/AL naming conventions 320
Variables 322
C/SIDE programming 327
Non-modifiable functions 328
Modifiable functions 328
Custom functions 330
C/AL syntax **337**
Assignment and punctuation 337
Expressions 338
Operators 339
Frequently used C/AL functions 344
The MESSAGE function 344
The ERROR function 345

The CONFIRM function	347
The STRMENU function	348
Record functions	349
FIND functions	352
Conditional statements	**356**
The BEGIN–END compound statement	356
The IF–THEN–ELSE statement	356
Indenting code	**357**
Some simple coding modifications	**358**
Adding field validation to a table	**358**
Adding code to a report	**363**
Lay out the new Report Heading	**364**
Save and test	**365**
Lookup Related table data	**365**
Layout the new report body	**366**
Save and test	368
Handling User-entered report options	368
Defining the Request Page	370
Finishing the processing code	**371**
Test the completed report	**372**
Output to Excel	**372**
Summary	**373**
Review questions	**374**
Chapter 7: Intermediate C/AL	**377**
C/AL Symbol Menu	**378**
Internal documentation	**380**
Validation functions	**384**
TESTFIELD	384
FIELDERROR	385
INIT	386
VALIDATE	387
Date and Time functions	**387**
TODAY, TIME, and CURRENTDATETIME functions	388
WORKDATE function	388
DATE2DMY function	389
DATE2DWY function	390
DMY2DATE and DWY2DATE functions	390
CALCDATE function	391
Data conversion and formatting functions	**392**
ROUND	392
FORMAT function	393
EVALUATE function	394

FlowField and SumIndexField functions	**395**
CALCFIELDS function	396
SETAUTOCALCFIELDS function	397
CALCSUMS function	398
CALCFIELDS and CALCSUMS comparison	398
Flow control	**399**
REPEAT-UNTIL	399
WHILE-DO	400
FOR-TO or FOR-DOWNTO	400
CASE-ELSE statement	401
WITH-DO statement	403
QUIT, BREAK, EXIT, and SKIP functions	404
QUIT function	404
BREAK function	404
EXIT function	405
SKIP function	405
Input and Output functions	**405**
NEXT function with FIND or FINDSET	406
INSERT function	406
MODIFY function	407
Rec and xRec	408
DELETE function	408
MODIFYALL function	408
DELETEALL function	409
Filtering	**409**
SETFILTER function	410
COPYFILTER and COPYFILTERS functions	411
GETFILTER and GETFILTERS functions	411
FILTERGROUP function	412
MARK function	413
CLEARMARKS function	413
MARKEDONLY function	413
RESET function	414
InterObject communication	**414**
Communication via data	414
Communication through function parameters	414
Communication via object calls	415
Enhancing the WDTU application	**416**
Modifying Table Fields	417
Add Validation logic	420
Creating the Playlist Subform page	423

Creating a function for our Factbox	431
Creating a Factbox page	435
Summary	**439**
Review questions	**440**
Chapter 8: Advanced NAV Development Tools	**443**
NAV process flow	**444**
Initial setup and data preparation	446
Transaction entry	446
Testing and posting the Journal batch	447
Utilizing and maintaining the data	447
Data maintenance	448
Role Center pages	**448**
The Role Center structure	449
The Role Center activities page	453
Cue Groups and Cues	454
Cue source table	455
Cue Group Actions	458
System Part	459
Page Parts	460
Page Parts not visible	460
Page Part Charts	461
Page Parts for user data	463
The Navigation Pane and Action menus	463
Action Designer	465
Create a WDTU Role Center Ribbon	468
The Navigation Pane	476
XMLports	**479**
XMLport components	480
XMLport properties	481
XMLport triggers	485
XMLport data lines	485
XMLport line properties	486
The Element or Attribute	490
XMLport line triggers	491
XMLport Request Page	493
Web services	**493**
Exposing a web service	495
Publishing a web service	496
Enabling web services	497
Determining what was published	497
XMLport – a web services integration example for WDTU	500
Summary	**507**
Review questions	**507**

Chapter 9: Successful Conclusions   **511**

Creating new C/AL routines   **512**
Callable functions   513
  Codeunit 358 – Date FilterCalc   513
  Codeunit 359 – Period Form Management   515
  Codeunit 365 – Format Address   516
  Codeunit 396 – NoSeriesManagement   518
  Function models to review and use   519
Management codeunits   520

Multi-language system   **521**
Multi-currency system   **522**
Navigate   **523**
Debugging in NAV 2015   **526**
Text Exports of Objects   527
Dialog function debugging techniques   529
  Debugging with MESSAGE and CONFIRM   529
  Debugging with DIALOG   530
  Debugging with text output   530
  Debugging with ERROR   531
The NAV 2015 Debugger   531
  Activating the Debugger   533
  Attaching the Debugger to a Session   534
  Creating Break Events   535
  The Debugger window   537
  Changing code while debugging   539

C/SIDE Test-driven development   **539**
Other Interfaces   **542**
Automation Controller   543
Linked Data Sources   544

NAV Application Server (NAS)   **544**
Client Add-ins   **544**
Client Add-in construction   545
WDTU Client Add-in   546
Client Add-in comments   561

Customizing Help   **562**
NAV development projects – general guidance   **563**
Knowledge is the key   563
Data-focused design   563
  Defining the needed data views   564
  Designing the data tables   564
  Designing the user data access interface   565
  Designing the data validation   565
  Data design review and revision   565

Designing the posting processes   566
Designing the supporting processes   566
Double-check everything   566
Design for efficiency   **567**
Disk I/O   567
Locking   568
Updating and upgrading   **569**
Design for updating   569
Customization project recommendations   570
Testing   571
Deliverables   575
Finishing the project   576
Plan for upgrading   576
Benefits of upgrading   577
Coding considerations   577
Good documentation   578
Low-impact coding   578
Supporting material   **579**
Summary   **580**
Review questions   **580**
Appendix: Review Answers   **583**
Index   **593**

Preface

Welcome to the worldwide community of Microsoft Dynamics NAV developers. This is a collegial environment populated by C/AL developers who readily and generously share their knowledge. There are formal and informal organizations of NAV-focused users, developers, and vendor firms scattered around the globe and active on the Web. Our community continues to grow and prosper, now including over 110,000 user companies worldwide.

The information in this book will help you to shorten your learning curve of how to program for the NAV 2015 ERP system using the C/AL language, the C/SIDE integrated development environment and their capabilities. We hope you enjoy working with NAV as much as we have.

A brief history of NAV

Each new version of Microsoft Dynamics NAV is the result of inspiration and hard work along with some good fortune and expert technical investment over the last thirty years.

The beginning

Three college friends, Jesper Balser, Torben Wind, and Peter Bang, from Denmark Technical University (DTU) founded their computer software business in 1984 when they were in their early twenties. This business was Personal Computing & Consulting (PC & C) and its first product was called PC Plus.

Single user PC Plus

PC Plus was released in 1985 with the primary goal of ease of use. An early employee said its functional design was inspired by the combination of a manual ledger journal, an Epson FX 80 printer, and a Canon calculator. Incidentally, Peter Bang is the grandson of one of the founders of Bang & Olufsen, the manufacturer of home entertainment systems par excellence.

PC Plus was a PC DOS-based single user system. PC Plus' design features included these:

- An interface resembling the use of documents and calculators
- Online help
- Good exception handling
- Minimal computer resources required

The PC Plus product was marketed through dealers in Denmark and Norway.

The multi-user Navigator

In 1987, PC & C released a new product, the multi-user Navigator and a new corporate name, Navision. Navigator was quite a technological leap forward. It included the following:

- Client/Server technology
- A relational database
- Transaction-based processing
- Version management
- High-speed OLAP capabilities (SIFT technology)
- A screen painter tool
- A programmable report writer

In 1990, Navision was expanding its marketing and dealer recruitment efforts in Germany, Spain, and the United Kingdom. Also in 1990, V3 of Navigator was released. Navigator V3 was still a character-based system, albeit a very sophisticated one. If you get an opportunity to study Navigator V3.x, you would instantly recognize the roots of today's NAV product. By V3, the product included these features:

- A design based on object-oriented concepts
- Integrated 4GL Table, Form, and Report Design tools (the IDE)
- Structured exception handling

- Built-in resource management
- The original programming language that became C/AL
- Function libraries
- The concept of regional or country-based localization

When Navigator V3.5 was released, it also included support for multiple platforms and databases. Navigator V3.5 would run on both Unix and Windows NT networks. It supported the Oracle and Informix databases, as well as the one developed in-house.

Around this time, several major strategic efforts were initiated. On the technical side, the decision was made to develop a GUI-based product. The first prototype of Navision Financials (for Windows) was shown in 1992. At about the same time, a relationship was established that would take Navision into distribution in the United States. The initial release in the US in 1995 was V3.5 of the character-based product, rechristened as Avista for the US distribution.

Navision Financials for Windows

In 1995, Navision Financials V1.0 for Microsoft Windows was released. This product had many (but not all) of the features of Navigator V3.5. It was designed for complete look-and-feel compatibility with Windows 95. There was an effort to provide the ease of use and flexibility of development of Microsoft Access. The new Navision Financials was very compatible with Microsoft Office and was thus sold as "being familiar to any Office user". Like any V1.0 product, it was quickly followed by a much improved V1.1.

In the next few years, Navision continued to be improved and enhanced. Major new functionalities were added, such as:

- Contact Relation Management (CRM)
- Manufacturing (ERP)
- Advanced Distribution (including Warehouse Management)

Various Microsoft certifications were obtained, providing muscle to the marketing efforts. Geographic and dealer base expansion continued apace. By 2000, according to the Navision Annual Report of that year, the product was represented by nearly 1,000 dealers (Navision Solution Centers) in 24 countries and used by 41,000 customers located in 108 countries.

Growth and mergers

In 2000, Navision Software A/S and its primary Danish competitor, Damgaard A/S, merged. Product development and new releases continued for the primary products of both original firms (Navision and Axapta). In 2002, the now much larger Navision Software, with all its products (Navision, Axapta, and the smaller, older C5, and XAL) was purchased by Microsoft, becoming part of the Microsoft Business Systems division along with the previously purchased Great Plains Software business and its several product lines. All the Navision and Great Plains products received a common rebranding as the Dynamics product line. Navision was renamed Dynamics NAV.

Continuous enhancement

As early as 2003, research began with the Dynamics NAV development team planning moves to further enhance NAV and take advantage of various parts of the Microsoft product line. Goals were defined to increase integration with products such as Microsoft Office and Microsoft Outlook. Goals were also set to leverage the functional capabilities of Visual Studio and SQL Server, among others. All the while, there was a determination not to lose the strength and flexibility of the base product.

NAV 2009 was released in late 2008, NAV 2013 in late 2012, followed by NAV 2015 in late 2014. The biggest hurdles to the new technologies have been cleared. A new user interface, the Role Tailored Client, was created as part of this renewal. NAV was tightly integrated with Microsoft's SQL Server and other Microsoft products such as Office, Outlook, and SharePoint. Development is more integrated with Visual Studio and more .NET compliant. The product is becoming more open and, at the same time, more sophisticated supporting features such as Web Services access, Web and tablet clients, the integration of third-party controls, RDLC, and Word-based reporting, and so on.

Microsoft continues to invest in, enhance, and advance NAV. More new capabilities and features are yet to come, continuing to build on the successes of the past. We will all benefit.

C/AL's Roots

One of the first questions asked by people new to C/AL is often "what other programming language is it like?" The best response is "Pascal". If the questioner is not familiar with Pascal, the next best response would be "C" or "C#".

At the time the three founders of Navision were attending classes at Denmark Technical University (DTU), Pascal was in wide use as a preferred language not only in computer courses, but also in other courses where computers were tools and software had to be written for data analyses. Some of the strengths of Pascal as a tool in an educational environment also served to make it a good model for Navision's business applications development.

Perhaps coincidentally (perhaps not) at DTU in this same time period, a Pascal compiler called Blue Label Pascal was developed by Anders Hejlsberg. That compiler became the basis for what was Borland's Turbo Pascal, which was the "everyman's compiler" of the 1980s because of its low price. Anders went with his Pascal compiler to Borland. While he was there, Turbo Pascal morphed into the Delphi language and the IDE tool set under his guidance.

Anders later left Borland and joined Microsoft, where he led the C# design team. Much of the NAV-related development at Microsoft is now being done in C#. So the Pascal-C/AL-DTU connection has come full circle, only now it appears to be C#-C/AL. Keeping it in the family, Anders' brother, Thomas Hejlsberg also works at Microsoft on NAV as a Software Architect. Each in their own way, Anders and Thomas continue to make significant contributions to Dynamics NAV.

In a discussion about C/AL and C/SIDE, Michael Nielsen of Navision and Microsoft, who developed the original C/AL compiler, runtime, and IDE, said that the design criteria were to provide an environment that could be used without the following:

- Dealing with memory and other resource handling
- Thinking about exception handling and state
- Thinking about database transactions and rollbacks
- Knowing about set operations (SQL)
- Knowing about OLAP (SIFT)

Paraphrasing some of Michael's additional comments, the goals of the language and IDE design were to do the following:

- Allow the developer to focus on design, not coding, but still allow flexibility
- Provide a syntax based on Pascal, stripped of complexities, especially relating to memory management
- Provide a limited set of predefined object types, reduce the complexity and learning curve

- Implement database versioning for a consistent and reliable view of the database
- Make the developer and end user more at home by borrowing a large number of concepts from Office, Windows, Access, and other Microsoft products

Michael is still working as part of the Microsoft team in Denmark on new capabilities for NAV. This is another example of how, once part of the NAV community, most of us want to stay part of this community.

What you should know

To get the maximum out of this book as a developer, you should have the following attributes:

- Be an experienced developer
- Know more than one programming language
- Have IDE experience
- Be knowledgeable about business applications
- Be good at self-directed study

If you have these attributes, this book will help you become productive with C/AL and NAV much more rapidly.

Even though this book is targeted first at developers, it is also designed to be useful to executives, consultants, managers, business owners, and others who want to learn about the development technology and operational capabilities of Dynamics NAV. If you fit into one of these or similar categories, start by studying *Chapter 1, An Introduction to NAV 2015*, for a good overview of NAV and its tools. Then you should review sections of other chapters as the topics apply to your specific areas of interest.

This book's illustrations are from the W1 Cronus database Dynamics NAV V2015.

What this book covers

Chapter 1, An Introduction to NAV 2015, starts with an overview of NAV as a business application system. This is followed by an introduction to the seven types of NAV objects, and the basics of C/AL and C/SIDE. Then we will do some hands-on work and define Tables, multiple Page types, and a Report. We'll close with a brief discussion of how backups and documentation are handled in C/SIDE.

Chapter 2, *Tables*, focuses on the foundation level of NAV data structure: Tables and their structures. We will cover Properties, Triggers (where C/AL resides), Field Groups, Table Relations, and SumIndexFields. We'll work our way through the hands-on creation of several tables in support of our example application. We will also review the types of tables found in the NAV applications.

Chapter 3, *Data Types and Fields*, we will learn about fields, the basic building blocks of the NAV data structure. We review the different Data Types in NAV. We will cover all the field properties and triggers in detail. We'll also review the three different Field Classes. We'll conclude with a discussion about the concept of filtering and how it should be considered in the database structure design.

Chapter 4, *Pages – The Interactive Interface*, we will review the different types of pages, their structures (Triggers, Properties) and general usage. We'll build several pages for our example application using Page Wizard and Page Designer. We will also study the different types of controls that can be used in the pages. In addition, we'll review how and where actions are added to the pages.

Chapter 5, *Queries and Reports*, we will learn about both Queries and Reports, two methods of extracting data for presentation to users. For Queries, we will study how they are constructed and some of the ways they are utilized. For Reports, we will walk through report data flow and the variety of different report types. We will study the two Report Designers, the C/SIDE Report Designer and the Visual Studio Report Designer and how a NAV report is constructed using both of these. We'll learn what aspects of reports use one designer and what aspects use the other. As in the previous studied objects, we will discuss Properties and Triggers. We will review how reports can be made interactive and will do some hands-on report creation.

Chapter 6, *Introduction to C/SIDE and C/AL*, we will learn about general Object Designer Navigation as well as the individual Designers (Table, Page, Report). We'll study C/AL code construction, syntax, variable types, expressions, operators, and functions. We will then take a closer look at some of the more frequently used built-in functions. The chapter will wrap up with an exercise on adding some C/AL code to a report objects created in an earlier exercise.

Chapter 7, *Intermediate C/AL*, we will dig deeper into C/AL development tools and techniques. We will review some more advanced built-in functions including those relating to dates and decimal calculations, both critical business application tools. We'll study the C/AL functions that support process flow control functions, input/output, and filtering. Then we'll do a review of methods of communication between objects. Finally, we'll apply some of what we've learned to enhance our example application.

Chapter 8, Advanced NAV Development Tools, we will review some of the more important elements of the Role Tailored User Experience, in particular the Role Center Page construction. We will dig into the components of a Role Center Page and how to build one. We'll also cover XMLports and Web Services, two of the powerful ways of connecting NAV applications to the world outside of NAV. To better understand these, we will not only review their individual component parts, but also go through the hands-on effort of building an example of each one.

Chapter 9, Successful Conclusions, we will study in detail how NAV functions are constructed and learn how to construct your own functions. We will learn more about tools and features built into C/AL and C/SIDE. We will study the new debugger, review the support for Test-Driven Development, and take a look at the ability to integrate .NET Client Add-ins. We will integrate a .NET Add-in into our example applications. Finally, we will review tips to design efficiently, update and upgrade the system with the goal of helping us to become more productive and high quality NAV developers.

Appendix, Review Answers, provides you with the answers to the questions given in each chapter.

What you need for this book

You will need some basic tools including at least the following:

- A license and database that you can use for development experimentation. The ideal license is a full Developer's license. If your license only contains the Page, Report, and Table Designer capabilities, you will still be able to do many of the exercises, but you will not have access to the inner workings of Pages and Tables and the C/AL code contained therein.

- A copy of the NAV Cronus demo/test database for your development testing and study. It would be ideal if you also had a copy of a production database at hand for examination as well. This book's illustrations are from the W1 Cronus database for V2015.

Access to other NAV manuals, training materials, websites, and experienced associates will obviously be of benefit, but they are not required for the time with this book to be a good investment.

Who this book is for

This book is for:

- The business applications software designer/developer who:
  - Wants to become productive in NAV C/SIDE—C/AL development as quickly as possible
  - Understands business applications and the type of software required to support these applications
  - Has significant programming experience
  - Has access to a copy of NAV 2015 including at least the Designer granules and a standard Cronus demo database
  - Is willing to do the exercises to get hands-on experience

- The Reseller manager or executive who wants a concise, in depth view of NAV's development environment and toolset
- The technically knowledgeable manager or executive of a firm using NAV that is about to embark on a significant NAV enhancement project
- The technically knowledgeable manager or executive of a firm considering the purchase of NAV as a highly customizable business applications platform
- The experienced business analyst or consultant or advanced student of applications software development who wants to learn more about NAV because it is one of the most widely used flexible business application systems available

The reader of this book:

- Does not need to be an expert in object-oriented programming
- Does not need previous experience with NAV, C/AL or C/SIDE

Conventions

In this book, you will find a number of styles of text that distinguish between different kinds of information. Here are some examples of these styles, and an explanation of their meaning.

Code words in text, database table names, folder names, filenames, file extensions, pathnames, dummy URLs, user input, and Twitter handles are shown as follows: "We can include other contexts through the use of the `include` directive."

A block of code is set as follows:

```
CalculateNewDate;
"Date Result" := CALCDATE("Date Formula to Test","Reference Date
for Calculation");
```

New terms and **important words** are shown in bold. Words that you see on the screen, in menus or dialog boxes for example, appear in the text like this: "In the **Description** column, we will put notes for the fields that need properties set later."

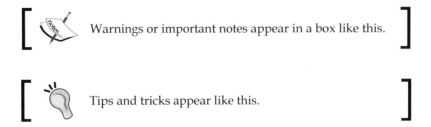

Warnings or important notes appear in a box like this.

Tips and tricks appear like this.

Reader feedback

Feedback from our readers is always welcome. Let us know what you think about this book—what you liked or disliked. Reader feedback is important for us as it helps us develop titles that you will really get the most out of.

To send us general feedback, simply e-mail feedback@packtpub.com, and mention the book's title in the subject of your message.

If there is a topic that you have expertise in and you are interested in either writing or contributing to a book, see our author guide at www.packtpub.com/authors.

Customer support

Now that you are the proud owner of a Packt book, we have a number of things to help you to get the most from your purchase.

Downloading the example code

You can download the example code files from your account at http://www. packtpub.com for all the Packt Publishing books you have purchased. If you purchased this book elsewhere, you can visit http://www.packtpub.com/support and register to have the files e-mailed directly to you.

Errata

Although we have taken every care to ensure the accuracy of our content, mistakes do happen. If you find a mistake in one of our books—maybe a mistake in the text or the code—we would be grateful if you could report this to us. By doing so, you can save other readers from frustration and help us improve subsequent versions of this book. If you find any errata, please report them by visiting `http://www.packtpub.com/submit-errata`, selecting your book, clicking on the **Errata Submission Form** link, and entering the details of your errata. Once your errata are verified, your submission will be accepted and the errata will be uploaded to our website or added to any list of existing errata under the Errata section of that title.

To view the previously submitted errata, go to `https://www.packtpub.com/books/content/support` and enter the name of the book in the search field. The required information will appear under the **Errata** section.

Piracy

Piracy of copyrighted material on the Internet is an ongoing problem across all media. At Packt, we take the protection of our copyright and licenses very seriously. If you come across any illegal copies of our works in any form on the Internet, please provide us with the location address or website name immediately so that we can pursue a remedy.

Please contact us at `copyright@packtpub.com` with a link to the suspected pirated material.

We appreciate your help in protecting our authors and our ability to bring you valuable content.

Questions

If you have a problem with any aspect of this book, you can contact us at `questions@packtpub.com`, and we will do our best to address the problem.

An Introduction to NAV 2015

1

"All truths are easy to understand once they are discovered; the point is to discover them."

– Galileo Galilei

"Everything really interesting that happens in software projects eventually comes down to people."

– James Bach

Microsoft Dynamics NAV has one of the largest installed user bases of any **enterprise resource planning (ERP)** system serving over 100,000 companies and one million plus individual users. The community of supporting organizations, consultants, implementers, and developers continues to grow and prosper. The capabilities of the off-the-shelf product increase with every release. The selection of the add-on products and services expands both in variety and depth.

The release of Microsoft Dynamics NAV 2015 continues its 20 plus year history of continuous product improvement. It provides more user options for access and output formatting. For new installations, NAV 2015 includes tools for rapid implementation. For all installations, it provides enhanced business functionality and more support for ERP computing in the cloud, including integration with Office 365. In addition, a new approach to upgrading that comes with NAV 2015 promises to lower the cost of ownership in the future.

Our goal in this chapter is to gain a *big picture* understanding of NAV 2015. You will be able to envision how NAV can be used by the managers (or owners) of an organization to help manage activities and the resources, whether the organization is for-profit or not-for-profit. You will also be introduced to the technical side of NAV from a developer's point of view.

In this chapter, we will take a look at NAV 2015, including the following:

- A general overview of NAV 2015
- A technical overview of NAV 2015
- A hands-on introduction to **Client/Server Integrated Development Environment (C/SIDE)** development in NAV 2015

NAV 2015 – an ERP system

NAV 2015 is an integrated set of business applications designed to service a wide variety of business operations. Microsoft Dynamics NAV 2015 is an ERP system. An ERP system integrates internal and external data across a variety of functional areas, including manufacturing, accounting, supply chain management, customer relationships, service operations, human resources management, as well as the management of other valued resources and activities. By having many related applications well integrated, a full featured ERP system provides an *enter data once, use many ways* information processing toolset.

NAV 2015 ERP addresses many functional areas. Some of them are listed as follows:

- Basic accounting functions (for example, general ledger, accounts payable, accounts receivable)
- Order processing and inventory (for example, sales orders, purchase orders, shipping, inventory, receiving)
- Relationship management (for example, vendors, customers, prospects, employees, contractors)
- Planning (for example MRP, sales forecasting, production forecasting)
- Other critical business areas (for example, manufacturing, warehouse management, marketing, cash management, fixed assets)

A good ERP system such as NAV 2015 is modular in design, which simplifies implementation, upgrading, modification, integration with third-party products, and expansion for different types of clients. All the modules in the system share a common database and, where appropriate, common data.

The groupings of individual NAV 2015 functions based on the department's menu structure is shown in the following figure. It is supplemented by information from Microsoft marketing materials and some of the groupings are a bit arbitrary. The important thing is to understand the overall components that make up the NAV 2015 ERP system.

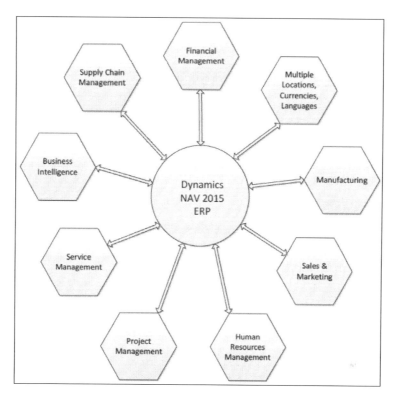

NAV 2015 has two quite different styles of **user interface** (**UI**). One UI, the Development Environment, targets developers. The other UI style, the RoleTailored Client, targets end users. In NAV 2015, there are three instances of the RoleTailored Client – for Windows, for Web interaction, and for tablet use. The example images in the following module descriptions are from the RoleTailored Client Departments menu in the Windows Client.

Financial Management

Financial Management is the foundation of any ERP system. No matter what the business is, the money must be kept flowing, and the flow of money must be tracked. The tools which help to manage the capital resources of the business are part of NAV 2015's Financial Management module. These include all or part of the following application functions:

- **General Ledger**: Manages overall finances of the firm
- **Cash Management and Banking**: Manages inventory of money
- **Accounts Receivable**: Tracks the incoming revenue
- **Accounts Payable**: Tracks the outgoing funds
- **Analytical Accounting**: Analyzes the various flows of funds
- **Inventory and Fixed Assets**: Manages the inventories of goods and equipment
- **Multi-Currency and Multi-Language**: Supports international business activities

The **Financial Management** section of the **Departments** menu looks as follows:

Financial Management	
General Ledger	Payables
Cash Management	Fixed Assets
Cost Accounting	Inventory
Cash Flow	Periodic Activities
Receivables	Setup

Manufacturing

NAV 2015 **Manufacturing** is general purpose enough to be appropriate for **Make to Stock (MTS)**, **Make to Order (MTO)**, **Assemble to Order (ATO)**, as well as various subsets and combinations of those. Although off-the-shelf NAV is not particularly suitable for most process manufacturing and some of the very high volume assembly line operations, there are third-party add-on and add-in enhancements available for these applications. As with most of the NAV application functions, Manufacturing can be implemented to be used in a basic mode or as a full featured system.

NAV Manufacturing includes the following functions:

- **Product Design (BOMs and Routings)**: Manages the structure of product components and the flow of manufacturing processes
- **Capacity and supply requirements planning**: Tracks the intangible and tangible manufacturing resources
- **Production scheduling (infinite and finite)**: Execution and tracking quantities and costs, plus tracking the planned use of manufacturing resources, both on an unconstrained and constrained basis

The **Manufacturing** section of the **Departments** menu looks as follows:

Supply Chain Management

Obviously, some of the functions categorized as part of NAV 2015 **Supply Chain Management (SCM)**, for example sales and purchasing, are actively used in almost every NAV implementation. The supply chain applications in NAV include all or parts of the following applications:

- **Sales order processing and pricing**: Supports the heart of every business
- **Purchasing (including requisitions)**: Includes planning, entering, pricing, and processing purchase orders
- **Inventory Management**: Manages inventories of goods and materials
- **Warehouse management including receiving and shipping**: Manages the receipt, storage, retrieval, and shipment of material and goods in warehouses

Even though we might consider **Assembly** to be part of **Manufacturing**, the standard NAV 2015 **Departments** menu includes it in the **Warehouse** section. The **Supply Chain Management** section of the **Departments** menu looks as follows:

As a whole, these functions constitute the base components of a system appropriate for distribution operations, including those which operate on an Assemble to Order basis.

Business Intelligence and reporting

Although Microsoft marketing materials identify **Business Intelligence (BI)** and reporting as though it were a separate module within NAV, it's difficult to physically identify it as such. Most of the components used for BI and reporting purposes are appropriately scattered throughout various application areas. In the words of one Microsoft document, "Business Intelligence is a strategy, not a product." Functions within NAV that support a BI strategy include the following:

- **Standard Reports**: These are distributed ready-to-use by end users
- **Account schedules and analysis reports**: These are a specialized report writer for General Ledger data
- **Query, XMLport, and Report Designers**: These are developer tools to support the creation of a wide variety of report formats, charts, XML, and CSV files
- **Analysis by dimensions**: This is a capability embedded in many of the other tools

- **Interfaces into Microsoft Office and Microsoft Office 365 including Excel**: These support the communications of data either into NAV or out of NAV

- **RDLC report viewer**: This provides the ability to present NAV data in a variety of textual and graphic formats; includes user interactive capabilities

- **Interface capabilities such as DotNet Interoperability and Web Services**: These are the technologies to support interfaces between NAV 2015 and external software products

Relationship Management

NAV's **Relationship Management (RM)** functionality is definitely the *little sister* (or, if you prefer, *little brother*) of the fully featured standalone Microsoft **Customer Relationship Management (CRM)** system. The big advantage of the NAV RM is its tight integration with NAV customer and sales data. For those who need the full Microsoft CRM, prior versions of NAV have had a module connecting it to NAV. The same connector has been released for NAV 2015.

Also falling under the heading of CRM is the NAV **Service Management (SM)** functionality. While the RM component shows up in the menu as part of sales and marketing, the SM component is identified as an independent function in the menu structure.

- NAV functions that support RM are as follows:

  - **Marketing campaigns**: Plans and manages promotions
  - **Customer activity tracking**: Analyzes customer orders
  - **To do lists**: Manages what is to be done and tracks what has been done

- NAV functions that support SM are as follows:

  - **Service contracts**: Supports service operations
  - **Labor and part consumption tracking**: Tracks the resources consumed by the service business
  - **Planning and dispatching**: Manages service calls

Human Resource management

NAV **Human Resources (HR)** is a very small module, but relates to a critical component of the business - employees. Basic employee data can be stored and reported via the master table (in fact, one can use HR to manage data about individual contractors in addition to employees). A wide variety of individual employee attributes can be tracked by the use of dimensions fields. NAV functions that support HR are as follows:

- **Employee tracking**: Maintains basic employee description data
- **Skills inventory**: Maintains an inventory of the capabilities of the employees
- **Absence tracking**: Maintains basic attendance information
- **Employee statistics**: Tracks government required employee attribute data such as age, gender, length of service, and so on

Project Management

The NAV project management module consists of the jobs functionality supported by the resources functionality. Projects can be short or long term. They can be external (in other words - billable) or internal. This module is often used by third-parties as the base for vertical market add-ons (such as construction or job-oriented manufacturing). This application area includes parts or all of the following functions:

- **Budgeting and cost tracking**: Manages project finances
- **Scheduling:** Plans project activities
- **Resource requirements and usage tracking**: Manages people and equipment
- **Project accounting**: Tracks the results

Significant changes in NAV 2015

NAV 2015 contains added capabilities in a variety of areas including business functionality, enhanced development tools, a tablet client, more Internet compatibility, and increased integration to other Microsoft products. For information on what was new in NAV 2013 R2, review the MSDN notes at:

- `http://msdn.microsoft.com/en-us/library/hh173994(v=nav.71).aspx`
- `http://msdn.microsoft.com/en-us/library/hh174007(v=nav.71).aspx`

Some of the mentioned items include Manual Payment Processing, bank reconciliation enhancement, SEPA Debit and Credit handling, Web Client Enhancements, new Windows PowerShell capabilities, a new Help Server, and features to better implement and manage NAV on Windows Azure.

Information on the minimum hardware and software requirements to install and run Microsoft Dynamics NAV 2015 are found in the embedded *Developer and IT Pro Help* topic *System Requirements for Microsoft Dynamics NAV 2015*. Following are some of the specific areas where NAV 2015 contains significant changes (this list is representative, not comprehensive).

Application changes

Significant changes to applications include:

- Mandatory indicator fields (required data elements)
- Auto-fill and hidden fields
- Document emailing
- Manage and create report layouts using Microsoft Word 2013, SQL Server Report Builder (RDLC), or Visual Studio Community Edition
- Simplified payment reconciliation
- Encryption functions
- Report scheduling
- Data exchange framework for easier implementation

Client enhancements

Significant client enhancements include:

- Tablet client for multiple tablet types (iPad, Android, Windows)
- Enhanced web client
- Office 365 integration
- UI elements removal capability
- Simplified user interface option
- Enhanced Role Center Cues including color and image options

Development tools

Significant new development tools include:

- Enhanced commenting capability
- Non-default property values display bold font
- New **Client Application Language (C/AL)** commands and functions

- New Development Environment commands
- New Report functions and status default to local status
- New Page field, action, and control properties
- New Table schema data synchronization options
- Windows PowerShell cmdlets and scripts include comparing and merging objects, caption management, and upgrading SQL server data when NAV table schema is changed

Other areas

Other new areas include:

- Major changes in Upgrade concepts and processes
- Deployment enhancements for Add-ins and .NET Framework
- PowerShell cmdlets for Exporting and Importing data selectively
- Licenses are now version specific
- RapidStart Services for implementation

A developer's overview of NAV 2015

From the point of view of a developer, NAV 2015 consists of about 4,000 potentially customizable off-the-shelf program objects plus the Integrated Development Environment (the C/SIDE development tools), which allow us to modify existing objects and create new ones.

The NAV 2015 system is an object-based system made up of the seven different object types available in NAV. Strictly speaking, NAV is not a full-featured object-oriented system. A full-featured object-oriented system would allow the definition and creation of new object types, while NAV only allows the creation and modification of instances of the seven predefined object types.

NAV object types

Let's start with basic definitions of the NAV 2015 object types:

- **Table**: Tables define the data structure and also contain the data records.

- **Page**: Pages are the way the data is formatted and displayed appropriately for each of the client types and user roles.

- **Report**: Reports provide display of the data to the user in hardcopy format, either on screen (preview mode) or via a printing device. Report objects can also update data in processes with or without data display.

- **Codeunit**: Codeunits are containers for code utilized by other objects. They are always structured in code segments called functions.

- **Query**: Queries support extracting data from one or more tables, making calculations, and outputting in the form of a new data structure. They can output data directly to charts, Excel, XML, and OData.

- **XMLport**: XMLports allow the importing and exporting of data to/from external files. The external file structure can be in XML or other file formats.

- **MenuSuite**: MenuSuites contain menu entries which refer to other types of objects. MenuSuites are different from other objects. Menus cannot contain any code or logic. MenuSuite entries display in the Departments page in the Navigation Pane in the Windows Client only. In the Web and Tablet clients, these are used to support Search functions.

The C/SIDE integrated development environment

NAV 2015 includes an extensive set of software development tools. The NAV development tools are accessed through C/SIDE which runs within the Development Environment client. This environment and its complement of tools are usually collectively referred to as C/SIDE. C/SIDE includes the C/AL compiler. All NAV programming uses C/AL. No NAV development can be done without using C/SIDE, but other tools are used to complement C/AL code (such as Visual Studio, .NET, COM controls, and OCX controls among others).

The C/SIDE is referred to as the **Object Designer** within NAV. It is accessed through a separate shortcut which is installed as part of a typical full system installation. When we open the Object Designer, we see the following screen:

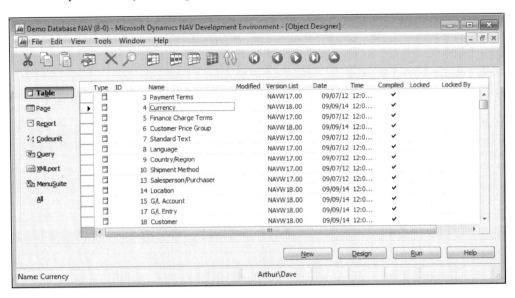

Object Designer tool icons

When we open an object in the applicable Designer (Table Designer, Page Designer, and so on) for that object, we will see a set of tool icons at the top of the screen. The following table lists those icons and the object types to which they apply. Occasionally, an icon will appear when it is of no use.

	C/AL Find	Properties	Field Menu	Symbol Table	C/AL Code
Table	✓	✓	✓ but no response	✓	✓
Page	✓	✓	✓	✓	✓
Report	✓	✓	✓	✓	✓
Codeunit	✓	✓	✓ but empty	✓	✓ Toggles debugger breakpoint
Query	✓	✓	✓	✓	✓
XMLport	✓	✓	✓ but no response	✓	✓
MenuSuite	✓ but of no use	No icon – *Alt+Enter*			

The C/AL programming language

The language in which NAV is coded is C/AL. A small sample of C/AL code within the **C/AL Editor** is shown next:

C/AL syntax is similar to Pascal syntax. Code readability is always enhanced by careful programmer attention to structure, logical variable naming, process flow consistent with that of the code in the base product, and good documentation both inside and outside of the code.

Good software developer focuses on design before coding and on accomplishing design goals with a minimum of code. Dynamics NAV facilitates that approach. In 2012, a team made up of Microsoft and NAV community members began the NAV Design Patterns project. As defined on Wikipedia, "a design pattern is a general reusable solution to a commonly occurring problem". Links to the NAV Design Patterns project information are as follows:

- `http://blogs.msdn.com/b/nav/archive/2013/08/29/what-is-the-nav-design-patterns-project.aspx`

- `https://community.dynamics.com/nav/w/designpatterns/default.aspx`

A primary goal of this project is to document patterns that exist within NAV. In addition, new *best practice* patterns have been suggested as ways to solve common issues we encounter during our customization efforts. Now, when working on enhancements of NAV, we will be aided by reference to the documentation of patterns within NAV. This allows us to spend more of our time designing a good solution using existing, proven functions (the documented patterns), and spending less time writing and debugging code. A good reference for NAV design and development using patterns can be found at `https://www.packtpub.com/application-development/microsoft-dynamics-nav-2013-application-design`.

To quote from the NAV 2015 Help:

> *"Reusing code makes developing applications both faster and easier. More importantly, if you organize your C/AL code as suggested, your applications will be less prone to errors. By centralizing the code, you will not unintentionally create inconsistencies by performing the same calculation in many places, for example, in several triggers that have the same table field as their source expression. If you have to change the code, you could either forget about some of these triggers or make a mistake when you modify one of them."*

Much of our NAV development work is done by assembling references to previously defined objects and functions, adding new data structure where necessary. As the tools for NAV design and development provided by both Microsoft and the NAV community continue to mature, our development work becomes more oriented to design and less to coding. The end result is that we are more productive and cost effective on behalf of our customers. Everyone wins.

NAV object and system elements

Following are some important terms used in NAV:

- **License**: A data file supplied by Microsoft that allows a specific level of access to specific object number ranges. NAV licenses are very clever constructs which allow distribution of a complete system, all objects, modules, and features (including development) while constraining exactly what is accessible and how it can be accessed. Each license feature has its price, usually configured in groups of features. Microsoft partners have access to *full development* licenses to provide support and customization services for their clients. End-user firms can purchase licenses allowing them developer access to NAV. A Training License can also be generated which contains any desired set of features and expires after a specified period of time.

License limits

The NAV license limits access to the C/AL code within tables, pages, and codeunits differently than the C/AL code buried within reports or XMLports. The latter can be accessed with a *lower level* license (that is, less expensive). If a customer has license rights to the Report Designer, which many do, they can access C/AL code within Report and XMLport objects. But access to C/AL code in a table, page, or codeunit requires a more expensive license with Developer privileges. As a result, C/AL code within tables, pages, and codeunits is more secure than that within report and XMLport objects.

All licenses are now version-specific. From the Microsoft Dynamics NAV 2015 Licensing Guide: "since the release of Microsoft Dynamics NAV 2013 R2 CU10, license keys are version-specific. A Microsoft Dynamics NAV 2015 license key is required to activate Microsoft Dynamics NAV 2015 software and a Microsoft Dynamics NAV 2015 license key will not activate any other versions of the software."

- **Field**: An individual data item, defined either in a table or in the working storage (temporary storage) of an object.
- **Record**: A group of fields (data items) handled as a unit in many operations. Table data consists of rows (records) with columns (fields).
- **Control**: In MSDN, a control is defined as "a component that provides (or enables) UI capabilities".
- **Properties**: These are the attributes of the element such as an object, field, record, or control that define some aspect of its behavior or use. Example of property attributes include display captions, relationships, size, position, and whether editable or viewable.

- **Trigger**: Mechanisms that initiate (fire) an action when an event occurs and is communicated to the application object. A trigger in an object is either empty, contains code that is executed when the associated event fires the trigger, or contains only comments (in a few cases, this affects the behavior of the trigger). Each object type, data field, control, and so on, may have its own set of predefined triggers. The event trigger name begins with the word *On* such as OnInsert, OnOpenPage, or OnNextRecord. NAV triggers have similarities to those in SQL, but they are not the same (similarly named triggers may not even serve similar purposes). NAV triggers are locations within objects where a developer can place comments or C/AL code. When we view the C/AL code of an object in its Designer, we can see non-trigger code groups that resemble NAV event-based triggers.

  - **Documentation**: It can contain comments only, no executable code. Every object type except MenuSuite has a single Documentation section at the beginning of the C/AL code.

  - **Functions**: It can be defined by the developer. They are callable routines which can be accessed by other C/AL code from either inside or outside the object where the called function resides. Many functions are provided as part of the standard product. As developers, we may add our own custom functions as needed.

- **Object numbers and field numbers**: All objects of the same object type are assigned a number unique within the object type. All fields within an object are assigned a number unique within the object (that is, the same field number may be repeated within many objects whether referring to similar or different data).

 In this book, we will generally use comma notation for these numbers (fifty thousand is 50,000). In C/AL, no punctuation is used.

The object numbers from 1 (one) to 50,000 and in the 99,000,000 (99 million) range are reserved for use by NAV as part of the base product. Objects in these number ranges can be modified or deleted with a developer's license, but cannot be created. Field numbers in standard objects often start with 1 (one). Historically, object and field numbers from 50,000 to 99,999 are generally available to the rest of us for assignment as part of customizations developed in the field using a normal development license.

(At the time of this writing, the Developer Help says that object numbers below 50,000 can be used, at least for reports, but the authors' testing doesn't agree.) Field numbers from 90,000 to 99,999 should not be used for new fields added to standard tables as those numbers are sometimes used in training materials. Microsoft allocates ranges of object and field numbers to **Independent Software Vendor** (**ISV**) developers for their add-on enhancements. Some such objects (the 14,000,000 range in North America, other ranges for other geographic regions) can be accessed, modified, or deleted, but not created using a normal development license. Others (such as in the 37,000,000 range) can be executed, but not viewed or modified with a typical development license.

The following table summarizes object numbering practice:

Object Number range	Usage
1 – 9,999	Base-application objects
10,000 – 49,999	Country-specific objects
50,000 – 99,999	Customer-specific objects
100,000 – 98,999,999	Partner-created objects
Above 98,999,999	Microsoft territory

- **Work Date**: This is a date controlled by the user operator. It is used as the default date for many transaction entries. The System Date is the date recognized by Windows. The Work Date, which can be adjusted at any time by the user, is specific to the workstation and can be set to any point in the future or the past. This is very convenient for procedures such as ending sales order entry for one calendar day at the end of the first shift, and then entering sales orders by the second shift dated to the next calendar day. There are settings to allow limiting the range of Work Dates allowed.

1. The Work Date can be set by clicking on arrowhead drop-down menu below the **Microsoft Dynamics** icon and selecting the **Set Work Date...** option.

2. Clicking on **Set Work Date...** in the drop-down options displays the **Set Work Date** screen. Or click on the date in the Status Bar at the bottom of the **Role Tailored Client (RTC)** window. In either case, we can enter a new Work Date:

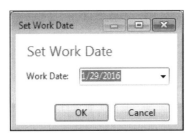

NAV functional terminology

For various application functions, NAV uses terminology more similar to accounting than to traditional data processing. Some examples are listed as follows:

- **Journal**: A table of unposted transaction entries, each of which represents an event, an entity, or an action to be processed. There are General Journals for general accounting entries, Item Journals for changes to inventory, and so on.

- **Ledger**: A detailed history of posted transaction entries that have been processed. For example, General Ledger, Customer Ledger, Vendor Ledger, Item Ledger, and so on. Some Ledgers have subordinate detail ledgers, typically providing a greater level of quantity and/or value detail.

- **Posting**: The process by which entries in a Journal are validated, and then entered into one or more Ledgers.

- **Batch**: A group of one or more Journal entries posted at the same time.

- **Register**: An audit trail showing the history, by Entry No. ranges, of posted Journal Batches.

- **Document**: A formatted page such as an Invoice, a Purchase Order, or a Payment Check, typically one page for each primary transaction (a page may require display scrolling to be fully viewed).

User interface

NAV 2015 UI is designed to be role oriented (also called role tailored). The term **role oriented** means tailoring the options available to fit the user's specific job tasks and responsibilities. If user access is via the Windows client, Web client, or Tablet client, the **Role Tailored Client** (**RTC**) will be employed. If the user access is via SharePoint or another client, the developer will have more responsibility to make sure the user experience is role tailored.

The first page that a user will meet is a Role Center Page. The Role Center Page provides the user with a view of work tasks to be done; it acts as the user's home page. The home Role Center Page should be tailored to the job duties of each user, so there will be a variety of Role Center Page formats for any installation.

Someone whose role is focused on Order Entry will likely see a different RTC home page than the user whose role focuses on Invoicing, even though both user roles are in what we generally think of as Sales and Receivables. The NAV 2015 RTC allows a great deal of flexibility for implementers, system administrators, managers, and individual users to configure and reconfigure screen layouts and the set of functions that are visible.

The following image is the out-of-the-box Role Center for a Sales Order Processor:

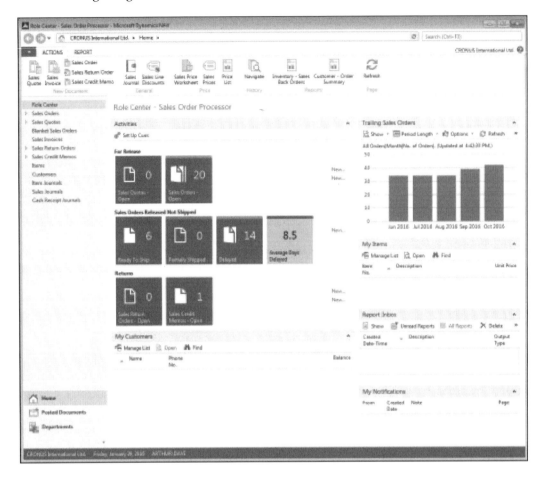

The key to properly designing and implementing any system, especially a role tailored system, is the quality of the User Profile analysis done as the first step in requirements analysis. User Profiles identify the day-to-day needs of each user's responsibilities relative to accomplishing the business' goals. Each user's tasks must be mapped to individual NAV functions or elements, identifying how those tasks will be supported by the system. A successful implementation requires the use of a proven methodology. It is very important that the upfront work be done and done well. Even the best programming cannot compensate for a bad definition of goals.

In our exercises, we will assume the upfront work has been well done and we will concentrate on addressing the requirements defined by our project team.

Hands-on development in NAV 2015

One of the best ways to learn a new set of tools, like those that make up a programming language and environment, is to experiment with them. We're going to have some fun doing that throughout this book. We're going to experiment where the cost of errors (otherwise known as learning) is small. Our development work will be a custom application of NAV 2015 for a relatively simple, but realistic application.

We're going to do our work using the Cronus demo database that is available with all NAV 2015 distributions and is installed by default when we install the NAV 2015 demo system. The simplest way to install the NAV 2015 demo is to locate all the components on a single workstation. A 64-bit system running Windows 7 Professional will suffice. Information about additional requirements is available in the MSDN library (`https://msdn.microsoft.com/en-gb/default.aspx`) under the heading *System Requirements for Microsoft Dynamics NAV 2015*. Other helpful information on installing NAV 2015 (the demo option is a good choice for our purposes) and addressing a variety of setup questions is available in the NAV 2015 area of the MSDN library. In fact, all the *Help information for NAV 2015* is accessible in the MSDN library.

The Cronus database contains all the NAV objects and a small, but reasonably complete set of data populated in most of the system's functional applications areas. Our exercises will interface very slightly with the Cronus data, but not depend on any specific data values.

To follow along with all our exercises as a developer, you will need a developer license for the system with rights allowing the creation of objects in the 50,000 to 50,099 number range. This license should also allow at least read access to all the objects numbered below 50,000. If you don't have such a license, check with your Partner or your Microsoft sales representatives to see if they will provide a training license for your use.

The NAV 2015 development exercise scenario

Our business is a small radio station that features a variety of programs, news, music, listener call-in, and other program types. Our station call-letters are WDTU. Our broadcast materials come from several sources and in several formats: vinyl records, CDs, MP3s, and downloaded digital (usually MP3s). While our station has a large library, especially of recorded music, sometimes our program hosts (also called disc jockeys or DJs) want to share material from other sources. For that reason, we need to be able to easily add items to our play lists (the list of what is to be broadcast) and also have an easy-to-access method for our DJs to preview MP3 material.

Like any business, we have accounting and activity tracking requirements. Our income is from selling advertisements. We must pay royalties for music played, fees for purchased materials such as prepared text for news, sports, and weather information, and service charges for our streaming Internet broadcast service. As part of our licensed access to the public airwaves, a radio station is required to broadcast public service programming at no charge. Often that is in the form of **Public Service Announcements (PSAs)** such as encouraging traffic safety or reduction in tobacco use. Like all radio stations, we must plan what is to be broadcast (create schedules) and track what has been broadcast (such as ads, music, purchased programming, PSAs) by date and time. We bill our customers for the advertising, pay our vendors their fees and royalties, and report our public service data to the appropriate government agency.

Getting started with application design

Our design for our radio station will start with a **Radio Show** table, a **Radio Show Card** page, a **Radio Show List** page, and a simple Radio Show List Report. Along the way, we will review the basics of each NAV object type.

When we open the NAV Development Environment for the first time or to work on a different database, we must define what database should be opened. Navigate to **File | Database | Open...**, as shown in the following image:

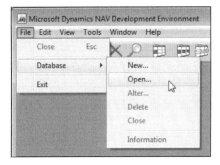

Application tables

Table objects are the foundation of every NAV application. Tables contain data structure definitions, as well as properties that describe the behavior of the data, including data validations and constraints.

More business logic is required in complex applications than in simple data type validation, and NAV allows C/AL code to be put in the table to control insertion, modification, and deletion of records as well as logic on the field level. When the bulk of the business logic is coded at the table level, it is easier to develop, debug, support, modify, and even upgrade. Good design in NAV requires that as much of the business logic as possible reside in the tables. Having the business logic coded at the table level doesn't necessarily mean the code is resident in the table. NAV 2015 Help recommends the following guidelines for placing C/AL code:

> In general, put the code in codeunits instead of on the object on which it operates. This promotes a clean design and provides the ability to reuse the code. It also helps enforce security. For example, typically, users do not have direct access to tables that contain sensitive data, such as the **General Ledger Entry** table, nor do they have permission to modify objects. If you put the code that operates on the general ledger in a codeunit, give the codeunit access to the table, and give the user permission to execute the codeunit, then you will not compromise the security of the table and the user will be able to access the table.
>
> If you must put the code on an object instead of in a codeunit, then put the code as close as possible to the object on which it operates. For example, put code that modifies records in the triggers of the table fields.

Designing a simple table

Our primary master data table will be the **Radio Show** table. This table lists our *inventory* of shows available to be scheduled.

First, open the NAV Development Environment, click **Tools | Object Designer** and select **Table**. We can view or modify the design of existing master tables in NAV by highlighting the table (for example, Table 18 - Customer, or Table 27 - Item) and clicking on **Design**.

Each master table has a standard field for the primary key (a Code data type field of 20 characters called **No**.) and has standard information regarding the entity the master record represents (for example, Name, Address, City, and so on for the **Customer** table and Description, Base Unit of Measure, Unit Cost, and so on, for the **Item** table).

The Radio Show table will have the following field definitions (we may add more later):

Field names	Definitions
No.	20 character text (code)
Type	10 character text (code)
Name	50 character text
Run Time	Duration
Host No.	20 character text (code)
Host Name	50 character text
Average Listeners	Integer
Audience Share	Decimal
Advertising Revenue	Decimal
Royalty Cost	Decimal

In the preceding list, three of the fields are defined as Code fields, which are text fields that limit the alphanumeric characters to upper case values. Code fields are used throughout NAV for primary key values. They are used to reference or be referenced by other tables (foreign keys). The **No.** will be the unique identifier in our table. We will utilize a set of standard internal NAV functions to assign a user-defined **No. Series** range that will auto increment the value on table insertion and possibly allow for user entry (as long as it is unique in the table) based on a setup value. **Host No.** references the standard **Resource** table and the **Type** field will reference a custom table we will create to allow for flexible **Type** values.

We will have to design and define the reference properties at the field level in the **Table Designer** window, as well as compile them, before the validation will work. At this point, let's just get started with these field definitions and create the foundation for the **Radio Show** table.

Creating a simple table

To invoke the table designer, open the NAV 2015 Development Environment and the database in which we will be doing our development. In the Object Designer, click **Table** (in the left column of buttons) and click **New** (in the bottom row of buttons). Enter the first field number as 10 (the default is 1), and increment each remaining field number by 10 (the default is 1). Sometimes it is useful to leave large gaps (such as jumping from 80 to 200 or 500) when the next set of fields have a particular purpose not associated with the prior set of fields.

NAV 2015 Help says to not leave gaps in field numbers. Based on many years of experience, the authors disagree. Leaving numbering gaps will allow us to later add additional fields between the existing fields, if necessary. The result will be data structures that are (at least initially) easier to read and understand. Once a table is referenced by other objects or contains any data, the field numbers of the previously defined fields should not be changed.

In the **Description** column, we will put notes for the fields that need properties set later. The following image shows our new table definition in the **Table Designer** window:

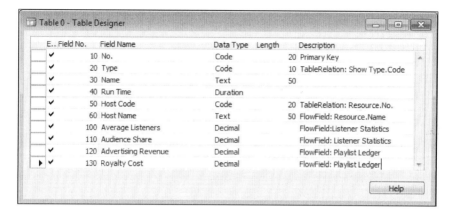

Now we can close the table definition (navigate to **File** | **Save** or *Ctrl + S* or press *ESC* or close the window. The first two options are the explicit methods of saving our work). We will see a message reminding us to save our changes, as shown in the following screenshot:

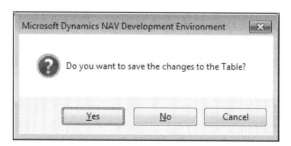

Click **Yes**. We must now assign the object number (use 50000) and a unique name (it cannot duplicate the same first 30 characters of another table object in the database). We will name our table Radio Show based on the master record to be stored in the table.

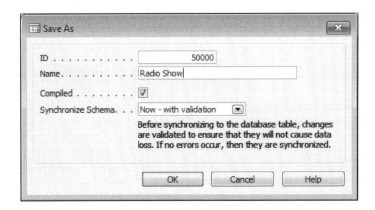

In the preceding screenshot, note that the **Compiled** option is automatically checked and the **Synchronize Schema** option is set to **Now – with validation**, which are the defaults for NAV. Once we press **OK** and the object is successfully compiled, it is immediately ready to be executed within the application. If the object we were working on was not ready to be compiled without error, we could unselect the **Compiled** option in the **Save As** window.

Uncompiled objects will not be considered by C/SIDE when changes are made to other objects. Until we have compiled an object, it is a work in progress, not an operable routine. There is a **Compiled** flag on every object that gives its compilation status. Even when we have compiled an object, we have not confirmed that all is well. We may have made changes that affect other objects which reference the modified object. As a matter of good work habit, we should recompile all objects before we end work for the day.

The **Synchronize Schema** option choice determines how table changes will be applied to the table data in SQL Server. When the changes are validated, any changes that could be destructive to existing data will be detected and handled either according to a previously defined upgrade codeunit or by generating an error message. The **Synchronize Schema** option choices are shown in the following image:

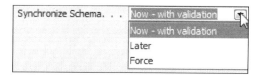

See the *Developer and IT ProHelp* section *Synchronizing Table Schemas* for more details.

Pages

Pages provide views of data or processes designed for on-screen display (or exposure as web services) and also allow for user data entry into the system. They act as containers for the action items (menu options).

There are several basic types of display/entry pages in NAV 2015, as listed next:

- **List**
- **Card**
- **Document**
- **Journal/Worksheet**
- **List Plus**
- **Confirmation dialog**
- **Standard dialog**

There are also page parts (they look and program like a page, but aren't intended to stand alone) as well as user interfaces that display like pages, but are not Page objects. The latter user interfaces are generated by various dialog functions. In addition, there are special Page types, such as Role Center pages and Navigate pages (for Wizards).

Standard elements of pages

A page consists of Page properties and triggers, controls, and control properties and triggers. Generally, Data controls are either labels displaying constant text or graphics, or containers that display data or other controls. Controls can also be buttons, action items, and page parts. While there are a few instances where we must include C/AL code within the page or page control triggers, it is good practice to minimize the amount of code embedded within pages. Any data-related C/AL code should be located in the table object rather than the page object.

List pages

List pages display a simple list of any number of records in a single table. The **Customer List** page (with its associated FactBoxes) in the following screenshot shows a subset of the data for each customer displayed. Often the List pages/forms do not allow entry or editing of the data. Journal/Worksheet pages look like List pages, but are intended for data entry. Standard List pages are always displayed with the navigation pane on the left. The **Customer List** page is shown in the following screenshot:

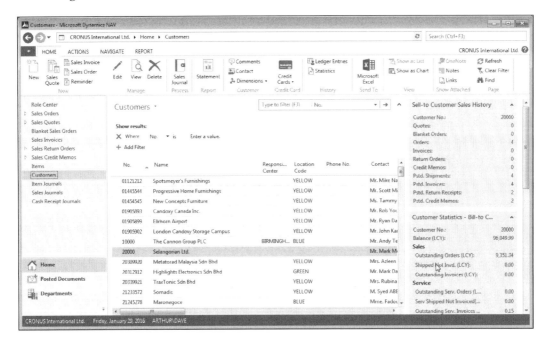

Card pages

Card pages display one record at a time. These are generally used for the entry or display of individual table records. Examples of frequently accessed Card pages include **Customer Card** for customer data, **Item Card** for inventory items, and **G/L Account Card** for General Ledger accounts.

Card pages often have FastTabs (one FastTab consists of a group of controls with each tab focusing on a different set of related customer data). FastTabs can be expanded or collapsed dynamically, allowing the data visible at any time to be controlled by the user. Important data elements can be promoted to be visible even when a FastTab is collapsed.

Card pages for the master records display all the required data entry fields. If a field is set to **ShowMandatory** (a control property we will discuss in *Chapter 4, Pages*), a red asterisk will display until the field is filled. Typically, Card pages also display FactBoxes containing summary data about related activity. Thus, Cards can be used as the primary inquiry point for the masterrecords. The following screenshot is a sample of a standard **Customer Card**:

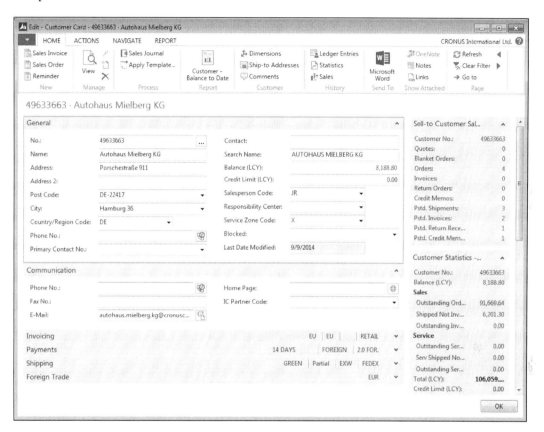

Document pages

A document page looks like a Card page with one tab containing a List page. An example is the **Sales Order** page shown in the following screenshot. In this example, the first tab and the last four tabs are in Card page format showing sales order data fields that have a single occurrence on the page (in other words, they do not occur in a repeating column).

The second tab from the top is in List page format (all fields are in repeating columns) showing the sales order line items. Sales order line items may include product to be shipped, special charges, comments, and other pertinent order details. The information to the right of the data entry area is related data and computations (FactBoxes) that have been retrieved and formatted. The top FactBox contains information about the ordering customer. The bottom FactBox contains information about the item on the currently highlighted sales line.

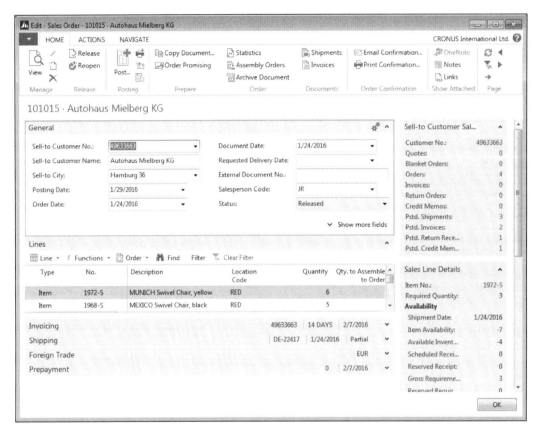

Journal/Worksheet pages

Journal and Worksheet pages look very much like List pages. They display a list of records in the body of the page. Many also have a section at the bottom that shows details about the selected line and/or totals for the displayed data. These pages may include a Filter pane and perhaps a FactBox. The biggest difference between the Journal/Worksheet pages and basic List pages is that Journal and Worksheet pages are designed to be used for data entry (though this may be a matter of personal or site preference). An example of the Requisition Worksheet page in Purchasing, is shown in the following screenshot. This Worksheet assists the user in determining and defining what purchases should be made.

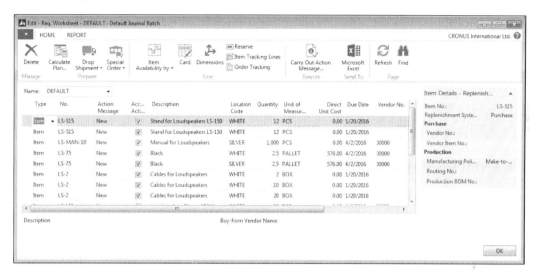

Creating a List page

Now we will create a List page for the table we created earlier. A List page is the initial page that is displayed when a user accesses any data table. The NAV Development Environment has Wizards (object generation tools) to help create basic pages. After our Wizard work is done, we will spend additional time in the Page design tool to make the layout ready for presentation to users.

Our first List page will be the basis for viewing our Radio Show master records. From **Object Designer**, click **Page**, and then click **New**. The **New Page** screen will appear. Enter the name (Radio Show) or table object ID (50000) in the **Table** field. This is the table to which the page will be bound. We can add additional tables to the page object C/AL Global Variables after we close the wizard, as then we will be working in **Page Designer**. Choose the option **Create a page using a wizard:** and select **List** as shown in the following image. Click **OK**.

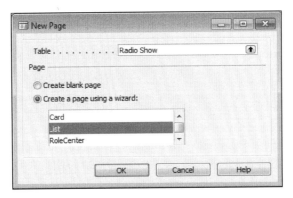

The next step in the wizard shows the fields available for the List page. We can add or remove any of the field columns by using the >, <, >>, and << buttons:

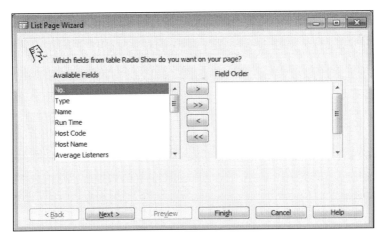

Add all the fields using **>>** and click **Next >**.

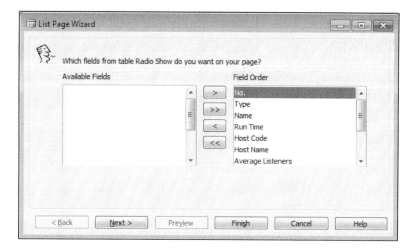

The next wizard step shows the Subforms, System FactBoxes, and Charts that are available to add to our page. (Subforms should properly be named Subpages. Such a change is being considered). We can add these later in **Page Designer** as needed. Click **Finish** to exit the wizard and enter **Page Designer**:

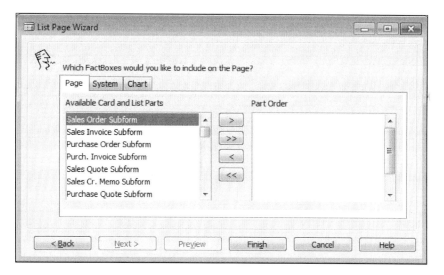

Click **Preview** to view the page with the default ribbon. Note that in the Preview mode, we cannot insert, modify, or delete any of the layout or enter data. The Preview page is not connected to the database data. We need to compile the page and run it to manipulate the data. In the following image of a Page Preview, some fields are out of sight at the right end:

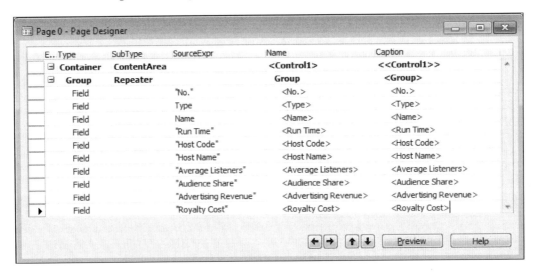

The Preview page is not connected to the database data. We need to compile the page and run it to manipulate the data. In the following image, some fields are out of sight at the right end:

The availability of some capabilities and icons (such as OneNote) will depend on what software is installed on our development workstation. Close the preview of the List page and close the window or press *ESC* to save. Number the page 50000 and name the object as Radio Show List, as shown in the following screenshot:

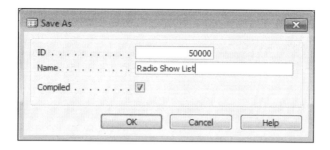

Creating a Card page

Next, let's create a Card page. The wizard process for a Card page is almost the same as for a List page, with one additional step. In **Object Designer**, with Pages selected, click **New** again. Enter the same table (Radio Show) and make sure the **Create a page using a wizard:** option is selected and Card is highlighted, as shown in the next screenshot:

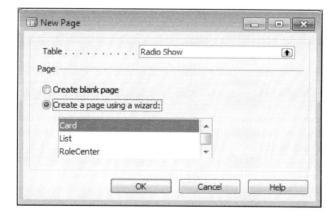

The next step in the Wizard is specific to Card pages, which allows us to create **FastTabs**. These are the display tools that allow the user to expand or collapse the window sections for ease of viewing. For our Radio Show Card, we will divide our table fields into two sections, General (primary key, description, resource information, and duration) and Statistics (data about the show), as shown in the following screenshot:

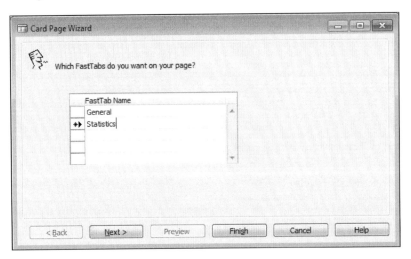

After defining the FastTab names, we must assign the data fields to the tabs on which they are to appear. We will populate the tabs based on the **FastTab Names** fields we assigned. We can select the fields from the **Available Fields** list and assign the order of appearance as we did in the List page wizard. Click the **Next >** button to proceed.

For the **General** FastTab, select the following fields: **No.**, **Type**, **Name**, **Run Time**, **Host Code**, and **Host Name**, as shown in the following screenshot:

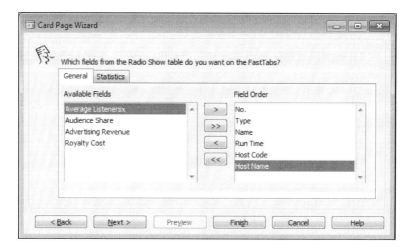

Click the **Statistics** tab to populate the **Statistics** FastTab, select **Average Listenersx**, **Audience Share**, **Advertising Revenue**, and **Royalty Cost**.

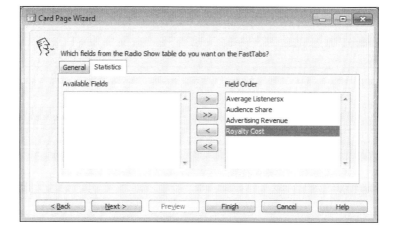

The last Card wizard step is to choose from the available Subforms (Subpages), **System** FactBoxes, and **Charts**. If we decide later that we want any of those, we will add them using **Page Designer**.

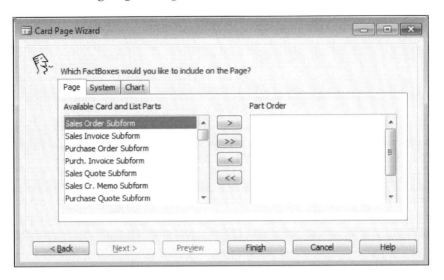

Click **Finish** to view the generated code in **Page Designer**.

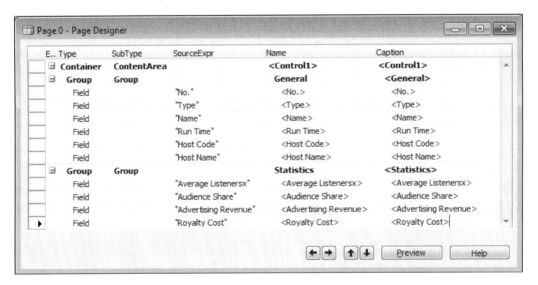

Click the **Preview button** to show a view-only display of the card page.

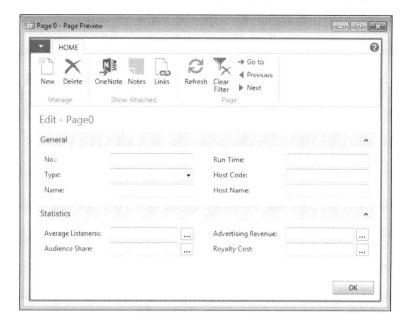

Exit out of the Preview and Page Designer. Save the page as **ID** 50001, and **Name** as Radio Show Card. Refer to the following screenshot:

Later on we can add an action to the List page which will link to the Card page for inserting and editing radio show records and also add the List page to the Role Center page for our radio station user.

Creating some sample data

Even though we haven't added all the bells and whistles to our Radio Show table and pages, we can still use them to enter sample data. The **Radio Show List** page will be the easiest to use for this.

In **Object Designer**, with Pages selected, highlight **Page 50000 – Radio Show List**, and click **Run**. Then click the **New** icon on the ribbon. An empty line will open up where we can enter our sample data. Of course, since our table is very basic at this point, without any validation functionality, table references, function calls, and so on, we will have to be creative (and careful) and enter all the individual data fields accurately and completely on our own.

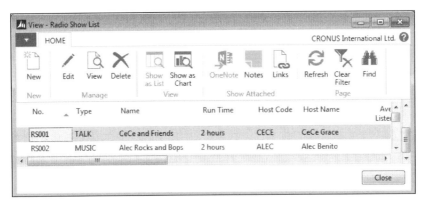

Enter the data shown in the following table so we can see what the page looks like when it contains data. Later on, after we add more capabilities to our table and pages, some fields will be validated, some will be either automatically entered or available on a lookup basis. But for now, simply key in each field value. If the data we key in now conflicts with the validations we create later (such as data in referenced tables), we may have to delete this test data and enter new test data later.

No.	Type	Description	Resource Code	Resource Name	Run Time
RS001	TALK	CeCe and Friends	CECE	CeCe Grace	2 hours
RS002	MUSIC	Alec Rocks and Bops	ALEC	Alec Benito	2 hours
RS003	CALL-IN	Ask Cole!	COLE	Cole Henry	2 hours
RS004	CALL-IN	What do you think?	CLARK	Clark Ernest	1 hour
RS005	MUSIC	Quiet Times	FAY	Fay Mae	3 hours
RS006	NEWS	World News	GOLDIE	Goldie Nickles	1 hour

Creating a List Report

Open **Object Designer**, select **Report** and click **New**. **Report Dataset Designer** is empty when it displays, so we need to add a **Data Source** (table) to the first blank row. Type 50000 or Radio Show into the **Data Source** column.

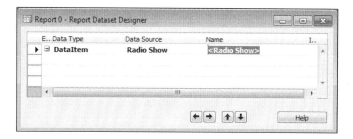

To add multiple data fields from the table, we can use **Field Menu** which is accessed via the icon on the toolbar or the **View | Field Menu** option. **Field Menu** will show a list of all the fields in the **Radio Show** table:

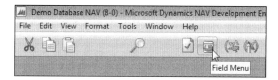

Highlight the first six fields on the **Field Menu**. Then click on the next blank line in **Report Dataset Designer**:

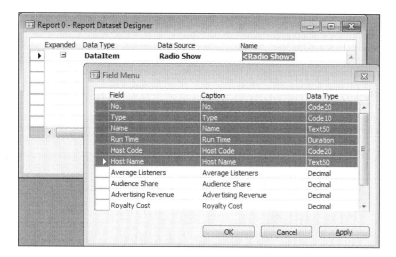

A confirmation box will appear asking if we want to add the fields selected. Click **Yes**.

The fields will appear in **Report Dataset Designer** without having to type them in manually:

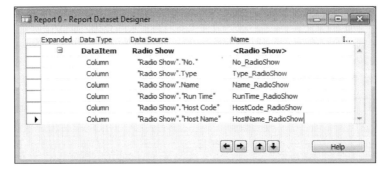

There are two options for RDLC Report Layout development tools: the current version of Visual Studio 2012 or 2014, or the free SQL Server Report Builder that matches the installed version of SQL Server. NAV defaults to using Visual Studio. But if the free SQL Server Report Builder is installed, it can be activated for NAV 2015 by accessing the **Options...** screen from the **Tools** menu option.

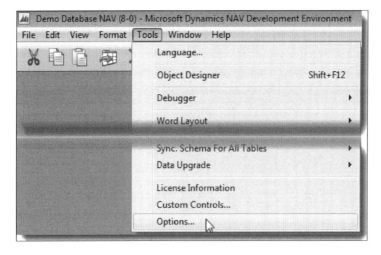

On the **Options** screen, set **Use Report Builder** to **Yes**.

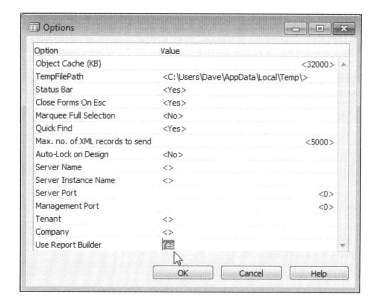

We can also now use the free Community version of Visual Studio, available at `https://www.visualstudio.com/en-us/downloads/visual-studio-2015-downloads-vs.aspx`.

If this link does not work, search the Web for **Visual Studio Community** or **Community Edition Visual Studio.** In this book, since we will use the free version of Community Visual Studio, we will not set **Use Report Builder** to **Yes**.

Click on **View | Layout** to proceed to the chosen report layout tool.

The RDLC Report Layout tool opens with a blank design surface and no visible dataset controls. Unlike **Page Designer**, there is no Report wizard to help with the layout of a new report. All the report layout design work must start from scratch with a blank design surface:

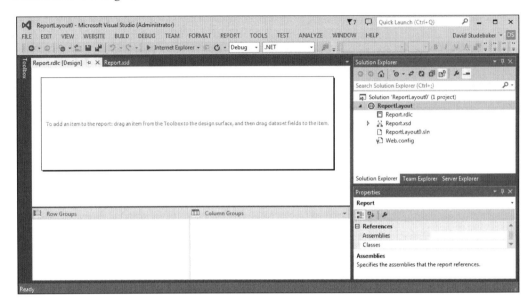

To show the dataset available from NAV, click **View** and select **Report Data** (the last item on the list). A new **Report Data** pane will show on the left of the **Visual Studio layout** window:

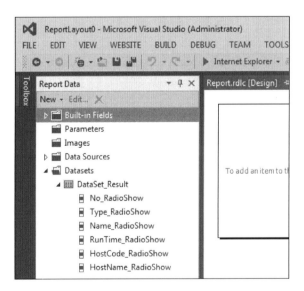

To create our simple list, we will insert a simple table object (a data region with fixed number of columns but variable number of rows) in the design surface. Right-click anywhere on the design surface and expand the **Insert** sub-menu to view the tools available on the report. Click the **Table** tool object, then use drag-and-drop to bring a control from the toolbox to the design surface, as shown in the following screenshot:

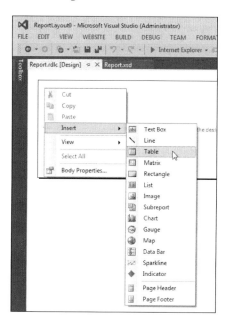

The table layout object defaults to three columns with a header row (repeated once) and a data row (repeated for each row of data retrieved from NAV.

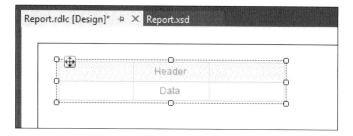

Drag and drop each of the six elements in `DataSet_Result` into columns in the table object. To add additional columns, right-click the table object header and select **Add Columns** (we could also drag-and-drop a field from the dataset to the table). The caption with the basic format of *Field Name Table Name* will default into the header row:

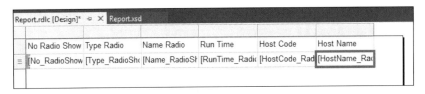

Let's do a little cleanup in the header row by making the captions look like they do in standard NAV reports, by manually typing in the field names.

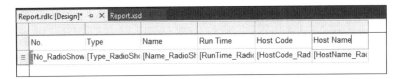

We will save our work by clicking on **File** | **Save All** or clicking on *Ctrl + Shift + S*) and then exit from Visual Studio (**File** | **Exit** or *Alt + F4*) Back in NAV Object Designer, we will exit out of the report or click on **File** | **Save**, then respond to two confirmation boxes. The first one asks if we want to save the report layout from Visual Studio. This allows us to load the RDLC report layout XML into the NAV database report object. Click **Yes**:

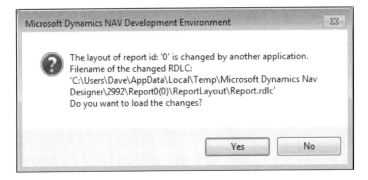

This is followed by the second confirmation screen. Enter 50000 for the **ID**, and **Name** the report **Radio Show List**. Click **OK** to save:

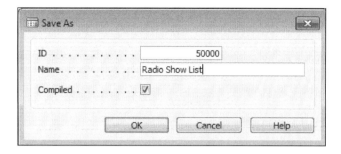

To view the report, make sure the new report object is selected, then click **Run** at the bottom of the **Object Designer** screen:

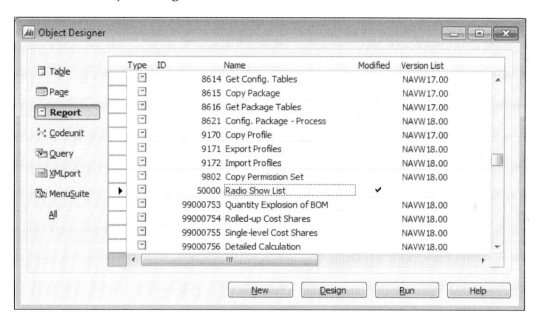

An instance of RTC will open with the Report Request Page showing. This is where the user can set filters, choose a sort sequence and choose the **Print..** options:

Click **Preview** to display the report on screen. The report will show our simple table layout with the fixed definition column captions showing exactly as we typed them.

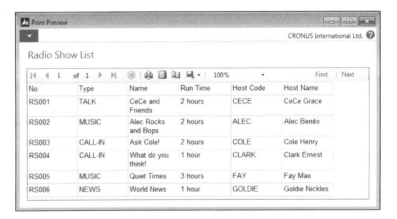

All we've done so far is scratch the surface. But you should have a pretty good overview of the development process for NAV 2015.

 You will be in especially good shape if you've been following along in your own system, doing a little experimenting along the way.

Other NAV object types

Let's finish up our introductory review of NAV's object types.

Codeunits

A codeunit is a container for *chunks* of C/AL code to be called from other objects. These chunks of code are called **Functions**. Functions can be called from any of the other NAV object types that can contain C/AL code. Codeunits can also be exposed (published) as web services. This allows the functions within a published codeunit to be invoked by external routines.

Codeunits are suited structurally to contain only functions. Even though functions could be placed in other object types, the other object types have superstructures that relate to their designed primary use as pages, reports, and so on.

Codeunits act only as a container for C/AL coded functions. They have no auxiliary functions, no method of direct user interaction, and no pre-defined processing. Even if we are creating only one or two functions and they are closely related to the primary activity of a particular object, if these functions are needed from both inside and outside of the report, the best practice is still to locate those functions in a Codeunit. For more guidance, see the *NAV Design Pattern of the Week – the Hooks Pattern* at `http://blogs.msdn.com/b/nav/archive/2014/03/16/nav-design-pattern-of-the-week-the-hooks-pattern.aspx`.

There are several codeunits delivered as part of the standard NAV product which are actually function libraries. These codeunits consist totally of utility routines, generally organized on some functional basis (for example, associated with Dimensions or some aspect of Manufacturing or some aspect of Warehouse management). Many of these can be found by filtering the Codeunit Names on the strings "Management" and "Mgt" (the same could be said for some of the Tables with the string "Buffer" in their name). When we customize a system, we should create our own function library codeunits to consolidate our customizations and make software maintenance easier. Some developers create their own libraries of favorite special functions and include a "function library" codeunit in systems on which they work.

If a Codeunit is structured very simply and can operate in a stand-alone mode, it is feasible to test it in the same way one would test a Report or a Page. Highlight the Codeunit and click the **Run** button. The codeunit will run for a single cycle. However, most codeunits are more complex and must be tested by a calling routine.

Queries

Queries are objects whose purpose is to create extracted sets of data from the NAV database and do so very efficiently. NAV 2015 Queries translate directly into T-SQL query statements and run on the server side rather than on the service tier. A Query can extract data from a single table or multiple tables. In the process of extracting data, it can do different types of Joins (Inner Join, Outer Join, Cross Join), can filter, can calculate FlowFields (special NAV calculations which are discussed in detail in *Chapter 3, Data Types and Fields)*, can sort, and can create sums and averages. Queries obey the NAV data structure business logic.

The output of a Query can be a CSV file (useful for Excel charts), an XML file (for charts or external applications), or an Odata file for a web service. Queries can be published for web service access in similar manner to Pages and Codeunits. The results of a Query can also be viewed by Pages (as described in *Chapter 5, Queries and Reports*) and Cues (as described in the **Help** *Walkthrough: Creating a Cue based on a Normal Field and a Query*), but are especially powerful when output to charts. With a little creativity, a Query can also be used to feed data to a report via use of a temporary table to hold the Query results.

MenuSuites

MenuSuites are the objects that are displayed in the navigation menus. They differ considerably from the other object types we have discussed earlier because they have a completely different structure and they are maintained differently. MenuSuite entries do not contain triggers. The only customization that can be done with them is to add, delete, or edit menu entries which are made up of a small set of properties.

In the RTC, the data in the MenuSuites object is presented in the Departments page.

XMLports

XMLports enable importing and exporting data. XMLports handle both XML structured data and other external text data formats. XML stands for **eXtensible Markup Language** which is the de facto standard for exchanging data between dissimilar systems. For example, XMLports could be used to communicate between our NAV ERP system and our accounting firm's financial analysis and tax preparation system.

XML is designed to be extensible, which means that we can create or extend the definition as long as we communicate the defined XML format to our correspondents. There is a standard set of syntax rules to which XML formats must conform. Much new software uses XML. For example, the new versions of Microsoft Office are quite XML friendly. All web services communications are in the form of an exchange of XML structured data.

The non-XML text data files handled by XMLports fall into two categories. One is known as *comma separated value* or *comma delimited* files (usually having a .csv file extension). Of course, the delimiters don't have to be commas. The other category is fixed format, in which the length and relative position of each field is pre-defined.

XMLports can contain C/AL logic for any type of appropriate data manipulation, either when importing or exporting. Functions such as editing, validating, combining, filtering, and so on, can be applied to the data as it passes through an XMLport.

Development backups and documentation

As with any system where we can do development work, careful attention to documentation and backing up of our work is very important. C/SIDE provides a variety of techniques for handling each of these tasks.

When we are working within Object Designer, we can back up individual objects of any type or groups of objects by exporting them. These exported object files can be imported in total, selectively in groups, or individually, to recover the original version of one or more objects.

NAV 2015 introduces Windows PowerShell cmdlets that support backing up data to the NAVData files. Complementary cmdlets support getting information or selectively retrieving data from previously created NAVData files. Although these tools promise to be very handy for repetitive development testing, they are challenging (or worse) to use in an environment of changing table or field definitions.

When objects are exported to text files, we can use a standard text editor to read or even change them. If, for example, we want to change all the instances of the field name **Customer** to **Patient**, we might export all the objects to text and execute a mass *Find and Replace*. Making such code changes in a text copy of an object is subject to a high probability of error, as we won't have any of the many safety features of the C/SIDE environment to limit what we can do.

Internal documentation (that is, inside C/SIDE) of object changes can be done in three areas. First is the *Object Version List*, a field attached to every object, visible in the Object Designer screen. Whenever a change (or set of changes) is made in an object, a notation should be added to the Version List.

The second area for documentation is the *Documentation trigger* that appears in every object type except MenuSuites. The Documentation trigger is at the top of the object and is the recommended location for noting a relatively complete description of any changes that have been made to the object. Such descriptions should include a brief description of the purpose of the change as well as technical information.

The third area we can place documentation at is inline with modified C/AL code. Individual comment lines can be created by starting the line with double forward slashes //. Whole sections of comments (or commented out code) can be created by starting and ending the section with a pair of curly braces{}. Depending on the type of object and the nature of the specific changes, we should generally annotate each change inline wherever the code is touched, so all the changes can be easily identified by the next developer.

In short, when doing development in NAV C/SIDE, everything applies of what we have learned earlier about good documentation practices. This holds true whether the development is new work or modification of existing logic.

Summary

In this chapter, we covered some basic definitions of terms related to NAV and C/SIDE. We followed it with the introduction of the seven NAV objects types (Tables, Pages, Reports, Codeunits, Queries, MenuSuites, and XMLports). We introduced Table, Page, and Report creation through review and hands-on use beginning a NAV application for the WTDU Radio Show programming management. Finally, we looked briefly at the tools that we use to integrate with external entities and discussed how different types of backups and documentation are handled in C/SIDE. Now that we have covered the basics, we will dive into the detail of the primary object types in the next few chapters.

In *Chapter 2*, *Tables,* we will focus on Tables, the foundation of a NAV system.

Review questions

Q 1. An ERP system such as NAV 2015 includes a number of functional areas. Which of the following are part of NAV 2015? Choose four.

    a.   Manufacturing

    b.   Order Processing

    c.   Planning

    d.   Computer Aided Design (CAD)

    e.   General Accounting

Q 2. New functionality in NAV 2015 includes (choose three):

    a.   Tablet client

    b.   Multi-language

    c.   Document emailing

    d.   Spell checker

    e.   Mandatory fields

Q 3. NAV 2015 development is done in the C/SIDE IDE and Visual Studio. True or False?

Q 4. Match the following table types and descriptions for NAV.

	Table types		Description
1	Journals	a	Audit trail
2	Ledgers	b	Validation process
3	Register	c	Invoice
4	Document	d	Transaction entries
5	Posting	e	History

Q 5. iPads can be used with NAV 2015 to display the Role Tailored Client. True or False?

Q 6. Which of the following describe NAV 2015? Choose two.

    a.   Customizable

    b.   Includes a Storefront module

    c.   Object based

    d.   C# IDE

    e.   Object oriented

Q 7. What are the seven NAV 2015 object types?

Q 8. All NAV objects except XMLports can contain C/AL code. True or False?

Q 9. NAV 2015 includes support for publishing objects as Web Services. True or False?

Q 10. What is the "home page" for a NAV 2015 user called? Choose one.

    a.   Role Home

    b.   Home Center

    c.   Main Page

    d.   Role Center

Q 11. Page Previews from the Development environment can be used for data entry and maintenance. True or False?

Q 12. For what work is Visual Studio used in NAV 2015? Choose one.

    a.   Report data definition

    b.   Report layout

    c.   Role Center design

    d.   Query processing

Q 13. Codeunits are the only NAV 2015 objects that can contain functions. True or False?

Q 14. Query output can be used as a Data Item for Reports. True or False?

Q 15. C/AL and C/SIDE are required for NAV 2015 development. True or False?

Q 16. What object number range is available for assignment to customer-specific objects? Choose two.

    a.   20-500

    b.   50000 – 60000

    c.   150000 – 200000

    d.   50000 – 99999

    e.   10000 – 100000

Q 17. XMLports can only process XML-formatted data. True or False?

Q 18. The Work Date can only be changed by the System Administrator. True or False?

Q 19. A Design Pattern is which of the following? Choose two.

    a.   Reusable code

    b.   Stripes and plaid together

    c.   A proven way to solve a common problem

    d.   User Interface guidelines

Q 20. NAV 2015 Reports are often generated automatically through the use of a wizard. True or False?

2
Tables

"Sometimes the questions are complicated and the answers are simple."

- Dr. Seuss (Theodor Seuss Geisel)

"The loftier the building, the deeper must the foundation be laid."

– Thomas à Kempis

The foundation of any system is the data structure definition. In NAV, the building blocks of this foundation are the **Tables** and the individual data fields that the tables contain. Once the functional analysis and process definition has been completed, any new design work must begin with the data structure. For NAV, that means the tables and their contents.

A NAV table includes much more than just the data fields and keys. A NAV table definition also includes data validation rules, processing rules, business rules, and logic to ensure referential integrity. The rules are in the form of properties and C/AL code.

In this chapter, we will learn about the structure and creation of tables. Details about fields, the components of tables, will be covered in the following chapter. Our topics in this chapter include:

- An overview of tables, including Properties, Triggers, Keys, SumIndexFields, and Field Groups

- Enhancing our scenario application by creating and modifying tables

- Types of tables; that is, Fully Modifiable, Content Modifiable, and Read-Only tables

An overview of tables

There is a distinction between the table (data definition and data container) and the data (the contents of a table). The **table definition** describes the identification information, data structure, validation rules, storage, and retrieval of the data which is stored in the table (container). The definition is defined by the design and can only be changed by a developer. The data is the variable content that originates from user activities. The place where we can see the data explicitly referenced independently of the table as a definition of structure is in the **Permissions** setup data. In the next image, the data is formally referred to as **Table Data**:

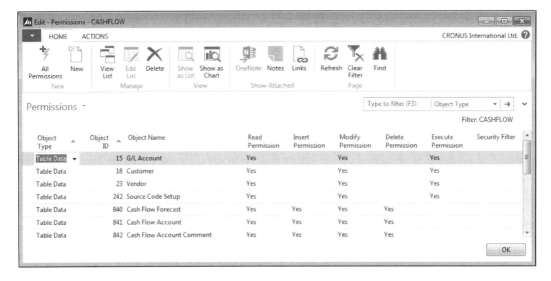

The table is not the data: it is the definition of data contained in the table (stored in the database as metadata). Even so, we commonly refer to both the data and the table as if they were one and the same. That is what we will do in this book.

All permanent data must be stored in a table. All tables are defined by the developer working in the development environment. As much as possible, critical system design components should be embedded in the tables. Each table should include the code that controls what happens when records are added, changed, or deleted, as well as how data is validated when records are added or changed. That includes functions to maintain the aspects of referential integrity that are not automatically handled.

The table object should also include the functions commonly used to manipulate the table and its data, whether for database maintenance or in support of business logic. In those cases where the business logic is either a modification applied to a standard (out-of-the-box) table or that same logic is also used elsewhere in the system, the code should be resident in a function library code unit and called from the table. Table structure as an architectural pattern is being developed and will be published in the Patterns wiki.

The table designer in C/SIDE provides tools for the definition of the data structure within the tables. We will explore these capabilities through examples and analysis of the structure of table objects. We find the approach of embedding control and business logic within the table object has a number of advantages:

- Clarity of design
- Centralization of rules for data constraints
- More efficient development of logic
- Increased ease of debugging
- Easier upgrading

Components of a table

A table is made up of Fields, Properties, Triggers (some of which may contain C/AL code), and Keys. Fields also have Properties and Triggers. Keys also have Properties.

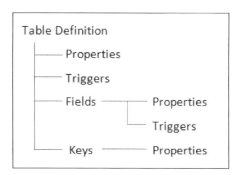

A table definition which takes full advantage of these capabilities reduces the effort required to construct other parts of the application. Good table design can significantly enhance the application's processing speed, efficiency, and flexibility.

A table can have:

- Up to 500 fields
- A defined record size of up to 8,000 bytes (with each field sized at its maximum)
- Up to 40 different keys

Naming a table

There are standardized naming conventions defined for NAV which we should follow. Names for tables and other objects should be as descriptive as possible, while keeping to a reasonable length. This makes our work more self-documenting.

Table names should always be singular. A table containing data about customers should not be named `Customers`, but `Customer`. The table we created for our WDTU Radio Station NAV enhancement was named `Radio Show`, even though it will contain data for all WDTU's radio shows.

In general, we should always name a table such that it is easy to identify the relationship between the table and the data it contains. For example, two tables containing the transactions on which a document page is based should normally be referred to as a **Header** table (for the main portion of the page) and a **Line** table (for the line detail portion of the page). As an example, the tables underlying a Sales Order page are the Sales Header and the Sales Line tables. The Sales Header table contains all the data that occurs only once for a Sales Order, while the Sales Line table contains all the lines for the order.

Additional information on table naming can be found in the old, but still useful, *Terminology Handbook for C/SIDE* and *C/AL Programming Guide,* which can be found on the Microsoft MSDN site at `http://social.msdn.microsoft.com/Search/en-US?query=Terminology%20Handbook%20for%20C%2FSIDE&ac=8` and `http://social.msdn.microsoft.com/Search/enUS?query=C%2FAL%20Programming%20Guide%20&ac=8`. These older documents may be obsolete in some areas. So of course, we should always refer first to the **Developer and IT Pro Help** included in NAV that is accessible from the Development Environment. The NAV 2015 Help is also on MSDN at `http://msdn.microsoft.com/en-us/library/hh173988(v=nav.80).aspx`. Much additional information can be found in the recently released C/AL Coding Guidelines at `https://community.dynamics.com/nav/w/designpatterns/156.cal-coding-guidelines`, including a **How do I** video.

Table numbering

There are no hard and fast rules for table numbering, except that we must only use the table object numbers that we are licensed to use. If all we have is the basic **Table Designer** rights, we are generally allowed to create tables numbered from 50000 to 50009 (unless our license was defined differently from the typical one). If we need more table objects, we can purchase licensing for table objects numbered up to 99999. **Independent Software Vendors (ISVs)** can purchase access to tables in other number ranges to use for their add-on products.

When creating several related tables, ideally, we should assign them related numbers in sequential order. We should let common sense be our guide to assigning table numbers. It requires considerable effort to renumber tables containing data.

Table properties

The first step in studying the internal construction of a table is to open it in Design mode. This is done as follows:

1. Open the **Development Environment** window.
2. Click on the **Table** button in the left column of buttons.
3. Highlight the table to work on (in this case, **Table 18 Customer**).
4. Click on the **Design** button at the bottom-right of the screen.

We now have the Customer table open in the Table Designer in Design mode. In *Chapter 1, An Introduction to NAV 2015*, we reviewed the function of the icons across the top of the **Table Designer**, but they are labeled in the following screenshot as a memory aid:

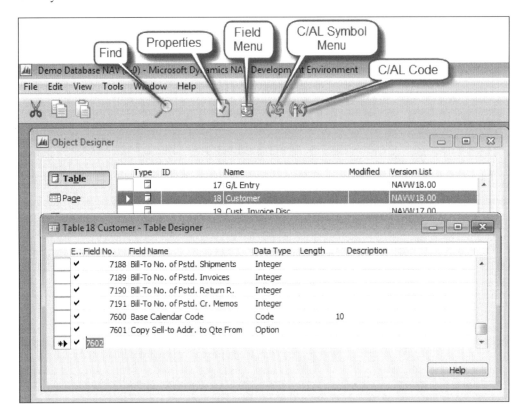

We can access the properties of a table while viewing the table in **Design** mode. Place the cursor on an empty field line (for example, the line below all the fields as shown in the preceding screenshot), and click on the Properties icon or press *Shift + F4* or use **View | Properties**. If we access properties while focus is on a field line, we will see the properties of that field (not the table).

This will take us to the **Table - Properties** display. The following screenshot is the **Table - Properties** display for the **Customer** table in the demonstration Cronus database:

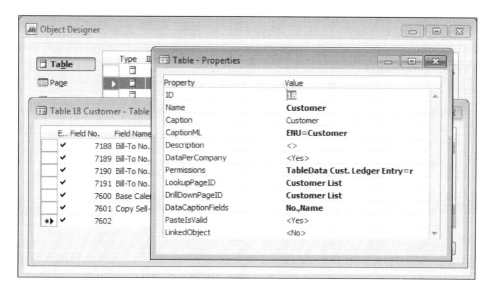

The table properties are as follows:

- **ID**: This is the object number of the table.

- **Name**: This is used for internal identification of the table object and acts as the default caption when data from this table is displayed.

- **Caption**: This contains the caption defined for the currently selected language. The default language for NAV is US English (ENU).

- **CaptionML**: This defines the **MultiLanguage** caption for the table. For an extended discussion on the language capabilities of NAV, refer to the section *MultiLanguage Development* in the online **Developer and IT Pro Help**.

- **Description**: This property is for optional documentation usage.

- **DataPerCompany**: This lets us define whether or not the data in this table is segregated by company (the default), or whether it is common (shared) across all companies in the database. The generated names of tables within SQL Server (not within NAV) are affected by this choice.

- **Permissions**: This allows us to grant users of this table different levels of access (**r**=read, **i**=insert, **m**=modify, and **d**=delete) to the table data in other table objects.

- **LookupPageID**: This allows us to define which Page is the default for looking up data in this table.

- **DrillDownPageID**: This allows us to define which Page is the default for drilling down into the supporting detail for the data that is summarized in this table.

- **DataCaptionFields**: This allows us to define specific fields whose contents will be displayed as part of the caption. For the Customer table, the No. and the Name will be displayed in the title bar at the top of a page showing a customer record.

- **PasteIsValid**: This property (Paste Is Valid) is not active in NAV 2015.

- **LinkedObject**: This lets us link the table to a SQL Server object. This feature allows the connection, for data access or maintenance, to a non-NAV system or an independent NAV system. For example, a LinkedObject could be an independently hosted and maintained special purpose database, and thus offload that processing from the main NAV system. When this property is set to **Yes,** then **LinkedInTransactionProperty** becomes available. **LinkedInTransactionProperty** should be set to **No** for any linkage to a SQL Server object outside the current database. The object being linked to must have a SQL Server table or view definition that is compatible with the Microsoft Dynamics NAV table definition.

As developers, we most frequently deal with the **ID**, **Name**, **LookupPageID**, **DrillDownPageID**, **Caption**, **CaptionML** (for languages other than American English), **DataCaption**, and **Permissions** properties. We rarely deal with the others.

Table triggers

To display the triggers with the table open in **Table Designer**, click on the **C/AL Code** icon or *F9* or **View | C/AL Code**. The first (top) table trigger is the **Documentation** trigger. This trigger is somewhat misleadingly named as it only serves as a location for needed documentation. No C/AL code in a **Documentation** trigger is executed. There are no syntax or format rules here, but we should follow a standard format of some type.

Every change to an object should be briefly documented in the **Documentation** trigger. The use of a standard format for such entries makes it easier to create them as well as to understand them two years later. For example:

```
CD.02 - 2015-03-16  Change to track when new customer added

  - Added field 50012 "Start Date"
```

The **Documentation** trigger has the same appearance as the four other triggers in a table definition, shown in the following screenshot, each of which can contain the C/AL code:

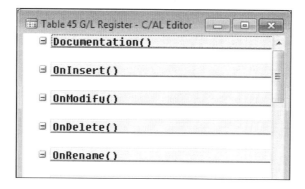

The code contained in a trigger is executed prior to the event represented by the trigger. In other words, the code in the `OnInsert()` trigger is executed before the record is inserted into the table. This allows the developer a final opportunity to perform validations and to enforce data consistency such as referential integrity. We can even abort the intended action if data inconsistencies or conflicts are found.

These triggers are automatically invoked when record processing occurs as the result of User action. But when table data is changed by C/AL code or by a data import, the C/AL code or import process determines whether or not the code in the applicable trigger is executed, as follows:

- **OnInsert()**: This is executed when a new record is to be inserted in to the table through the User Interface. (In general, new records are added when the last field of the primary key is completed and focus leaves that field. See the `DelayedInsert` property in *Chapter 4*, *Pages - the Interactive Interface* for an exception).

- **OnModify()**: This is executed when a record is rewritten after the contents of any field other than a primary key field have been changed. The change is determined by comparing `xRec` (the image of the record prior to being changed) to `Rec` (the current record copy). During our development work, if we need to see what the "before" value of a record or field is, we can reference the contents of `xRec` and compare that to the equivalent portion of `Rec`. These variables (`Rec` and `xRec`) are System-Defined Variables.

- **OnDelete()**: This is executed before a record is to be deleted from the table.

- **OnRename()**: This is executed when some portion of the primary key of the record is about to be changed. Changing any part of the primary key is a Rename action. This maintains a level of referential integrity. Unlike some systems, NAV allows the primary key of any master record to be changed, and automatically maintains all the affected foreign key references from other records.

There is an internal inconsistency in the handling of data integrity by NAV. On one hand, the `OnRename()` trigger automatically maintains one level of referential integrity when any part of the primary key is changed (that is, the record is "renamed"). This happens in a "black box" process, an internal process that we cannot see or touch.

However, if we delete a record, NAV doesn't automatically do anything to maintain referential integrity. For example, child records could be orphaned by a deletion, left without any parent record. Or if there are references in other records back to the deleted record, they could be left with no target. In this latest version of NAV, code has been added to the **OnDelete()** trigger of many (perhaps all) tables to handle this aspect of referential integrity. As developers, we are responsible for ensuring this part of referential integrity in our customizations.

When we write the C/AL code in one object that updates data in another (table) object, we can control whether or not the applicable table update trigger fires (executes). For example, if we were adding a record to our Radio Show table and used the following C/AL code, the **OnInsert()** trigger would fire:

```
"RadioShow".INSERT(TRUE);
```

However, if we use either of the following C/AL code options instead, the `OnInsert()` trigger would not fire and none of the logic inside the trigger would be executed:

```
"RadioShow".INSERT(FALSE);
```

or,

```
"RadioShow".INSERT;
```

It's always a good habit to write code explicitly so there is no doubt what the intended action is; in other words, use the explicit `true` or `false`.

The automatic "black box" logic enforcing primary key uniqueness will happen whether or not the `OnInsert()` trigger is fired.

Keys

Table keys are used to identify records, and to speed up filtering and sorting. Having too few keys may result in painfully slow inquiries and reports. However, each key incurs a processing cost because the index containing the key must be updated every time information in a key field changes. Key cost is measured primarily in terms of increased index maintenance processing. There is also additional cost in terms of disk storage space (usually not significant) and additional backup/recovery time (sometimes very important).

When a system is optimized for processing speed, it is critical to analyze the SQL Server indexes that are active because that is where the updating and retrieval time are determined. The determination of the proper number and design of keys and indexes for a table requires a thorough understanding of the types and frequencies of inquiries, reports, and other processing for that table.

Every NAV table must have at least one key — the primary key. The primary key is always the first key in the key list. By default, the primary key is made up of the first field defined in the table. In many of the **Reference** tables, there is only one field in the primary key and the only key is the primary key. An example is the **Payment Terms** table. Highlight **Table 3 Payment Terms**, then click on the **Design** button to see the **Keys** window, and click on **View | Keys**:

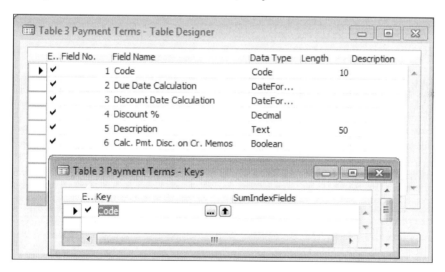

The primary key must have a unique value in each table record. We can change the primary key to be any field, or any combination of fields up to 16 fields totaling up to 900 bytes, but the uniqueness requirement must be met. It will automatically be enforced by NAV because NAV will not allow us to add a record in to a table with a duplicate primary key.

When we examine the primary keys in the supplied tables, we see that many of them consist only of or terminate in a **Line No.**, an **Entry No.**, or another data field whose contents make the key unique. For example, the **G/L Entry** table in the following screenshot uses just the **Entry No.** as the primary key. It is a NAV standard that the **Entry No.** fields contain a value that is unique for each record.

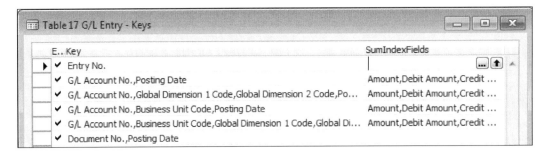

The primary key of the **Sales Line** table shown in the following screenshot is made up of several fields, with the **Line No.** of each record as the terminating primary key field. In NAV, the **Line No.** fields are assigned a unique number within the associated document. **Line No.** combined with the preceding fields in the primary key (usually including fields, such as **Document Type** and **Document No**, which relate to the parent Header record) makes each primary key entry unique. The logic supporting the assignment of the **Line No.** values is done within explicit C/AL code. It is not an automatic feature. The **No. Series** pattern documentation can be found at `https://community.dynamics.com/nav/w/designpatterns/74.no-series.aspx`.

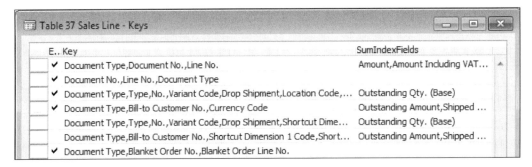

All keys except the primary key are secondary keys. There is no required uniqueness constraint on secondary keys. There is no requirement to have any secondary keys. If we want a secondary key not to have duplicate values, our C/AL code must check for duplication before completing the new entry.

The maximum number of fields that can be used in any one key is 16 with a maximum total length of 900 bytes. At the same time, the total number of different fields that can be used in all the keys combined cannot exceed 16. If the primary key includes three fields (as in the preceding screenshot), then the secondary keys can use up to 13 other fields (16 minus 3) in various combinations, plus any or all of the fields in the primary key. If the primary key has 16 fields, then the secondary keys can only consist of different groupings and sequences of those 16 fields. The first release of the NAV 2015 C/AL compiler allows up to 20 fields in a key, but the last 4 fields are ignored by SQL Server. Behind the scenes, each secondary key has the primary key appended to the backend. A maximum of 40 keys is allowed per table.

 Database maintenance performance is faster with fewer fields in keys, especially the primary key. The same is true when there are fewer keys. This must be balanced against improved performance in processes by having the optimum key contents and choices.

A number of SQL Server-specific key-related parameters have been added to NAV. These key properties can be accessed by highlighting a key in the Keys form, then clicking on the **Properties** icon or pressing *Shift + F4*. We can also display these properties in the **Keys** screen by accessing **View | Show Column** and selecting the columns we want displayed. The following screenshot shows both the **Show Column** choice form and the resulting **Keys** form with all the available columns displayed:

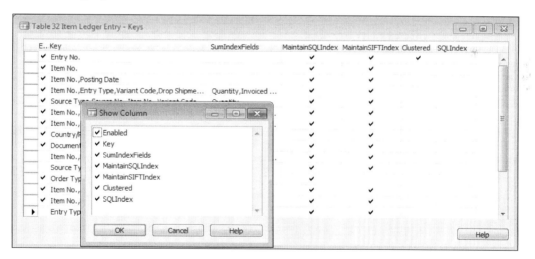

SumIndexFields

Since the beginning of NAV (formerly Navision), one of its unique capabilities has been the **SumIndexField Technology** (SIFT) feature These fields serve as the basis for FlowFields (automatically accumulating totals) and are unique to NAV. This feature allows NAV to provide almost instantaneous responses to user inquiries for summed data, calculated on the fly at runtime, related to the SumIndexFields. The cost is primarily that of the time required to maintain the SIFT indexes when a table is updated.

NAV 2015 maintains SIFT totals using **SQL Server Indexed Views**. An indexed view is a view that has been preprocessed and stored. NAV 2015 creates one indexed view for each enabled SIFT key. SIFT keys are enabled and disabled through the **MaintainSIFTIndex** property. SQL Server maintains the contents of the view when any changes are made to the base table, unless the **MaintainSIFTIndex** property is set to No.

SumIndexFields are accumulated sums of individual fields (columns) in tables. When the totals are automatically precalculated, they are easy to use and provide very high-speed access for inquiries. If users need to know the total of the **Amount** values in a **Ledger** table, the **Amount** field can be attached as a **SumIndexField** to the appropriate keys. In another table such as Customer, **FlowFields** can be defined as display fields take the advantage of the **SumIndexFields** property. This gives the users a very rapid response for calculating a total Balance amount inquiry based on detailed **Ledger Amounts** tied to those keys. We will discuss the various data field types and **FlowFields** in more detail in a later chapter.

In a typical ERP system, many thousands, millions, or even hundreds of millions of records might have to be processed to give such results, taking considerable time. In NAV, only a few records need to be accessed to provide the requested results. The processing is fast and the programming is greatly simplified.

SQL Server SIFT values are maintained through the use of SQL Indexed Views. By use of the **Key** property **MaintainSIFTIndex**, we can control whether or not the SIFT index is maintained dynamically (faster response) or only created when needed (less ongoing system performance load). The C/AL code is the same whether the SIFT is maintained dynamically or not. In NAV 2015, SIFT indexes can be built by SQL Server on-the-fly, but at the cost of having the full SIFT construction happen at one time rather than incrementally as records are added to the table. To define permanent SIFT indexes or not is a design choice that must be made carefully.

Too many Keys or SIFT fields can negatively affect system performance for two reasons. The first, which we already discussed, is the index maintenance processing load. The second is the table locking interference that can occur when multiple threads are requesting update access to a set of records that update SIFT values.

Conversely, the lack of necessary Keys or SIFT definitions can also cause performance problems. Having unnecessary data fields in a SIFT key creates many extra entries, affecting performance. Integer fields usually create an especially large number of unique SIFT index values and the **Option** fields create a relatively small number of index values.

The best design for a SIFT index has the fields which will be used most frequently in queries positioned on the left-hand side of the index in order of descending frequency of use. In a nutshell, we should be careful in our design of Keys and SIFT fields. While a system is in production, applicable SQL Server statistics should be monitored regularly and appropriate maintenance actions taken. NAV 2015 automatically maintains a count for all SIFT indexes, thus speeding up all **COUNT** and **AVERAGE** FlowField calculations.

The **MaintainSQLIndex** and **MaintainSIFTIndex** properties shown in the previous image allow the developer and/or system administrator to determine whether or not a particular key or SIFT field will be continuously maintained or will be recreated only when needed. Indexes that are not maintained, minimize record update time but require longer processing time to dynamically create the indexes when they are used. This level of control is useful for managing indexes that are only needed occasionally. For example, a Key or SIFT index that is used only for monthly reports can be disabled and no index maintenance processing be done on a day-to-day basis. If the month end need is for a single report, the particular index will be recreated automatically when the report is run. If the month end need is for a number of reports, the system administrator might enable the index, process the reports, then disable the index again.

Field Groups

When a user starts to enter data in a field where the choices are constrained to existing data (for example, an Item No., a Salesperson Code, a Unit of Measure code, a Customer No., and so on), good design dictates that the system will help the user by displaying the universe of acceptable choices. Put simply, a lookup list of choices should be displayed.

In the Role Tailored Client, the lookup display (a drop-down control) is generated dynamically when its display is requested by the user's effort to enter data in a field that references a table through the **TableRelation** property (which will be discussed in more detail in the next chapter). The format of the drop-down is a basic list. The fields that are included in that list and their left-to-right display sequence are either defined by default, or by an entry in the **Field Groups** table.

The **Field Groups** table is part of the NAV table definition much like the list of Keys. In fact, the **Field Groups** table is accessed very similarly to the Keys, via **View | Field Groups**.

If we look at **Field Groups** for **Table 27 - Item**, we see the drop-down information defined in **Field Group**, which must be named DropDown (without a hyphen):

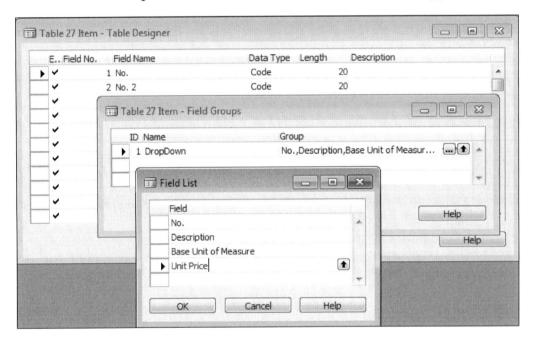

The drop-down display created by this particular Field Group is shown in the following screenshot of the Sales Order page, contains fields in the same order of appearance as in the Field Group definition.

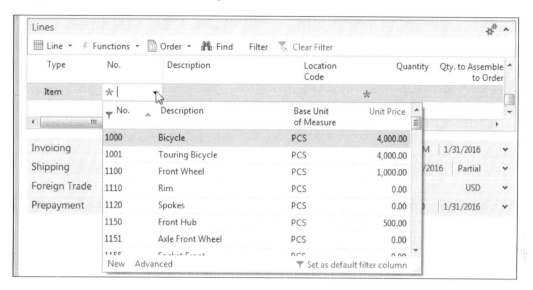

If no Field Group is defined for a table, the system defaults to using the primary key plus the **Description** field (or **Name** field).

Since Field Groups can be modified, they provide another opportunity for tailoring the user interface. As we saw in the preceding screenshot, the standard structure for the fields in a Field Group is to have the primary key appear first. The user can choose any of the displayed fields to be the default filter column, the defacto lookup field.

As a system option, the drop-down control provides a find-as-you-type capability, where the set of displayed choices filters and redisplays dynamically as the user types, character by character. The filter applies to the default filter column. Whatever field is used for the lookup, the referential field defined in the page determines what data field contents are copied into the target table. In the preceding image example, the reference table/field is the Sales Line table/field "No." and the target table/field is the Item table/field "No.".

As developers, we can change the order of appearance of the fields in the drop-down display. We can also add or delete fields by changing the contents of the Field Group. For example, we could add a capability to our page that provides an "alternate search" capability (where if the match for an Item No. isn't found in the **No.** field, the system will look for a match based on another field). In NAV 2015, fields in a field group no longer must be in a key.

Consider this situation: the customer has a system design where the Item No. contains a hard to remember, sequentially assigned code to uniquely identify each item. But the **Search Description** field contains a product description that is relatively easy for the users to remember. When the user types, the find-as-you-type feature helps them to focus and find the specific Item No. to be entered for the order. In order to support this, we simply need to add the **Search Description** field to the Field Group for the Item table as the first field in the sequence. The following screenshot shows that change in the **Item Field Group** table:

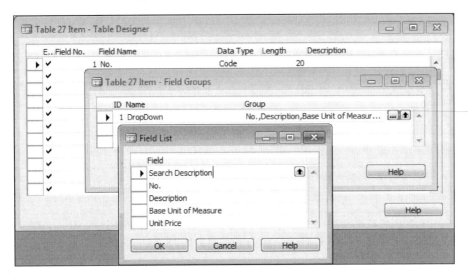

The effect of this change can be seen in the following screenshot which shows the revised drop-down control. The user has begun entry in the **No.** field, but the lookup has focused on the newly added **Search Description** field. Find-as-you-type has filtered the displayed items down to just those that match the data string entered so far (user has entered st; Field Group has filtered to items with **Search Description** starting with st).

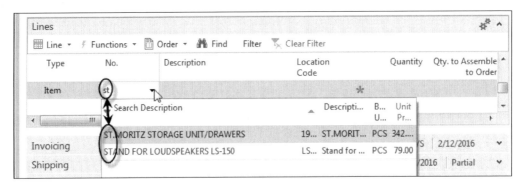

The result of our change allows the user to lookup the items by their **Search Description**, rather than by the harder to remember **Item No**. Obviously, any field in the Item table could have been used, including our custom fields.

Enhancing our sample application

Now we can take our knowledge of tables and expand our WDTU application. Our base Radio Show table needs to be added to and modified. We also need to create and reference additional tables.

Although we want to have a realistic design in our sample application, we will focus on changes that illustrate the features in the NAV table design which the authors feel are among the most important. If there are capabilities or functionalities that you feel are missing, feel free to add them. Adjust the examples as much as you wish to make them more meaningful to you.

Creating and modifying tables

In *Chapter 1, An Introduction to NAV 2015*, we created the Radio Show table for the WDTU application. At that time we used the minimum fields that allowed us to usefully define a master record. Now, let's set properties on existing data fields, add more data fields, and create an additional data table to which the Radio Show table can refer.

Our new data fields are shown in the following layout table:

Field No.	Field Name	Description
1000	Frequency	An Option data type (Hourly, Daily, Weekly, Monthly) for the frequency of a show; Hourly to be used for a show segment such as news, sports, or weather that is scheduled every hour. A space/ blank is used for the first option to allow a valid blank field value.
1010	PSA Planned Quantity	A number (stored as an Integer) of Public Service Announcements to be played per show; this will be used by playlist generation and posting logic.
1020	Ads Planned Quantity	A number (stored as an Integer) of advertisements to be played per show; this will be used by playlist generation and posting logic.
1030	News Required	Is headline news required to be broadcast during the show (a Boolean)?

Field No.	Field Name	Description
1040	**News Duration**	The duration (stored as a Duration) of the news program embedded within the show.
1050	**Sports Required**	Is sports news required to be broadcast during the show (a Boolean)?
1060	**Sports Duration**	The duration (stored as a Duration) of the sports program embedded within the show.
1070	**Weather Required**	Is weather news required to be broadcast during the show (a Boolean)?
1080	**Weather Duration**	The duration (stored as a Duration) of the weather program embedded within the show.
1130	**Date Filter**	A date FlowFilter (stored as a `Data Type Date`, `Data Class FlowFilter`) that will change the calculations of the flow fields based on the date filter applied. More on `FlowFilters` in *Chapter 3, Data Types and Fields*.

After we have completed our Radio Show table, it will look like the following image:

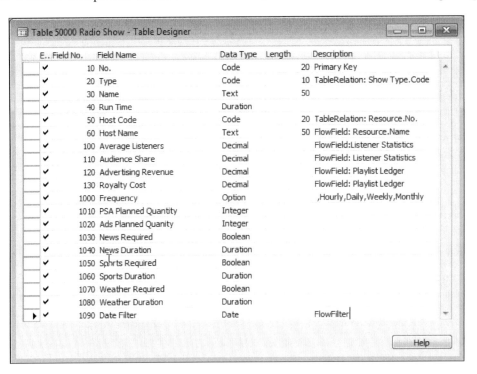

Next we need to fill the **OptionString** and **Caption** properties for the **Option** field
Frequency. Highlight the **Frequency** field, then click on the **Properties** icon or press
Shift + F4. Enter the values for the **OptionString** property as shown in the next
screenshot; don't forget to include the leading space followed by a comma to get
a space/blank as the first option. Be sure to copy and paste the same information
to the **OptionCaption** property. The **OptionCaptionML** property will be filled
in automatically with a copy of that information (since we do not have a second
language installed). Note that the properties that have been changed from the default
are displayed in bold. This new feature makes it much easier for developers to see
what properties have been modified.

Next we want to define the reference table we are going to tie to the **Type** field. The table will contain a list of the available Radio Show Types such as Music, Talk, Sports, and so on. We will keep this table very simple, with **Code** as the unique key field and **Description** as the text field. Both fields will be of the default length as shown in the following layout. Create the new table and save it as Table 50001 with the name of Radio Show Type.

Field No.	Field Name	Description	Data Type	Length
10	Code	Primary key of data type Code	Code	10
20	Description	A text field	Text	30

Before we can use this table as a reference from the Radio Station table, we need to create a list page that will be used for both data entry and data selection for the table. We will use **Page Designer**, and **Page Wizard** to create a **List** page. We should be able to do this pretty quickly. Click on **Pages**, click on the **New** button, enter 50001 in the **Table** field (the table field will redisplay the table name), then choose the wizard to create a page type of **List**.

Populate the page with all the fields from the Radio Show Type table. Our designed page should look like the following screenshot:

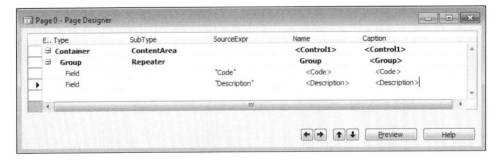

Save the page as number `50002`, and exit **Page Designer**, naming the page **Radio Show Types**. Test the page by highlighting it in the Object Designer, then clicking on the **Run** button. The new page will be displayed. While the page is open, enter some data (by clicking on **New**) such as the examples shown in the following screenshot:

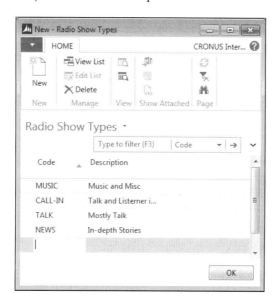

Now we'll return to the Radio Show Type table and set the Table's Properties for **LookupPageID** and **DrillDownPageID** to point to the new page we have just created. As a reminder, we will use **Design** to open the table definition, then focus on the empty line below the description field, and either click on the Properties icon or press *Shift + F4*.

In the value for each of the two `PageID` properties, we can either enter the page name (`Radio Show Types`) or the page number (`50002`). Either entry will work, but as you can see in the following screenshot, the appearance depends on what you enter:

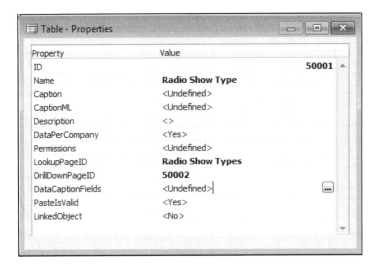

After the table has been saved, the next time we view these two `PageID` properties, they look like the following image:

Assigning a Table Relation property

Finally, we open the Radio Show table again by highlighting the table line and clicking on the **Design** button. This time highlight the **Type** field and access its **Properties** screen. Highlight the **TableRelation** property and click on the **ellipsis** button (the three dots). We see the **Table Relation** screen with four columns, as shown in the following image. The middle two columns are headed **Table** and **Field**. In the top line in the Table column, enter `50001` (the table number) or `Radio Show Type` (the table name). In the same line, in the **Field** column, click on the up-arrow button and choose **Code**.

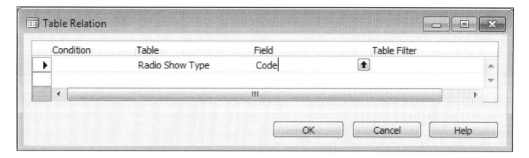

We exit the **Table Relation** screen (by clicking the **OK** button) and return to the **Type - Properties** page that looks like the following image. Save and exit the modified table.

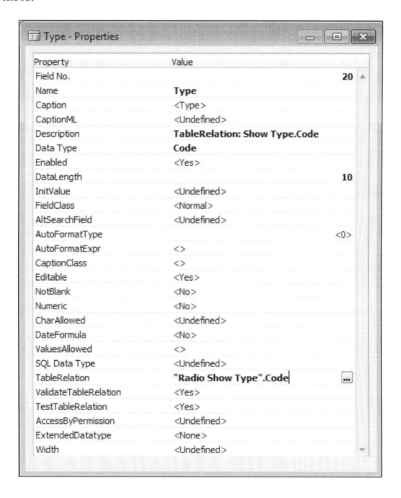

To check that **TableRelation** is working properly, we could run the Radio Show table (that is, highlight the table name and click on the **Run** button). We could also run the **Radio Show List** page and have almost exactly the same view of the data. This is because the Run of a table creates a temporary list page which includes all the fields in the table: thus, it contains the same data fields as the page we created using the **Page** Wizard. In either one, we should highlight the **Radio Show Type** field and click on the drop-down arrow to view the list of available entries. The following image is of our **Radio Show List** page; you should also try it using the **Run** function on the **Radio Show** table:

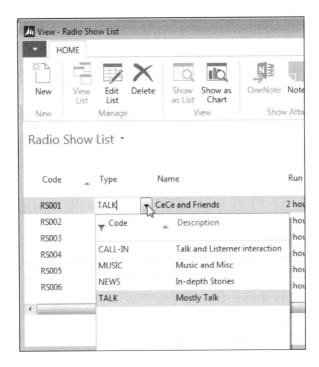

If all has gone according to plan, the Radio Show Type field will display a drop-down arrow (the downward pointing arrowhead button). Whether we click on that button or press *F4*, we will invoke the drop-down list for the Radio Show Type table, as shown before.

Assigning an InitValue property

Another property we can define for several of the Radio Show fields is **InitValue**. WDTU has a standard policy that news, sports, and weather be broadcast for a few minutes each at the beginning of every hour in the day. We want the Boolean (Yes/No) fields for News Required, Sports Required, and Weather Required to default to Yes. We also want the default time value of the News Duration, Sports Duration, and Weather Duration to be 2 minutes, 2 minutes, and 1 minute, respectively. That way the first 5 minutes of every hour can be spent on keeping the listeners informed of the latest happenings.

Setting the default for a field to a specific value simply requires setting the **InitValue** property to the desired value. In the case of the "Required" Boolean fields, that value is set to Yes. Using the Table Designer, we must Design the Radio Station table, and access the **Properties** screen for the **News Required** field. Repeat this for the **Sports Required** and **Weather Required** fields. After we have filled in the values for the three fields, exit the **Properties** screen, exit **Table Designer**, and save the changes.

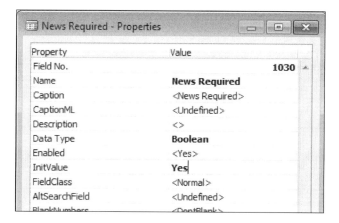

In the case of the "Duration" fields, we will set **InitValue** to 2 minutes each for **News Duration** and **Sports Duration**, and 1 minute for **Weather Duration**. Duration fields require both the time span numeric and the time unit of measure (seconds, minutes, hours, and so forth). Our entries will look like 2 minutes (or 2 minute, both are acceptable).

Adding a few activity-tracking tables

Our WDTU organization is a profitable and productive radio station. We track historical information about our advertisers, royalties owed, and listenership. We track the music that is played, the rates we charge for advertisements based on the time of day, and we provide a public service by broadcasting a variety of government and other public service announcements.

We aren't going to cover all these features and functions in the following detailed exercises. However, it's always good to have a complete view of the system on which we are working, even if we are only working on one or two components. In this case, the parts of the system not covered in detail in our exercises will be opportunities for you to extend your studies and practice on your own.

Any system development should start with a Design Document that completely spells out the goals and the functional design details. Neither system design nor project management will be covered in this book, but when we begin working on production projects proper attention to both of these areas will be critical to success. Use of a proven project management methodology can make a project much more likely to be on time and within budget.

Based on the requirements our analysts have given us, we need to expand our application design. We started with a Radio Show table, one reference table (Radio Show Type), and pages for each of them. We earlier entered some test data and added a few additional fields to the Radio table (which we will not add to our pages here).

Now we will add a supplemental table, document (header and line) tables, plus a ledger (activity history) table relating to Playlist activities. Following that, we will also create some pages for our new data structures.

Our WDTU application will now include the following tables:

- **Radio Show**: A master list of all programs broadcast by our station.
- **Radio Show Type**: A reference list of possible types of radio shows.
- **Playlist Header**: A single instance of a Radio Show with child data in the form of Playlist Lines.
- **Playlist Line**: Each line represents one of a list of items and/or durations per Radio Show.
- **Playlist Item Rate**: A list of rates for items played during a show as determined by our advertising sales staff or the royalty organization we use.

- **Radio Show Ledger**: A detailed history of all the time spent and items played during the show, with any related royalties owed or advertisement revenue expected.

- **Listenership Ledger**: A detailed history of estimated listenership provided by the ratings organization to which we subscribe.

- **Publisher**: A reference list of the publishers of content that we use. This will include music distributors, news wires, sports and weather sources, as well as WDTU (we use material that we publish).

Remember, one purpose of this example system is for you to follow along in a hands-on basis in your own system. You may want to try different data structures and other object features. For example, you could add functionality to track volunteer activity, perhaps even detailing the type of support the volunteers provide.

For the best learning experience, you should be creating each of these objects in your development system to learn by experimenting. In the course of these exercises, it will be good if you make some mistakes and see some new error messages. That's part of the learning experience. A test system is the best place to learn from mistakes, at the minimum cost.

New tables for our WDTU project

First, we create a **Playlist Header** table (Table number **50002**), which will contain one record for each scheduled Radio Show:

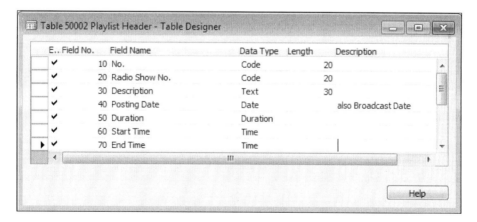

Then we will create the associated **Playlist Line** table (Table number **50003**). This table will contain the child records for the **Playlist Header** table. Each **Playlist Line** record represents one scheduled piece of music, advertisement, public service announcement, or embedded show within the scheduled Radio Show, as defined in the **Playlist Header** table. The description for each of the **Option** fields shows the information that needs to be entered into the **OptionString, OptionCaption,** and **OptionCaptionML** properties for those fields.

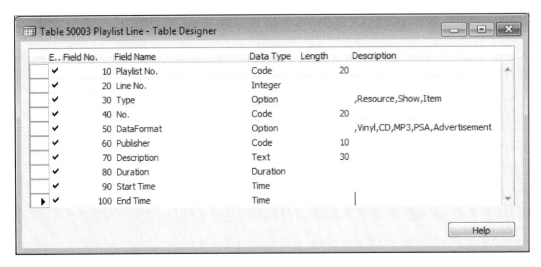

Now we'll create our **Playlist Item Rate** table. These rates include both what we charge for ad time and what we must pay in royalties for material we broadcast.

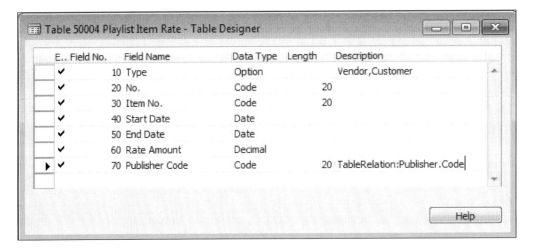

A Ledger table contains the detailed history of processed activity records. In this case, the data is a detailed history of all the **Playlist Line** records for previously broadcast shows.

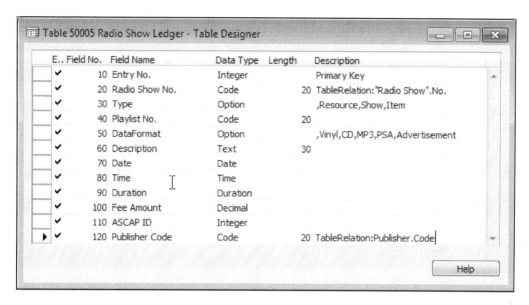

Now we'll create one more Ledger table to retain the data we receive from the listenership rating service.

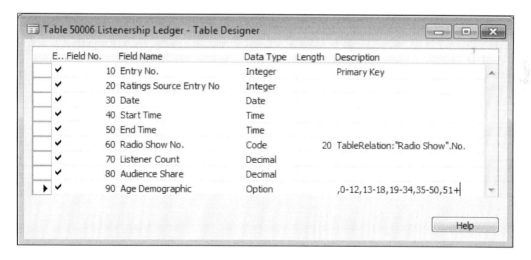

Finally, the last new table definition for now, our **Publisher** table, is shown in the next screenshot:

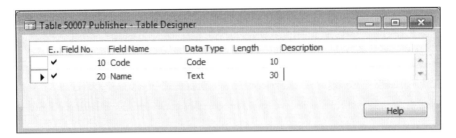

New list pages for our WDTU project

Each of the new tables we have created should be supported with an appropriately named List Page. As part of our WDTU project work, we should create the following pages:

- **50003 Playlist Document**
- **50005 Playlist Item Rates**
- **50006 Radio Show Ledger**
- **50007 Listenership Ledger**
- **50008 Publishers**

Keys, SumIndexFields, and table relations in our examples

Thus far, we have created basic table definitions and associated pages for the WDTU project. The next step is to flesh out those definitions with additional keys, SIFT field definitions, table relations, and so on. The purpose of these are to make our data easier and faster to access, to take advantage of the special features of NAV to create data totals and to facilitate relationships between various data elements.

Secondary keys and SumIndexFields

The **Playlist Line** table default primary key was the one field **Playlist No**. In order for the primary key to be unique for each record, another field is needed. For a Line table, the additional field is the **Line No.** field which is incremented via the C/AL code for each record. So we'll change the key for table 50003 accordingly.

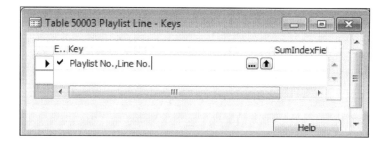

We know a lot of reporting will be done based on the data in the Radio Show Ledger. We also know that we want to report on data by Radio Show and by the Type of entry (individual song, specific ad, and so on). So we will add secondary keys for each of these, including the **Date** field so we can rapidly filter the data by Date. The reporting that is financial in nature will need totals for the **Fee Amount** field, so we'll put that in the **SumIndexFields** column for our new keys.

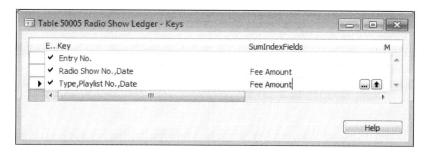

We know that to do the necessary Listenership analysis, the Listenership Ledger needs an additional key combined with **SumIndexFields** for totaling listener statistics.

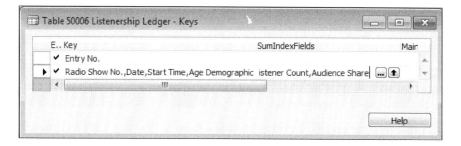

To utilize **SumIndexFields** we have just defined, we will need to define corresponding FlowFields in other tables. We will leave that part of the development effort for the next chapter where we are going to discuss Fields, Flowfields, and FlowFilters in detail.

Table relations

For those tables where we defined fields intended to refer to data in other tables for lookups and validation, we must define the relationships in the referring tables. Sometimes these relationships are complicated, dependent on other values within the record.

In Table 50003, Playlist Line, we have the field **No.** If the **Type** field contains **Resource**, then the **No.** field should contain a Resource No. If the **Type** field contains **Show**, then the **No.** field should contain a Show Code. And, if the **Type** field contains **Item**, the **No.** field should contain an Item No. The pseudo-code (approximate syntax) for that logic can be written as:

```
IF Type = 'Resource' THEN No. := Resource.No.
   ELSE IF Type = 'Show' THEN No. := Radio Show.No.
      ELSE IF Type = 'Item' THEN No. := Item.No.
```

Fortunately, a tool built into the C/SIDE editor makes it easy for us to build that complex logic in the **TableRelation** property. When we click on the **TableRelation** property, then click on the ellipsis button (three dots), we get a **Table Relation** screen we can use to construct the necessary logic structure:

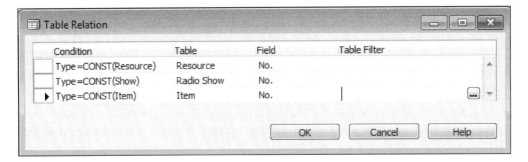

When we exit the **Table Relation** screen by clicking on the **OK** button, the **TableRelation** line looks like the following image:

Table 50004, Playlist Item Rate, has a similar **Table Relation** requirement for the field **No.** in that table. In this case, the **No.** field will refer to **Vendor No.** if **Type = Vendor**, or to the **Customer No.** if **Type = Customer**.

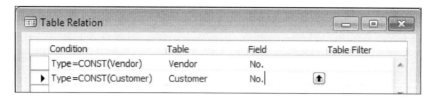

When we exit the **Table Relation** screen this time (by clicking on the **OK** button), the **TableRelation** line looks like the following image:

If in the process of making these changes (or some future changes), we realize that we need to change the Data Type of a field and try to do so, we may get the following error message:

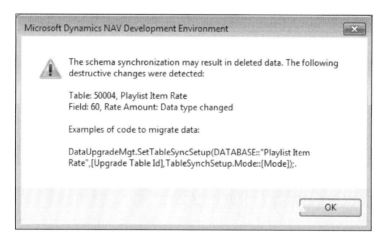

The intent of this message is to keep us from unintentionally deleting or corrupting data through a change in the table definition. After checking that we really aren't going to make that mistake, perhaps making a backup of the data about to be affected, we can override the system's error checking and force the change to be done by choosing the Synchronize Schema. The **Force** option in the **Save Changes** screen as shown following.

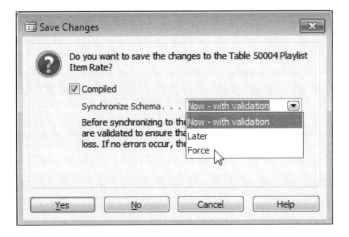

Modifying a standard table

One of the big advantages to the NAV system development environment is the fact that we are allowed to enhance the tables that are part of the standard product. Many package software products do not provide this flexibility. Nevertheless, with privilege comes responsibility. When we modify a standard NAV table, we must do so carefully.

In our system, we are going to use the standard **Item table – Table 27**, to store data about recordings such as music, advertisements, and PSAs which we have available for broadcast. One of the new fields will be an **Option** field. Another will refer to the Publisher table we created earlier. When the modifications to the Item table design are completed, they will look like the following image:

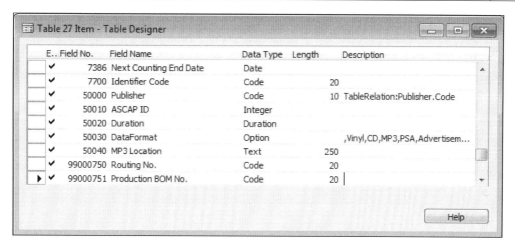

E..	Field No.	Field Name	Data Type	Length	Description
✔	7386	Next Counting End Date	Date		
✔	7700	Identifier Code	Code	20	
✔	50000	Publisher	Code	10	TableRelation:Publisher.Code
✔	50010	ASCAP ID	Integer		
✔	50020	Duration	Duration		
✔	50030	DataFormat	Option		,Vinyl,CD,MP3,PSA,Advertisem…
✔	50040	MP3 Location	Text	250	
✔	99000750	Routing No.	Code	20	
✔	99000751	Production BOM No.	Code	20	

Note that we were careful not to touch any of the standard fields that were already defined in the Item table. Plus, we numbered all our new fields in the range of 50000 to 99999, making them easy to identify as belonging to a Partner modification.

Version list documentation

In *Chapter 1, An Introduction to NAV 2015*, we mentioned the importance of good documentation; one component being the assignment of version numbers to modifications and enhancements. Frequently, modifications are identified with a combination letter number code, the letters indicating who did the modification (such as the NAV Partner initials — or, in this case, the book authors' combined initials) and a sequential number for the specific modification. Our Partner initials are CD, so all our modifications will have a version number of CDxx. We will use the Chapter number of this book for the sequential number, such as:

- CD01 – Chapter 01
- CD02 – Chapter 02
- CD01, 02 – Chapters 01 and 02

When applied to the table objects we have created so far, our Version List entries look like the following for the tables (Table 27 Item not shown):

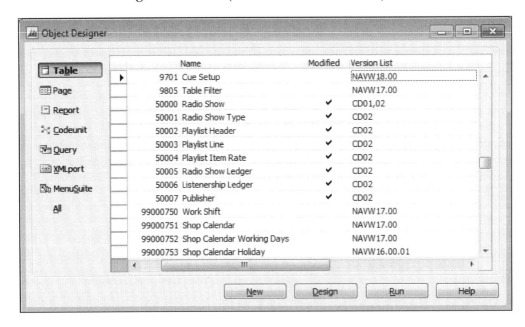

Similar version numbers should be assigned to the pages and reports that have been created thus far.

When working on a customer's system, a more general purpose versioning structure should be used in the same general format as the one used by Microsoft for the product. Such a structure would be in the format CD8.00.01 (CD company, NAV version 8, minor version 00 (no Service Pack), build 01). The next release of objects would then be CD8.00.02. In the **Documentation** trigger, there should be a sequential list of changes showing each incremental version followed by a list of all the features implemented for that version. This approach provides a standardized Version list externally and the full detail of changes internally. Done properly and combined with good external documentation describing the reasons and intended outcomes of each modification, the result is a system that is much easier to maintain.

Types of tables

For this discussion, we will divide table types into three categories: Fully Modifiable, Content Modifiable and Read-Only. As developers, we can change the definition and the contents of the first category (the Fully Modifiable Tables). We cannot change the definition of the base fields of the second category (the Content Modifiable Tables), but we can change the contents and add new fields. The third category (the Read-Only Tables) can be accessed for information, but neither the definition nor the data within is modifiable.

Fully Modifiable tables

The following tables are included in the fully modifiable tables category which includes the following table types:

- Master
- Journal
- Template
- Ledger
- Reference
- Register
- Posted document
- Setup
- Temporary

Patterns have been defined for Master and Setup table types. Other table patterns are likely to be defined over time.

Master

The Master table type contains primary data (such as Customers, Vendors, Items, Employees, and so on). In any enhancement project, these are the tables that should be designed first because everything else will be based on these tables. When working on a modification, necessary changes to Master tables should be defined first. Master tables always use card pages as their primary user input method. The Customer table is a Master table. A Customer record is shown in the following screenshot:

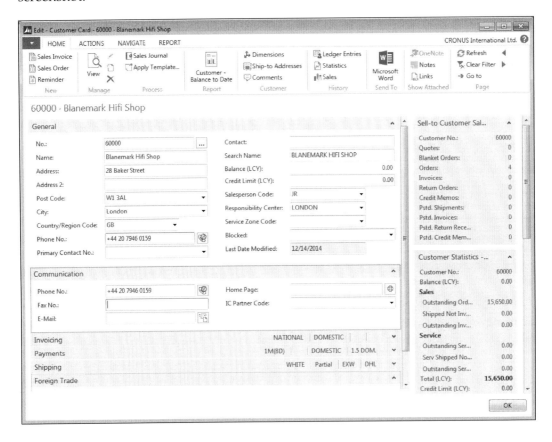

The preceding screenshot shows how the card page segregates the data into categories on different FastTabs (such as **General**, **Communication**, and **Invoicing**) and includes primary data fields (for example, **No.**, **Name**, **Address**), reference fields (for example, **Salesperson Code**, **Responsibility Center**), and a FlowField (for example, **Balance (LCY)**).

Journal

The Journal table type contains unposted activity detail—data that other systems refer to as **transactions**. Journals are where most repetitive data entry occurs in NAV. In the standard system, all Journal tables are matched with corresponding Template tables (one Template table for each Journal table). The standard system includes journals for Sales, Cash Receipts, General Journal entries, Physical Inventory, Purchases, Fixed Assets, and Warehouse Activity, among others.

The transactions in a Journal can be segregated into batches for entry, edit review, and processing purposes. Journal tables always use Worksheet pages as their primary user input method. The next two screenshots show two Journal Entry screens. They both use the **General Journal** table, but each has quite a different appearance, and are based on different pages and different templates.

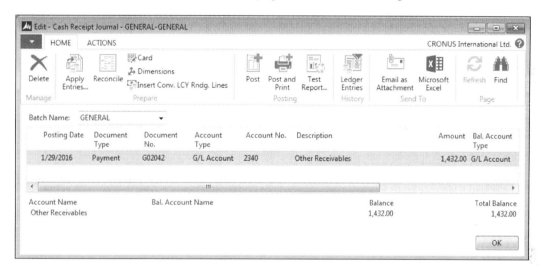

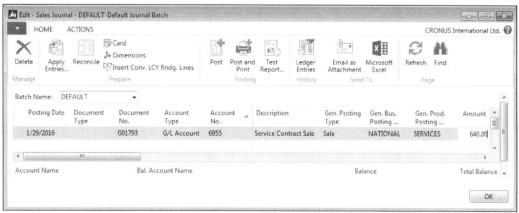

Comparing the preceding two screenshots, the differences include not only which fields are visible, but also what logic applies to data entry defaults and validations.

Template

The Template table type operates behind the scenes, providing control information for a Journal, which operates in the foreground. By using a Template, multiple instances of a Journal can each be tailored for different purposes. Control information contained in a Template includes the following:

- The default type of accounts to be updated (for example, Customer, Vendor, Bank, General Ledger)
- The specific account numbers to be used as defaults, including balancing accounts
- The transaction numbering series that will be used
- The default encoding to be applied to transactions for the Journal (for example, Source Code, Reason Code)
- Specific Pages and Reports to be used for data entry and processing of both edits and posting runs

For example, **General Journal Templates** allow the General Journal table to be tailored in order to display fields and perform validations that are specific to the entry of particular transaction categories such as **Cash Receipts**, **Payments**, **Purchases**, **Sales**, and other transaction entry types. Template tables always use tabular pages for user input. The following screenshot shows a list of the various General Journal Templates defined in the Cronus International Ltd. demonstration database:

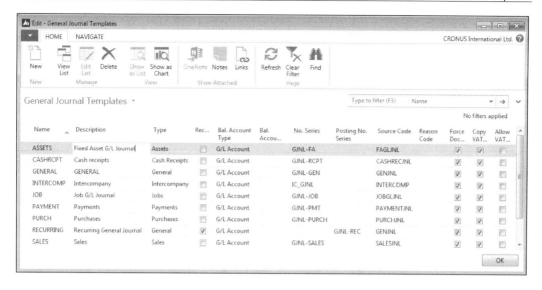

In addition to the Templates, there are Batch tables which allow us to set up any number of batches of data under each journal template. The Batch, Template, Journal Line structure provides a great deal of flexibility in data organization and definition of required fields while utilizing a common underlying table definition (the General Journal).

Ledger

The Ledger table type contains posted activity detail: the data other systems call history. NAV data flows from a Journal through a Posting routine into a Ledger. A significant advantage of NAV Ledger design is the fact that it allows retention of all detail indefinitely. While there are routines supporting compression of the Ledger data, if at all feasible we should retain the full historical detail of all activity. This allows users to have total flexibility for historical comparative or trend data analysis.

Ledger data is considered accounting data in NAV. We are not allowed to directly enter the data into a Ledger or change the existing data in a Ledger, but must "Post" to a Ledger. Posting is done by creating Journal Lines, validating the data as necessary, then posting those journal lines into the appropriate ledgers. Although we can physically force data into a Ledger with our Developer tools, we should not do so.

Because Ledger data is **accounting data**, we are not permitted to delete data from a Ledger table. Corrections are done by posting adjustments or reversing entries. We can compress or summarize Ledger data (very carefully), eliminating detail, but we should not change anything that would affect accounting totals for money or quantities.

User views of Ledger data are generally through use of List pages. The following screenshots show a **Customer Ledger Entries** list (financially oriented data) and an **Item Ledger Entries** list (quantity-oriented data). In each case, the data represents historical activity detail with accounting significance. There are other data fields in addition to those shown in the following screenshots. The fields shown here are representative. The users can utilize page-customization tools (which we will discuss in *Chapter 4, Pages - the Interactive Interface*) in order to create personalized page displays in a wide variety of ways. First, the **Customer Ledger Entries** list:

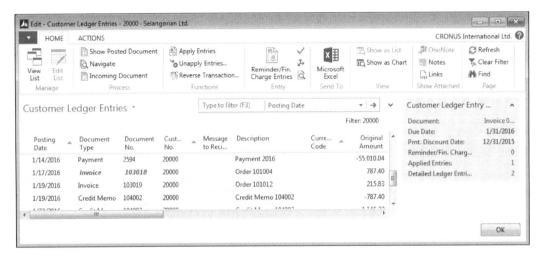

Second, the **Item Ledger Entries** list:

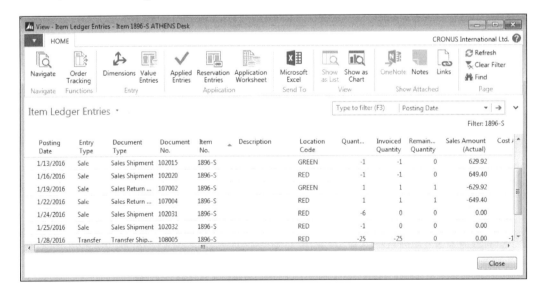

The **Customer Ledger Entries** page displays critical information such as **Posting Date** (the effective accounting date), **Document Type** (the type of transaction), **Customer No.**, and the **Original** and **Remaining Amount** of the transaction. The record also contains **Entry No.**, which uniquely identifies each record. The **Open** entries are those where the transaction amount has not been fully applied, such as an Invoice amount not fully paid or a Payment amount not fully consumed by Invoices.

The **Item Ledger Entries** page displays similar information pertinent to inventory transactions. As previously described, **Posting Date**, **Entry Type**, and **Item No.**, as well as the assigned **Location** for the Item, control the meaning of each transaction. Item Ledger Entries are expressed both in **Quantity** and **Amount** (Value). **Open** entries here are tied to **Remaining Quantity**, such as material that has been received but is still available in stock. In other words, the **Open** entries represent current inventory. Both the Customer Ledger Entry and Item Ledger Entry tables have underlying tables that provide additional details for entries affecting values.

Reference tables

The **Reference** (also called **Supplemental**) table type contains lists of codes, descriptions, or other validation data. Reference table examples are postal zone codes, country codes, currency codes, currency exchange rates, and so on. Reference tables are often accessed by means of one of the **Setup** menu options because they must be set up prior to being used for reference purposes by other tables. In our WDTU example, tables 50001 Radio Show Type and 50007 Publisher are Reference tables.

The following screenshots show some sample Reference tables for **Locations**, **Countries**, and **Payment Terms**. Each table contains data elements that are appropriate for its use as a Reference table, plus, in some cases, fields that control the effect of referencing a particular entry. These data elements are usually entered as part of a setup process and then updated over time as appropriate.

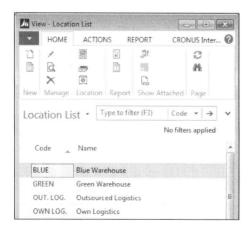

Location List in the preceding screenshot is a simple validation list of the Locations for this implementation. Usually, they represent physical sites, but depending on the implementation, they can also be used simply to segregate types of inventory. For example, locations could be **Refrigerated** versus **Unrefrigerated,** or there could be locations for **Awaiting Inspection**, **Passed Inspection,** and **Failed Inspection**.

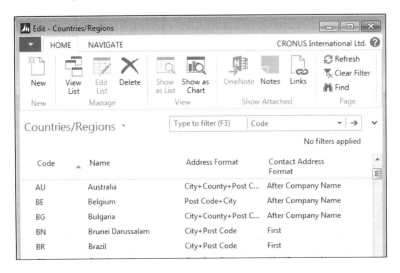

The **Countries/Regions** list in the preceding screenshot is used as validation data, defining the acceptable country codes. It also provides control information for the mailing **Address Format** (general organization address) and the **Contact Address Format** (for an individual contact's address).

The **Payment Terms** table shown in the following screenshot provides a list of payment terms codes along with a set of parameters that allows the system to calculate specific terms. In this set of data, for example, the **1M (8D)** code will yield payment terms of due in 1 month with a discount of **2%** applied for payments processed within 8 days of the invoice date. In another instance, **14D** payment terms will calculate the payment as due in 14 days from the date of invoice with no discount available.

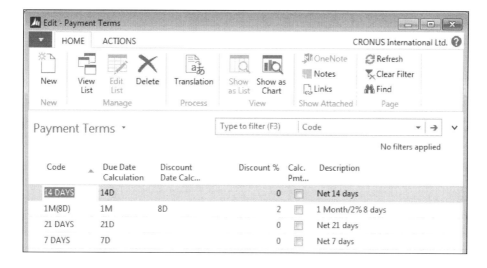

Register

The Register table type contains a record of the range of transaction ID numbers for each batch of posted Ledger entries. Register data provides an audit trail of the physical timing and sequence of postings. This, combined with the full detail retained in the Ledger, makes NAV a very auditable system because we can see exactly what activity was done and when it was done.

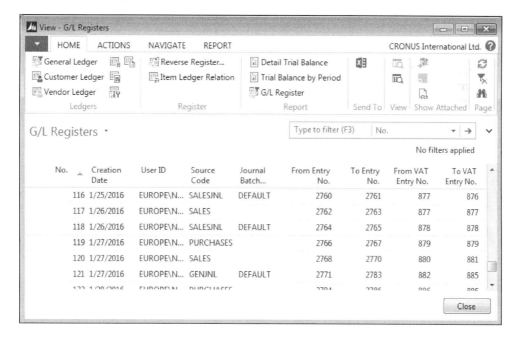

The user views **Register** through a tabular page, as shown in the previous screenshot. We see that each Register entry has **Creation Date**, **Source Code**, **Journal Batch Name**, and the identifying **Entry No.** range for all the entries in that batch. Another NAV feature, the **Navigate** function, which we will discuss in detail in *Chapter 4*, *Pages - the Interactive Interface*, also provides a very useful auditing tool. The **Navigate** function allows the user (who may be a developer doing testing) to highlight a single Ledger entry and find all the other Ledger entries and related records that resulted from the posting that created that highlighted entry.

Posted Document

The Posted Document type contains the posted copies of the original documents for a variety of data types such as Sales Invoices, Purchase Invoices, Sales Shipments, and Purchase Receipts. Posted documents are designed to provide an easy reference to the historical data in a format similar to what would have stored in paper files. A Posted Document looks very similar to the original source document. For example, a Posted Sales Invoice will look very similar to the original Sales Order or Sales Invoice. The Posted Documents are included in the **Navigate** function.

The following screenshots show a **Sales Order** before Posting and the resulting **Posted Sales Invoice** document. Both documents are in a header/detail format, where the information in the header applies to the whole order and the information in the detail is specific to the individual Order Line. As part of the **Sales Order** page, there is information displayed to the right of the actual order. This is designed to make the user's life easier by providing related information without requiring a separate lookup action.

First, we see the **Sales Order** document ready to be Posted:

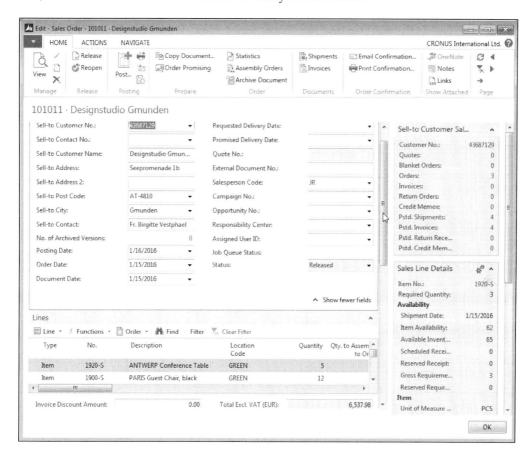

The following screenshot is that of the partial shipment **Sales Invoice** document after the Invoice has been posted for the shipped goods:

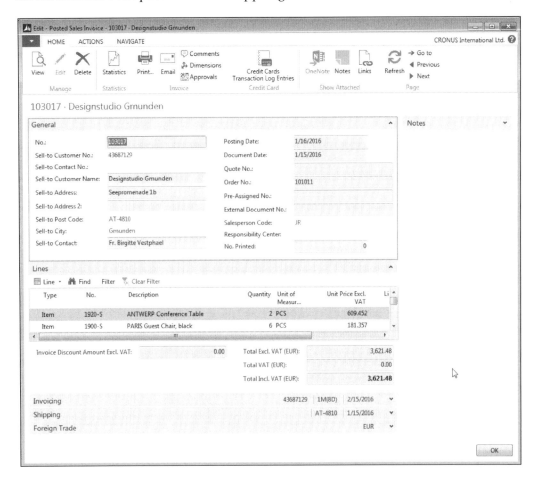

Setup

The Setup table type contains system or functional application control information. There is one Setup table per functional application area, for example, one for **Sales and Receivables**, one for **Purchases and Payables**, one for **General Ledger**, one for Inventory, and so on. Setup tables contain only a single record. Since a Setup table has only one record, it can have a primary key field which has no value assigned (this is how all the standard NAV Setup tables are designed). The Singleton (Setup) table Design Pattern can be found at:

```
https://community.dynamics.com/nav/w/designpatterns/151.singleton-
table.
```

The **Inventory Setup** page is shown in the following screenshot:

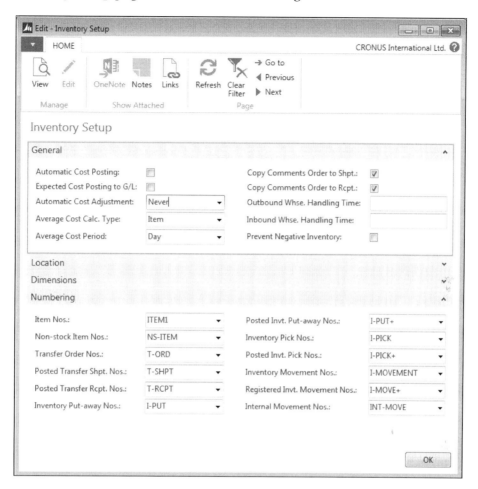

Temporary

The Temporary table is used within objects to hold temporary data. A Temporary table does not exist outside the instance of the object where it is defined using a permanent table as the source of the table definition. The Temporary table has exactly the same data structure as the permanent table after which it is modeled.

Temporary tables are created empty when the parent object execution initiates, and they disappear along with their data when the parent object execution terminates (that is, when the Temporary table variable goes out of scope).

Temporary tables are not generally accessible to users except on a display only basis. They can directly be the target of Reports, Pages, and XML ports. In general, Temporary tables are intended to be work areas and as such, are containers of data. The definition of a Temporary table can only be changed by changing the definition of the permanent table on which it has been modeled. A YouTube video was created about Temporary Dataset usage in NAV 2013 R2. It is still applicable. It is located at `https://www.youtube.com/watch?v=QHn5oEOJv0Q`.

There is a Temporary table technique used by advanced developers to define a new temporary table format without consuming a (paid for) licensed table slot. Define the new table in an unlicensed number range. If the current production license allows for tables 50000 through 50099, assign the new layout to 50500 (for example). That layout can then be used to define a temporary table in an object. The layout cannot be used to actually store data in the database, but only to provide a convenient data format design for some special intermediate process.

Content modifiable tables

There is only one table type included in the Content Modifiable Table category.

System

The System table type contains user-maintainable information that pertains to the management or administration of the NAV application system. System tables are created by NAV; we cannot create System tables. However, with full developer license rights, we can modify System tables to extend their usage. With full system permissions, we can also change the data in System tables.

An example is the User table, which contains user login information. This particular System table is often modified to define special user access routing or processing limitations. Other System tables contain data on report-to-printer routing assignments, transaction numbers to be assigned, batch job scheduling, and so on. The following are examples of System tables for which definition and content can be modified. The first three relate to system security functions.

- **User**: The table of identified users and their security information
- **Permission Set**: The table containing a list of all the permission sets in the database
- **Permission**: The table defining what individual Permission Sets are allowed to do, based on object permission assignments

- **Access Control**: The table of the Security roles that are assigned to each Windows Login

The following tables are used to track a variety of system data or control structures:

- **Company**: The companies in this database. Most of the NAV data is automatically segregated by Company.
- **Chart**: This defines all the chart parts that have been set up for use in constructing pages.
- **Web Service**: This lists the pages, queries, and code units that have been published as web services.
- **Profile**: This contains a list of all the active profiles and their associated Role Center pages. A profile is a collection of NAV users who are assigned to the same Role Center.
- **User Personalization**: In spite of its name, this table does not contain information about user personalization that has occurred. Instead, this table contains the link between the user ID and the Profile ID, the language, the company, and the debugger controls. (A **personalization** is a change in the layout of a page by a user, such as adding or removing fields, page parts, restructuring menus, resizing columns, and so on. This information is in the User Metadata table.)

The following tables contain information about various system internals. Their explanation is outside the scope of this book.

- Send-to Program
- Style Sheet
- User Default Style Sheet
- Record Link
- Object Tracking
- Object Metadata
- Profile Metadata
- User Metadata

Read-only tables

There is only one table type included in the Read-only table category.

Virtual

The Virtual table type is computed at runtime by the system. A Virtual table contains data and is accessed like other tables, but we cannot modify either the definition or the contents of a Virtual table. We can think of the Virtual tables as system data presented in the form of a table so it is readily available to C/AL code. Some of these tables (such as the *Database File, File,* and *Drive* tables) provide access to information about the computing environment. Other Virtual tables (such as the *Table Information, Field,* and *Session* tables) provide information about the internal structure and operating activities of our database. A good way to learn more about any of these tables is to create a list or card page bound to the table of interest. Include all the fields in the page layout, **Save** the page and **Run** it. We can then view the field definition and data contents of the target virtual table.

Some virtual tables (such as *Date* and *Integer*) provide tools that can be used in our application routines. The Date table provides a list of calendar periods (such as days, weeks, months, quarters, and years) to make it much easier to manage various types of accounting and managerial data handling. The Integer table provides a list of integers from -1,000,000,000 to 1,000,000,000. As we explore standard NAV reports, we will frequently see the Integer table being used to supply a sequential count in order to facilitate a reporting sequence (often in a limited numeric range such as 1 or 1 to 10).

We cannot see these tables presented in the List of Table objects, but can only access them as targets for Pages, Reports, or Variables in C/AL code. Knowledge of the existence, contents, and usage of these Virtual tables is not useful to an end user. However, as developers, we will regularly use some of the Virtual tables. There is educational value in studying the structure and contents of these tables, as well as having the ability to create valuable tools with knowledge of and by accessing of one or more Virtual tables.

The following screenshot shows a list of most of the Virtual and System tables:

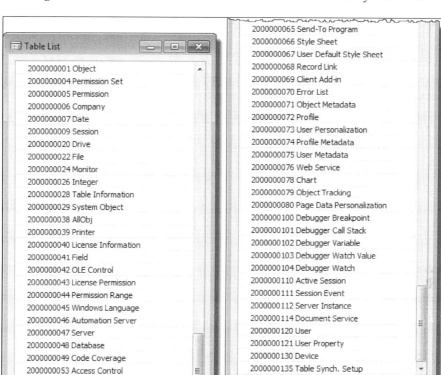

Summary

In this chapter, we have focused on the foundation level of NAV data structure: tables and their internal structure. We have worked our way through the hands-on creation of a number of tables and their data definitions in support of our WDTU application. We have briefly discussed Field Groups and how they are used.

We have identified the essential table structure elements including Properties, Object Numbers, Triggers, Keys, and SumIndexFields. Finally, we have reviewed several categories of tables found in NAV 2015.

In the next chapter, we will dig deeper into the NAV data structure to understand how fields and their attributes are assembled to make up tables. We will also focus on what can be done with Triggers. Then we will explore how other object types use tables, working towards developing a full featured NAV development toolkit.

Review questions

Q.1. Which of the following is a correct description of a table in NAV 2015? Choose two.

    a.   A NAV table is the definition of data structure

    b.   A NAV table includes a built-in data entry page

    c.   A NAV table can contain C/AL code, but that should be avoided

    d.   A NAV table should implement many of the business rules of a system

Q.2. All primary keys should contain only one data field. True or False?

Q.3. With which property is it possible to link a NAV table to a table outside of the NAV database? Choose one.

    a.   DatabaseLink

    b.   ObjectPointer

    c.   LinkedObject

    d.   C# Codelet

Q.4. System Tables cannot be modified. True or False?

Q.5. Which of the following are Table triggers? Choose two.

    a.   OnInsert

    b.   OnChange

    c.   OnNewKey

    d.   OnRename

Q.6. Keys can be enabled or disabled in executable code. True or False?

Q.7. Because Setup Tables only contain one record, they do not need to have a Primary Key. True or False?

Q.8. Table numbers intended to be used for customized table objects should only range between 5000 and 9999. True or False?

Q.9. Which of the following tables can be modified by Partner developers? Choose three.

     a. Customer

     b. Date

     c. User

     d. Item Ledger Entry

Q.10. The DropDown display on a field lookup in the RTC can be changed by modifying the table's Field Groups. True or False?

Q.11. Temporary table data can be saved in a special database storage area. True or False?

Q.12. Which of the following Virtual Tables are commonly used in NAV development projects? Choose two.

     a. Date

     b. GPS Location

     c. Integer

     d. Object Metadata

Q.13. SumIndexFields can be used to calculate totals. True or False?

Q.14. Table Permissions (for access to another table's data) include which of the following permissions. Choose three.

     a. read

     b. sort

     c. delete

     d. modify

Q.15. The TableRelation property allows a field in one table to reference data in another table. True or False?

Q.16. Tables can be created or deleted dynamically. True or False?

Q.17. Only Tables have Triggers, and only Fields have Properties. True or False?

Q.18. Ledger data in NAV can be freely updated through either posting routines or direct data entry. True or False?

Q.19. SQL Server for NAV supports SIFT by which mechanism? Choose one.

      a. SQL SIFT indexes

      b. SQL Dynamic Indexes

      c. SQL Indexed Views

      d. SIFT not supported in SQL

Q.20. Reference Tables and Virtual Tables are simply two different names for the same type of table. True or False?

3

Data Types and Fields

It's the little things that make the big things possible. Only close attention to the fine details of any operation makes the operation first class.

- J. Willard Marriott

Always design a thing by considering it in its next larger context - a chair in a room, a room in a house, a house in an environment, an environment in a city plan.

- Eliel Saarinen

The design of an application should begin at the simplest level, with the design of the data elements. The type of data your development tool supports has a significant effect on our design. Since NAV is designed for financially oriented business applications, NAV data types are financial and business oriented.

In this chapter, we will cover many of the data types that we use within NAV. For each data type, we will cover some of the more frequently modified field properties and how particular properties, such as FieldClass, are used to support application functionality. FieldClass is a fundamental property that defines whether the contents of the field are data to be processed or control information to be interpreted. In particular, we will cover the following topics:

- Basic definitions
- Fields
- Data types
- FieldClass properties
- Filtering

Basic definitions

First, let's review some basic NAV terminology:

- **Data type**: This defines the kind of data that can be held in a field, whether it is a numeric (such as an integer or a decimal), text, table RecordID, time, date, Boolean, and so forth. The data type defines what constraints can be placed on the contents of a field, determines the functions in which the data element can be used (not all data types are supported by all functions), and defines what the results of certain functions will be.

- **Fundamental data type**: This is a simple, single-component structure that consists of a single value at any point in time, for example, a number, a string, or a Boolean value.

- **Complex data type**: This is a structure made up of or relating to simple data types, for example, records, program objects such as Pages or Reports, **Binary Large OBjects** (**BLOBs**), DateFormulas, external files, and indirect reference variables.

- **Data Element**: This is an instance of a data type that may be a Constant or a Variable.

- **Constant**: This is a data element that is explicitly defined in the code by a literal value. Constants are not modifiable during execution, only by a developer using C/SIDE. All the simple data types can be represented by constants. Examples are "MAIN" (Code or Text), 12.34 (Decimal), and "+01-312-444-5555" (Text).

- **Variable**: This is a data element that can have a value assigned to it dynamically during execution. Except for special cases, a variable will be a single, unchanging, and specific data type.

Fields

A field is the basic element of data definition in NAV—the atom in the structure of a system. The elemental definition of a field consists of its number, its description (name), its data type, and, of course, any properties required for its particular data type. A field is defined by the values of its properties and the C/AL code contained in its triggers.

Field properties

The specific properties that can be defined for a field depend on the data type. There are a minimum set of universal properties. We will review these first. Then, we will review the rest of the more frequently used properties, some that are data dependent and some that are not. You can check out the remaining properties by using **Developer and IT Pro Help** within the **Table Designer**.

We can access the properties of a field while viewing the table in Design mode by highlighting the field and then clicking on the **Properties** icon, or by clicking on **Properties** under **View**, or by pressing *Shift + F4*. All of the property screenshots in this section were obtained this way for fields within the standard **Customer** table. As we review various field properties, you will learn more if you follow along in your NAV system using the **Object Designer**. Explore different properties and the values they can have. Make good use of NAV 2015's **Help** functions liberally for additional information and examples.

The property value that is enclosed within < > (less than and greater than brackets) is the default value for that property. When we set a property to any other value, < > should not be present unless they are supposed to be part of the property value (for example, as part of a text string value). When a property has been changed from its default value, the NAV 2015 C/AL Editor displays the new property value in bold.

All of the fields, of any data type, have the following properties:

- **Field No.**: The identifier for the field within the containing table object.
- **Name**: This is the label by which the C/AL code references the field. A name can consist of up to 30 characters, including special characters. The name can be changed by a developer at any time and NAV will automatically ripple that change throughout the system. If no caption value has been defined, the name is used as the default caption when data from this field is displayed. Changing names that are used as literals in C/AL code can cause problems with some functions, such as web services and GETFILTERS, in which the reference is based on the field name rather than the field number.
- **Caption**: This contains the defined caption for the currently selected language. It will always be one of the defined multilanguage captions. The default language for a NAV installation is determined by the combination of a set of built-in rules and the languages available in the installation.

- **CaptionML**: This defines the multilanguage caption for the table. It also identifies the language in use; for example, ENU for US English (as shown in the following screenshot).

- **Description**: This is an optional use property for our internal documentation.

- **Data Type**: This defines what type of data format applies to this field (for example, Integer, Date, Code, Text, Decimal, Option, or Boolean).

- **Enabled**: This determines whether or not the field is activated for user generated events. The property defaults to **<Yes>** and is rarely changed.

- **AccessByPermission**: This determines the permission mask required for a user to access this field in pages or in the user interface.

The following screenshot shows the properties for the **Picture** field of the **Data Type** BLOB in the **Company Information** table (this field is often used to store a company's logo image):

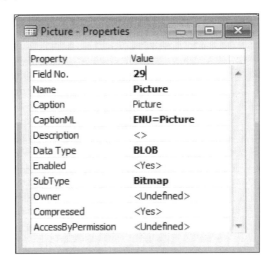

The set of properties shown for a **BLOB** data type field is the simplest set of field properties. After the properties that are shared by all of the data types, appear the BLOB-specific properties scan be seen; these are **SubType**, **Owner**, and **Compressed**.

- **SubType**: This defines the type of data stored in the **BLOB** and sets a filter in the import/export function for the field. The three **SubType** choices are **Bitmap** (for bitmap graphics), **Memo** (for text data), and **User-Defined** (for anything else). User-Defined is the default value.

- **Owner**: This defines the NAV Server user who owns the object in the **BLOB** field.

- **Compressed**: This defines whether the data stored in the **BLOB** is stored in a compressed format. If we want to access **BLOB** data with an external tool (from outside of NAV), this property must be set to No.

The properties of **Code** and **Text** data type fields are quite similar to one another. This is logical, since both represent types of textual data. The following images are from the Customer table:

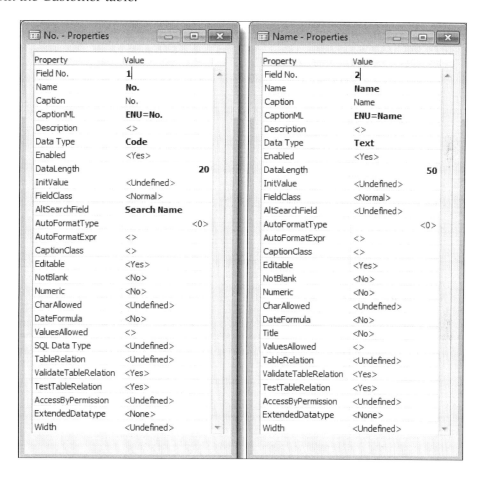

The following are some properties common to both the **Code** and **Text** data types:

- **DataLength**: This specifies the maximum number of characters the field can contain. This is 250 characters in a table, if no maximum limit is specified for a Text field, there is no length limitation for a variable stored only in memory (working storage). Code fields in memory cannot exceed 1024 characters in length.

- **InitValue**: This is the value that the system will supply as a default when a field is initialized.

- **AltSearchField**: This has been replaced by Field Groups (described in *Chapter 2, Tables*) in the Role Tailored Client; it was a feature implemented in the old Classic Client. Presumably, it was left in place for backward compatibility.

- **Caption Class**: This can be set up by the developer to allow users to dynamically change the caption for a text box or a check box. **Caption Class** defaults to empty. For more information on this, refer to **Developer and IT Pro Help**. Used in base NAV in the **Dimensions** fields.

- **Editable**: This is set to No when we don't want to allow a field to be edited; for example, if it is a computed or assigned value field that the user should not change. **Editable** defaults to Yes.

- **NotBlank**, **Numeric**, **CharAllowed**, **DateFormula**, and **ValuesAllowed**: Each of these allows us to place constraints on the data that can be entered into the field by a user. They do not affect data updates driven by the application's C/AL code.

- **SQL Data Type**: This applies to the **Code** fields only. **SQL Data Type** allows you to define what data type will be allowed in a particular Code field and how it will be mapped to a SQL Server data type. This controls the sorting and display. Options are Varchar, Integer, BigInteger, and Variant. Varchar is the default and causes all of the data to be treated as a text. Integer and BigInteger allow only numeric data to be entered. A Variant can contain any data type from a wide range of NAV data types. In general, once set, this property should not be changed. These settings should not affect any data handling that is done in SQL Server external to NAV, but the conservative approach is not to make changes here.

- **TableRelation**: This is used to specify a relationship to the data in the specified target table. The target table field must be in the primary key. The relationship can be conditional and/or filtered; it can be used for validation, lookups, and data-change propagation.

- **ValidateTableRelation**: If a **TableRelation** is specified, set this to `Yes` in order to validate the relation when data is entered or changed. (In other words, confirm that the entered data exists in the target table.) If a **TableRelation** is defined, and this property is set to `No`, the automatic table referential integrity will not be maintained. Note that application code can be written that will bypass this validation.

- **TestTableRelation**: This is a property that has been left over from earlier versions and no longer has any use or value.

- **ExtendedDataType**: This property allows the optional designation of an extended data type that automatically receives special formatting and validation. Type options include an e-mail address, a URL, a phone number, a report filter, a progress bar ratio, or a masked entry (as dots). An **Action Icons** may also be displayed, when three fields are defined with **ExtendedDataType**, as shown in the following screenshot:

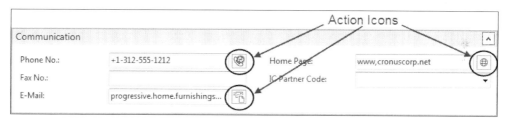

Let's take a look at the properties of two more data types, Decimal and Integer, especially the properties related to numeric content:

- **DecimalPlaces**: This sets the minimum and maximum number of decimal places (min:max) for storage and display in a **Decimal** data item. The default is 2 (2:2), the minimum is 0, and the maximum is 255.

- **BlankNumbers, BlankZero**, and **SignDisplacement**: This can be used to control the formatting and display of the data field on a page. **BlankNumbers** and **BlankZero** all fields of the chosen values to be displayed as blank. **SignDisplacement** allows data positioning to be shifted for negative values.

- **MinValue** and **MaxValue**: When set, these constrain the range of data values allowed for user entry. The available range depends on the field data type.

- **AutoIncrement**: This allows you to define one **Integer** field in a table to automatically increment for each entered record. When used, which is not often, it almost always supports the automatic updating of the filled that is used as the last field in a primary key, enabling the creation of a unique key. The use of this feature does not ensure a contiguous number sequence. Under some circumstances, the use of this feature can lead to table locking conflicts. When the property is set to `Yes`, the automatic functionality should not be overridden in code.

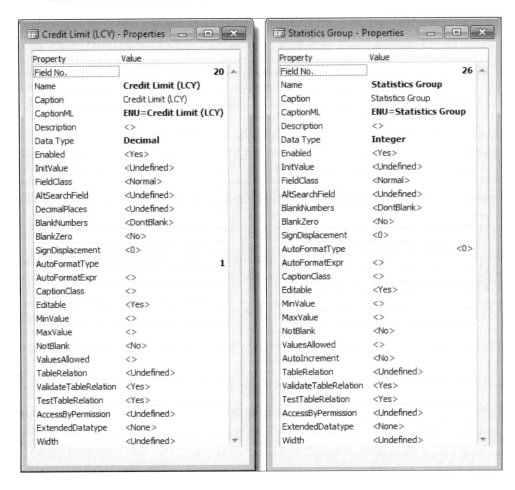

The properties for an **Option** data type are similar to those of other numeric data types. This is reasonable because an Option is stored as an integer, but there are also properties that are specific to **Option**:

- **OptionString**: This details the text interpretations for each of the stored integer values that are contained in an Option field.

- **OptionCaption** and **OptionCaptionML**: These serve the same captioning and multilanguage purposes as caption properties do for other data types.

Internally, options are stored as integers, which are tied to each option's position in the **OptionString** starting with position **0**, **1**, **2**, and so on. The **OptionString** and **OptionCaption** properties are shown in the following screenshot:

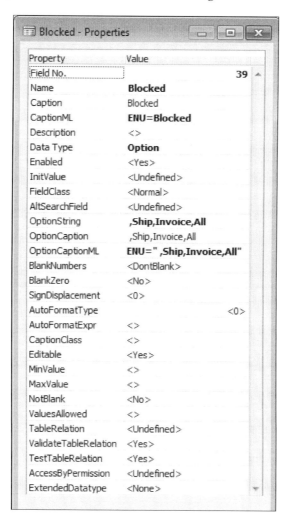

Field triggers

To see field triggers, let us look at our Table **50000 - Radio Show**. Open the table in the **Design** mode, highlight the **No.** field, press *F9*, and you will see the following screenshot:

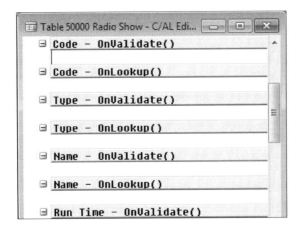

Each field has two triggers, the OnValidate() trigger and the OnLookup() trigger, which function as follows:

- OnValidate(): The C/AL code in this trigger is executed whenever an entry is made by the user. Its intended use is to validate that the entry conforms to the design parameters for the field. It can also be executed under program control through the use of the VALIDATE function (which we will discuss later).

- OnLookup(): OnLookup behavior can be triggered by pressing *F4* or *Shift + F4* from an ellipsis button or by clicking on the lookup arrow in a field, as shown in the following screenshot:

- If the field's **TableRelation** property refers to a table, then the default behavior is to display a drop-down list to allow the selection of a table entry to store it in this field. The list will be based on the Field Groups defined for the table. We may choose to override that behavior by coding different behavior for a special case. We must be careful because any entry whatsoever in the body of an OnLookup() trigger, even a comment line, will eliminate the default behavior of this trigger.

Data structure examples

Some good examples of tables in the standard product to review for particular features are as follows:

- Table 18 – Customer, for a variety of data types and Field Classes. This table contains some fairly complex examples of C/AL code in the Triggers table. A wide variety of field property variations can be seen in this table as well.

- Table 14 – Location and Table 91 – User Setup both have good examples of OnValidate trigger C/AL code, as do all of the primary master tables (Customer, Vendor, Item, Job, and so on.)

Field numbering

The number of each field within its parent table object is the unique identifier that NAV uses internally to identify that field. We can easily change a field number when we initially define a table layout. However, after other objects such as pages, reports, or code units reference the fields in a table, it becomes difficult to change the numbers of referenced fields. Deleting a field and reusing its field number for a different purpose is not a good idea and can easily lead to programming confusion.

> We cannot easily safely change the definition, renumber, or delete a field that has data present in the database. The same can be said for reducing the defined size of a field to less than the largest size of data that is already present in that field. However, if we force the change, the force function will override the system's built-in safeguards. This action can truncate or delete data.

When we add new fields to standard NAV product tables (those shipped with the product), the new field numbers must be in the 50,000 to 99,999 number range, unless we have been explicitly licensed for another number range. Field numbers for fields in new tables that we create can be anything from 1 to 999,999,999 (in all cases without the commas).

When a field representing the same data element appears in related tables (for example, Table 37 – Sales Line and Table 113 – Sales Invoice Line), the same field number should be assigned to that data element for each of the tables. Not only is this consistent approach easier for reference and maintenance, but it also supports the TRANSFERFIELDS function. TRANSFERFIELDS allows you to copy data from one table's record instance to another table's record instance by doing record-to-record mapping based on the field numbers.

If we plan ahead and number the fields logically and consistently from the beginning of our design work and provide an entry in the Description column for each field, we will create code that's easier to maintain. It's a good idea to leave frequent gaps in field number sequences within a table. This allows easier insertion of new fields that are numerically adjacent to related, previously defined fields. In turn, this makes it easier for the following developer to understand the modification's data structure.

For additional information, please see *Object Numbering Conventions* in the **Developer and IT Pro Help** in the Development Environment.

Field and Variable naming

In general, the rules for naming fields (data elements in a table) and variables (data elements within the working storage of an object) are the same, and we will discuss them on that basis. The **Developer and IT Pro Help** section's *Naming Conventions* describes many recommended best practices for naming within NAV. A lot of additional information can also be found in the recently released C/AL Coding Guidelines at `https://community.dynamics.com/nav/w/designpatterns/156.cal-coding-guidelines`, which includes a **How do I** video.

Variables in NAV can either be global (with a scope across the breadth of an object) or local (with a scope only within a single function). Variable names should be unique within the sphere of their scope. There must not be any duplication between global and local names. Even though the same local name can be used in more than one function within the same object, doing so is not a good idea and will almost certainly confuse the next developer that follows. Therefore, we should make our working variable names unique within the object.

Uniqueness includes not duplicating reserved words or system variables. Refer to the *C/AL Reserved Words* list in the **Developer and IT Pro Help**. Avoid using as a variable name, any word that appears as an UPPER CASE word in either the **Developer and IT Pro Help** or any of the published NAV technical documentation. For example, we shouldn't use the words **Page** or **Image** as variable names.

Variable names in NAV are not case sensitive. There is now a 128-character limit on variable names (but still a 30-character limit on field names in tables). Variable names can contain all ASCII characters except for control characters (which can contain ASCII values from 0 to 31 and 255) and the double quotes (ASCII value 34) as well as some Unicode characters that are used in languages other than English. Characters outside the standard ASCII set (0-127) may display differently on different systems.

Note that the compiler won't tell us that an asterisk (*, ASCII value 42) or question mark (?, ASCII value 63) cannot be used in a variable name. However, since both the asterisk and the question mark can be used as **wildcards** in many expressions, especially filtering, neither one should be used in a variable name.

The first character of a variable name must be a letter between A and Z (upper or lower case) or an underscore (_, ASCII value 95) unless the variable name is enclosed in double quotes when it is referenced in code (and such names should be avoided). Alphabets other than the 26-character English alphabet may interpret the ASCII values to characters other than A to Z and may include more than 26 characters. A variable name's first character can be followed by any combination of the legal characters.

If we use any characters other than the A-Z alphabets, numerals, and underscore, we must surround our variable name with double quotes each time we use it in the C/AL code (for example, *Cust List*, which contains an embedded space, or **No.**, which contains a period).

When we create a variable with a complex data type such as Record, Report, Codeunit, Page, XMLport, Query, or Testpage, and do not supply a name; the variable name will be automatically generated according to C/AL Coding Guidelines by the Development Environment.

See *Naming Conventions* in the **Developer and IT Pro Help** for additional guidance to name C/AL variables.

Data types

We are going to segregate the data types into several groups. We will first look at Fundamental data types and then at Complex data types.

Fundamental data types

Fundamental data types are the basic components from which the complex data types are formed. They are grouped into Numeric, String, and Date/Time data types.

Numeric data

Just like other systems, NAV supports several numeric data types. The specifications for each NAV data type are defined for NAV, independent of the supporting SQL Server database rules. However, some data types are stored and handled somewhat differently from a SQL Server point of view than the way they appear to us as NAV developers and users. For more details on the SQL Server-specific representations of various data elements, refer to the **Developer and IT Pro Help**. Our discussion will focus on NAV representation and handling for each data type.

The various numeric data types are as follows:

- **Integer**: This is an integer number ranging from -2,147,483,646 to +2,147,483,647

- **Decimal**: This is a decimal number in the range of +/- 999,999,999,999,999.99. Although it is possible to construct larger numbers, errors such as overflow, truncation, or loss of precision might occur. In addition, there is no facility to display or edit larger numbers.

- **Option**: This is a special instance of an integer, stored as an integer number ranging from 0 to +2,147,483,647. An option is normally represented in the body of our C/AL code as an option string. We can compare an option to an integer in C/AL, rather than using the option string. However, this is not a good practice because it eliminates the self-documenting aspect of an option field.

  An option string is a set of choices listed in a comma-separated string, one of which is chosen and stored as the current option. Since the maximum length of this string is 250 characters, the practical maximum number of choices for a single option is less than 125 characters. The currently selected choice within the set of options is stored in the option field as the ordinal position of that option within the set. For example, selection of an entry from the option string of red, yellow, and blue would result in the storing of 0 (red), 1 (yellow), and **2** (blue). If red were selected, 0 would be stored in the variable and if blue were selected, 2 would be stored. Quite often, an option string starts with a blank to allow an effective choice of "none chosen". An example of this (blank, Hourly, Daily,...) is as follows:

| | ✔ | 1000 Frequency | Option | ,Hourly,Daily,Weekly,Monthly | |

- **Boolean**: A Boolean variable is stored as 1 or 0. In a C/AL code, it is programmatically referred to as True or False, but sometimes, it is referred in properties as Yes or No. Boolean variables may be displayed as Yes or No (language dependent), P or blank, or True or False.

- **BigInteger**: 8-byte Integer, as opposed to the 4 bytes of Integer. BigIntegers are for very big numbers (from -9,223,372,036,854,775,807 to 9,223,372,036,854,775,807).

- **Char**: This is a numeric code between 0 and 65535 (hexadecimal FFFF) that represents a single 16-bit Unicode character. Char variables can operate either as text or numbers. Numeric operations can be done on Char variables. Char variables can also be defined with individual text character values. Char variables cannot be defined as permanent variables in a table; they can only be defined as working storage variables within C/AL objects.

- **Byte**: This is a single 8-bit ASCII character with a value ranging from 0 to 255. Byte variables can operate either as text or numbers. Numeric operations can be done on Byte variables. Byte variables can also be defined with individual text character values. Byte variables cannot be defined as permanent variables in a table, but only as working storage variables within C/AL objects.

- **Action**: This is a variable returned from a PAGE RUNMODAL function or RUNMODAL (Page) function that specifies what action a user performs on a page. The possible values are OK, Cancel, LookupOK, LookupCancel, Yes, No, RunObject, and RunSystem.

- **ExecutionMode**: This specifies the mode in which a session runs. The possible values are Debug or Standard.

String data

The following are the data types included in String data:

- **Text**: This contains any string of alphanumeric characters. In a table, a Text field can be from 1 to 250 characters long. In working storage within an object, a Text variable can be any length if no length is defined. If a maximum length is defined, it must not exceed 1024. NAV 2015 does not require a length to be specified, but if we define a maximum length, it will be enforced. When calculating the 'length' of a record for design purposes (relative to the maximum record length of 8,000 bytes), the full defined field length should be counted.

- **Code**: Although the Help says that the length constraints for Code variables are the same as those for text variables, the C/AL Editor enforces length limits of 1 to 250 characters. All of the letters are automatically converted to uppercase when data is entered into a Code variable; any leading or trailing spaces are removed.

Date/Time data

The following are the data types included in Date/Time data:

- **Date**: This contains an integer number, which is interpreted as a date ranging from January 1, 1754 to December 31, 9999. A 0D (numeral zero, letter D) represents an undefined date (stored as a SQL Server **DateTime** field) that is interpreted as January 1, 1753. According to the **Developer and IT Pro Help** that, NAV 2015 supports a Date of 1/1/0000 (presumably as a special case for backward compatibility, but it is not supported by SQL Server).

  A date constant can be written as the letter D preceded by either six digits in the format *MMDDYY* or eight digits as *MMDDYYYY* (where *M* = month, *D* = day, and *Y* = year). For example, 011915D or 01192015D both represent January 19, 2015. Later, in **DateFormula**, we will find *D* interpreted as day, but here the trailing D is interpreted as the date (data type) constant. When the year is expressed as *YY* rather than *YYYY*, the century portion (in this case, 20) is 20 if the two digit year is from 00 to 29, or 19 if the year is from 30 through 99.

  NAV also defines a special date called the **Closing** date, which represents the point in time between one day and the next. The purpose of a closing date is to provide a point at the end of a day, after all of the real date- and time-sensitive activity is recorded — the point when accounting *closing* entries can be recorded.

  Closing entries are recorded, in effect, at the stroke of midnight between two dates — this is the date of closing accounting books, and it is designed so that one can include or exclude, at the user's option, closing entries in various reports. When sorted by date, the closing date entries will get sorted after all normal entries for a day. For example, the normal date entry for December 31, 2015 would display as 12/31/15 (depending on the date format masking), and the closing date entry would display as C12/31/15. All of the C12/31/15 ledger entries would appear after all normal 12/31/15 ledger entries. The following screenshot shows two 2014 closing date entries mixed with normal entries from December 2015 and January through April 2015. (This data is from the Cronus demo. The 2014 Closing entries have an "Opening Entry" description, which shows that these were the first entries for the demo data in the respective accounts. This is not a normal set of production data.)

- **Time**: This contains an integer number, which is interpreted on a 24-hour clock, in milliseconds plus 1, from 00:00:00 to 23:59:59:999. A 0T (numeral zero, letter T) represents an undefined time and is stored as 1/1/1753 00:00:00.000.

- **DateTime**: This represents a combined Date and Time, stored in **Coordinated Universal Time (UTC)**, and it always displays local time (that is, the local time on our system). DateTime fields do not support NAV Closing dates. DateTime is helpful for an application that must support multiple time zones simultaneously. DateTime values can range from January 1, 1754 00:00:00.000 to December 31, 9999 23:59:59.999, but dates earlier than January 1, 1754 cannot be entered (don't test with dates late in 9999 as an intended advance to the year 10000 won't work). Assigning a date of 0DT will yield an undefined or blank DateTime.

- **Duration**: This represents the positive or negative difference between two DateTime values, in milliseconds, stored as a BigInteger. Durations are automatically output in the text format as *DDD* days *HH* hours *MM* minutes *SS* seconds.

Complex data types

Each complex data type consists of multiple data elements. For ease of reference, we will categorize them into several groups of similar types.

Data structure

The following data types are in the data structure group:

- File: This refers to any standard Windows file outside the NAV database. There is a reasonably complete set of functions to allow to create, delete, open, close, read, write, and copy (among other things) data files. For example, we could create our own NAV routines in C/AL to import or export data from or to a file that had been created by some other application.

> With the three-tier architecture of NAV 2015, business logic runs on the server and not the client. We need to keep this in mind any time we refer to local external files, because they will be on the server by default. Use of **Universal Naming Convention** (**UNC**) paths can make this easier to manage.

- **Record**: This refers to a single data row within a NAV table that consists of individual fields. Quite often, multiple variable instances of a Record (table) are defined in working storage to support a validation process, allowing access to different records within the table at one time in the same function.

Objects

Page, Report, Codeunit, Query, and XMLPort, each represents an object data type. Object data types are used when there is a need to refer to an object or a function in another object. Examples:

- Invoking a Report or an XMLPort from a Page or a Report
- Calling a function for data validation or processing is coded as a function in a Table or a Codeunit

Automation

The following are Automation data types (these are not supported by the NAV Web client.) OCX and Automation data types are supported in NAV 2015 for backward compatibility only:

- **OCX**: This allows the definition of a variable that represents and allows access to an ActiveX or OCX custom control. Such a control is typically an external application object that we can invoke from our NAV object.

- **Automation**: This allows us to define a variable that we can access similar to an OCX. The application must act as an Automation Server and be registered with the NAV client or server that calls it. For example, we can interface from NAV into the various Microsoft Office products (Word, Excel, and so on) by defining them in Automation variables.

- **DotNet**: This allows us to define a variable for .NET Framework interface types within an assembly. It supports accessing .NET Framework type members, including methods, properties, and constructors from C/AL. These can be members of the global assembly cache or custom assemblies.

Input/Output

The following are the Input/Output data types:

- **Dialog**: This supports the definition of a simple user interface window without the use of a Page object. Typically, Dialog windows are used to communicate processing progress or allow a brief user response to a go/no-go question, though this latter use could result in bad performance due to locking. There are other user communication tools as well, but they do not use a Dialog type data item.

- **InStream** and **Outstream**: These allow us to read from and write to external files, BLOBS, and objects of the Automation and OCX data types.

DateFormula

DateFormula provides for the definition and storage of a simple, but clever, set of constructs to support the calculation of runtime-sensitive dates. A DateFormula is stored in a nonlanguage dependent format, thus supporting multilanguage functionality. A DateFormula is a combination of:

- Numeric multipliers (for example, 1, 2, 3, 4, and so on)
- Alpha time units (all must be in uppercase)
    - D for a day
    - W for a week
    - WD for day of the week, that is, from day 1 to day 7 (either in the future or in the past, but not today). Monday is day 1 and Sunday is day 7.
    - M for calendar month

- ○ Y for year
- ○ CM for current month, CY for current year, CW for current week
- Math symbols interpretation
  - ○ + (plus) as in CM + 10D means the Current Month end plus 10 days (in other words, the tenth of the next month)
  - ○ – (minus) as in (-WD3) means the date of the previous Wednesday (which is the 3rd day of the past week).
- Positional notation (D15 means the 15th day of the month and 15D means 15 days)

Payment Terms for Invoices support full use of `DateFormula`. All `DateFormula` results are expressed as a date based on a reference date. The default reference date is the system date and not the Work Date.

Here are some sample `DateFormulas` and their interpretations (displayed dates are based on the US calendar) with a reference date of July 10, 2015, a Friday:

- CM is the last day of Current Month, 07/31/15
- CM + 10D is the tenth of the next month, 08/10/15
- WD6 is the next sixth day of the week, 07/11/15
- WD5 is the next fifth day of the week, 07/17/15
- CM – M + D is the end of the current month minus one month plus one day, 07/01/15
- CM – 5M is the end of the current month minus five months, 02/28/15

Let us take the opportunity to use the `DateFormula` data type to learn a few NAV development basics. We will do so by experimenting with some hands-on evaluations of several `DateFormula` values. We will create a table to calculate dates using `DateFormula` and Reference Dates.

To do this, navigate to **Tools | Object Designer | Tables**. Then, click on the **New** button and define the fields shown in the following screenshot. Save it as **Table 50009**, named **Date Formula Test**. After we are done with this test, we will save this table for some later testing.

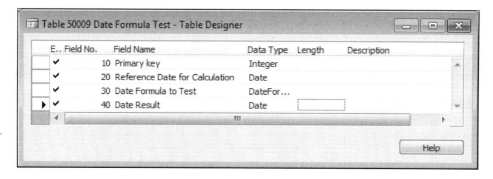

Now, we will add some simple C/AL code to our table so that when we enter or change either the Reference Date or the DateFormula data, we can calculate a new result date.

First, access the new table via the **Design** button. Then, go to the global variables definition form through the **View** menu option, the **C/AL Globals** sub-option, and finally, choose the **Functions** tab. Type in our new function name as **CalculateNewDate** on the first blank line, as shown in the following screenshot, and then exit (by means of the *Esc* key) from this form back to the list of data fields:

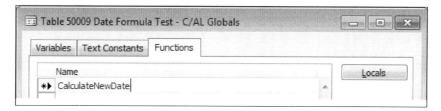

From the **Table Designer** form that displays the list of data fields, either press *F9* or click on the **C/AL Code** icon:

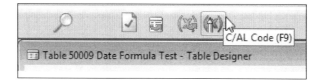

This will take us to the following screen, where we can see all of the field triggers plus the trigger for the new function that we just defined. The table triggers will not be visible, unless we scroll up to show them. Note that our new function was defined as a LOCAL function. This means that it cannot be accessed from another object unless we change it to a GLOBAL function.

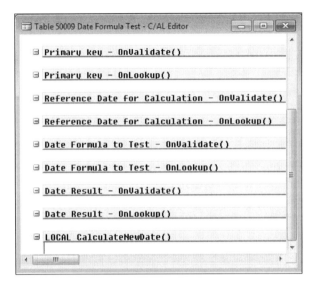

Since our goal now is to focus on experimenting with the DateFormula, we will not go into detail and explain the logic of what we are creating. The logic that we're going to code is as follows:

> When an entry is made (new or changed) in either the "Reference Date" field or in the "Date Formula to Test field", invoke the CalculateNewDate function to calculate a new "Result Date" value based on the entered data.

First, you need to create the logic within our new function, CalculateNewDate(), to evaluate and store a **Date Result** based on the DateFormula and Reference Date that you enter into the table.

Just copy the C/AL code exactly as shown in the following screenshot, exit, compile, and save the table:

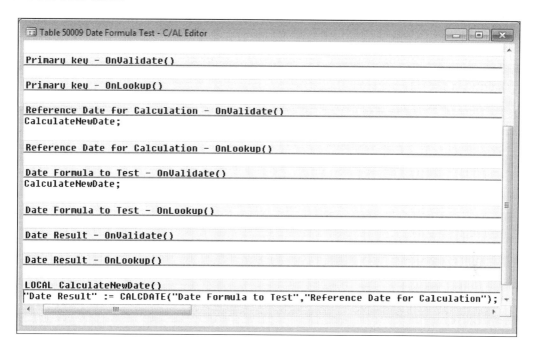

If you get an error message of any type when you close and save the table, you probably have not copied the C/AL code exactly as it is shown in the screenshot (also shown in the following code for ease of copying.)

```
CalculateNewDate;
"Date Result" := CALCDATE("Date Formula to Test","Reference Date
for Calculation");
```

This code will cause the `CalculateNewDate()` function to be called via the **OnValidate** trigger when an entry is made in either the **Reference Date for Calculation** or the **Date Formula to Test** fields. The function will place the result in the **Date Result** field. The use of an integer value in the redundantly named **Primary Key** field allows us to enter any number of records into the table (by manually numbering them 1, 2, 3, and so forth).

Let's experiment with several different date and date formula combinations. We will access the table via the **Run** button. This will cause NAV to generate a default format page and run it in the Role Tailored Client.

Enter a **Primary Key** value of 1 (one). In **Reference Date for Calculation**, enter either an upper or lower case T for Today and the system date. The same date will appear in the **Date Result** field because at this point, no Date Formula has been entered. Now, enter 1D (number 1 followed by uppercase or lowercase D (C/SIDE will make it uppercase) in the Date Formula to Test field. We will see that the **Date Result** field contents are changed to be one day beyond the date in the Reference Date for **Calculation** field.

Now, for another test entry, start with a 2 in the **Primary Key** field. Again, enter the letter T (for Today) in the **Reference Date for Calculation** field, and enter the letter W (for Week) in the **Date Formula to Test field**. We will get an error message telling us that our formulas should include a number. Make the system happy and enter 1W. We will now see a date in the **Date Result** field that is one week beyond our system date.

Set the system's Work Date to a date in the middle of a month (remember, we discussed setting the Work Date in Chapter 1). Start another line with the number 3 as the **Primary Key**, followed by a W (for Work Date) in the **Reference Date for Calculation** field. Enter cm (or CM or cM or Cm, it doesn't matter) in the **Date Formula to Test field**. Our result date will be the last day of our Work Date month. Now, enter another line using the Work Date, but enter a formula of -cm (the same as before but with a minus sign). This time, our result date will be the first day of our Work Date month. Note that the DateFormula logic handles month end dates correctly, including a leap year. Try starting with a date in the middle of February 2016 to confirm this. The following screen shows the **Date Formula Test** window:

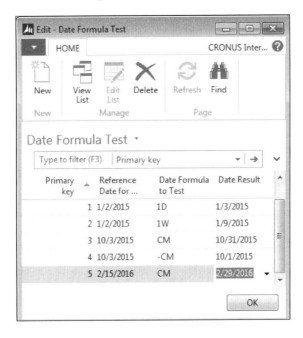

Now, enter another line with a new **Primary Key**. Skip over the **Reference Date for Calculation** field and just enter 1D in the **Date Formula to Test** field. So, what happens when you do this? We get an error message stating that **You cannot base a date calculation on an undefined date.** In other words, NAV cannot make the requested calculation without a Reference Date. Before we put this function into production, we want our code to check for a Reference Date before calculating. We could default an empty date to the System Date or the Work Date and avoid this particular error.

The preceding and following screenshots show different sample calculations. Build on these and then experiment. We can create a variety of different algebraic date formulae and get some very interesting results. One NAV user has due dates on Invoices for the tenth of the next month. Invoices are dated at various times during the month than they are actually printed. By using the DateFormula of CM + 10D, the due date is always automatically calculated to be the tenth of the next month:

5	2/15/2016	CM	2/29/2016
6	2/15/2015	CM	2/28/2015
7	4/6/2015	1M	5/6/2015
8	4/6/2015	-1M	3/6/2015
9	9/3/2015	-1W-1D	8/26/2015
10	8/26/2015	1W+1D	9/3/2015
42	10/3/2015	-1W	9/26/2015
55	1/15/2016	-CM-1D	12/31/2015
56	1/15/2016	-1Y-CM	1/1/2015

Don't forget to test with WD (weekday), Q (quarter), and Y (year) as well as D (day), W (week), and M (month). For our code to be language independent, we should enter the date formulae with < > delimiters around them (for example, <1D+1W>). NAV will translate the formula into the correct language codes using the installed language layer.

Although our focus for the work we just completed was the Date Formula data type, we've accomplished a lot more than simply learning about that one data type:

- We created a new table just for the purpose of experimenting with a C/AL feature that we might use. This is a technique that comes in handy when we are learning a new feature or trying to decide how it works or how we might use it.

- We put some critical OnValidate logic in the table. When data is entered in one area, the entry is validated and, if valid, the defined processing is done instantly.

- We created a common routine as a new LOCAL function. This function is then called from all the places to which it applies.

- We did our entire test with a table object and a default tabular page that is automatically generated when we **Run** a table. We didn't have to create a supporting structure to do our testing. Of course, when we design a change to a complicated existing structure, we will have a more complicated testing scenario. One of our goals will always be to simplify our testing scenarios, both to minimize the setup effort and to keep our test narrowly focused on the specific issue.

- Finally, and most specifically, we saw how NAV tools make a variety of relative date calculations easy. These are very useful in business applications, many aspects of which are date centered.

References and other data types

The following data types are used for advanced functionality in NAV, sometimes supporting an interface with an external object:

- **RecordID**: This contains the object number and primary key of a table.

- **RecordRef**: This identifies a row in a table, a record. RecordRef can be used to obtain information about the table, the record, the fields in the record, and the currently active filters on the table.

- **FieldRef**: This identifies a field in a table; thus, it allows access to the contents of that field.

- **KeyRef**: This identifies a key in a table and the fields in that key.

Since the specific record, field, and key references are assigned at runtime, RecordRef, FieldRef, and KeyRef are used to support logic which can run on tables that are not specified at design time. This means that one routine built on these data types can be created to perform a common function for a variety of different tables and table formats.

- **Variant**: This defines variables that are typically used to interface with Automation and OCX objects. Variant variables can contain data of various C/AL data types to pass them to an Automation or OCX object as well as external Automation data types that cannot be mapped to C/AL data types.

- **TableFilter**: For variables which can only be used for setting security filters from the Permissions table.

- **Transaction Type**: This has optional values of **UpdateNoLocks**, **Update**, **Snapshot**, **Browse**, and **Report** that define SQL Server behavior for a NAV Report or XMLport transaction from the beginning of the transaction.

- **BLOB**: This can contain either specially formatted text, a graphic in the form of a bitmap, or other developer-defined binary data up to 2 GB in size. The term **Binary Large Object (BLOB)**. BLOBs can only be included in tables and not used to define working storage Variables. Refer to **Developer and IT Pro Help** for additional information.

- **BigText**: This can contain large chunks of text up to 2 GB in size. BigText variables can only be defined in the working storage within an object, but they cannot be included in tables. BigText variables cannot be directly displayed or seen in the debugger. There is a group of special functions that can be used to handle BigText data. Refer to **Developer and IT Pro Help** for additional information.

 To handle text strings in a single data element that are greater than 250 characters in length, use a combination of BLOB and BigText variables.

- **GUID**: This is used to assign a unique identifying number to any database object. **Globally Unique Identifier (GUID)**, a 16-byte binary data type that is used for unique global identification of records, objects, and so on. GUID is generated by an algorithm developed by Microsoft.

- **TestPage**: This is used to store a test page, which is a logical representation of a page that does not display a user interface. Test pages are used for NAV application testing, using the automated testing facility that is part of NAV.

Data type usage

About forty percent of the data types can be used to define the data that is either stored in tables or in working storage data definitions (that is, in a Global or Local data definition within an object). Two data types, BLOB and TableFilter, can only be used to define table-stored data, but not working storage data. About sixty percent of the data types can only be used for working storage data definitions.

The following list shows which data types can be used for table (persisted) data fields and which ones can be used for working storage (variable) data:

Table Data Types	Working Storage Data Types
	Action
	Automation
BigInteger	BigInteger
	BigText
BLOB	
Boolean	Boolean
	Byte
	Char
Code	Code
	Codeunit
Date	Date
DateFormula	DateFormula
DateTime	DateTime
Decimal	Decimal
	Dialog
	DotNet
Duration	Duration
	ExecutionMode
	FieldRef
	File
GUID	GUID
	Instream
Integer	Integer
	KeyRef
	OCX
Option	Option
	Outstream
	Page
	Query
	Record
RecordID	RecordID
	RecordRef
	Report
TableFilter	
	TestPage
Text	Text
Time	Time
	TransactionType

FieldClass property options

Almost all data fields have a `FieldClass` property. FieldClass has as much effect on the content and usage of a data field as the data type; in some instances, it has more effect. In the next chapter, we'll cover most of the field properties, but we'll discuss the `FieldClass` property options now.

FieldClass – Normal

When the FieldClass is Normal, the field will contain the type of application data that's typically stored in a table—the contents we would expect based on the data type and various properties.

FieldClass – FlowField

FlowFields must be dynamically calculated. FlowFields are virtual fields that are stored as metadata; they do not contain data in the conventional sense. A FlowField contains the definition of how to calculate (at runtime) the data that the field represents and a place to store the result of that calculation. Generally, the Editable property for a FlowField is set to `No..`

Depending on the `CalcFormula` method, this could be a value, a reference lookup, or a Boolean. When the `CalcFormula` method is `Sum`, the `FieldClass` connects a data field to a previously defined `SumIndexField` in the table defined in the `CalcFormula`. The FlowField processing speed will be significantly affected by the key configuration of the table being processed. While we must be careful not to define extra keys, having the right keys defined will have a major effect on system performance and thus, on user satisfaction.

A FlowField value is always 0, blank, or false, unless it has been calculated. If a FlowField is displayed directly on a page, it is calculated automatically when the page is rendered. FlowFields are also automatically calculated when they are the subject of predefined filters as part of the properties of a data item in an object. (This will be explained in more detail in the chapters covering Reports and XMLports.) In all other cases, a FlowField must be forced to calculate using the `C/AL RecordName.CALCFIELDS(FlowField1, [FlowField2],...)` function or by the use of the `SETAUTOCALCFIELDS` function. This is also true if the underlying data is changed after the initial display of a page (that is, the FlowField must be recalculated to take a data change into account).

 Because a FlowField does not contain actual data, it cannot be used as a field in a key. In other words, we cannot include a FlowField as part of a key. In addition, we cannot define a FlowField that is based on another FlowField, except in special circumstances.

When a field has its FieldClass set to `FlowField`, another directly associated property becomes available—CalcFormula. (Conversely, the **AltSearchField**, **AutoIncrement**, and **TestTableRelation** properties disappear from view when **FieldClass** is set to `FlowField`). The `CalcFormula` method is the place where we can define the formula for calculating the FlowField. On the `CalcFormula` property line, there is an ellipsis button. Clicking on that button will bring up the following screen:

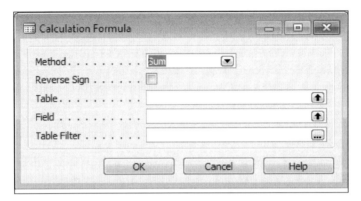

Click on the drop-down button to show the seven `FlowField` methods:

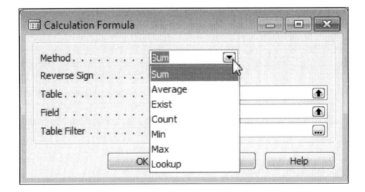

The seven FlowFields are described in the following table:

FlowField Method	Field data type	Calculated value as it applies to the specified set of data within a specific column (field) in a table
Sum	Decimal	The sum total
Average	Decimal	The average value (the sum divided by the row count)
Exist	Boolean	Yes or No / True or False - does an entry exist?
Count	Integer	The number of entries that exist
Min	Any	The smallest value of any entry
Max	Any	The largest value of any entry
Lookup	Any	The value of the specified entry

The Reverse Sign control allows us to change the displayed sign of the result for FlowField types **Sum** and **Average** only; the underlying data is not changed. If a Reverse Sign is used with the FlowField type **Exists**, it changes the effective function to *does not Exist*.

Table and **Field** allow us to define the Table and the Field within that table to which our Calculation Formula will apply. When we make the entries in our **Calculation Formula** screen, no validation checking is done by the compiler to check whether we have chosen an eligible table and field combination. This checking doesn't occur until runtime. Therefore, when we create a new FlowField, we should test it as soon as we have defined it.

The last, but by no means the least significant component of the FlowField calculation formula is the **Table Filter**. When we click on the ellipsis in the table filter field, the window shown in the following screenshot will appear:

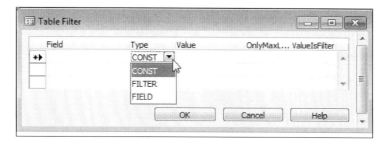

When we click on the **Field** column, we will be invited to select a field from the table that was entered into the **Table** field earlier. The **Type** field choice will determine the type of filter. The **Value** field will have the filter rules defined on this line, which must be consistent with the **Type** choices described in the following table:

Filter type	Value	Filtering action	OnlyMax-Limit	Values-Filter
Const	A constant which will be defined in the Value field	This uses the constant to filter for equally valued entries		
Filter	A filter that will be spelled out as a literal in the Value field	This applies the filter expression from the Value field		
Field	A field from the table within which the FlowField exists	This uses the contents of the specified field to filter equally valued entries	False	False
		If the specified field is a FlowFilter and the OnlyMaxLimit parameter is True, then the FlowFilter range will be applied on the basis of only having a MaxLimit, that is, having no bottom limit. This is useful for the date filters for the Balance Sheet data. (Refer to *Balance at Date* field in the **G/L Account** table for an example)	True	False
		This causes the contents of the specified field to be interpreted as a filter (See *Balance at Date* field in the **G/L Account** table for an example)	True or False	True

FieldClass – FlowFilter

FlowFilters control the calculation of FlowFields in the table (when the FlowFilters are included in the CalcFormula). FlowFilters do not contain permanent data, but instead, they contain filters on a per-user basis, with the information stored in that user's instance of the code that is being executed. A FlowFilter field allows a filter to be entered at a parent record level by the user (for example, G/L Account) and applied (through the use of FlowField formulas, for example) to constrain what child data (for example, G/L Entry records) is selected.

A FlowFilter allows us to provide flexible data selection functions to the users. The user does not need to have a full understanding of the data structure to apply filtering in intuitive ways to both the primary data table and the subordinate data. Based on our C/AL code design, FlowFilters can be used to apply filtering on multiple tables that are subordinate to a parent table. Of course, it is our responsibility as developers to make good use of this tool. As with many C/AL capabilities, a good way to learn more is by studying the standard code designed by the Microsoft developers of NAV and then experimenting.

A number of good examples on the use of FlowFilters can be found in the **Customer** (Table 18) and **Item** (Table 27) tables. In the **Customer** table, some of the FlowFields using FlowFilters are **Balance**, **Balance (LCY)**, **Net Change**, **Net Change (LCY)**, **Sales (LCY)**, and **Profit (LCY)** where **LCY** stands for **local currency**. The **Sales (LCY)** FlowField FlowFilter usage is shown in the following screenshot:

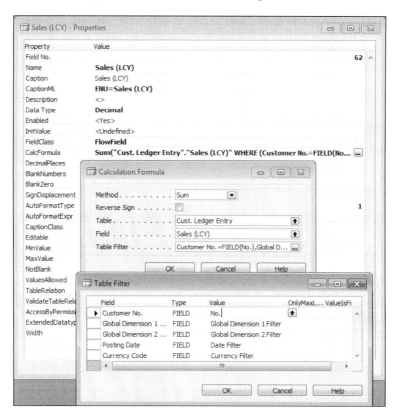

Similarly constructed FlowFields using FlowFilters in the **Item** table include
`Inventory, Net Invoiced Qty., Net Change, Purchases (Qty.),` as well
as other fields.

Throughout the standard code, there are FlowFilters in most of the master
table definitions; there are the Date Filters and Global Dimension Filters (global
dimensions are user-defined codes that facilitate the segregation of accounting data
by groupings such as divisions, departments, projects, customer type, and so on).
Other FlowFilters that are widely used in the standard code related to Inventory
activity such as **Location Filter**, **Lot No. Filter**, **Serial No. Filter**, and **Bin Filter**.

The following pair of images shows two fields from the **Customer** table, both with a
Data Type of **Date**. On the left side of the screenshot is the **Last Date Modified** field
(FieldClass of Normal) and on the right side of the screenshot is the **Date Filter** field
(FieldClass of FlowFilter). It's easy to see that the properties of the two fields are very
similar, except for the properties that differ because one is a **Normal** field and the
other is a **FlowFilter** field.

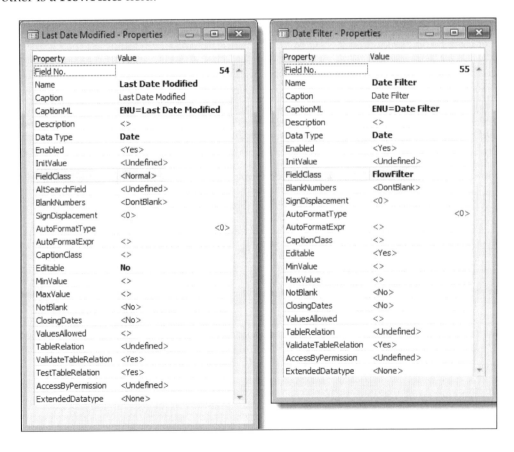

FlowFields and a FlowFilter for our application

In our application, we have decided to have several FlowFields and a FlowFilter in Table 50000 – Radio Show. The reason for having these fields is to provide instant analysis for individual shows based on the detailed data stored in subordinate tables. In Chapter 2, we showed Table 50000 with fields 100 through 130 and 1090 but didn't provide any information about how the fields should be constructed. Let's go through the construction process now. Here's how the fields 100 through 130 and 1090 should look when we open Table 50000 in the Table Designer. If you didn't add these fields during the Chapter 2 exercise, do that now.

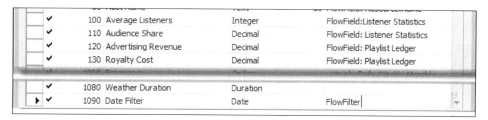

These five fields will be used for statistical analysis for each Radio Show, as follows:

- **Field 100 – Average Listeners**: The average number of listeners that are reported by the ratings agency

- **Field 110 – Audience Share**: The percentage of one station's total estimated listening audience per time slot

- **Field 120 – Advertising Revenue**: The sum total of the advertising revenue generated by the show

- **Field 130 – Royalty Cost**: The sum total of the royalties incurred by the show for playing copyrighted material

- **Field 1090 – Date Filter**: A filter to restrict the data calculated for the preceding four fields

To begin with, we will set the calculation properties for the first FlowField, **Average Listeners**.

1. If Table 50000 isn't already open in the Table Designer, then open it by navigating to **Tools | Object Designer** and select the **Table** button on the left as the object type. Find **table 50000, Radio Show**, select it, and then click on **Design**.

2. Scroll down to field **100**, select it, and click on the properties icon at the top of the screen, or press *Shift + F4*. Highlight the **FieldClass** property, click on the drop-down arrow 🔽 and select **FlowField**. A new property called **CalcFormula** will appear, directly underneath the **FieldClass** property. An **Assist Edit ellipsis** button 🔳 will appear. Click on it and the **Calculation Formula** form will appear as follows:

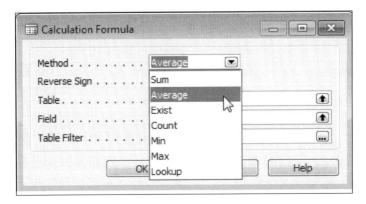

3. Select **Average** from the **Method** dropdown, leave the **Reverse Sign** field unchecked, and type `Listenership Ledger` or `50006` into the **Table** field. We can either type `Listener Count` or click the **Lookup** arrow button 🔼 to select the **Listener Count** field from the table. Lastly, we need to define a filter to allow the Radio Show statistics to be reviewed, based on a user-definable date range. Click on the **Assist Edit ellipsis** button on the **Table Filter** field, and the following **Table Filter** screen will appear:

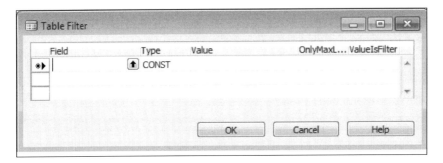

4. Click on the Lookup arrow in the **Field** column and select **Date** from the **Listenership Ledger – Field List**.

5. In the **Type** column, click on the drop-down arrow. You will see three choices for defining what type of filter to apply: **CONST**, **FILTER**, **FIELD**. In this case, we need to apply a field filter, so choose **FIELD**.

6. The last part of the **Table Filter** definition is the **Value** column. Click on the Lookup arrow in the **Value** column and choose **Date Filter** from the **Radio Show – Field List**. This will cause the **Date Filter** field value in the Radio Show record to be applied to the values in the **Date** field in the **Listenership Ledger**, to control what data to use for the **FlowField Average** calculation.

7. Click on **OK** and our **Calculation Formula** screen should look like this:

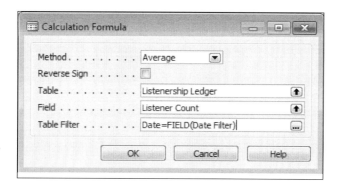

8. Click on **OK** and the **CalcFormula** property will fill in with the following text:

> Average("Listenership Ledger"."Listener Count" WHERE (Date=FIELD(Date Filter)))

9. Since this is a text field, we can enter the syntax manually, but it's much easier and less error prone to use the **Calculation Formula** screen.

10. Set the **Editable** property to No.

11. For **Field 110 – Audience Share**, repeat the procedure that we just went through, but for **Field**, select **Audience Share** from the **Listenership Ledger – Field List**. Our result should look like the following screenshot:

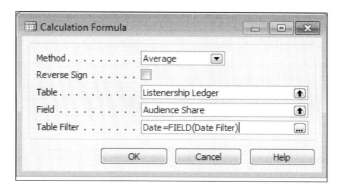

12. For the fields **120, Advertising Revenue**, and **130, Royalty Cost**, the FlowField calculation is a sum with multiple fields that have filters applied to them. For each field, the first step will be to set the **FieldClass** property to FlowField, then click on the **Assist Edit** button in the **CalcFormula** property to call up the **Calculation Formula** screen.

13. For **Advertising Revenue**, make the **Method** as **Sum** and for **Table**, enter **Radio Show Ledger** or the table number, 50005, and then set **Field** to **Fee Amount**.

14. Click on the **Assist Edit** button for the table filter. Fill in the first row with the **Field** as Date, the **Type** as FIELD, and the **Value** with **Date Filter**. Fill in the second row with **Field** set to DataFormat, Type to FILTER, and Advertisement in the Value column (since we are filtering for a single value, we could have also used CONST for the Type value). The FlowField will now add up all the Fee Amount values that have a **Format** option selected as Advertisement and fall within the range of the date filter applied from the Radio Show table.

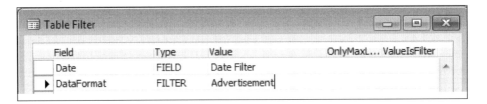

Advertisement is an available value for the **DataFormat** field (Data Type Option). In the Radio Show Ledger, we typed a value that was not an Option value such as Commercial, an error would have displayed showing us what the available Option choices were.

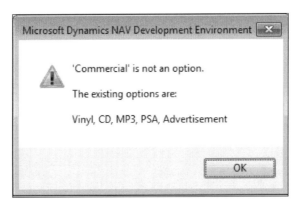

We can use this feature as a development aid when we don't remember what the option values are. We can enter a known incorrect value (such as 'xxx'), press *F11* to compile, and find out all the correct Option values.

15. Click on **OK** on the **Table Filter** form, and **OK** again on the **Calculation Formula** form.

16. Start `Royalty Cost` the same way (**Method** is **Sum**) all the way through the Table (table 50005) and Field choices in the **Calculation Formula** form. Click on the **Assist Edit** button for the table filter. Just as before, fill in the first row with the Field as Date, the Type as **FIELD**, and the **Value** with **Date Filter**.

17. Fill in the second row set **Field** to **Format** and **Type** to **FILTER**. In the **Value** column, enter `Vinyl|CD|MP3`. This means that we will filter for all records where the field **Format** contains a value equal to `Vinyl` OR `CD` OR `MP3` (the Pipe symbol is translated to the Boolean "OR"). As a result, this FlowField will sum up all the Fee Amount values that have a Format option selected as `Vinyl`, `CD`, or `MP3` and a date that satisfies the **Date Filter** specified in the **Radio Show** table.

18. The last field that we will define in this exercise is the **Date Filter** field. We have already been referencing this Radio Show table field as a source of a user-defined date selection to help analyze the data from the listenership, payable, and revenue data, but we have not yet defined the field. This one is much easier than the FlowFields as no calculation formula is required.

19. Select the properties for the **Date Filter** field and set the **FieldClass** property to **FlowFilter,** as shown here:

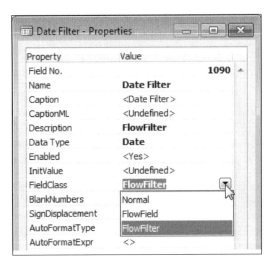

20. Close the **Date Filter - Properties** window and exit Table Designer, compiling the Radio Show table as we do so. If we do not previously exit and compile our table modifications through this exercise, we will get an error message beginning with "The schema synchronization may result in deleted data. The following destructive changes were detected:" This is followed by a list of all the fields in which we made changes that could affect previously stored data. In this case, that is a list of all the fields that were changed from **Normal** to either **FlowField** or **FlowFilter**. This is because a Normal field can store normal data, but the other two field types do not do this. Since we have no data in any of the changed fields, we should choose the **Synchronize Schema** option of **Force** to override the error message and complete the save-and-compile step. Ideally, we should also update the **Version List** field of the table object to indicate that we've made additional changes to this table.

Filtering

Filtering is one of the most powerful tools within NAV. Filtering is the application of defined limits on the data that is to be considered in a process. When we apply a filter to a Normal data field, we will only view or process records where the filtered data field satisfies the limits defined by the filter. When we apply a filter to a FlowField, the calculated value for that field will only consider data that satisfies the limits defined by the filter. Filter structures can be applied in at least three different ways, depending on the design of the process.

The first way is for the developer to fully define the filter structure and the value of the filter. This can be done in a report designed to show information on only a selected group of customers, such as those with an unpaid balance. The **Customer** table would be filtered to report only customers who have an outstanding balance greater than zero.

The second way is for the developer to define the filter structure, but allow the user to fill in the specific value to be applied. This approach would be appropriate in an accounting report that was to be tied to specific accounting periods. The user would be allowed to define the periods to be considered for each report run.

The third way is the ad hoc definition of a filter structure and value by the user. This approach is often used for general analysis of ledger data where the developer wants to give the user total flexibility in how they slice and dice the available data.

It is common to use a combination of the different filtering types. For example, the report just mentioned lists only customers with an open Balance (via a developer-defined filter) could also allow the user to define additional filter criteria. If the user wants to see only Euro currency customers, they would filter on the **Customer Currency Code** field.

Filters are an integral part of the implementation of both FlowFields and FlowFilters. These flexible, powerful tools allow the NAV designer to create pages, reports, and other processes that can be used under a wide variety of circumstances. In most competitive systems, standard user inquiries and processes are quite specific. The NAV C/AL toolset allows us to have relatively generic user inquiries and processes; it then allows the user to apply filtering to generate results that fit their specific needs.

The user sees FlowFilters filtering referred to as **Limit Totals** onscreen. Application of filters and ranges may give varying results depending on Windows settings or the SQL Server collation setup. A good set of examples of filtering options and syntax can be found in **Developer and IT Pro Help** in the section titled *Entering Criteria in Filters*.

Experimenting with filters

Now, it's time for some experimenting with filters. We want to accomplish a couple of things through our experimentation. First, get more comfortable with how filters are entered, and second, see the effects of different types of filter structures and combinations. If we had a database with a large volume of data, we could also test the speed of filtering on fields in keys and fields not in keys. However, the amount of data in the basic Cronus database is small, so any speed differences will be difficult to see in these tests.

We could experiment on any report that allows filtering. A good report for this experimentation is the **Customer/Item List**. This reports which Customer purchased what items. The **Customer/Item List** can be accessed on the Role Tailored Client Departments menu by navigating to **Sales & Marketing** | **Sales** | **Reports** | **Customer** | **Customer/Item Sales**.

When we initially run **Customer/Item Sales**, we will see just three data fields listed for the entry of filters on the **Customer** table, as shown in the following screenshot:

There are also two data fields listed for the entry of filters on the **Item Ledger Entry** table, as shown in the following screenshot (which has the **Item Ledger Entry** FastTab that can be expanded by clicking on it so we can see its predefined filter entry options):

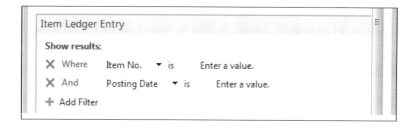

For both the **Customer** and **Item Ledger Entry**, these are the fields that should be emphasized as per the developer of this report. If we run the report without entering any filter constraints at all, using the standard Cronus data, the first page of the report will resemble the following:

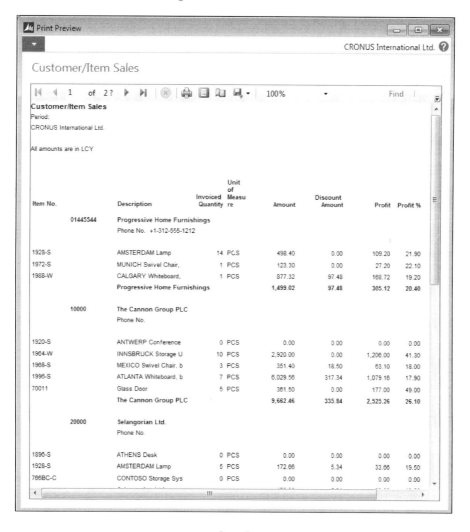

If we want to print information only for customers whose names begin with the letter A, our filter will be very simple, similar to the following screenshot:

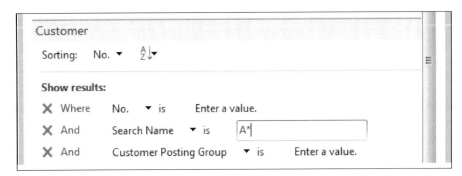

The resulting report will be similar to the following screenshot and show only the data for the two customers on file whose names begin with the letter A:

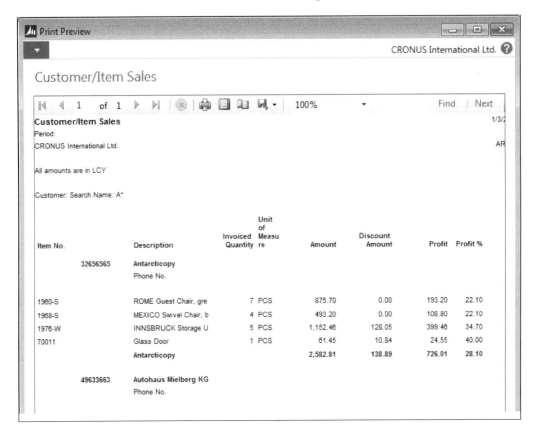

If we want to expand the customer fields to which we can apply filters, we can access the full list of other fields in the customer table. We can either click on the drop-down symbol next to a filter field that is not already in use or click on the **Add Filter** button to add a new filter field with a drop-down list access. If the number of fields available for filtering is longer than what the initial list display allows, the bottom entry in the list is **Additional Columns**. If we click on that, we might end up with a display like the following. Note that the lists are in alphabetical order, based on the field names. If the list of available fields is too long to display in the second column, that column can be scrolled up and down.

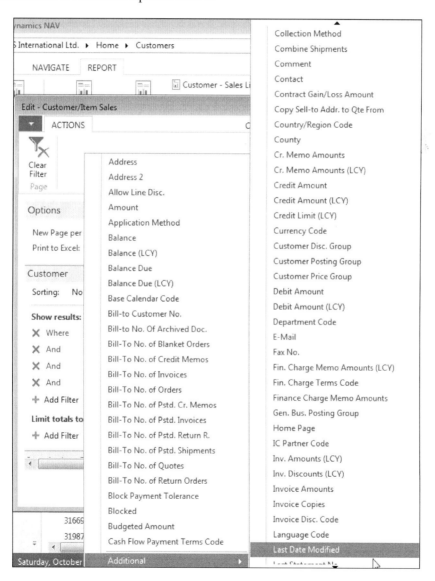

From these lists, we can choose one or more fields and then enter filters on those fields. If we choose **Territory Code**, for example, then the **Request Page** would look similar to the following screenshot. And, if we clicked on the lookup arrow in the **Filter** column, a screen would pop up, allowing us to choose from the data items in the related table — in this case, **Territories**:

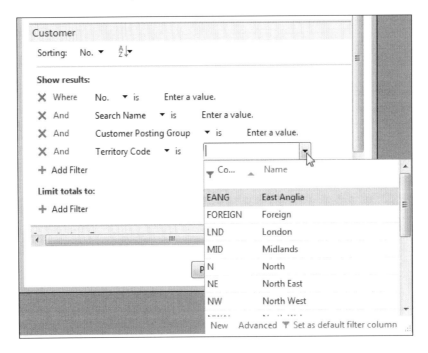

This particular **Request Page** has FastTabs for each of the two primary tables in the report. Click on the **Item Ledger Entry** FastTab to filter the Item-related data. If we filter on the **Item No.** for item numbers that contain the letter **W**, the report will be similar to the following screenshot:

Downloading the example code.

You can download the example code files from your account at http://www.packtpub.com for all the Packt Publishing books you have purchased. If you purchased this book elsewhere, you can visit http://www.packtpub.com/support and register to have the files e-mailed directly to you.

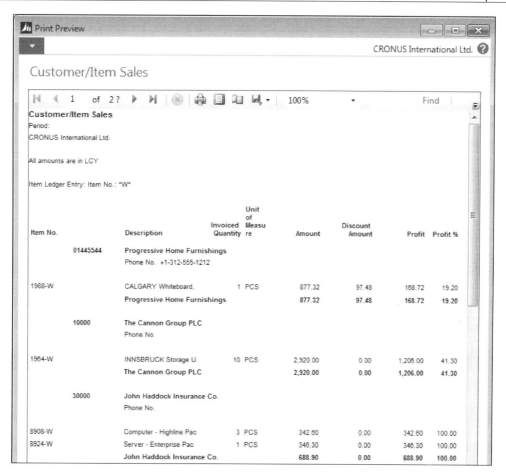

If we want to see all of the items containing either the letter W or the letter S, our filter would be ***W* | *S***. If we made the filter **W | S**, then we would get only entries that are exactly equal to **W** or **S** because we didn't use any wildcards.

You should go back over the various types of filters that we discussed and try each one and try them in combination. Get creative! Try some things that you're not sure may work and see what happens. Explore a variety of reports or list pages in the system by applying filters to see the results of your experiments. A good page on which to apply filters is the **Customer List** (**Sales & Marketing** menu | **Sales** | **Customers**). This filtering experimentation process is safe (you can't hurt anything or anyone) and a great learning experience.

Accessing filter controls

NAV 2015 has two very different approaches to set up filtering—one for the Development Environment and the other for the Role Tailored Client. Since we develop in the former, we will briefly cover filtering there. As we target our development for use in the Role Tailored Client, we need to be totally comfortable with filtering there; that is the interface for our users.

Development Environment filter access

There are four buttons at the top of the screen that relate to filtering; there is another one to choose the active key (that is, current sort sequence). Depending on the system configuration (OS and setup), they will look similar to those in the following screenshot:

From left to right, they are:

- **Field Filter** (*F7*): To highlight a field, press *F7* (or select **View** | **Field** Filter), and the data in that field will display as being ready for us to define a filter on that data field. We can freely edit the filter before clicking on **OK**.

- Table Filter (*Ctrl* + *F7*): Press the *Ctrl* key and *F7* simultaneously (or select **View** | **Table Filter**). We will get a screen that allows us to choose fields in the left column and enter related filters in the right column. Each filter is the same as would have been created by using the **Field Filter** option. The multiple filters for the individual fields are **ANDed** together (that is, they all apply simultaneously). If we invoke the **Table Filter** form when any **Field Filters** are already applied, they will be displayed in the form.

- Flow Filter (*Shift* + *F7*): Since we cannot view any data containing FlowFields in the Development Environment, using the Flow Filter in the Development Environment is not useful.

- Show All (*Shift* + *Ctrl* + *F7*): This will remove all Field Filters, but it will not remove any Flow Filters.

- Sort (*Shift* + *F8*): This allows us to choose key that is active on a displayed data list.

When we are viewing a set of data (such as a list of objects) and want to check whether any filters are in effect, we should check the bottom of the screen for the word **FILTER**.

Role Tailored Client filter access

The method of accessing fields to use in filtering in the Role Tailored Client (RTC) is quite different from that in the Development Environment.

When a page such as the **Customer List** is opened, the filter section at the top of the page looks like the following screenshot. On the upper-right corner is a place to enter single-field filters. This is the **Type to filter** (also referred to as **Quick**), which is essentially equivalent to the Field Filter in the Development Environment. The fields available for filtering are the same as the visible columns showing in the List.

If we click on the chevron circle button in the upper-right corner to expand the Filter Pane, the result will look similar to the following screenshot. This filter display includes an additional filtering capability, **Show Results**, that allows entry of filters of the **Limit Totals** to type:

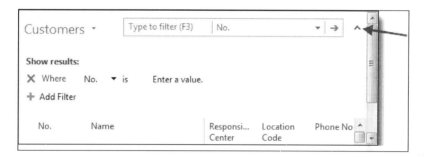

If we go to the Filter Pane header line (where the Page's Menu Caption is **Customers** in this page) and click on the drop-down symbol, we will see a set of selection options (the filter menu), similar to that in the following screenshot. The **Advanced filter** provides for the entry of multiple Field Filters (essentially the same as the Development Environment Table Filter). The **Limit Totals** filter provides for the entry of FlowFilter constraints.

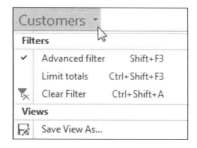

This is one of two places in which we can clear filters of all types (we can also enter *Ctrl + Shift + A* as indicated in the filter menu). The **Save View As...** option allows the user to save the filtered view, name it, and add it to an **Activity Group** in the Navigation pane. The following image shows a series of Saved Views on **Sales Orders** (most of them are out of the box). The **Euro Orders** entry is a Saved View created by a user.

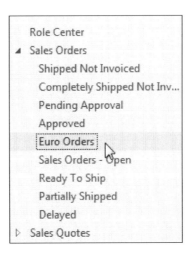

If we click on **Limit Totals** (or press *Ctrl + Shift + F3*), the **Limit Totals to:** portion of the Filter pane will be displayed. When we click on the drop-down arrow, we will get a list of all the FlowFields to which we can apply one or more **Limit totals** (FlowFilters).

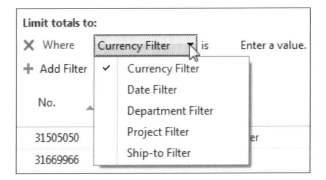

Depending on the specific page and functional area, Flowfield filtering can be used to segregate data on Dimension fields. For example, in the page shown in the preceding screenshot, we can filter data regarding a single Department or Project (both of which are Dimension fields), a range of Departments or Projects, or a range of Customer Ship-to locations.

Summary

In this chapter, we focused on the basic building blocks of the NAV data structure: fields and their attributes. We reviewed the types of data fields, properties, and trigger elements for each type of field. We walked through a number of examples to illustrate most of these elements though we had postponed the exploration of triggers until later, when we had more knowledge of C/AL. We covered Data Type and FieldClass, properties which determine what kind of data can be stored in a field.

We reviewed and experimented with the date calculation tool that gives C/AL an edge in business applications. We discussed filtering, how filtering is considered as we design our database structure, and how the users will access data. Finally, more of our NAV Radio Show application was constructed.

In the next chapter, we will look at the many different types of Pages in more detail. We'll put some of that knowledge to use to further expand our example NAV application.

Review questions

Q.1. The maximum length for a C/AL field or variable name is 250 characters. True or False?

Q.2. The Table Relation property defines the reference of a data field to a table. The related table data field must be: (choose one)

    a.   In any key in the related table

    b.   Defined in the related table but not in a key

    c.   In the Primary Key in the related table

    d.   The first field in the primary key in the related table

Q.3. How many of the following Field Data Types support storing application data such as names and amounts 1, 2, 3 or 4?

    a.   FlowFilter

    b.   Editable

    c.   Normal

    d.   FlowField

Q.4. The ExtendedDataType property supports designation of all but one of the following data types, displaying an appropriate action icon. (Choose the one that is not supported.)

a. Email address

b. Website URL

c. GPS location

d. Telephone number

e. Masked entry

Q.5. Choose one of the following that is not a FlowField Method.

a. Median

b. Count

c. Max

d. Exist

e. Average

Q.6. It is important to have a consistent, well-planned approach to field numbers, especially if the application will use the TransferFields function. True or False?

Q.7. Field Filters and Limit totals cannot be used at the same time. True or False?

Q.8. Which property is used to support the multi-language feature of NAV? (choose one)

a. Name

b. CaptionML

c. Caption

d. LanguageRef

Q.9. Which of the following are Field Triggers? (Choose two)

a. OnEntry

b. OnValidate

c. OnDeletion

d. OnLookup

Q.10. Which of the following are complex data types? (Choose three)

    a.   Records

    b.   Strings of text

    c.   DateFormula

    d.   DateTime data

    e.   Objects

Q.11. Every table must have a Primary Key. A Primary Key entry can be defined as unique or duplicates allowed, based on a table property. True or False?

Q.12. Text and Code variables can be of any length.

    a.   In a memory variable (working storage)? True or False?

    b.   In a table field? True or False?

Q.13. FlowField results are not stored in the NAV table data. True or False?

Q.14. The following two filters are equivalent. True or False?

    a.   (*W50?|I?5|D*)

    b.   (I?5) OR (D*) OR (*W50?)

Q.15. Limit totals apply to FlowFilters. True or False?

Q.16. All Data Types can be used to define data in tables and working storage. True or False?

Q.17. DateFormula alpha time units include which of the following? (Choose two.)

    a.   C for century

    b.   W for week

    c.   H for holiday

    d.   CM for current month

Q.18. FlowFilter data is stored in the database. True or False?

Q.19. Option data is stored as alpha data strings. True or False?

Q.20. Which of the following are numeric data types in NAV 2015? (Choose two.)

a. Decimal

b. Option

c. Hexadecimal

d. BLOB

Q.21. Which of the following acts as wildcards in NAV 2015? (Choose two.)

a. Decimal Point (.)

b. Question Mark (?)

c. Asterisk (*)

d. Hash Mark (#)

4
Pages – The Interactive Interface

"The best journey is the one with the fewest steps. Shorten the distance between the user and their goal."

– Author Unknown

"It takes less time to do a thing right than to explain why you did it wrong."

– H.W. Longfellow

Pages are NAV 2015's object type for interactively presenting information. The page rendering routines that *paint* the page on the target display handle much of the data presentation detail. This allows a variety of clients to be created by Microsoft, such as Web browser resident clients, Windows RTC clients, and new tablet clients (iPad, Android, Windows). **Independent Software Vendors (ISVs)** have created mobile clients and even clients targeted to devices other than video displays.

One of the benefits of Page technology is the focus on the user experience rather than the underlying data structure. As always, the designer/developer has the responsibility of using the tools to their best effect. Another advantage of NAV 2015 pages is the flexibility they provide the user for personalization, allowing him/her to tailor what is displayed and how it is organized.

In this chapter, we will explore the various types of pages offered by NAV 2015. We will review many options for formatting, data accessing, and tailoring the pages. We will also learn about the Page Designer tools and the inner structures of the pages. Topics we will cover include:

- Page design and structure overview
- Types of Pages
- Page Designer
- Page components
- Page controls
- Page actions
- WDTU Page enhancement exercises

Page design and structure overview

Pages serve the purpose of input, output, and control. They are views of data or process information designed for on-screen display only. They are also user data entry vehicles.

Pages are made up of various combinations of controls, properties, actions, triggers, and C/AL code.

- Controls provide the user with ways to view, enter, and edit data, choose options or commands, initiate actions, and view status
- Properties are attributes or characteristics of an object that define its state, appearance, or value
- Actions are menu items (which may be icons)
- Triggers are predefined functions that are executed when certain actions or events occur

The internal structure of a page maps to an XML structure, some of which is readily visible in the Page Designer display while the rest is in the background.

Page design guidelines

C/SIDE allows us to create pages with a number of different look and feel attributes. The standard NAV application only uses a few of the possibilities, and closely follows a set of **Graphical User Interface (GUI)** guidelines that provide consistency throughout the system. These guidelines are described in an interactive document named Microsoft Dynamics NAV 2015 User Experience Guidelines (UX Guide for short). Obtain a copy of this guide from the MSDN Library (`https://msdn.microsoft.com/en-us/library/jj651618(v=nav.80).aspx`) and study it.

Good design practice dictates that enhancements integrate seamlessly with the existing software unless there is an overwhelming justification for being different. When we add new pages or change the existing pages, the changes should have the same look and feel as the original pages unless the new functionality requires significant differences. This consistency not only makes the user's life easier, it also makes support, maintenance, and training more efficient.

There will be instances where we will need to create a significantly different page layout in order to address a special requirement. Maybe we need to use industry specific symbols, or we need to create a screen layout for a special display device. Perhaps we are going to create a special *dashboard* display to report on the status of work queues. Even when we are going to be different, we should continue to be guided by the environment and context in which our new work will operate.

The NAV 2015 page structure

Let's take a look at what makes up a typical page in the NAV 2015 Role Tailored Client. The page in the following screenshot includes a List page at its core (the content area).

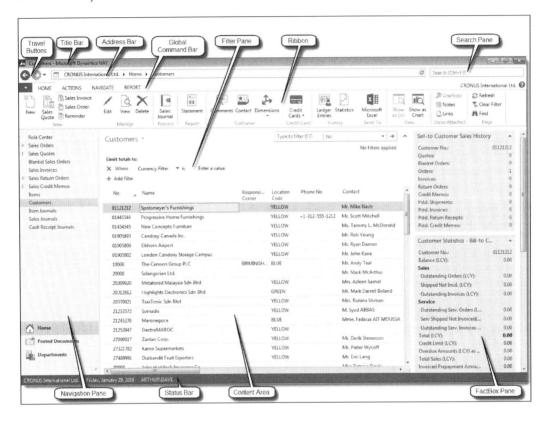

Following is a brief description of all these options:

- **Travel Buttons**: They serve the same purpose as in the Explorers, that is to move backward or forward through the previously displayed pages.

- **Title Bar**: This displays Page Caption and product identification.

- **Address Bar**: This is also referred to as the Address Box and it displays the navigation path that led to the current display. It defaults to the following format, which is sometimes referred to as the breadcrumb path:

If we click on one of the right-facing arrowheads in the Address Bar, the child menu options will be displayed in a drop-down list (as can be seen in the following screenshot). The same list of options subordinate to **Sales Orders** is displayed both in the drop-down menu from the address bar, and in the detailed list of options in the navigation pane.

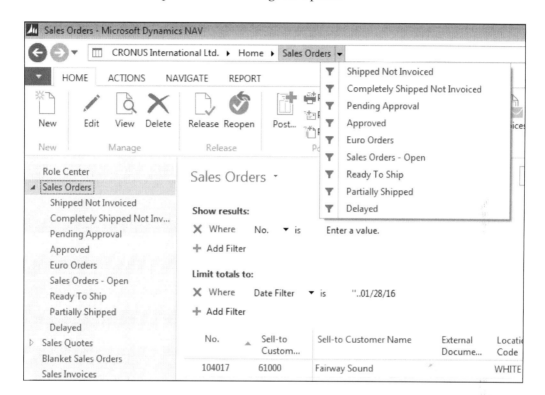

If we click in the blank space in the Address Bar to the right of the breadcrumbs, the path display will change to a traditional path format, as shown next:

- **Global Command Bar**: This provides access to a general set of menu options, which varies slightly based on what is in the content area. The left-most menu in the Command Bar is accessed by clicking on the drop-down arrow at the left end of the Global Command Bar. It provides access (as shown in the next screenshot) to some basic application information and administration functions.

- **FilterPane**: This is where the user controls the filtering to be applied to the page display.
- **Ribbon**: This contains shortcut icons to actions. These same commands will be duplicated in other menu locations, but are in the Ribbon for quick and easy access. The Ribbon can be collapsed (made not visible) or expanded (made visible) under user control.
- **Search Field**: This allows the users to find pages, reports, or views based on the object's name (full or partial). Search finds only those objects that are accessible from the Navigation Pane.
- **Navigation Pane**: This contains menu options based on the active Role Center (which is tied to the user's login). It also contains activity buttons, at a minimum the **Home** and **Departments** buttons. The **Departments** button and its menu items are generated based on the contents of the NAV MenuSuite.
- **Status Bar**: This shows the name of the active company, the work date, and the current user ID. If we double-click on the company name, we can change the companies. If we double-click on the work date, we can change the work date.

- **Content Area**: This is the focus of the page. It may be a Role Center, a List page, or a Departments menu list.
- **FactBox Pane**: This can appear on the right side of certain page types (Card, List, ListPlus, Document, Navigate, or Worksheet). A FactBox can only display a CardPart, ListPart, System Part, or a limited set of predefined charts. Fact Boxes can provide no-click and one-click access to related information about the data in focus in the Content Area.

Types of pages

Let's review the types of pages available for use in an application. Then we will create several examples for our WDTU Radio Station system.

Each time we work on an application design, we need to carefully consider which page type is best to use for the functionality we are creating. Types of pages available include RoleCenter, List, Card, ListPart, CardPart, ListPlus, Document, Worksheet, Navigate, ConfirmationDialog, and StandardDialog. Pages can be created and modified by the developer and can be personalized by the administrator, super user, or user.

Role Center page

A user's assigned Role Center page is their home page in NAV, the page where they land when first logging into NAV 2015. The purpose of a Role Center page is to provide a task-oriented home base which focuses on the tasks that the user typically needs in order to do his/her job on a day to day basis. All the user's common tasks should be no more than one or two clicks away.

The standard NAV 2015 distribution includes twenty-three predefined Role Center pages, including generic roles such as Bookkeeper, Sales Manager, and Production Planner. Some of the provided Role Centers are richly featured and have been heavily tailored by Microsoft as illustrations of what is possible. On the other hand, some of the provided Role Centers are only skeletons, acting essentially as place holders.

 It is critical to understand that the provided Role Center pages are intended to be templates, not final deliverables.

Role Centers that are specific to the customer's organization structure and user role profiles should be created for every NAV implementation. We should take advantage of the guidance for the design and creation of Role Center pages that is part of the Microsoft MSDN documentation (such as `https://msdn.microsoft.com/en-us/library/jj128066(v=nav.80).aspx` and its *See Also* references) or is in various blogs. Even though this material is brief, it provides much useful information.

Central to each Role Center page is the **Activities** area. The **Activities** area provides the user with a visual overview of their primary tasks. Central to the **Activities** part are the **Cues**. Each blue Cue icon represents a filtered list of documents in a particular status, indicating the amount of work to be handled by the user. The grey Cue icons display a calculated value.

The following screenshot shows a **Role Center** page for the user role profile of **Sales Order Processor**:

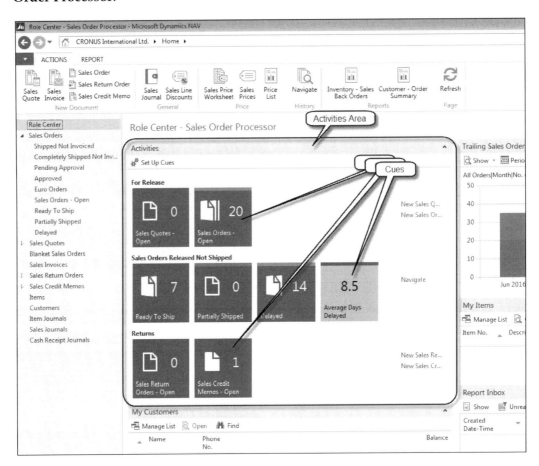

List page

List pages are the first pages accessed when choosing any menu option to access data. This includes all the entries under the **Home** Button on the Navigation Pane. A List page displays a list of records (rows), one line per record, with each displayed data field in a column.

When a List page is initially selected, it is not editable. When we double-click an entry in a List, either an editable Card page or an editable List page entry is displayed. Examples of this latter behavior are the Reference table pages such as Post Codes, Territories, and Languages. A List page can also be used to show a list of master records to allow the user to visually scan through the list of records, or to easily choose a record on which to focus.

List pages may optionally include FactBoxes. Some NAV 2015 List pages, such as Customer Ledger Entries (Page 25), allow editing of some fields (for example, Invoice Due Dates) and not of others.

The following screenshot shows a typical list page—the Item List, Page 31:

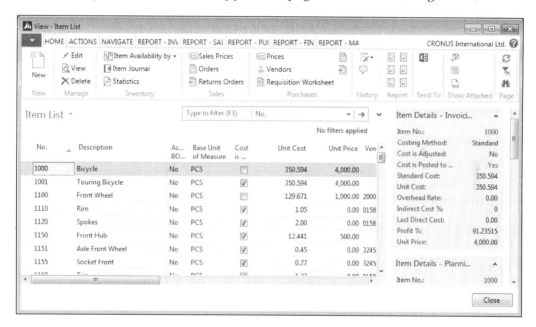

Card page

Card pages display and allow updating of a single record at a time. They are used for master tables and setup data. Complex cards can contain multiple FastTabs and FactBoxes, as well as display data from subordinate tables. An example of Card page image for the **Customer Card** – Page 21 follows, with the **General** FastTab expanded and the other FastTabs collapsed:

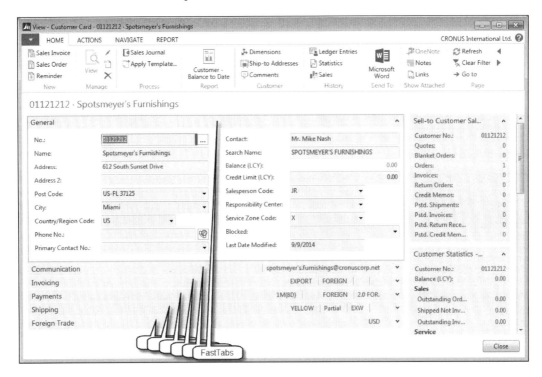

Document page

Document (task) pages have at least two FastTabs in a header/detail format. The FastTab at the top contains the header fields in a card style format, followed by a FastTab containing multiple records in a list style format (a ListPart page). Examples are Sales Orders, Sales Invoices, Purchase Orders, Purchase Invoices, and Production Orders. The Document page type is appropriate whenever we have a parent record tied to a subordinate child records in a one-to-many relationship. A Document page may also have FactBoxes. An example of Sales Order Document page follows (Sales Order – Page 42):

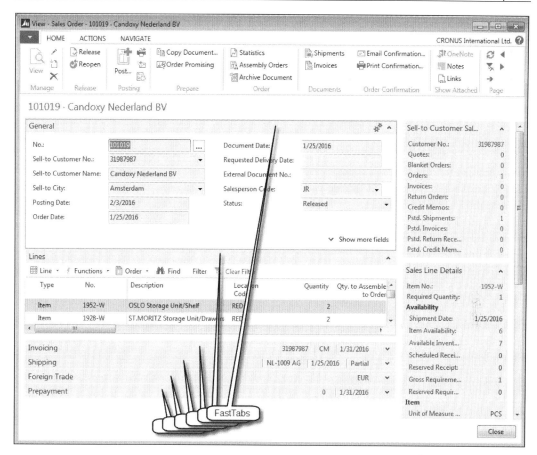

FastTab

FastTabs, as shown in the preceding **Customer Card** and **Sales Order** screenshots, are collapsible/expandable replacements for traditional left-to-right forms tabs. They are often used to segregate data by subject area on a Card page or a Document page. In this Sales Order image, the **General** and **Lines** FastTabs are expanded and the remaining FastTabs are collapsed. Individually important fields can be Promoted so they display on the FastTab header when the tab is collapsed, allowing the user to see this data with minimal effort. Examples appear on all the Sales Order's collapsed FastTabs. Promoted field displays disappear from the FastTab header when the FastTab is expanded.

ListPlus page

A ListPlus page is similar in layout to a Document page, as it will have at least one FastTab with fields in a card type format and one FastTab in a list page format. Unlike a Document page that can only have a single list style subpage, a ListPlus page may have more than one FastTab with card format fields and one or more FastTabs with a list page format. The card format portion of a ListPlus page often contains control information determining what data is displayed in the associated list, such as in Page 113 – Budget, shown in the following image:

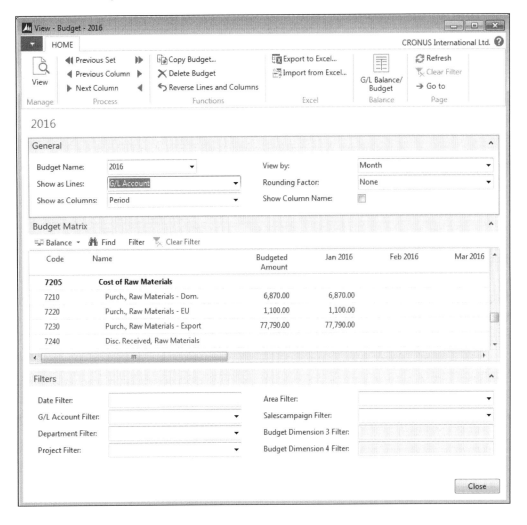

A ListPlus page may also have FactBoxes. Other examples of ListPlus pages are **Page 155 – Customer Sales** and **Page 157 – Item Availability** by Periods.

Worksheet (Journal) page

Worksheet pages are widely used in NAV to enter transactions. The Worksheet page format consists of a list page style section showing multiple record lines in the content area, followed by a section containing either additional detail fields for the line in focus or containing totals. All the Journals in NAV use Worksheet pages. Data is usually entered into a Journal/Worksheet by keyboard entry, but in some cases via a batch process.

The following screenshot shows a Worksheet page, **Sales Journal – Page 253**:

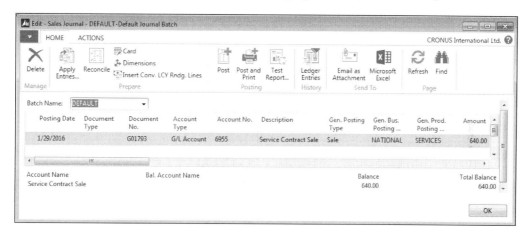

ConfirmationDialog page

This is a simple display page embedded in a process. It is used to allow a user to control the flow of a process. Following is a sample ConfirmationDialog page:

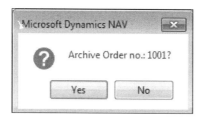

StandardDialog page

The StandardDialog page is also a simple page format to allow the user to control a process, such as **Copy Tax Setup** (Page 476). The StandardDialog page allows the entry of control data such as that shown in the following screenshot:

NavigatePage

The primary use of the NavigatePage page type in NAV 2015 is as the basis for Wizard pages. All the instances of Wizard pages in NAV 2015 are in the Marketing functionality area of the system. Some Wizard page examples are pages: 5077 – Create Interaction, 5097 – Create To-do, 5126 – Create Opportunity, 5129 – Update Opportunity, and 5146 – Assign Opportunity. A Wizard page consists of multiple user data entry screens linked together to provide a series of steps necessary to complete a task.

Two screens from a Wizard page (Page 5126 – **Create Opportunity**) are shown in the following screenshots:

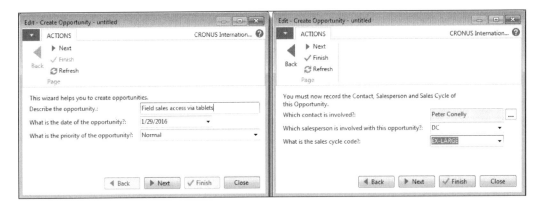

Navigate page 344

The Navigate function has been a very powerful, unique feature of NAV since the 1990s. Somewhat confusingly, in NAV 2015 the Navigate function is implemented using the ListPlus page type, not the NavigatePage page type which was used in the earlier NAV releases.

The **Navigate page (Page 344)** allows the user (who may be a developer operating in user mode) to view a summary of the number and type of posted entries having the same document number and posting date as a related entry or as a user-entered value. The user can drill down to examine the individual entries. Navigate is a terrific tool for tracking down related posted entries. It can be productively used by a user, an auditor, or even by a developer. A sample Navigate page is shown in the following screenshot:

Special pages

There are two special purpose page types. One is a component of other objects, and the second is automatically generated.

Request page

A Request page is a simple page that allows the user to enter information to control the execution of a Report or XMLport object. Request pages can have multiple FastTabs, but can only be created as part of a Report or XMLPort object. All Request page designs will be similar to the following image for the **Item Price List (Report 715)** Request page:

Departments page

The Departments page is a one-of-a-kind, system-generated page. We don't directly create a Departments page because it is automatically generated from the entries in the MenuSuite object. When we create new objects and add appropriate entries to the MenuSuite, we provide the material needed to update the Departments menu/page. The look and feel of the Departments page cannot be changed (though individual entries can be added, changed, moved, or deleted).

The Departments page acts as a *site map* to the NAV system for the user. When we add new objects to the MenuSuite (thus to the Departments menu), NAV UX design guidelines encourage the entry of duplicate links within whichever sections the user might consider looking for that page (we will later discuss the Search function which makes this task even easier). An example of a **Departments** page is shown in the following screenshot:

Page parts

Several of the page types we have reviewed thus far contain multiple panes with each pane including special purpose parts. Let's look at some of the component page parts available to the developer.

> Some page parts compute the displayed data on the fly, taking advantage of Flow Fields which may require considerable system resources to process the FlowField calculations. As developers, we need to be careful about causing performance problems through overuse of such displays.

FactBox Area

The FactBox Area can be defined on the right side of certain page types including Card, List, List Plus, Document, and Worksheet. A FactBox Area can contain Page parts (CardPart or ListPart), Chart parts, and System parts (Outlook, Notes, MyNotes, or Record Links). A variety of standard CardParts, ListParts, and Charts are available which can be used in FactBoxes. System parts cannot be modified. All the others can be enhanced from the standard instances, or new ones may be created from scratch.

CardParts and ListParts

CardParts are used for FactBoxes that don't require a list. They display fields or perhaps a picture control. (NAV 2015 Help contains an example of including a DotNet add-in within a FactBox to display a chart) An example of the **Customer Statistics** FactBox **(Page 9082 – Customer Statistics Factbox)** is shown in the following screenshot:

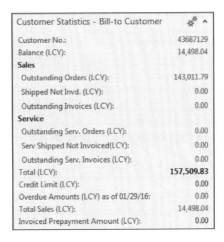

ListParts are used for FactBoxes that require a list. A list is defined as columns of repeated data. No more than two or three columns should appear in a FactBox list. A screenshot of the three-column **My Items** FactBox **ListPart - Page 9152** follows:

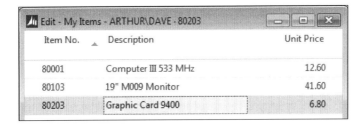

Charts

In NAV 2015, there are two standard ways of including charts in our pages. The first one, Chart parts, is a carry-over from NAV 2009. The second one, the Chart Control Add-in, was new in NAV 2013.

Chart part

A Chart part displays list data in graphic form. It is a default optional component of all FactBox Areas; it is not a Page Type. If a FactBox exists, it has a Chart part option available. Chart parts are populated by choosing one of the available charts stored in the **Chart table (Table 2000000078)**. Some charts require range parameters while others do not (they default to a defined data range). Most of the supplied charts are two-dimensional, but a sampling of three-dimensional, dynamic charts is included. A MSDN NAV Team blog provides an extensive description of chart construction and a utility for creating new charts (`http://blogs.msdn.com/b/nav/archive/2011/06/03/chart-generator-tool-for-rtc-cgtrtc.aspx`). There is also a YouTube video on the topic, available at `https://www.youtube.com/watch?v=RwOv3dLdXAw&x-yt-cl=85114404&x-yt-ts=1422579428`. Though both of these were created for the previous releases of NAV, they are useful for NAV 2015 as well. A sample standard chart is shown in the following screenshot:

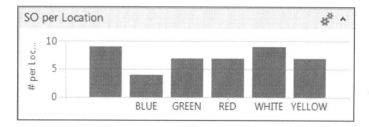

Chart Control Add-in

The NAV 2015 distribution includes a charting capability that is based on a Control Add-in (created with .NET code written outside of C/SIDE and integrated into NAV). An example is the Trailing Sales Orders chart in a **Factbox Page part (Page 760)** that appears in the **Order Processor Role Center (Page 9006)**. Following is a screenshot of that chart:

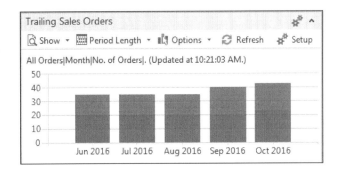

The *Cash Flow Chart Example* in the NAV 2015 **Developer and IT Pro Help** describes how to create charts using the Chart Control Add-in.

Page names

Card pages are named similarly as the table with which they are associated, plus the word *Card*. Examples include Customer table and Customer Card, Item table and Item Card, and Vendor table and Vendor Card.

List pages are named similarly as the table with which they are associated. List pages which are simple noneditable lists have the word *list* associated with the table name. Examples are Customer List, Item List, and Vendor List. For each of these, the table also has an associated card page. Where the table has no associated card page, the list pages are named after the tables, but in the plural format. Examples include Customer Ledger Entry table and Customer Ledger Entries page, Check Ledger Entry table and Check Ledger Entries page, Country/Region table and Countries/Regions page, and Production Forecast Name table and Production Forecast Names page.

The single-record Setup tables that are used for application control information throughout NAV are named after their functional area, plus the word *Setup*. The associated Card page should also be (and generally is) named similarly to the table. For example, General Ledger Setup table and General Ledger Setup page, Manufacturing Setup table and Manufacturing Setup page, and so on.

Journal entry (worksheet) pages are given names tied to their purpose, plus the word *Journal*. In the standard product, several Journal pages for different purposes are associated with the same table. For example, the Sales Journal, Cash Receipts Journal, Purchases Journal, and Payments Journal, all use the General Journal Line table as their SourceTable (they are different pages all tied to the same table).

If there is a Header and Line table associated with a data category such as Sales Orders, the related page and subpage ideally should be named to describe the relationship between the tables and the pages. However, in some cases, it's better to tie the page names directly to the function they perform rather than the underlying tables. An example is the two pages making up the display called by the Sales Order menu entry—the Sales Order page is tied to the Sales Header table, and the Sales Order Subform page is tied to the Sales Line table. The same tables are involved for the Sales Invoice page and Sales Invoice Subform page.

 The use of the word *Subform* rather than *Subpage*, as in Sales Invoice Subform, is a left-over term from the previous versions of NAV which had forms rather than pages.

Sometimes, while naming pages, we will have a conflict between naming pages based on the associated tables and naming them based on the use of the data. For example, the menu entry Contacts invokes a main page/subpage named Contact Card and Contact Card Subform. The respective tables are the Contact table and the Contact Profile Answer table. The context usage should take precedence in the page naming as was done here.

Page Designer

The Page Designer is accessed from within the Development Environment through **Tools | Object Designer | Page**. It can be opened either for creation of a new page by using the **New** button or for editing an existing page by highlighting the target object, then clicking the **Design** button.

New Page Wizard

When we click on the **New** button, or *F3*, or **Edit | New**, we bring up the **New Page** Wizard.

We can proceed to the Page Designer with the PageType property set to **Card** and no SourceTable defined by clicking on **OK** with **Create blank page** selected, and not entering a Table Name or Number. Or we could enter a Table Name or Number, select **Create a page using a wizard**, and select a Page Type. That will take us to the Page Wizard with the PageType property set to our choice and the SourceTable assigned to the table we entered. There is almost always less effort to use the Wizard to create at least a rough version of a page design, then modify the generated object structure and code to get the ultimate desired result.

To use the Page Wizard, first we enter the name or number of the table to which we want our page to be bound. Then we choose what PageType we want to create – Card, List, RoleCenter, CardPart, ListPart, Document, Worksheet, ListPlus, ConfirmationDialog, StandardDialog, or NavigatePage. The subsequent steps the Page Wizard will take us through depend on the PageType chosen. The following chart shows which options are available for each Page Type through use of the Wizard:

Page Type	Fast Tabs	Fields to Display	FactBoxes	Page Designer
RoleCenter	-	-	-	✓
Card	✓	✓	✓	✓
List	-	✓	✓	✓
Document	✓	✓	✓	✓
ListPlus	✓	✓	✓	✓

Page Type	Fast Tabs	Fields to Display	FactBoxes	Page Designer
Worksheet	-	✓	✓	✓
ConfirmationDialog	✓	✓	-	✓
StandardDialog	-	-	-	✓
NavigatePage	✓	✓	✓	✓
CardPart	-	✓	-	✓
ListPart	-	✓	-	✓

To see what the Page Wizard looks like, we'll step through an example definition of a Card page based on our Table 50000 – Radio Show (this example is only done to illustrate the Page Wizard process – we aren't creating a page that we'll keep for our Radio Show application).

Invoke the Page Designer Wizard by clicking on the **New** button with the **Page** button highlighted. Enter 50000 in the **Table** field, select the **Create a page using a wizard**: option, select **Card**, and click on the **OK** button. The next screen allows us to define FastTabs. It displays a default first FastTab titled **General**. For our example, we'll add two more FastTabs, **Tab 1** and **Tab 2**.

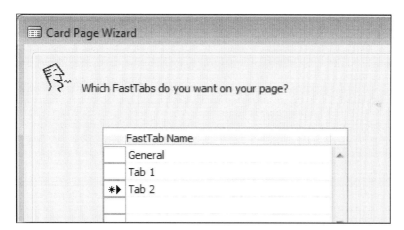

We click **Next** and proceed to the screen to assign fields from our bound table to each of the individual tabs. The single arrow buttons move one field either onto or off of the selected tab. The double arrow buttons move all the fields in the chosen direction. In the following screenshot, five fields have been selected and assigned to the **General** tab:

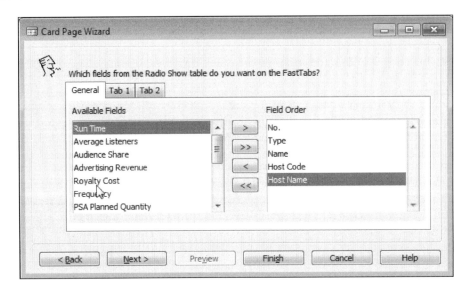

We can move fields back and forth between the chosen and available sets, as well as reposition them in the Field Order until we are satisfied with the result. If we realize that we should have defined our tabs differently, we can click on the **Back** button and return to the FastTab definition screen to revise the tab assignments.

After all the desired fields have been assigned to the appropriate tab in the desired order, we will click **Next** and move on to the screen that allows us to assign FactBoxes to the Page. Many different page components are made available by the Wizard for assignment as FactBoxes.

As we will see in the next screenshot, many of the choices are not appropriate for use in most pages. We can only select previously created page parts for FactBoxes. This leads to an important concept.

 Even though we can add component parts later, it's good practice to plan our page design layout ahead of time and construct the component parts first (start with just place holder page parts now and modify them later to be fully functional).

If we had not yet defined the FactBoxes for our current page design, we could pick other similar page components and then make the appropriate code replacement later in the **Page Designer**.

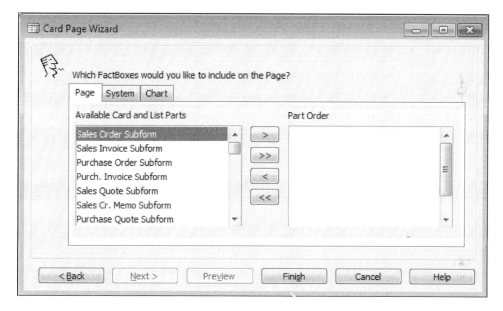

Once we have done all the assignment work that is feasible within the Page Wizard, we will click **Finish**. The Page Wizard will generate the object structure and C/AL code for our defined page and present the results to us in the **Page Designer**, as shown in the following screenshot:

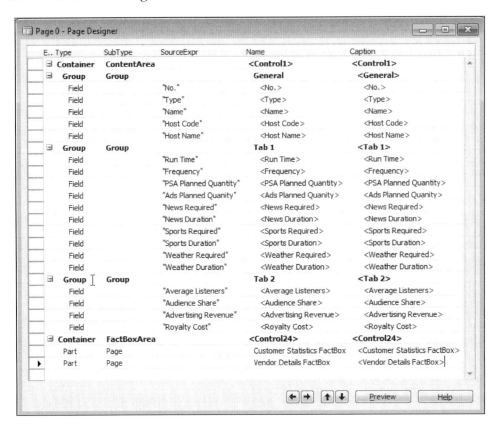

We realize now that it would have been more efficient to have planned ahead and created our custom FactBox page parts before we used the Wizard to create our card page. The alternative we used was to simply add a couple of FactBox page parts as place holders which we could replace later. That gave us the structure we wanted and compensated for our lack of planning. We could wait and just add the FactBoxes later, but we wouldn't be taking advantage of the help the Wizard can provide.

Page components

All pages are made up of certain common components. The basic elements of a page object are the page triggers, page properties, controls, control triggers, and control properties.

Page Triggers

The following screenshot shows the page triggers. The **Help** section **Page and Action Triggers** provides good general guidance to the event which causes each page trigger to fire. Note that the **OnQueryClosePage** trigger isn't related to any Query object action.

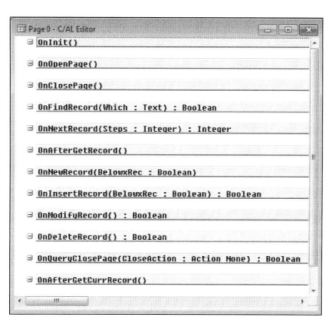

In general, according to best practices, we should minimize the C/AL code placed in Page triggers, putting the code in a Table or Field trigger or calling a Codeunit Library function instead. However, many standard pages include a modest amount of code supporting page specific filter or display functions. When we develop a new page, it's always a good idea to look for similar pages in the standard product and be guided by how those pages operate internally. Sometimes special display requirements result in complex code being required within a page. It is important that the code in a page be there for only managing the data display and not for data modification.

Page properties

We will now look at the properties of the **Radio Show List** page we created earlier. The list of available page properties is the same for all page types. The values of these properties vary considerably from one page to another, even more from one page type to another. The following screenshot shows the **Page - Properties** screen of our **Radio Show List page (Page 50000)**. This screen is accessed by opening Page 50000 in the Page Designer, highlighting the first empty line in the **Controls** list, and Clicking on the **Properties** icon (or *Shift + F4* or **View | Properties**).

We can see that many of these properties are still in their default condition (they are not highlighted in bold). Following are the properties with which we are most likely to be concerned:

- **ID**: This is the unique object number of the page.

- **Name**: This is the unique name by which this page is referenced in C/AL code.

- **Caption** and **CaptionML**: This refers to the page name to be displayed, depending on the language option in use.

- **Editable**: This determines whether or not the controls in the page can be edited (assuming the table's **Editable** properties are also set to **Yes**). If this property is set to **Yes**, the page allows the individual the control to determine the appropriate **Editable** property value.

- **Description**: This is for internal documentation only.

- **Permissions**: This is used to instruct the system to allow the users of this page to have certain levels of access (r=read, i=insert, m=modify, d=delete) to the TableData in the specified table objects. For example, users of Page 499 (Available - Sales Lines) are allowed to only read or modify (Permissions for Sales Line = rm) the data in the Sales Line table.

 Whenever defining special permissions, be sure to test with an end-user license. In fact, it's always important to test with an end user license.

- **PageType**: This specifies how this page will be displayed, using one of the available ten page types (RoleCenter, Card, List, ListPlus, Worksheet, ConfirmationDialog, StandardDialog, NavigatePage, CardPart, and ListPart).

- **CardPageID**: This is the ID of the Card page that should be launched when the user double-clicks on an entry in the list. This is only used on List pages.

- **RefreshOnActivate**: When set to **Yes**, This causes the page to refresh when the page is activated. This property is unsupported by the Web Client.

- **PromotedActionCategoriesML**: This allows the language to be changed for Promoted Action Categories from the default English (ENU) to another language, or to extend the number of Promoted Action Categories from the standard three options (New, Process, and Reports) to seven more categories. See the **Help** section *How to: Define Promoted Action Categories Captions for the Ribbon*.

- **SourceTable**: This is the name of the table to which the page is bound.

- **SourceTableView**: This can be utilized to automatically apply defined filters and/or open the page with a key other than the Primary Key.

- **ShowFilter**: This is set to **No** to have the Filter pane default to not visible. The user can still make the Filter pane visible.

- **DelayedInsert**: This delays the insertion of a new record until the user moves focus away from the new line being entered. If this value is no, then a new record will automatically be inserted into the table as soon as the primary key fields have been completed. This property is generally set to **Yes** when **AutoSplitKey** (see the second last point of this list) is set to **Yes**. It allows complex new data records to be entered with all the necessary fields completed.

- **MultipleNewLines**: When set to **Yes**, This supposedly allows the insertion of multiple new lines between existing records. However, it is set to **No** in the standard Order forms from Microsoft. This indicates that this property is no long active in NAV 2015.

- **SaveValues**: If set to **Yes**, This causes user-specific entered control values to be retained and redisplayed when the page is invoked another time.

- **AutoSplitKey**: This allows for the automatic assignment of a primary key, provided the last field in the primary key is an integer (there are rare exceptions to this, but we won't worry about them in this book). This feature enables each new entry to be assigned a key so it will remain sequenced in the table following the record appearing above it. Note that **AutoSplitKey** and **DelayedInsert** are generally used jointly. On a new entry at the end of a list of entries, the trailing integer portion of the primary key, often named Line No., is automatically incremented by 10,000 (the increment value cannot be changed). When a new entry is inserted between two previously existing entries, their current key-terminating integer values are summed and divided by two (hence the term **AutoSplitKey**) with the resultant value being used for the new entry key terminating integer value. Since 10,000 (the automatic increment) can only be divided by two and rounded to a non-zero integer result 13 times, only 13 new automatically numbered entries can be inserted between two previously recorded entries by the **AutoSplitKey** function.

- **SourceTableTemporary**: This allows use of a temporary table as the SourceTable for the page. This can be very useful where there is a need to display data based on the structure of a table, but not using the table data as it persists in the database. Examples of such an application are Page 634—Chart of Accounts Overview and Page 6510—Item Tracking Lines. Note that the temporary instance of the source table is empty when the page opens up, so our code must populate the temporary table in memory.

Page Preview tool

The Page Designer in NAV 2015 has a Page Preview tool which is very helpful in defining our control placement and action menu layout.

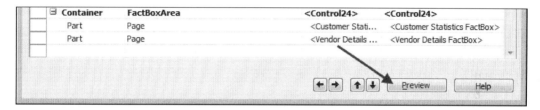

If we click on the **Preview** button while we have a page open in the **Page Designer**, a preview of that page's layout will display. The controls and actions are not active in the preview (this is display only), but we can display all the ribbon tabs and their controls.

The Preview screen is interactively linked to the **Page Designer** and its subordinate **Action Designer**. When we click on a control line in the **Page Designer** or an Action line in the **Action Designer**, the **Page Preview** highlights the generated object. Or when we click on a control or action displayed in the previewed page, the corresponding line in the **Page Designer** or **Action Designer** is highlighted. An example of a highlighted control is shown in the following partial page screenshot:

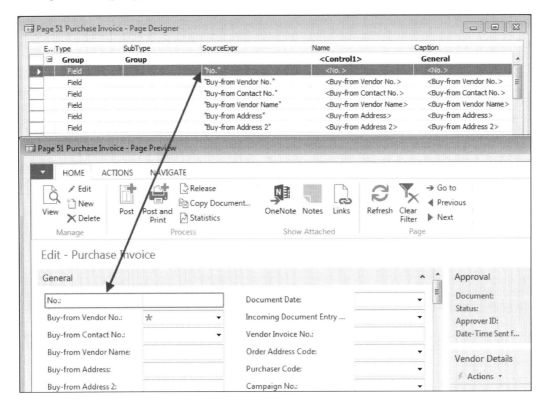

In the following screenshot, an action is highlighted in the **Preview** page:

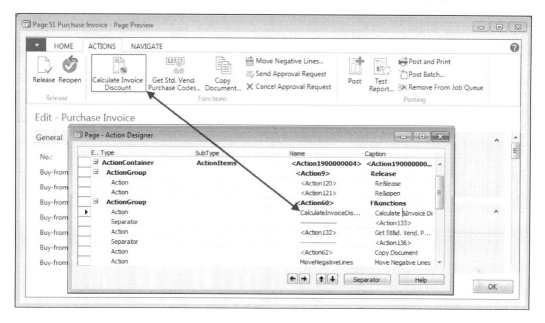

Inheritance

One of the attributes of an object oriented system is the inheritance of properties. While NAV is object-based rather than object-oriented, the properties that affect data validation are inherited. Properties such as decimal formatting are also inherited. If a property is explicitly defined in the table, it cannot be less restrictively defined elsewhere.

Controls that are bound to a table field will inherit the settings of the properties that are common to both the field definition and the control definition. This basic concept applies to inheritance of data properties – beginning from fields in tables to pages and reports, and then from pages and reports to controls within the pages and reports. Inherited property settings that involve data validation cannot be overridden, but all others can be changed. This is another example of why it is generally best to define the properties in the table, for consistency and ease of maintenance, rather than defining them for each instance of use in a page or a report.

WDTU Page Enhancement – part 1

Before we move on to learn about controls and actions, let's do some basic enhancement work on our WDTU Radio Show application. Back in *Chapter 1, An Introduction to NAV 2015*, we created several minimal pages, then later added new fields to our **Radio Show master table (Table 50000)**. We'll now enhance the Radio Show List and Card to include those added fields.

Because our previous page development work resulted in simple pages, we have the opportunity to decide whether we want to start with the New Page Wizard and replace our original pages or use the Page Designer to modify the original pages. If we had done any significant work on these pages previously in the Page Designer, the choice to go right to the Page Designer would be easy. Let's do a quick evaluation to help us make our decision. First, let's take a look at the existing **Radio Show List** page, as can be seen in the following screenshot:

We want to compare the list of fields that exist in the source table **(Radio Show – 50000)** to what is already in the page. If there are only a couple of fields missing, it will be more efficient to do our work in the Page Designer. The quickest way to inspect the fields of the source table is to use the **About This Page** Help information available from the drop-down at the left end of the Global Command Bar:

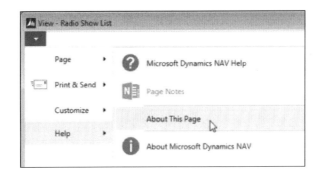

When we click **About This Page** (or *Ctrl + Alt + F1*), the following screen displays:

When we scroll down the list of fields in Table 50000 (which are displayed alphabetically, not by field number or in order of placement in the page), we see that there are quite a few fields in the table that aren't in our page. This makes it easy to conclude that we should use the Page Wizard to create the new version of our **Page 50000 – Radio Show List**.

Although the Wizard allows us to choose and sequence fields in our new list form, for the sake of simplicity, we will just insert all the fields at once in the order in which they appear in the table. In other words, we will choose the **>>** button to include all the fields. Then, because we know that the **Date Filter** field is only for filter control of related tables and will not contain visible data, we will remove that field. Our Wizard screen will look like the following screenshot:

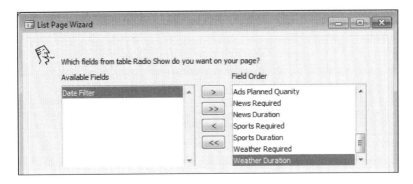

Finish the Page, Saving it as Page 50000, Radio Show List, overwriting the old version. If we wanted to be very safe, before making any changes, we would have done an Export of the original version of Page 50000 as a .fob file (using **File | Exprort**).

Next we want to also create a new layout for the Radio Show Card. We'll make the same choice for the same reasons, to use the Page Wizard to create a new version of the card page. When we review the data fields, we decide that we should have three FastTabs: **General**, **Requirements**, and **Statistics**. As before, the **Date Filter** field should not be on the page. After we have generated, compiled, and saved our new Radio Show Card, it looks like the following screenshot:

Our final step at this point is to connect the Radio Show Card to the **Radio Show List** page so that when the user double-clicks on a list entry, the Card page will be invoked show the list selected entry. This is a simple matter of opening our new Page 50000 in the Page Designer, highlighting the first empty line in the Controls list, and Clicking on the **Properties** icon (or *Shift + F4* or **View | Properties**).

In the list of page properties displayed, we will find **CardPageID**. Fill in that property with either the name (Radio Show Card) or Object ID number (50001) of the target card, save and compile, and run. We should see a ribbon as shown in the following screenshot with both **Edit** and **Edit List** showing:

Clicking on **Edit** will bring up the Radio Show Card. Clicking on **Edit List** will make the line in the list editable in place. If we don't want the user to be able to edit within the list, we could change the List page property **Editable** to **No** and the **Edit List** option will not be available, as shown in the following image:

Page controls

Controls on pages serve a variety of purposes. Some controls display information on pages. This can be data from the database, static material, pictures, or the results of a C/AL expression. Container controls can contain other controls. Group controls make it easy for the developer to handle a set of contained controls as a group. A FastTabs control also makes it easy for the user to consider a set of controls as a group. The user can make all the controls on a FastTab visible or invisible by expanding or collapsing the FastTab.

The user also has the option to show or not to show a particular FastTab as a part of the page customizing capability. The **Help** sections *Pages Overview* and *How to: Create a Page* provide good background guidance on the organization of controls within page types for NAV 2015.

The following screenshot from the Page Designer shows all the data controls on the **Fixed Asset Card (Page 5600)**. The first column, Expanded, is a **+** or **–** indicating whether the section is expanded or not. Type and **SubType** define how this control is interpreted by the Role-Tailored Client. **SourceExpr** defines the value of the control. Name is the internal reference name of the control. Caption is what will appear on the screen. The default values for **Name** and **Caption** originate from the table definition.

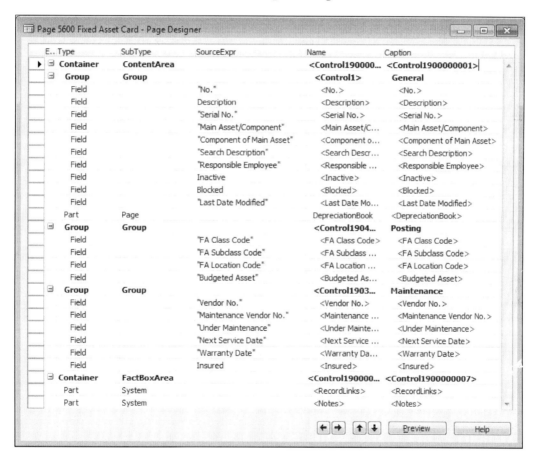

The page's control structure can be seen in the indented format shown in the preceding image. The **Container** controls define the primary parts of the page structure. The next level of structure is the **Group** control level. In this page, those are the **General**, **Posting**, and **Maintenance** groups (each of which represents a FastTab). Indented under each **Group** control are **Field** controls.

The **Fixed Asset Card** page, complete with the action ribbon, displays as the following screenshot:

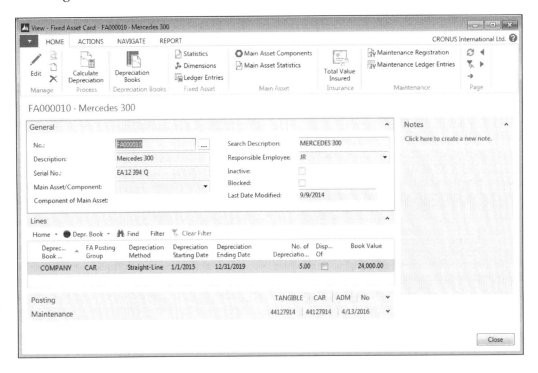

The **Group – FastTab** correlation here is obvious. The **Lines – FastTab** connection is less obvious. It comes from the line where Type equals **Part**, **SubType** equals **Page**, and **Name** equals **DepreciationBook**. This control line embeds a page part as though it were defined as another Group. The **Part – Page** line has the same indentation level as the Group entries, thus is displayed at the same level as the Groups.

Control types

There are four primary types of page controls are `Container`, `Group`, `Field`, and `Part`. `Container`, `Group`, and `Field` controls are used to define the content area of the pages. Part controls are used to define FactBoxes and embedded subpages. When designing pages that may be used by different client types (such as the Web Client), we need to be aware that some controls operate differently or are not supported in all the different clients.

Container controls

Container controls can be one of three subtypes: `ContentArea`, `FactBoxArea`, or `RoleCenterArea`. Container controls define the root-level primary structures within a page. All page types start with a Container control. The `RoleCenterArea` Container control can only be used on a RoleCenter page type. A page can only have one instance of each Container subtype.

Group controls

Group controls provide the second level of structure within a page. Group controls are the home for fields. Almost every page has at least one **Group** control. The following screenshot, from **Page 5600 – Fixed Asset Card** (with all the **Group** controls collapsed), shows two **Container** controls and three **Group** controls. Also showing is a page Part control which displays a **PagePart** as a FastTab.

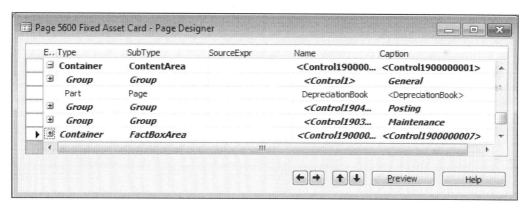

The properties of a **Group** control are shown in the following image:

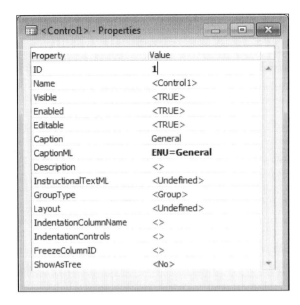

Several of the **Group** control properties are particularly significant because of their effect on all the fields within the group.

- **Visible**: TRUE or FALSE, defaulting to TRUE. The Visible property can be assigned a Boolean expression, which can be evaluated during processing. This allows for dynamically changing the visibility of a group of fields during processing based on some variable condition (dynamic processing must occur in either the **OnInit**, **OnOpenPage**, or **OnAfterGetCurrRecord** trigger and the variable must have its **IncludeInDataSet** property set to **Yes**).

- **Enabled**: TRUE or FALSE, defaulting to TRUE. The **Enabled** property can be assigned a Boolean expression to allow dynamically changing the enabling of a group of fields.

- **Editable**: TRUE or FALSE, defaulting to TRUE. The **Editable** property can be assigned a Boolean expression to allow dynamically changing the editability of a group of fields.

- **GroupType**: It will be one of the five choices—**Group**, **Repeater**, **CueGroup**, **FixedLayout**, or **GridLayout**. The **GroupType** property is visible on the Page Designer screen in the column headed SubType (see the earlier Page Designer screenshot).

  ○ **Group** is used in Card type pages as the general structure for fields, which are then displayed in the sequence in which they appear in the Page Designer group.

- ○ **Repeater** is used in List type pages as the structure within which fields are defined and then displayed as repeated rows.

- ○ **CueGroup** is used for Role Center pages as the structure for the actions that are the primary focus of a user's work day. CueGroups are found in page parts, typically having the word *Activities* in their name and included in RoleCenter page definitions. The following screenshot shows two **CueGroups** defined in the **Page Designer**:

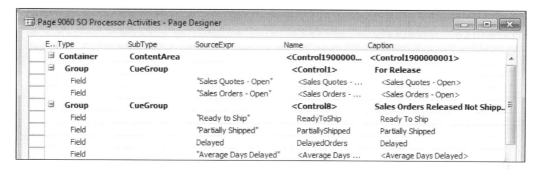

These CueGroups are displayed in the RTC as follows:

- ° **FixedLayout** is used at the bottom of List pages, following a Repeater group. The **FixedLayout** group typically contains totals or additional line-related detail fields. Many Journal pages, such as **Page 39 – General Journal**, **Page 40 – Item Journal**, and **Page 201 – Job Journal** have FixedLayout groups. The **Item Journal FixedLayout** group only shows Item Description (which is also available in a Repeater column), but could easily display other fields as well. A **FixedLayout** group can also display a lookup or calculated value like many of the Statistics pages (for example, **Page 151 – Customer Statistics** and **Page 152 – Vendor Statistics**).

- ° **GridLayout** provides additional formatting capabilities to layout the fields row by row, column by column, spanning rows or columns and hiding or showing captions. Page 970 is one example of GridLayout use. To learn more about GridLayout use, search Help for *Gridlayout*.

- **IndentationColumnName** and **IndentationControls**: These allow a group to be defined in which fields will be indented, as shown in the following screenshot of the Chart of Accounts page. Examples of pages that utilize the indentation properties include **Page 16 – Chart of Accounts and Page 18 – G/L Account List**.

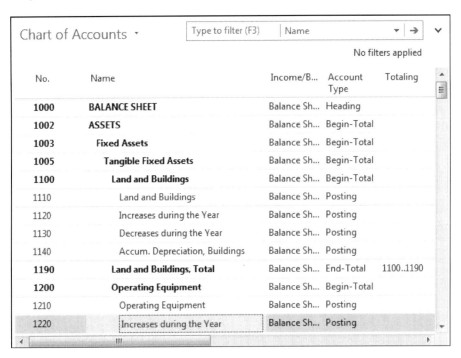

- **FreezeColumnID**: This freezes the identified column and all the columns to its left, so they remain in a fixed position while the columns to the right can be scrolled horizontally. This is similar to freezing a pane in an Excel worksheet. Users can also freeze columns as part of personalization.

- **ShowAsTree**: This works together with the indentation property. **ShowAsTree** allows an indentation set of rows to be expanded or collapsed dynamically by the user for easier viewing. Examples are **Page 583 – XBRL Taxonomy Lines**, **Page 634 – Chart of Accounts Overview**, and **Page 5522 – Order Planning**.

Field controls

All field controls appear in the same format in the Page Designer. The **SubType** column is empty and the **SourceExpr** column contains the data expression that will be displayed.

All the field control properties are listed for each field, but individual properties only apply to the data type for which they make sense. For example, the **DecimalPlaces** property only applies to fields where the data type is decimal. Following is a split screenshot of the properties for field controls:

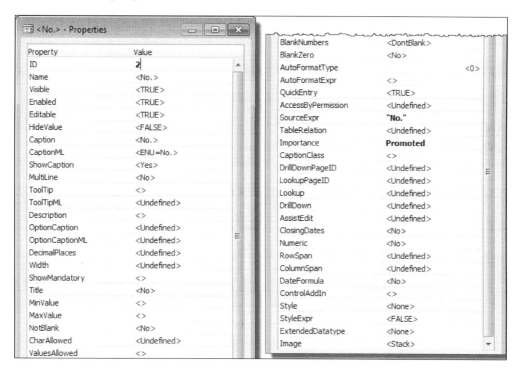

We'll review those field control properties that are more frequently used or are more significant in terms of effect:

- **Visible**, **Enabled**, and **Editable**: These have the same functionality as the identically named group controls, but only apply to individual fields. If the group control is set to **FALSE**, either statically (in the control definition within the page) or dynamically by an expression evaluated during processing, the Group control's **FALSE** condition will take precedence over the equivalent Field control setting. Precedence applies in the same way at the next, higher levels of identically named properties at the Page level, and then at the Table level. For example, if a data field is set to **Non-Editable** in the table, that setting will take precedence over (override) other settings in a page, control group, or control.

- **HideValue**: This allows the value of a field to be optionally displayed or hidden, based on an expression that evaluates to **TRUE** or **FALSE**.

- **Caption** and **CaptionML**: These define the caption that will be displayed for this field (in English or the current system language if not English).

- **ShowCaption**: Set to **Yes** or **No**, this determines whether or not the caption is displayed.

- **MultiLine**: This must be set to **TRUE** if the field is to display multiple lines of text.

- **OptionCaption** and **OptionCaptionML**: These set the text string options that are displayed to the user. The captions that are set as page field properties will override those defined in the equivalent table field property. The default captions are those defined in the table.

- **DecimalPlaces**: This applies to decimal fields only. If the number of decimal places defined in the page is smaller than that defined in the table, the display is rounded accordingly. If the field definition is the smaller number, it controls the display.

- **Width**: This allows the setting of a specific field display width – the number of characters that can be included. It is especially useful for Control SubType of GridLayout.

- **ShowMandatory**: This shows a red asterisk in the field display to indicate a required (mandatory) data field. **ShowManadatory** can be based on an expression that evaluates to **TRUE** or **FALSE**. This property does not enforce any validation of the field. Validation is left to the developer.

- **QuickEntry**: This allows the field to optionally receive focus or be skipped, based on an expression that evaluates to **TRUE** or **FALSE**.

- **AccessByPermission**: This determines the permission mask required for a user to view or access this field.

- **Importance**: This controls the display of a field. This property only applies to individual (nonrepeating) fields located within a FastTab. Importance can be set to Standard (the default), Promoted, or Additional:

- **Standard**: This is the normal display. Implementations of the rendering routines for different targets may utilize this differently.

- **Promoted**: If the property is set to **Promoted** and the page is on a collapsed FastTab, then the field contents will be displayed on the FastTab line. If the FastTab is expanded, the field will display normally.

- **Additional**: If the property is set to **Additional** and the FastTab is collapsed, there is no effect on the display. If the FastTab is expanded, then the user can determine whether or not the field is displayed by clicking on the **Show More Fields** or **Show Fewer Fields** display control in the lower-right corner of the FastTab.

- **RowSpan** and **ColumnSpan**: These are used in conjunction with GridLayout controls as layout parameters.

- **ControlAddIn**: When the field represents a control add-in, this contains the name and public token key of the control add-in.

- **ExtendedDatatype**: This allows a text field to be categorized as a special data type. The default value is None. If **ExtendedDatatype** is selected, it can be any one of the following:
  - **Phone No.**
  - **URL**
  - **E-Mail**
  - **Filter**: Used on reports.
  - **Ratio**: For a processing progress bar display.
  - **Masked**: This fills the field with bold dots in order to mask the actual entry. The number of masking characters displayed is independent of the actual field contents. The contents of a masked field cannot be copied. If **ExtendedDatatype** is **Phone No.**, **URL**, or **E-Mail**, an active icon is displayed on the page following the text field providing access to call the phone number, access the URL in a browser, or invoke the email client. Setting **ExtendedDatatype** will also define the validation that will automatically be applied to the field.

- **Image**: This allows the display of an image on a Cue for a Field control in a CueGroup control. It only applies to a Cue control field of an integer data type. If no image is wanted, choose the value of **None**.

Page Part controls

Page Parts are used for FactBoxes and SubPages. Many of the properties of Page Parts are similar to the properties of other NAV components and operate essentially the same way in a Page Part as they operate elsewhere. Those properties include **ID**, **Name**, **Visible**, **Enabled**, **Editable**, **Caption**, **CaptionML**, **ToolTip**, **ToolTipML**, and **Description**.

Following is a list of the other properties which are specific to Page Part controls :

- **SubPageView**: This defines the table view that applies to the named subpage (see WhseMovLines Part in **Page 7315 – Warehouse Movement**).

- **SubPageLink**: This defines the field(s) that links to the subpage and the link (based on a constant, a filter, or another field). Also in Page 7315.

- **ProviderID**: This contains the ID of another Page Part control within the current page. This enables us to link a subordinate part to a controlling parent part. For example, **Page 42 – Sales Order** uses this property to update the Sales Line FactBox by defining a ProviderID link from the FactBox to the SalesLines FastTab. Other pages with similar links include **Page 41 - Sales Quote** and Pages 43, 44, 50, 507, and 5768. In the following screenshot, we see the SalesLines PagePart (Control ID 58) linked to by the SalesLine Factbox.via the ProviderID value of 58:

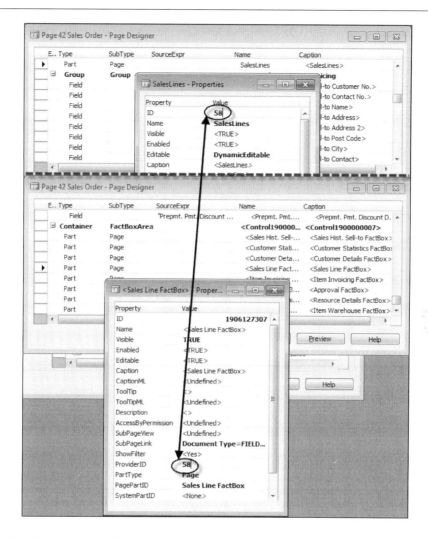

- **PartType**: This defines the type of part to be displayed in a FactBox. There are three options. Each option also requires another related property to be defined:

PartType Option	Required property
Page	PagePartID
System	SystemPartID
Chart	ChartPartID

- **PagePartID**: This must contain the page object ID of a FactBox part, if the **PartTypeOption** is set to **Page**.

- **SystemPartID**: This must contain the name of a predefined system part if the **PartTypeOption** is set to **System**. Available choices are **Outlook**, **Notes**, **MyNotes**, and **RecordLinks**.

- **ChartPartID**: This must contain a chart ID if the **PartTypeOption** is set to **Chart**. The **Chart ID** is a link to the selected entry in the Chart table (Table number 2000000078).

- **UpdatePropagation**: This allows updating the parent page from the child (subordinate) page. A value of Subpage updates the subpage only. A value of Both will cause the parent page to be updated and refreshed at the same time as the subpage.

 The NAV 2015 Chart Control Add-in provides significant additional charting capability. Information can be found in the **Help** section *Displaying Charts Using the Chart Control Add-in*.

Page control triggers

The following screenshot shows Page Control triggers. There are five triggers for each Field control. Container, Group, and Part controls do not have associated triggers.

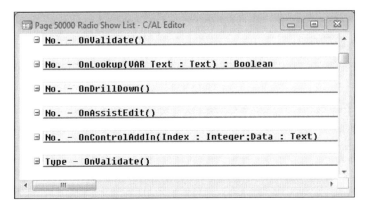

The guideline for the use of these triggers is the same as the one for Page triggers—if there is a choice, don't put C/AL code in a Control trigger. Not only will this make our code easier to upgrade in the future, but it will also make it easier to debug and easier for the developer following us to decipher our changes.

Bound and Unbound Pages

Pages can be created as bound (associated with a specific table), or unbound (not specifically associated with any table). Typically, a Card or List page will be bound, but Role Center pages will be unbound. Other instances of unbound pages are rare. Unbound pages may be used for communicating status information or initiating a process. Examples of unbound pages are **Page 476 - Copy Tax Setup** and **Page 1040 – Copy Job** (both of which have a **PageType** property of **StandardDialog**).

WDTU Page Enhancement – part 2

Now that we have additional understanding of page structures, let's do a little more enhancing of our WDTU application pages. We've decided that it would be useful to keep track of specific listener contacts, a *fan* list. First we need to create a table of Fan information which we will save as Table 50010 – Radio Show Fan and which will look like the following screenshot:

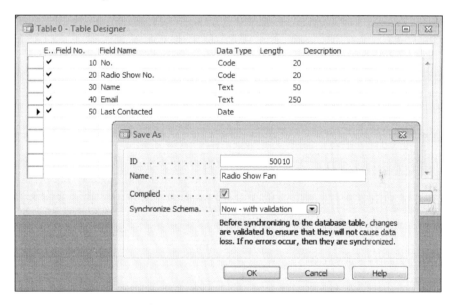

We want to be able to review the Fan list as we scan the Radio Show List. This requires adding a FactBox area to Page 50000. In turn, that requires a Page Part which will be displayed in the FactBox. The logical sequence is to create the Page Part first, then add the FactBox to Page 50000. Since we just want a simple **ListPart** with three columns, we can use the Page Wizard to create our Page Part which we will save as Page 50080 – Radio Show Fan **ListPart**, including just the `Name`, `E-mail`, and `Last Contacted` fields.

Next we will use the Page Designer to add a FactBox area to Page 50000, populate the FactBox area with our **PagePart – Page 50080**, and set the properties for the Page Part to link to the highlighted record in the Radio Show List page.

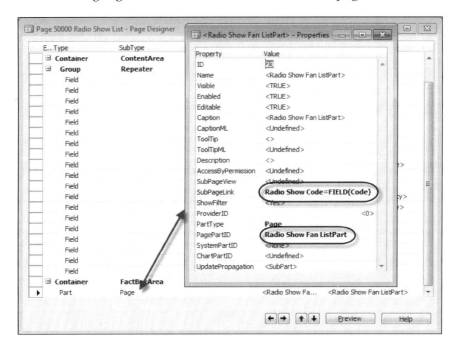

If we **Run** Table 50010 and insert a few test records first, and then run Page 50000, we should see something similar to the following screenshot:

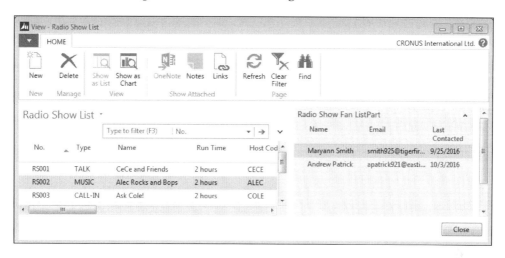

Before finishing this part of our enhancement effort, we will create a List page that we can use to view and maintain the data in Table 50010 in the future (assign it as **Page 50009 – Radio Fan List**).

One other enhancement we can do now is to promote some fields in the Radio Show Card so they can be seen when the FastTabs are collapsed. All we have to do is choose the fields we want to promote, then change the page control property of **Importance** to **Promoted**. If we choose the fields No., Type, Description, and Avg. Listener Share and promote these, our card with collapsed FastTabs will look similar to the following screenshot (we don't have any Listener Share data yet):

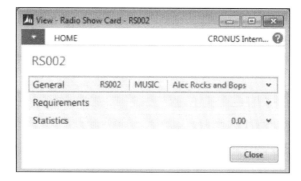

Page Actions

Actions are the menu items of NAV 2015. Action menus can be found in several locations. The primary location is the Ribbon appearing at the top of most pages. Other locations for actions are the Navigation Pane, Role Center Cue Groups, and the Action menu on FactBox page parts.

The **Action Designer**, where actions are defined, is accessed from the **Page Designer** form, by clicking **View** and selecting **Page Actions** or **Control Actions** (Control Actions can only be used for Role Center Cue Group actions and for NavigatePage wizard actions). When we click **Page Actions** (or *Ctrl + Alt + F4*) for the Fixed Asset page (Page 5600), we will see a list of Ribbon actions in the following screenshot as they appear in the **Action Designer**.

The associated Ribbon tabs for the preceding **Page Action** list are shown in the following images. First, the **Home** tab:

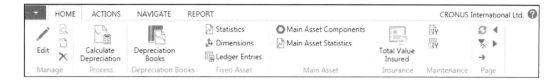

Second, the **Actions** tab:

Third, the **Navigate** tab:

Finally, the **Reports** tab:

There are two default Ribbon tabs created for every Ribbon: Home and Actions. Which actions appear by default is dependent on the PageType.

Actions defined by the developer appear on a Ribbon tab and tab submenu section based on a combination of the location of the action in the Page Actions structure and the property settings of the individual action. There are a lot of possibilities, so it is important to follow some basic guidelines. These are:

- Maintain the look and feel of the standard product wherever feasible and appropriate
- On the **Home** tab, put the actions that are expected to be used the most

- Be consistent in organizing actions from tab to tab and page to page
- Provide the user with a complete set of action tools, but don't provide so many options that it's hard to figure out which one to use

Page Action Types and Subtypes

Page Action entries can have one of four Types: ActionContainer, ActionGroup, Action, or Separator. At this time, Separators don't seem to have any effect in the rendered pages. A Page Action Type uses an indented hierarchical structure like shown in the following table:

Action Types	Description
ActionContainer	Primary Action grouping
ActionGroup	Secondary Action grouping
Action	Action
Action Group	Secondary groups can be set up within an Action list for dropdown menus of Actions (a tertiary level)
Action	The indentation indicates this is part of a dropdown menu
Separator	
Action	Action
Separator	
Action Group	Back to the Secondary grouping level
ActionContainer	Back to the Primary grouping level

An ActionContainer action line type can have one of six **SubType** values as shown in the following image. The SubTypes of HomeItems and ActivityButtons only apply to RoleCenter pages.

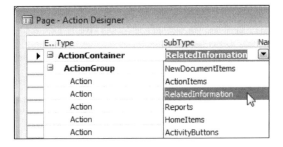

- Actions in a **Reports** SubType will appear on the Ribbon **Reports** tab, Actions in a **RelatedInformation** SubType will appear on the on the Ribbon Navigate tab

- Actions in an **ActionItems** SubType will appear on the Ribbon **Actions** tab

- Actions in a **NewDocumentItems** SubType will appear on the Ribbon in a New Documents submenu section on the **Actions** tab

Action Groups

Action Groups provide a submenu grouping of actions within the assigned tab. In the following screenshot, the **Page Preview** is highlighting the submenu **Main Asset** which is the Caption for the associated ActionGroup. In the **RelatedInformation** ActionContainer, we can see the other **ActionGroups**, **Fixed Asset**, **Insurance**, and **History**, matching the submenu groups on the ribbon's **Navigate** tab.

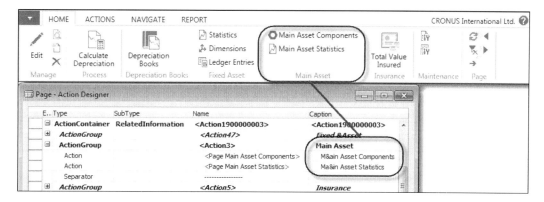

Action properties

Following are the **ActionContainer** properties:

- **ID**: The automatically assigned unique object number of the action

- **Name** and **Caption**: Displayed in the Action Designer

- **CaptionML**: The action name displayed, depending on the language option in use

- **Description**: For internal documentation

Following are the **ActionGroup** properties:

- **ID**: The automatically assigned unique object number of the action.

- **Name** and **Caption**: Displayed in the Action Designer.

- **Visible** and **Enabled**: TRUE or FALSE, defaulting to TRUE. The **Visible** property can be assigned a Boolean expression, which can be evaluated during processing.

- **CaptionML**: The action name displayed, depending on the language option in use.

- **Description**: For internal documentation.

- **Image**: Can be used to assign an icon to be displayed. The icon source is the Activity Button Icon Library, which can be viewed in detail in the **Developer and IT Pro Help**.

Next is a screenshot of the Properties for an action from **Page 5600 – Fixed Asset Card**:

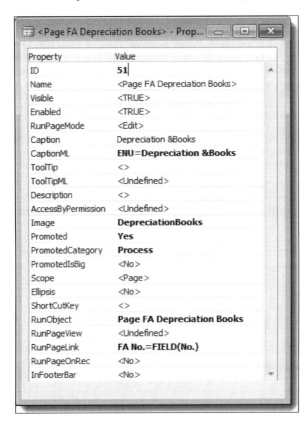

Following is an explanation of the **Action** properties displayed in the preceding image:

- **ID**: The automatically assigned unique object number of the action.

- **Name** and **Caption**: Displayed in the Action Designer.

- **CaptionML**: The action name displayed, depending on the language option in use.

- **Visible** and **Enabled**: **TRUE** or **FALSE**, defaulting to **TRUE**. The **Visible** property can be assigned a Boolean expression, which can be evaluated during processing.

- **RunPageMode**: Can be **View** (no modification), **Edit** (the default), or **Create** (New).

- **ToolTip** and **ToolTipML**: For helpful display to the user.

- **Description**: For internal documentation.

- **Image**: Can be used to assign an icon to be displayed. The icon source is the Action Icon Library, which can be viewed in detail in the **Developer and IT Pro Help**.

- **Promoted**: If **Yes**, show this action on the ribbon **Home** tab.

- **PromotedCategory**: If Promoted is **Yes**, defines the Category on the **Home** tab in which to display this action.

- **PromotedIsBig**: If Promoted is **Yes**, indicates if the icon is to be large (**Yes**) or small (**No** – the default).

- **Ellipsis**: If **Yes**, displays an ellipsis after the Caption.

- **ShortCutKey**: Provides a shortcut key combination for this action.

- **RunObject**: Defines what object to run to accomplish the action.

- **RunPageView**: Sets the table view for the page being run.

- **RunPageLink**: Defines the field link for the object being run.

- **RunPageOnRec**: Defines a linkage for the run object to the current record.

- **InFooterBar**: Places the action icon in the page footer bar. This only works on pages with the PageType of NavigatePage.

To summarize a common design choice, individual Ribbon actions can be promoted to the **Home** ribbon tab based on two settings. First, set the **Promoted** property to **Yes**. Second, set the **PromotedCategory** property to define the category on the **Home** tab where the action is to be displayed. This promotion results in the action appearing twice in the ribbon, once where defined in the action structure hierarchy and once on the **Home** tab. See the preceding screenshot for example settings assigning **Depreciation Books** action to the Process category in addition to appearing in the Fixed Assets category on the **Navigation** tab.

Navigation Pane Button actions

In the Navigation Pane on the left side of the Role Tailored Client display, there is a Home Button where actions can be assigned as part of the Role Center page definition. The Navigation Pane definition is part of the Role Center. When defining the actions in a Role Center page, we can include a group of actions in an **ActionContainer** group with the **SubType** of **HomeItems**. These actions will be displayed in the Home Button menu on the Navigation Pane.

Additional Navigation Pane buttons can also be easily defined in a Role Center page action list. First, define an **ActionContainer** with the **SubType** of **ActivityButtons**. Each **ActionGroup** defined within this **ActionContainer** will define a new Navigation Pane Activity button. The next screenshot is a combination showing a) the RTC for the Sales Order Processor Role Center on the left, focused on the Navigation Pane, and b) the Action Designer contents that define the **Home** and **Posted Documents** buttons showing on the right.

The actions that appear on the right, which aren't visible in the Navigation Pane on the left, are in submenus indicated by the small outline arrowheads to the far left of several entries including Sales Orders and Sales Quotes. NAV will automatically do some of this grouping for us based on the pages referenced by the actions, including Cue Group Actions.

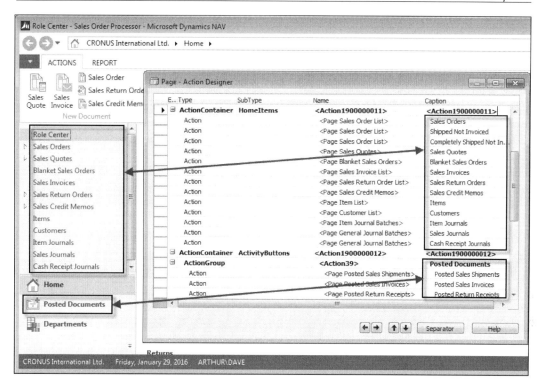

Actions Summary

The primary location where each user's job role-based actions should appear is the Navigation Pane. The Role Center action list provides detailed action menus for the Home button and any appropriate additional Navigation Pane button. Detailed page/task specific actions should be located in the Ribbon at the top of each page.

As mentioned earlier, a key design criterion for the NAV Role Tailored Client is for a user to have access to the actions they need to get their job done; in other words, tailor the system to the individual users' roles. Our job as developers is to take full advantage of all these options, to make life easier for the user. In general, it's better to go overboard in providing access to useful capabilities, than to make the user search for the right tool or use several steps in order to get to it. The challenge is to not clutter up the first-level display with too many things, but still have the important user tools no more than one click away.

Learning more

Descriptions follow of several excellent ways to learn more about pages.

UX (User Experience) Guidelines

The **User Experience Design Guidelines** documents developed by Microsoft are available for download from various Internet locations. The **Microsoft Dynamics NAV 2015 User Experience Guidelines** is available from the MSDN at `https://msdn.microsoft.com/en-us/library/jj128065(v=nav.80).aspx`. These UX (User Experience) Guidelines serve both as a summary tutorial to the construction of pages and as recommendations for good design practices.

Creative plagiarism and patterns

When we want to create new functionality, the first task is obviously to create functional specifications. Once those are in hand, we should look for guidelines to follow. Some sources which are readily available are:

- The NAV Design Patterns Wiki (`https://community.dynamics.com/nav/w/designpatterns/default.aspx`)

- C/AL Coding Guidelines as used internally by Microsoft in the development of NAV application functionality (`https://community.dynamics.com/nav/w/designpatterns/156.cal-coding-guidelines.aspx`)

- Blogs and other materials available in the Microsoft Dynamics NAV Community (`https://community.dynamics.com/nav/default.aspx`)

- The NAV system itself is always good to start with an existing pattern or object that has capabilities similar to our requirements and study the existing logic and the code. In many lines of work, the term plagiarism is a nasty term. But when it comes to modifying an existing system, plagiarism is a very effective research and design tool. This approach allows us to build on the hard work of the many skilled and knowledgeable people who have contributed to the NAV product. In addition, this is working software, and it eliminates at least some of the errors we would make if starting from scratch.

  When designing modifications for NAV, studying how the existing objects work and interact is often the fastest way to create new working models. We should allocate some time both for studying material in the NAV Design Patterns Wiki and for exploring the NAV Cronus demo system.

Search through the Cronus demonstration system (or an available production system) in order to find one or more pages that have the feature we want to emulate (or a similar feature). If there are both complex and simple instances of pages that contain this feature, we should concentrate our research on the simple instance first. Make a test copy of the page. Read the code. Use the Page Preview feature. Run the page. Make a minor modification. Preview again; run it again. Continue this until our ability to predict the results of changes eliminates surprises or confusion.

Experimenting on our own

If you have followed along with the exercises so far in this book, it's time for you to do some experimenting on your own. No matter how much information someone else describes, there is no substitute for a personal, hands-on experience. You will combine things in a new way from what was described here. You will either discover a new capability that you would not have learned otherwise, or you will have an interesting problem to solve. Either way, the result will lead to significantly gaining more knowledge about pages in NAV 2015.

Don't forget to make liberal use of the **Help** information while you are experimenting. A majority of the available detailed NAV documentation is in the help files that are built into the product. Some of the help material is a bit sparse, but it is being updated on a frequent basis. In fact, if you find something missing or something that you think is incorrect, please use the **Documentation Feedback** function built into the NAV help system. The product team responsible for Help pay close attention to the feedback they receive and use it to improve the product. Thus, we all benefit from your feedback.

Experimentation

Start with the blank slate approach, because that allows you to focus on specific features and functions. Since we've already gone through the mechanical procedures of creating new pages of the card and list types and using the Page Designer to add controls and modify control properties, we won't detail those steps here. But as you move the focus for experimentation from one feature to another, you may want to review what was covered in this chapter.

Let's walk through some examples of experiments you could do now, then you can build on as you get more adventuresome. Each of the objects you create at this point should be assigned into an object number range that you are reserving for testing.

1. Create a new Table 50050 (try using 50009 if your license won't allow 50050). Do this by opening Table 50004 in the Table Designer, then saving it as 50050 with the name Playlist Item Rate Test.

2. Enter a few test records into Table 50050, Playlist Item Rate. This can be done by highlighting the table, then clicking on Run.

3. Create a list page for Table 50050 with at least three or four fields.

4. Change the **Visible** property of a field, by setting it to **False**.

5. Save and run the page.

6. Confirm that the page looks as what was expected. Go into **Edit** mode on the page. See if the field is still invisible.

7. Use the page Customization feature (from the Dropdown icon on the upper-left corner of the page) in order to add the invisible field, and also remove a field that was previously visible. Exit Customization. View the page in various modes (such as **View**, **Edit**, and **New**).

8. Go back into the **Page Designer** and design the page again.

9. One or two at a time, experiment with setting the **Editable, Caption, ToolTip**, and other control properties.

10. Don't just focus on text fields. Experiment with other data types as well. Create a text field that's 200 characters long. Try out the **MultiLine** property.

11. After you get comfortable with the effect of changing individual properties, try changing multiple properties to see how they interact.

When you feel you have thoroughly explored individual field properties in a list, try similar tests in a card page. You will find that some of the properties have one effect in a list, while they may have a different (or no) effect in the context of a card (or vice-versa). Test enough to find out. If you have some "Aha!" experiences, it means that you are really learning.

The next logical step is to begin experimenting with the group level controls. Add one or two to the test page, then begin setting the properties for that control, again experimenting with only one or two at a time, in order to understand very specifically what each one does. Do some experimenting to find out which properties at the group level override the properties at the field level, and which do not override.

Once you've done group controls, do part controls. Build some FactBoxes using a variety of the different components that are available. Use the System components and some Chart Parts as well. There is a wealth of pre-built parts that come with the system. Even if the parts that are supplied aren't exactly right for the application, they can often be used as a model for the construction of custom parts. Remember that using a model can significantly reduce both the design and the debugging work when doing custom development.

After you feel you have a grasp of the different types of controls in the context of cards and lists, consider checking out some of the other page types. Some of those won't require too much in the way of new concepts. Examples of these are the ListPlus, List Parts, Card Parts, and, to a lesser extent, even Document pages.

You may now decide to learn by studying samples of the page objects that are part of the standard product. You could start by copying an object, such as **Page 22 – Customer List** to another object number in your testing range, then begin to analyze how it is put together and how it operates. Again, you should tweak various controls and control properties in order to see how that affects the page. Remember, you should be working on a copy, not the original! Plus, it's a good idea to back up your work one way or another before making additional changes. An easy way to backup individual objects is to highlight the object, then export it into a `.fob` file (**File | Export**). The restore is the reverse: that is import the `.fob` file.

Another excellent learning option is to choose one of the Patterns that has a relationship with the area about which you want more knowledge. If, for example, you are going to create an application that has a new type of document (such as a Radio Program Schedule), you should study the **Document Pattern**. You might also want to study the Create Data from Templates Pattern. At this point, it has become obvious that there are a variety of sources and approaches to supplement the material in this text.

Summary

You should now be relatively comfortable in the navigation of NAV and with the use of the Object Designer. You should be able to use the Page Wizard as an advanced beginner. If you have taken full advantage of the various opportunities to create tables and pages, both with our guidance and experimentally on your own, you are beginning to become a NAV Developer.

We have reviewed different types of pages and worked with some of them. We have reviewed all of the controls that can be used in pages and have worked with several of them. We also lightly reviewed page and control triggers. We've had a good introduction to the Page Designer and significant insight into the structure of some types of pages. With the knowledge gained, we have expanded our WDTU application system, enhancing our pages for data maintenance and inquiry.

In the next chapter, we will learn to find our way around the NAV Query and Report Designers. We will dig into the various triggers and controls that make up reports. We will also do some Query and Report creation work to better understand what makes them tick and what we can do within the constraints of the Query and Report Designer tools.

Review questions

Q.1. Once a Page has been developed using the Page Wizard, the developer has very little flexibility in the layout of the Page. True or False?

Q.2. Different actions appear on the Role Center screen in several places. Choose two:

    a.   Address Bar

    b.   Ribbon

    c.   Filter Pane

    d.   Navigation Pane

    e.   Command Bar

Q.3. A user can choose their Role Center when they login. True or False?

Q.4. An Action can only appear in one place - in the Ribbon or in the Navigator Pane. True or False?

Q.5. When developing a new page, choose the two Page Part types that are available:

    a.   Chart part

    b.   Map part

    c. Social part

    d. System part

Q.6. All page design and development is done within the C/SIDE Page Designer. True or False?

Q.7. Document pages are for word processing. True or False?

Q.8. Two Activity Buttons are always present in the Navigation Pane. Which two?

    a. Posted Documents

    b. Departments

    c. Financial Management

    d. Home

Q.9. The Filter Pane includes the "Show results – Where" and "Limit totals to" options. True or False?

Q.10. The C/AL code placed in pages should only be used for controlling display characteristics, not for modifying data. True or False?

Q.11. Inheritance is the passing of property definition defaults from one level of object to another. If a field property is explicitly defined in a table, it cannot be less restrictively defined for that field displayed on a page. True or False?

Q.12.Which of the following are true about the control property Importance? Choose two.

    a. Applies only to Card and CardPart pages

    b. Can affect FastTab displays

    c. Has three possible values: Standard, Promoted, and Additional

    d. Applies to Decimal fields only

Q.13 FactBoxes are delivered as part of the standard product. They cannot be modified nor can new FactBoxes be created. True or False?

Q.14. RTC Navigation Pane entries always invoke which one of the following page types?

    a. Card

    b. Document

    c. List

    d. Journal/Worksheet

Q.15. The Page Preview tool can be used as a drag and drop page layout design tool. True or False?

Q.16. Some field control properties can be changed dynamically (as the object executes). Which ones? Choose three.

      a.   Visible

      b.   HideValue

      c.   Editable

      d.   Multiline

      e.   DecimalPlaces

Q.17. Which property is normally used in combination with the AutoSplitKey property? Choose one.

      a.   SaveValues

      b.   SplitIncrement

      c.   DelayedInput

      d.   MultipleNewLines

Q.18. Ribbon tabs and menu sections are predefined in NAV and cannot be changed by the developer. True or False?

Q.19. Inheritance between tables and pages operates two ways – tables can inherit attributes from pages and pages can inherit from tables. True or False?

Q.20. For the purpose of testing, pages can be run directly from the Development Environment. True or False?

5
Queries and Reports

To design is to communicate clearly by whatever means you can control or master.

– Milton Glaser

Complexity is the problem. Ease of use is the solution. Productivity is the result.

– Unknown

In NAV 2015, **Reports** and **Queries** are two ways to extract and output data for the purpose of presentation to a user (Reports can also modify data). Each of these objects uses tools and processes that are NAV based for the data extraction (XMLports, which also can extract and modify data, will be covered in a later chapter). In this chapter, we will focus on understanding the strengths of each of these tools and when and how they might be used. We will cover the NAV side of both Queries and Reports in detail to describe how to obtain the data we need to present to our users. We will cover output formatting and consumption of that data in less detail. There are currently no wizards available for either Query building or Report building; therefore, all the work must be done step by step, using programming tools and our skills as designers/developers. The topics we will cover include the following:

- Queries and Reports
- Report components – overview
- Report data flow
- Report components – detail
- Creating and modifying Reports

Queries

Reports have always been available in NAV as a data retrieval tool. Reports have been used to process and/or manipulate the data (through the Insert, Modify, or Delete functions) with the option of presenting the data in a formatted, printable format. Prior to NAV 2013, data selection could only be done using C/AL code or DataItem properties to filter individual tables as datasets (retrieved from the database with simple T-SQL statements generated by the C/AL compiler), and to perform loops to find the data required for the purpose.

The Query object, new in NAV 2013, was created with performance in mind. Instead of multiple calls to SQL to retrieve multiple datasets to then be manipulated in C/AL, Queries allow us to utilize familiar NAV tools to create advanced T-SQL queries.

A NAV developer can utilize the new Query object as a source of data both in NAV and externally. Some external uses include the following:

- As a web service that is cloud compatible
- As a web service source for XML or Odata. Odata is different from XML in that it contains the field definitions and styles along with the data itself
- Feeding data to external reporting tools such as Excel, SharePoint, and SSRS

Internally, NAV Queries can be used as follows:

- A direct data source for Charts
- Providers of data to which Cues (displayed in Role Centers) are bound. See the **Help** article titled *Walkthrough: Creating a Cue Based on a Normal Field and a Query*
- As a dataset variable in C/AL to be accessed by other object types (Reports, Pages, Codeunits, and so on). See `http://msdn.microsoft.com/en-us/library/hh167210(v=nav.70).aspx` for guidance on using the READ function to consume data from a Query object.

Query objects are more limited than the stored procedures of SQL. Queries are more similar to SQL View. Some compromises in the design of the Query functionality were made for better performance. Data manipulation is not supported in Queries. Variables, subqueries, and dynamic elements (such as building a query based on selective criteria) are not allowed within a Query object.

The closest SQL Server objects that Queries resemble are SQL Views. One of the new features that allows for NAV to generate advanced T-SQL statements is the use of **SQL Joins**. These include the following Join methods:

- **Inner**: The query compares each row of table A with each row of table B to find all the pairs of rows that satisfy the Join criteria

- **Full Outer**: It does not require each record in the two Joined tables to have a matching record, so that all records from both table A and table B will appear at least once

- **Left Outer Join**: Every record from table A will appear at least once, even if a matching record from table B is not found

- **Right Outer Join**: Every record from table B will appear at least once, even if a matching record from Table A is not found

- **Cross Join**: It returns the Cartesian product of the sets of rows from tables A and B (the Cartesian product is a set made up of rows that include the columns of each row in table A along with the columns of each row in table B for a number of rows; in other words, it includes the columns of the rows in table A plus those in table B)

 Union (joins all records from tables A and B without the Join criteria) is not available at this time.

Building a simple Query object

Sometimes, it is necessary to quickly retrieve detailed information from one or more ledgers that may contain hundreds of thousands to many millions of records. The Query object is the perfect tool for such a data selection as it is totally scalable and can retrieve the selected fields from multiple tables at once. The following example (using Cronus data) will show the aggregated quantity per bin of the lot-tracked items in stock. This query could be presented to a user by means of either a report or a page.

First, it is necessary to know what inventory is in stock and contains a lot number. This is accomplished using the **Item Ledger Entry** table. However, the **Item Ledger Entry** record does not contain any bin information. This information is stored in the **Warehouse Ledger Entry** table. The **Location Code, Item No.**, and **Lot No.** are used to match the **Item Ledger Entry** and **Warehouse Ledger Entry** records to make sure the correct items are selected. In order to determine which bins are designated as pick bins, the Bin Type records that are marked as **Pick** = True need to be matched with the bins in **Warehouse Ledger Entry**. Lastly, **Quantity** of each **Warehouse Entry** record needs to be summed according to **Location Code, Zone Code, Bin Code, Item No.**, and **Lot No.** in order to show the total number of items available in each bin.

The first step is to define the primary DataItem in the Data Source column. The first DataItem is the Item Ledger Entry table. We can either type in the table name or the table number (32). Query may select from multiple tables (as we do in this example). All DataItems except the first must be indented. Each successively indented DataItem must have a link defined to a lesser-indented DataItem (because Union joins are not supported).

After defining the first DataItem, we focus on the first blank line, and **Type** will default to Column. Column is a field from the DataItem table that will be output as an available field from the Query dataset. The other **Type** option is Filter, which allows us to use a source column as a filter and does not output this column in the dataset. Use the Lookup arrow or the Field menu to add the two following fields under **Item Ledger Entry**: **Item No.** and **Lot No.**.

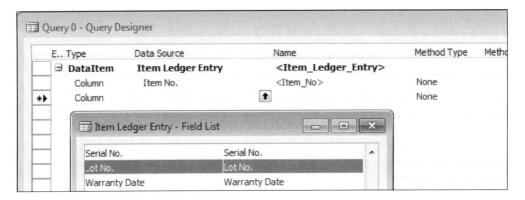

The next `DataItem` that we need is the `Warehouse Entry` table. We must join it to the `Item Ledger Entry` by filling in the **DataItemLink** property. Link the `Location Code`, `Item No.`, and `Lot No.` fields between the two tables, as shown in the following image:

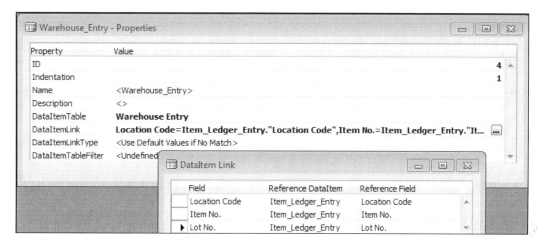

The following steps will define the rest of the `DataItems`, `Columns`, and `Filters` for this query.

1. Select **Entry No.**, **Location Code**, **Zone Code**, **Bin Code**, and **Quantity** as **Columns** under **Warehouse Entry DataItem**.

2. Add the `Bin` table as the next `DataItem`.

3. Set `DataItem Link` between `Bin` and `Warehouse Entry` as the `Bin` table `Code` field linked to the `Bin Code` field for the Warehouse Entry table.

4. Add the **Bin Type** table as the last `DataItem` for this query. Create a `DataItem` Link between the `Bin Type` table `Code field` and the `Bin` table `Bin Type Code` field.

5. Set the `DataItem Filter` as `Pick = CONST(Yes)` to only show the quantities for bins that are enabled for picking.

6. For the dataset returned by Query, we only want the total quantity per combination of Location, Zone, Bin, Item, and Lot. For Column - Quantity in Warehouse Entry DataItem, set the Method Type column to Totals. The **Method** will default to Sum, and the columns above Quantity will be marked with **Group By** checked. This shows the grouping criteria for the aggregation of the Quantity field:

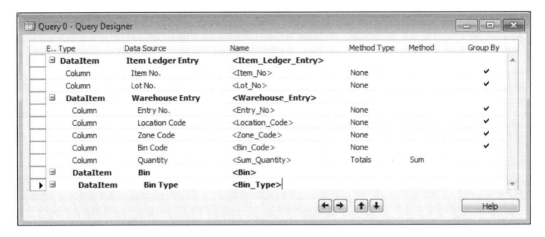

Once DataItems and Columns have been selected, Query can be compiled and saved in the same manner as Tables and Pages are compiled and saved. Number and name the Query object as shown following. Query can be tested simply by highlighting it in **Object Designer** and clicking on **Run**:

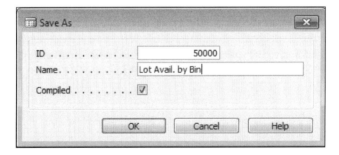

This query can be utilized internally in NAV 2015 as an indirect data source in a Page or a Report object. Although DataItems in Pages and Reports can only be database tables, we can define Query as a variable and then, use the Query dataset result to populate a temporary **Sourcetable**. In a page, we define the **SourceTableTemporary** property to Yes and then, load the table via the C/AL code located in the **OnOpenPage** trigger, or in a report that we might utilize as a virtual table, such as the Integer table, to step through the Query result.

In our example, we use the **Warehouse Entry** table to define our temporary table because it contains all the fields of the Query dataset. In the **Page Properties**, we set the **SourceTableTemporary** to Yes (if we neglect marking this table as temporary, we are quite likely to corrupt the Warehouse Entry table). In the **OnOpenPage** trigger, the Query object (LotAvail) is filtered and opened. As long as the Query object has a dataset line available for output, the Query column values can be placed in the temporary record variable and be available for display, as shown in the following image. Because this code is located in the **OnOpenPage** trigger, the temporary table is empty when this code is executed. If the code were invoked from another trigger, the statement Rec.DELETEALL would be needed at the beginning in order to clear out any previously loaded data from the table:

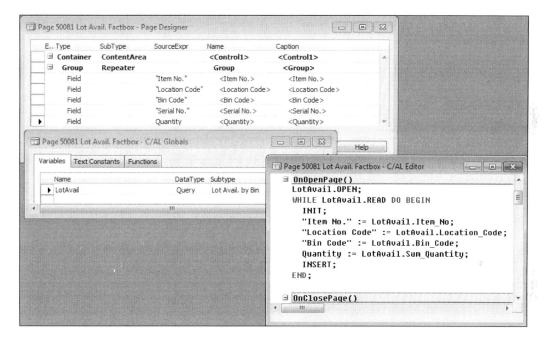

As the Query dataset is read, the temporary record dataset will be displayed on the page as follows:

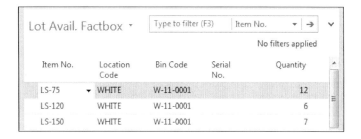

When Query is used to supply data to Report, `Integer DataItem` is defined to control stepping through the Query results. Before the report read loop begins, Query is filtered and invoked so that it begins processing. As long as the Query object continues to deliver records, `Integer DataItem` will continue looping. At the end of the Query output, the report will proceed to its **OnPostDataItem** trigger processing, just as though it had completed processing a table rather than a Query-created dataset. This approach is a faster alternative to a design that would use several FlowFields, particularly if those FlowFields were only used in one or two periodic reports.

A similar approach to using a Query object to supply data to a report is described in Mark Brummel's Blog Tip #45 at `https://markbrummel.wordpress.com/2015/03/24/tip-45-nav2015-report-temporary-property/`

Query and Query component properties

There are several Query properties that we should review.

Query properties

The properties of a Query object can be accessed by highlighting the first empty line and clicking on the **Properties** icon (or clicking *Shift + F4* or **View** | **Properties**). The **Properties** of the Query that we created earlier look like the following:

We'll review three of these properties:

- **OrderBy**: Provides the capability to define a sort, data column by column, and ascending or descending, giving the same result as if a key were defined for the Query result, but without the requirement for a key.

- **TopNumberOfRows**: Allows the specification of the number of data rows that will be presented by the Query object. A blank or 0 value shows all rows. Specifying a limit can make the Query object execution complete much faster. This property can also be set dynamically from the C/AL code.

- **ReadState**: Controls the state (committed or not) of data that is included and the type of lock that is placed on the data read.

The DataItem properties

Query Line can be one of three types: DataItem, Column, and Filter. Each has its own property set. The Query DataItem properties can be accessed by highlighting a DataItem line and clicking on the **Properties** icon (or clicking *Shift + F4* or **View | Properties**).

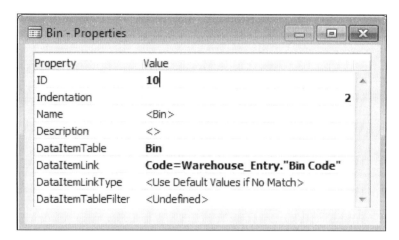

Again, we'll review a selected subset of these properties.

- **Indentation**: Indicates the relative position of this line within the Query object's data hierarchy. The position in the hierarchy combined with the purpose of the line (data, lookup, or total) determines the sequence of processing within the Query object.

- **DataItemLinkType**: Can only be used for the subordinate DataItem relative to its parent DataItem; in other words, it only applies to a Query object that has multiple DataItems. There are three value options:
  - **Use Default Values if No Match**: Includes the parent DataItem row, even when there is no matching row in the subordinate DataItem
  - **Exclude Row if No Match**: Skips the parent DataItem row if there is no matching row in the subordinate DataItem
  - **SQL Advanced Options**: Enables another property, the SQLJoinType property
- **SQLJoinType**: Allows the specification of one of the five different SQL Join Types (Inner, Left Outer, Right Outer, Full Outer, or Cross Join). More information is available in the Help sections titled **SQLJoinType Property** and **SQL Advanced Options for Data Item Link Types**.
- **DataItemTableFilter**: Provides the ability to define filters to be applied to the DataItem.

Column properties

The following image shows a Column Property screen showing the Quantity Column for our simple Query object (the **MethodType** and **Method** properties are used here):

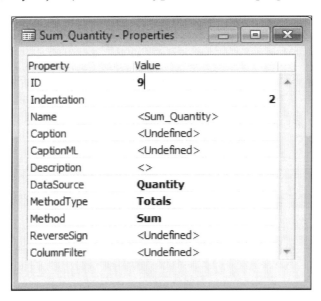

The properties specific to Query Column controls are as follows:

- **MethodType**: Controls the interpretation of the following **Method** property. This can be `Undefined`/`None`, `Date`, or `Totals`.

- **Method**: Is dependent on the value of the **MethodType** property:

    ◦ If **MethodType** = `Date`, then **Method** assumes that Column accesses a date value. The value of **Method** can be `Day`, `Month`, or `Year` and the Query result for Column will be the extracted day, month, or year from the source date data.

    ◦ If **MethodType** = Totals, then **Method** can be Sum, Count, Avg, Min, or Max. The result in Column will be based on the appropriate computation. See the Help section for **Method Property** for more information

- **ReverseSign**: Reverses the sign of the Column value for numeric data

- **ColumnFilter**: Allows the application of a filter to limit the rows in the Query result. Filtering here is similar to, but more complicated than, the filtering rules that apply to DataItemTableFilter. Static ColumnFilters can be dynamically overridden and can also be combined with DataItemTableFilters. See the **Help** section for **ColumnFilter Property** for more detailed information.

Reports

Some consider the standard library of reports provided in the NAV product distribution from Microsoft to be relatively simple in design and limited in its features. Others feel that the provided reports satisfy most needs because they are simple but flexible. Their basic structure is easy to use. They are made much more powerful and flexible by taking advantage of NAV's filtering and SIFT capabilities. There is no doubt that the existing library can be used as a foundation for many of the special reports that customers require to match their own specific business management needs.

The fact remains that NAV's standard reports are basic. In order to obtain more complex or more sophisticated reports, we must use the features that are part of the product or feed processed data to external reporting tools. Through creative use of these features, many different types of complex report logic may be implemented.

First, we will review different types of reports and the components that make up the reports. We'll look in detail at the triggers, properties, and controls that make up NAV report data processing. SQL Server Report Builder is installed by default when the NAV system is installed. We will work with this tool for our report layout work. However, for those who are experienced with Visual Studio Report Designer, it also integrates into NAV 2015 and can be used instead.

We'll create some reports with our Report Designer tools. We'll modify a report or two using Report Designer. We'll examine the data flow of a standard report and the concept of reports used for processing only (with no printed or displayed output). Further, we'll take a look at the Microsoft Word 2013 Report Layout design capability, which is new in NAV 2015.

What is a report?

A report is a vehicle for organizing, processing, and displaying data in a format suitable for outputting to the user. Reports may be displayed on-screen in the Preview mode, output to a file in the Word or PDF format (or, when appropriately designed, output in the CSV or XML format), e-mailed to a user (or other consumer of the information), or printed to hardcopy the old-fashioned way. All the report screenshots in this book were taken from Preview mode reports.

Once generated, the data contents of a report are static. When a NAV 2015 Report is output in the Preview mode, the report can have interactive capabilities. These capabilities only affect the presentation of the data; they do not change the actual data contents included in the report dataset. Interactive capabilities include dynamic sorting, visible/hidden options, and detail/summary expand/collapse functions. All specifications of the data selection criteria for a report must be done at the beginning of the report run, before the report view is generated. NAV 2015 also allows a dynamic functionality for drill down into the underlying data, drill through to a page, and even drill through into another report.

In NAV, report objects can be classified as **Processing Only** (such as report 795 Adjust Cost – Item Entries) by setting the correct report property (that is, by setting the **ProcessingOnly** property to **Yes**). A **ProcessingOnly** report will not display data to the user but will simply process and update data in the tables. Report objects are convenient to use for processing because the report's automatic **read-process-write** loop and the built-in Request page reduce the coding that would otherwise be required. A report can add, change, or delete data in tables, irrespective of whether the report is **ProcessingOnly** or a typical report that generates output for viewing.

In general, reports are associated with one or more tables. A report can be created without being externally associated with any table, but this is an exception. Even if a report is associated with a particular table, it can freely access and display data from other referenced tables.

Four NAV report designers

Any NAV 2015 report design project uses at least two Report Designer tools. The first is **Report Designer** that is part of the C/SIDE development environment. The second is the developer's choice of **Visual Studio Report Designer** or **SQL Server Report Builder** or **Microsoft Word 2013**. Refer to Microsoft Dynamics NAV Development Environment Requirements for information about the choice of tools for handling RDLC report layouts for NAV 2015. SQL Server Report Builder is installed by default during a NAV system install. There is also a free version of Visual Studio available at `https://msdn.microsoft.com/en-us/visual-studio-community-vs.aspx`

For our work, we are going to use a combination of C/SIDE Report Designer (C/SIDE RD) and SQL **Server Report Builder (SSRB)**. Access to SQL Server Report Builder is enabled by going to **Tools | Options** and setting **Use Report Builder** to **Yes,** as shown in the following screenshot:

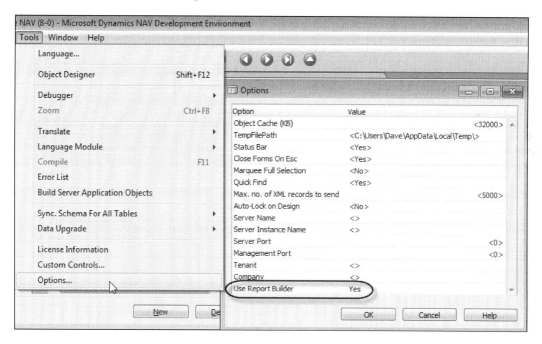

The new option, using **Microsoft Word 2013**, is aimed at supporting quick, simple changes in format with the goal of allowing customers to be more self-sufficient while requiring less technical expertise. Because our focus is on becoming qualified NAV Developers, we will leave the discussion of layout formatting with Word for later.

> The report development process for a NAV 2015 report begins with the data definition in C/SIDE RD. All the data structures, working data elements, data flows, and C/AL logic are defined there. We must start in C/SIDE RD to create or modify report objects. Once all of the elements of the dataset definition and Request page are in place, the development work proceeds to SSRB or VS RD or Word where the display layout work is done (including any desired dynamic options).

When a report is developed, SSRB and VS RD each build a definition of the report layout in the XML-structured **Report Definition Language Client-side** (**RDLC**). If Word is used to build a NAV 2015 Report layout, the result is a custom XML part, which is used to map the data into a report at run time. When we exit the layout design tool, the latest copy of the RDLC code is stored in the current C/SIDE Report object. When we exit C/SIDE Report Designer and save our Report object, C/SIDE RD saves the combined set of report definition information, C/SIDE and RDLC, in the database.

If we export a report object in the text format, we will be able to see the two separate sets of report definition. XML-structured RDLC is quite obvious (beginning with the heading RDLDATA).

```
  }
CODE
{
  UAR
    LastFieldNo@1000 : Integer;
    EmployeeFilter@1001 : Text;
    Employee___BirthdaysCaptionLbl@7301 : TextConst 'ENU=Employee - Birthdays';
    CurrReport_PAGENOCaptionLbl@8565 : TextConst 'ENU=Page';
    Full_NameCaptionLbl@8418 : TextConst 'ENU=Full Name';
    Employee__Birth_Date_CaptionLbl@1647 : TextConst 'ENU=Birth Date';

  BEGIN
  END.
}
RDLDATA
{
    <?xml version="1.0" encoding="utf-8"?>
<Report xmlns:rd="http://schemas.microsoft.com/SQLServer/reporting/reportdesigner
  <AutoRefresh>0</AutoRefresh>
  <DataSources>
    <DataSource Name="DataSource">
      <ConnectionProperties>
        <DataProvider>SQL</DataProvider>
        <ConnectString />
      </ConnectionProperties>
      <rd:SecurityType>None</rd:SecurityType>
      <rd:DataSourceID>b3d0e809-2738-4fe0-ae5d-c8879f2acc45</rd:DataSourceID>
    </DataSource>
  </DataSources>
```

For an experienced NAV Classic Client report developer who is moving to Role Tailored Client projects, it is initially a challenge to learn exactly which tasks are done using which report development tool and to learn the intricacies of the SQL Server or Visual Studio report designer layout tools. The biggest challenge is the fact that there are no wizards to help with the NAV 2015 report layout. All our report development must be done manually, one field or format at a time. If we would like Microsoft to invest in report layout wizards for future releases, we should tell them.

 We can submit suggestions on any Dynamics NAV-related topic through Microsoft Connect at `http://connect.microsoft.com/directory/`.

NAV allows us to create reports of many types with different *look and feel* attributes. The consistency of the report look and feel does not have the same level of design importance as it has for pages. There may be Patterns developed that relate to reports, so before starting a new report format, it is best to check whether there is an applicable Pattern.

Good design practice dictates that enhancements should integrate seamlessly in both process and appearance unless there is an overwhelming justification for being different. There are still many opportunities for reporting creativity. The tools available within NAV for accessing and manipulating data for reports are very powerful. Of course, there is always the option to output report results to other processing/presentation tools such as Excel or third-party products.

NAV report types

The standard NAV application uses only a few of the possible report styles, most of which are in a relatively basic format. The following are the types of reports included in NAV 2015:

- **List**: A formatted list of data. A standard list is the **Inventory - List** report (Report 701)

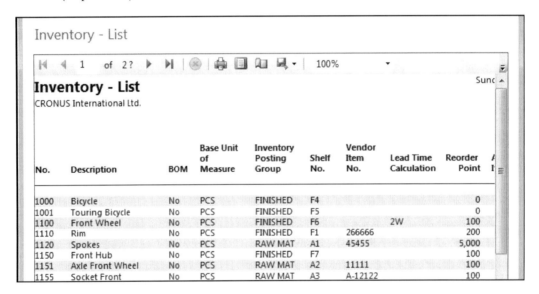

- **Document**: Is formatted along the lines of a pre-printed form, where a page (or several pages) contains a header, details, and footer section with dynamic content. Examples are Customer Invoice, Packing List (even though it's called a list, it's a document report), Purchase Order, and Accounts Payable Check

The following screenshot shows a Customer **Sales-Invoice** document report preview:

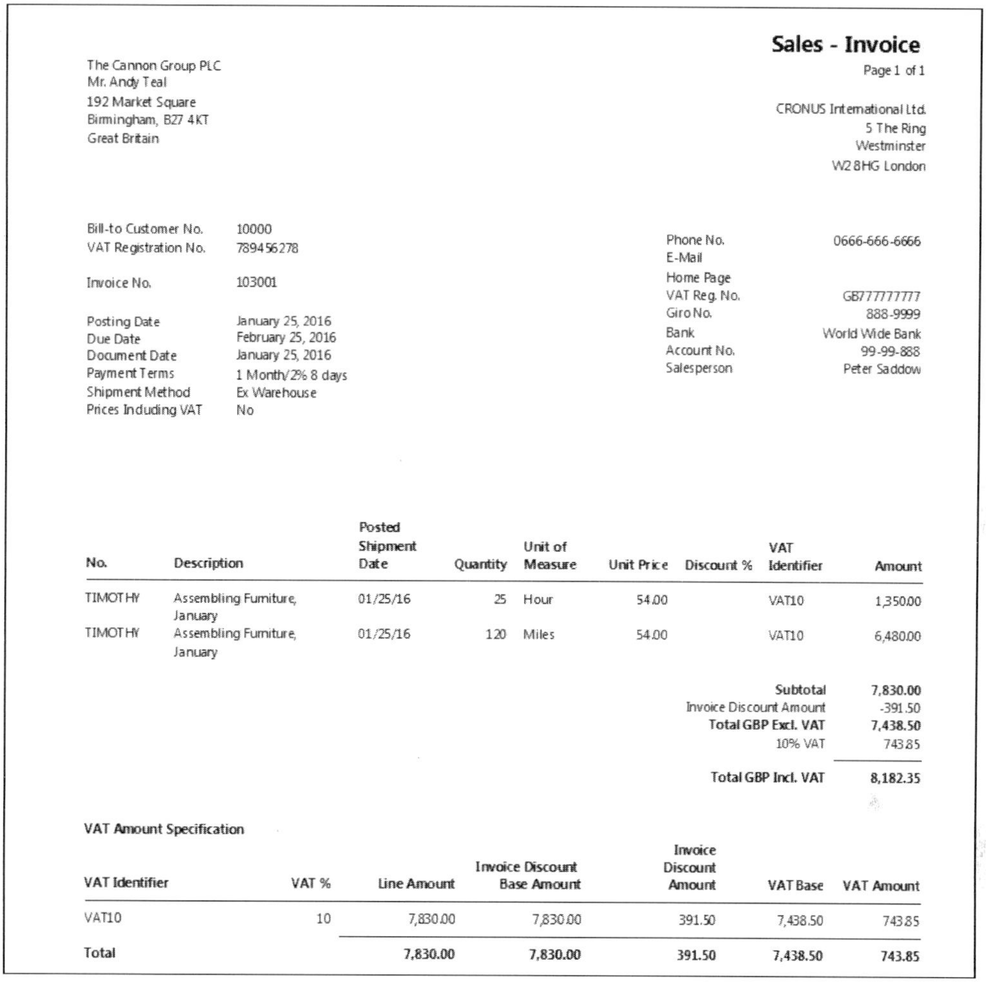

Sales - Invoice

Page 1 of 1

The Cannon Group PLC
Mr. Andy Teal
192 Market Square
Birmingham, B27 4KT
Great Britain

CRONUS International Ltd.
5 The Ring
Westminster
W2 8HG London

Bill-to Customer No.	10000		Phone No.	0666-666-6666
VAT Registration No.	789456278		E-Mail	
			Home Page	
Invoice No.	103001		VAT Reg. No.	GB777777777
			Giro No.	888-9999
Posting Date	January 25, 2016		Bank	World Wide Bank
Due Date	February 25, 2016		Account No.	99-99-888
Document Date	January 25, 2016		Salesperson	Peter Saddow
Payment Terms	1 Month/2% 8 days			
Shipment Method	Ex Warehouse			
Prices Including VAT	No			

No.	Description	Posted Shipment Date	Quantity	Unit of Measure	Unit Price	Discount %	VAT Identifier	Amount
TIMOTHY	Assembling Furniture, January	01/25/16	25	Hour	54.00		VAT10	1,350.00
TIMOTHY	Assembling Furniture, January	01/25/16	120	Miles	54.00		VAT10	6,480.00

Subtotal	7,830.00
Invoice Discount Amount	-391.50
Total GBP Excl. VAT	7,438.50
10% VAT	743.85
Total GBP Incl. VAT	8,182.35

VAT Amount Specification

VAT Identifier	VAT %	Line Amount	Invoice Discount Base Amount	Invoice Discount Amount	VAT Base	VAT Amount
VAT10	10	7,830.00	7,830.00	391.50	7,438.50	743.85
Total		7,830.00	7,830.00	391.50	7,438.50	743.85

The List and Document report types are defined on the basis of their layouts. The next three report types are defined on the basis of their usage rather than their layout.

- **Transaction**: Provides a list of ledger entries for a particular Master table. For example, a Transaction list of the Item Ledger entries for all of the items matching a particular criterion, or a list of General Ledger entries for some specific accounts, as shown in the following screenshot:

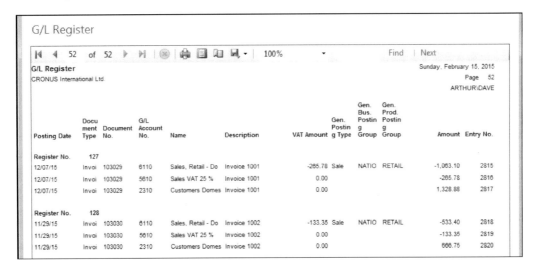

- **Test**: These reports are printed from the `Journal` tables prior to posting the transactions. Test reports are used to pre-validate data before posting. The following is a Test report for a **General Journal – Sales** batch.

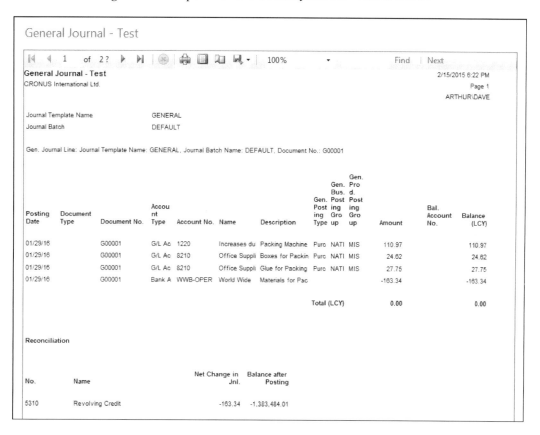

- **Posting**: Reports are printed as an audit trail as part of a "Post and Print" process. Posting report printing is controlled by the user's choice of either a **Posting Only** option or a **Post and Print** option. The Posting portions of both options work in a similar manner. Post and Print runs a report that is selected in the application setup (in the applicable Templates page in columns that are hidden by default). The default setup uses the same report that one would use as a Transaction (history) report (like G/L Register shown earlier). This type of posting audit trail report, which is often needed by accountants, can be regenerated completely and accurately at any time.

Report types summarized

The following list describes the different basic types of reports available in
NAV 2015.

Type	Description
List	Used to list volumes of similar data in a tabular format, such as Sales Order Lines, a list of Customers, or a list of General Ledger Entries.
Document	Used in "record-per-page header" + "line item detail" situations, such as Sales Invoice, Purchase Order, Manufacturing Work Order, or Customer Statement.
Transaction	Generally presents a list of transactions in a nested list format, such as a list of General Ledger Entries grouped by GL Account, Physical Inventory Journal Entries grouped by Item, or Salesperson To-Do List by Salesperson.
Test	Prints in a list format as a prevalidation test and data review, prior to a Journal Posting run. A Test Report option can be found on any Journal page such as General Journal, Item Journal, or Jobs Journal. Test reports show errors that must be corrected prior to posting.
Posting	Prints in a list format as a record of which data transactions were posted into permanent status (that is, moved from a journal to a ledger). A posting report can be archived at the time of original generation or regenerated as an audit trail of posting activity.
Processing Only	Only processes data; does not generate a report output. Has the **ProcessingOnly** report property set to `Yes`.

Many reports in the standard system don't fit neatly within the preceding categories
but are variations or combinations. Of course, this is also true of many custom reports.

Report naming

Simple reports are often named the same as the table with which they are primarily
associated, plus a word or two describing the basic purpose of the report. Common
key report purpose names include the words Journal, Register, List, Test, and
Statistics. Some examples are as follows: **General Journal–Test**, **G/L Register**,
and **Customer – Order Detail**.

When there are conflicts between naming that is based on the associated tables and
naming that is based on the use of the data, the usage context should take precedence
in naming reports, just as it does with pages. One absolute requirement for names is
that they must be unique; no duplicate names are allowed for a single object type.

Report components – overview

What we generally refer to as the report or report object created with SSRB or VS RD is technically referred to as **RDLC Report**. RDLC Report includes the information describing the logic to be followed when processing the data (the data model), the dataset structure that is generated by C/SIDE, and the output layout designed with SQL Server Report Builder (or Visual Studio). RDLC Reports are stored in the NAV database. Word report XML layouts are also stored in the NAV database. NAV 2015 allows multiple RDLC and Word formats for a single report. We will use the term "report" irrespective of whether we mean the output, the description, or the object.

Reports share some attributes with pages including aspects of the designer, features of various controls, some of the triggers, and even some of the properties. Where those parallels exist, we should take notice of them. Where there is consistency in the NAV toolset, it makes it easier to learn and to use.

Report structure

The overall structure of NAV RDLC Report consists of the following elements:

- Report properties
- Report triggers
- Request page
    - Request page properties
    - Request page triggers
    - Request page controls

- Request page control triggers
- DataItems
    - DataItem properties
    - DataItem triggers
    - Data columns

- Data column properties
- SSRB (RDLC) layout
    - SSRB (RDLC) controls
- SSRB (RDLC) control properties

- Word layout

    ◦ Word layout template
    ◦ Word controls

- Word control properties

Report data overview

Report components such as Report Properties and Triggers, Request Page Properties and Triggers, and DataItems and their Properties and Triggers define the data flow and overall logic for processing the data. Another set of components, Data Fields and Working Storage, are defined as subordinate to DataItems (or Request Page). These are all designed in **C/SIDE Report Dataset Designer (C/SIDE RD)**.

Data Fields are defined in this book as the fields contained in DataItems (application tables). **Working Storage** (also referred to as Working Data or variables) fields are defined in this book as the data elements that are defined within a report (or other object) for use in that object. The contents of Working Storage data elements are not permanently stored in the database. All of these are collectively referred to in NAV Help as columns.

These components define the data elements that are made available to **SQL Server Report Builder (SSRB)** as a dataset to be used in the layout and delivery of results to the user. In addition, Labels (text literals) for display can be defined separately from any DataItem and included in the dataset passed to SSRB. Labels must be **Common Language Specification (CLS)**-compliant names (that means labels can contain only alpha and decimal and underscore characters and must not begin with an underscore). If the report is to be used in a multilanguage environment, the CaptionML label must be properly defined to support the alternate languages.

SSRB cannot access any data elements that have not been defined within C/SIDE RD. Each data element passed to SSRB in the dataset, whether Data Field or Working Data, must be associated with DataItem (except for Labels).

The Report Request Page is displayed when a report is invoked. Its purpose is to allow users to enter information to control the report. Control information entered through Request Page may include filters, control dates, other parameters, and specifications as well as formatting or processing options to use for this report run. Request Page appears once at the beginning of a report at run time. The following is a sample Request Page, the one associated with **Customer - List (Report 101)**:

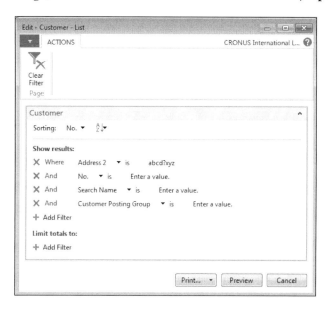

Report Layout overview

The Report Layout is designed in SSRB using data elements defined in Dataset DataItems by C/SIDE RD and then, made available to SSRB. Report Layout includes Page Header, Body, and Page Footer.

In most cases, the body of the report is based on an RDLC Table layout control defined in SSRB. The SSRB Table control is a data grid used for layout purposes and is not the same as a data table stored in the NAV database. The terminology can be confusing. When the NAV Help files regarding reports refer to a table, we have to read very carefully to determine which meaning for "table" is intended. Further, in this book, references to SSRB also apply in general to Visual Studio Report Designer.

Within the Report body, there can be none, one, or more Detail rows. There can also be Header and Footer rows. The Detail rows are the definition of the primary, repeating data display. A report layout may also include one or more Group rows, used to group and total data that is displayed in the Detail rows.

All of the report formatting is controlled in Report Layout. The Font, field positioning, visibility options (including the expand/collapse sections), dynamic sorting, and graphics are all defined as part of Report Layout. The same is true for pagination control, headings and footers, some totaling, column-width control, font, color, and many other display details.

Of course, if the display target changes dramatically, for example, from a desktop workstation display to a browser on a phone, the appearance of Report Layout will change dramatically as well. One of the advantages of the NAV reporting layout toolset is to support the required flexibility. Since we must expect significant variability in our users' output devices (desktop video, browser, or tablet), we should design and test any report (or other User Interface) modifications or additions to make sure they are compatible with the various categores of output devices.

Report data flow

One of the principal advantages of the NAV report is its built-in data flow structure. At the beginning of any report, we define DataItems (the tables) that the report will process. We can create a processing-only report that has no data items (if no looping-through database data is required), but this situation often calls for a code unit to be used. In a report, NAV automatically creates a data flow process for each DataItem, or table reference. This automatically created data flow provides specific triggers and processing events for each data item:

- Preceding DataItem
- After reading each record of DataItem
- Following the end of DataItem

The underlying "black-box" report logic (the part that we can't see or affect) automatically loops through the named tables, reading and processing one record at a time. Therefore, any time, we need a process that steps through a set of data one record at a time, it is often easier to use a report object.

The reference to a database table in a report is referred to as **DataItem**. The report data flow structure allows us to nest data items (to create a hierarchical grandparent, parent, and child structure). If DataItem2 is nested within DataItem1 and is related to DataItem1, then for each record in DataItem1, all the related records in DataItem2 will be processed.

The following example uses tables from our WDTU system. The design is for a report to list all the scheduled instances of a Radio Show playlist grouped by Radio Show, in turn grouped by Show Type. Thus, **Radio Show Type** is the primary table (**DataItem1**). For each Radio Show Type, we want to list all Radio Shows of this type (**DataItem2**). Further, for each **Radio Show**, we want to list all the scheduled instances of the show recorded in **Playlist Header** (**DataItem3**).

Open Object Designer, select the Report object type, and click the New button. On the Report Dataset Designer screen, we first enter the table name **Radio Show Type** (or table number **50001**), as we can see in the following screenshot. The DataItem Name, to which the C/AL code will refer, is **DataItem1** in our example here. Then, we enter the second table, **Radio Show**, which is automatically indented relative to the data item above (the "superior" or parent data item). This indicates the nesting of the processing of the indented (child) data item within the processing of the superior data item.

For our example, we have renamed DataItems to better illustrate the report data flow. The normal behavior would be for **Name** in the right column to default to the table name shown in the left column (for example, Name for Radio Show would be **<Radio Show>** by default). This default DataItem Name would only need to be changed if the same table appeared twice within the DataItem list. If there were a second instance of Radio Show for example, we could simply name it **RadioShow2** (but it would be much better to give it a name describing its purpose in context).

For each record in the parent dataitem, the indented dataitem will be fully processed, depending on the filters and the defined relationships between the superior and the indented tables. In other words, the visible indentation is only part of the necessary parent-child definition.

For our example, we enter a third table, **Playlist Header**, and our example name of **DataItem3**:

The following chart shows the data flow for this DataItem structure. The chart boxes are intended to show the nesting that results from the indenting of DataItems in the preceding screenshot. **Radio Show DataItem** is indented under **Radio Show Type DataItem**. This means that for every processed Radio Show Type record, all of the selected Radio Show records will be processed. That same logic applies to the Playlist Header records and Radio Show records (that is, for each Radio Show record processed, all selected Playlist records are processed):

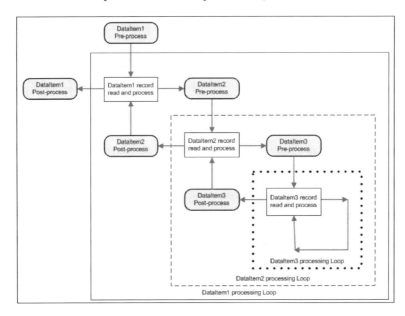

The blocks visually illustrate how the data item nesting controls the data flow. As we can see, the full range of processing for DataItem2 occurs for each DataItem1 record. In turn, the full range of processing for DataItem3 occurs for each DataItem2 record.

In the NAV 2015 Role Tailored Client, report processing occurs in two separate steps, the first tied primarily to what has been designed in C/SIDE RD, the second tied to what has been designed in the SSRB. The data processing represented in the preceding image all occurs in the first step, yielding a complete dataset containing all the data that is to be rendered for the output.

Once the dataset is processed for display by the RDLC code created by the SSRB, if the output is to be displayed in NAV Client for Windows, the results are handed off to Microsoft Report Viewer. Microsoft Report Viewer provides the NAV 2015 reporting capabilities such as various types of graphics; interactive sorting and expand/collapse sections; output to PDF, Word, and Excel; and other advanced features. Other clients are served by rendering tools that address each client's capabilities and limitations.

Report components – detail

Earlier, we reviewed a list of the components of a Report object. Now, we're going to review detailed information about each of these components. Our goal here is to understand how the pieces of the report puzzle fit together.

C/SIDE Report properties

The C/SIDE RD Report Properties are shown in the following screenshot. Some of these properties have essentially the same purpose as similarly named properties in pages and other objects:

The properties in the preceding image are defined as follows:

- **ID**: The unique report object number.
- **Name**: The name by which this report is referred to within the C/AL code.
- **Caption**: The name that is displayed for this report; **Caption** defaults to Name.
- **CaptionML**: The **Caption** translation for a defined alternative language.
- **Description**: For internal documentation.

- **UseRequestPage**: Yes or No, controlling whether or not the report will begin with Request Page for the user parameters to be entered.

- **UseSystemPrinter**: Determines whether the default printer for the report should be the defined system printer, or whether NAV should check for a setup-defined User/Report printer definition. More on User/Report printer setup can be found in the NAV application help.

- **EnableExternalImages**: If Yes, this allows links to external (non-embedded) images on the report. Such images can be outside the NAV database.

- **EnableHyperLinks**: If Yes, this allows links to other URLs, including other reports or to pages.

- **EnableExternalAssemblies**: If Yes, this allows the use of external custom functions as part of the report.

- **ProcessingOnly**: Set to Yes when the report object is being used only to process data and no reporting output is to be generated. If this property is set to Yes, then it overrides any other property selections that would apply in a report-generating situation.

- **ShowPrintStatus**: If this property is set to Yes and the **ProcessingOnly** property is set to No, then a **Report Progress** window, including a Cancel button, is displayed. When **ProcessingOnly** is set to Yes, if we want a Report Progress Window, we must create our own dialog box.

- **TransactionType**: This can be in one of the four basic options: **Browse**, **Snapshot**, **UpdateNoLocks**, and **Update**. These control the record locking behavior to be applied in this report. The default is **UpdateNoLocks**. This property is generally only used by advanced developers.

- **Permissions**: This provides report-specific setting of permissions, which are the rights to access data, subdivided into **Read**, **Insert**, **Modify**, and **Delete**. This allows the developer to define report and processing permissions that override the user-by-user permissions security setup.

- **PaperSourceFirstPage**, **PaperSourceDefaultPage**, and **PaperSourceLastPage**: All allow the choice of the paper source tray based on information in the fin.stx file (**fin.stx** is an installation file that contains the active language messages and reserved words in addition to some system control parameters that are defined by Microsoft and are not modifiable by anyone else).

- **PreviewMode**: Specifies the choice of the default Normal or PrintLayout, causing the report to open up in either the interactive view allowing manipulation or in a fixed format on a printer.

- **DefaultLayout**: Specifies whether the report will use either the Word or the RDLC layout.
- **WordMergeDataItem**: Defines the table on which the outside processing loop will occur for a Word layout (equivalent to the effect of the first DataItem on an RDLC layout).

SQL Server Report Builder – Report properties

The SSRB **Properties** Window is docked by default on the right-hand side of the screen (as with most SSRB windows, it can be redocked, hidden, or float).

By highlighting various report elements (individual cells, rows, columns, and so on), we can choose which set of properties we want to access, those of the whole **Report**, **Body**, **Tablix**, or individual **Text Boxes**. Once we have chosen the desired set of properties, we can access these properties in one of two ways. The obvious way is through the window that opens up when we choose which control properties to display. The following screenshot shows the properties of **Text Box** with the **Font** properties highlighted and expanded.

The **Font** properties are the properties most often accessed to change the appearance of a report layout, although a variety of other field formatting properties are also utilized:

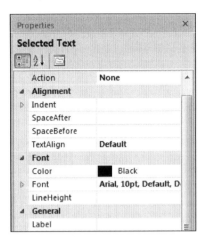

Another way to access property details is to highlight the element of interest, right click and select the Properties option for that element. This opens up a control-specific **Properties** window, which includes a menu of choices of property categories to access. In the following image, **Text Box Properties** were opened and the **Font** properties accessed for display:

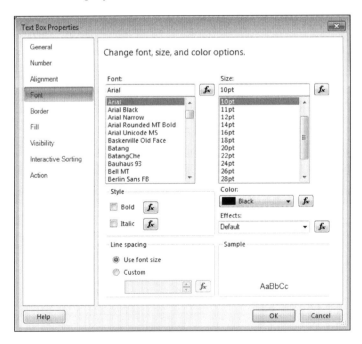

Some may feel it's easier to find and change all the properties options here. This applies to Report-level properties controlling macro elements, such as **Paper Orientation,** as well as to control-level properties controlling micro elements such as font size. Report-level properties also include the facility to include expressions that affect the behavior or controls. The expression shown in the following image is generated by NAV to support C/SIDE field formatting properties such as Blank When Zero:

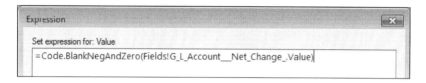

Report triggers

The following screenshot shows the C/SIDE RD Report triggers available in a report:

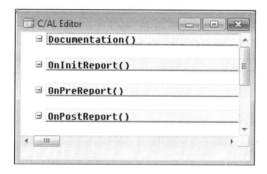

Report Trigger can be explained as follows:

- **Documentation()**: Documentation is technically not a trigger, since it can hold no executable code. It will contain whatever documentation we care to put in there. There are no format restrictions.
- **OnInitReport()**: Executes once when the report is opened.
- **OnPreReport()**: Executes once after Request Page completes. All the DataItem processing follows this trigger.
- **OnPostReport()**: If the report is completed normally, this trigger executes once at the end of all of the other report processing. All the DataItem processing precedes this trigger.

Request Page Properties

The Request Page properties are a subset of the Page properties that are covered in detail in *Chapter 4, Pages – The Interactive Interface*. Usually, most of these properties are not changed simply because the extra capability is not needed. An exception is the **SaveValues** property, which, when set to Yes, causes the entered values to be retained and redisplayed when the page is invoked another time. A screenshot of the **Request Page** properties follows:

Request page triggers

Request Pages have a full complement of triggers, thus allowing for complex pre-report processing logic. Because of their comparatively simplistic nature, Request Pages seldom need to take advantage of these trigger capabilities.

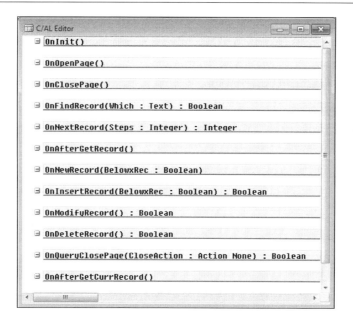

DataItem properties

The following screenshot shows the properties of DataItem:

The following are descriptions of frequently used DataItems properties:

- **Indentation**: This shows the position of the referenced DataItem in the hierarchical structure of the report. A value of **0** (zero) indicates that this DataItem is at the top of the hierarchy. Any other value indicates that the subject DataItem is subordinate to (that is nested within) the preceding DataItem.

- **DataItemTable**: This is the name of the NAV table assigned to this DataItem.

- **DataItemTableView**: This is the definition of the fixed limits to be applied to the DataItem (the key, ascending or descending sequence, and that filters that can be applied to this field).

> If we don't define a key, then the users can choose a key to control the data sequence to be used during processing. If we do define a key in the DataItem properties and in the **ReqFiltgerFields** property, we do not specify any Filter Field names to be displayed; this DataItem will not have FastTab displayed as part of Request Page. This will stop the user from filtering this DataItem, unless we provide the capability in the C/AL code.

- **DataItemLinkReference**: This names the parent DataItem to which this DataItem is linked.

- **DataItemLink**: This identifies the field-to-field linkage between this DataItem and its parent DataItem. This linkage acts as a filter because only those records in this table will be processed that have a value that matches with the linked field in the parent data item. If no field linkage filter is defined, all the records in the child table will be processed for each record processed in its parent table.

- **ReqFilterFields**: This property allows us to choose certain fields to be named in Report Request Page, to make it easier for the user to access them as filter fields. As long as Report Request Page is activated for DataItem, the user can choose any available field in the table for filtering, irrespective of what is specified here.

- **CalcFields**: This names FlowFields that are to be calculated for each record processed. Because FlowFields do not contain data, they have to be calculated to be used. When FlowField is displayed on a page, NAV automatically does the calculation. When FlowField is to be used in a report, we must instigate the calculation. This can either be done here in this property or explicitly within the C/AL code.

- **MaxIteration**: This can be used to limit the number of iterations that the report will make through this DataItem. For example, we would set this to 7 for processing with the virtual Date table to process one week's data.

- **PrintOnlyIfDetail**: This should only be used if this DataItem has a child DataItem, that is, DataItem indented/nested below it. If **PrintOnlyIfDetail** is Yes, then controls associated with this DataItem will only print when data is processed for the child DataItem.

- **Temporary**: Specifies that a temporary table is supplying the dataset to populate the columns for this DataItem.

DataItem triggers

Each DataItem has the following triggers available:

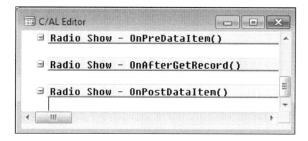

DataItem triggers are where most of the flow logic is placed for a report. Developer-defined functions may be freely added, but generally, they will be called from within these three triggers.

- **OnPreDataItem()** is the logical place for any preprocessing to take place that can't be handled in Report or DataItem properties or in the two report preprocessing triggers

- **OnAfterGetRecord()** is the data "read + process loop". The code placed here has full access to the data of each record, one record at a time. This trigger is repetitively processed until the logical end of table is reached for this DataItem. This is where we would typically access data in related tables. This trigger is represented on our report Data Flow diagram as any one of the boxes labeled **DataItem Processing Loop**.

- **OnPostDataItem()** executes after all the records in this DataItem are processed, unless the report is terminated by means of a User **Cancel** or by execution of a C/AL BREAK or QUIT function, or by an error.

Creating a Report in NAV 2015

Because our NAV report layouts will all be developed in SSRB or Visual Studio, our familiarity with NAV C/SIDE will only get us part way to having NAV report development expertise. We've covered most of the basics for the C/SIDE part of NAV report development. Now, we need to dig into the RDLC part. If you are already an SSRB or Visual Studio reporting expert, you will not spend much time on this part of the book. If you know little or nothing about either of these tools, you will need to experiment and practice.

Learn by experimentation

One of the most important learning tools available is experimentation. Report development is one area where experimentation will be extremely valuable. We need to know which report layouts, control settings, and field formats work well and which do not. The best way to find out is by experimentation.

Create a variety of test reports, beginning with the very simple and getting progressively more complex. Document what you learn as you make discoveries. You will end up with your own personal Report Development Help documentation. Once we've created a number of simple reports from scratch, we should modify the test copies of some of the standard reports that are part of the NAV system.

We must always make sure that we are working on test copies, not the originals!

Some reports will be relatively easy to understand, others that are very complex will be difficult to understand. The more we test, the better we will be able to determine which standard NAV report designs can be borrowed for our work and where we will be better off starting from scratch. Of course, we should always check to see whether there is a Pattern that is applicable to the situation on which we are working.

Report building – phase 1

Our goal is to create a report for our WDTU data that will give us a list of all the scheduled radio show instances organized within **Radio Show** organized by **Radio Show Type,** as shown in the following screenshot:

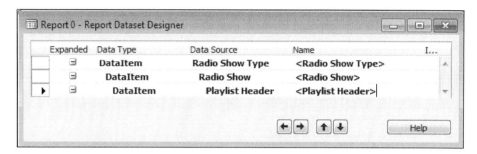

The easy way to create the preceding report data structure definition is simply type the letter D in the Data Type column, tab to the Data Source column, enter the target table number (in this case 50001, then 50000, and then 50002) in the **Data Source** column, drop to the next line, and do it again. Then, save the new report skeleton as Report **50001**, **Shows by Type**.

Before we go any further, let's make sure that we've got some test data in our tables. To enter data, we can either use the pages that we built earlier or, if those aren't done yet, we can just **Run** the tables and enter some sample data. The specifics of our test data aren't critical.

We simply need a reasonable distribution of data so that our report test will be meaningful. The following is an example minimal set of data:

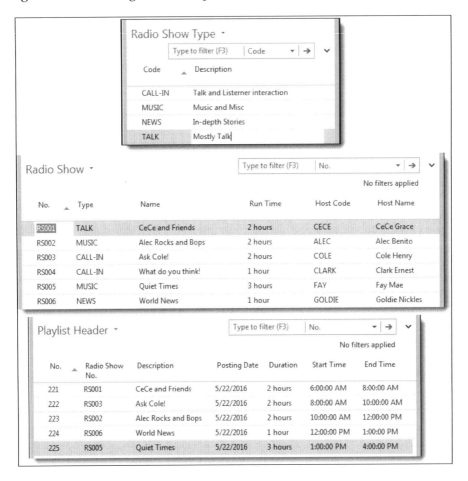

Since the C/SIDE part of our report design is relatively simple, we can do it as part of our Phase 1 effort. It's simple because as we aren't building any processing logic, we don't have any complex relationships to address. We just want to create a nice, neat, nested list of data.

Our next step is to define the data fields that we want available for processing and output by SSRB. By clicking on the **Include Caption** column, we can cause the **Caption** value for each field to be available for use in SSRB. At this point, we should do that for all the data fields. If some are not needed in our layout design, we can later return to this screen and remove the check marks, where unnecessary. Please note that the **Name** column value will end up as the SSRB dataset field name; to make sure that it is easy to understand, describe what the data is and its source.

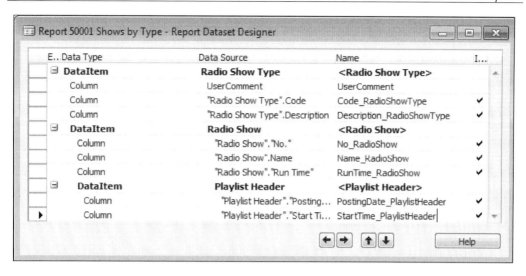

Each of the subordinate nested DataItems must be properly linked to its parent
DataItem. **Playlist Header** DataItem is joined to **Radio Show** DataItem by the
Playlist Header **Radio Show No.** field and the Radio Show "No." field. Radio Show
DataItem is joined to Radio Show Type DataItem by the Radio Show "Type" field and
the Radio Show Type "Code" field. The Radio Show portion of the dataset returned is
limited by setting **PrintOnlyIfDetail** to Yes. This will skip the Radio Show record so
that it will not be sent to SSRB (if no Playlist Header records are associated with this
Radio Show).

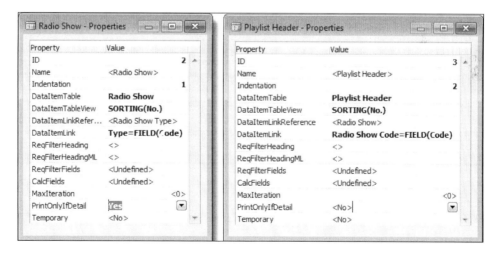

The other data that we can pass from C/SIDE RD to SSRB are the labels. Labels will be used later as captions in the report and are enabled for multilanguage support. Let's create a title label to hand over the fence to SQL Server Report Builder. Go to the **View** menu, choose **Labels** to open **Report Label Designer**. Enter the following label definition:

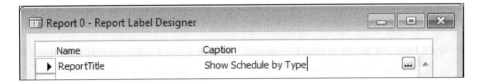

Now that we have our C/SIDE dataset definition completed, we should save and compile our work before doing anything else. Then, before we begin our SSRB work, it's a good idea to check that we don't have any hidden errors that will get in our way later. The easiest way to do that is just to **Run** what we have now. What we expect to see is a basic Request Page display allowing us to run an report with no layout defined.

Report building – phase 2

As mentioned earlier, there are several choices of tools to use for NAV report layout development. The specific screen appearance depends somewhat on which tool is being used.

To begin our report development work in SQL Server Report Builder, we must have our C/SIDE dataset definition open in the **Design** mode. Then, go to **View | Layout** to open **SQL Server Report Builder**. If we have previously done SSRB development work on this report and saved it, that work will be displayed in SSRB ready for our next effort. In this case, since we are just starting, we will see the following:

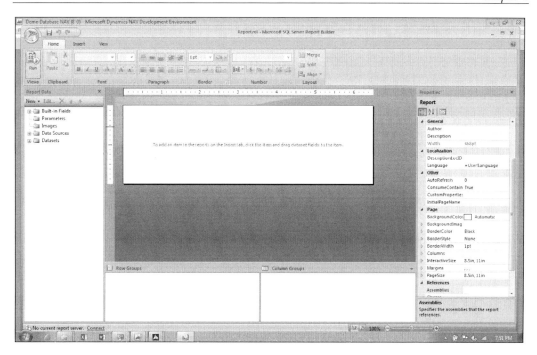

At the top of the screen is a tab labeled **Insert**. When we click on this tab, the ribbon shown in the next image will be displayed:

Before we start on our sample report SSRB work here, study some of the information on report design in **NAV Developer and IT Pro Help**. In particular, you should review *Walkthrough: Designing a Customer List Report* and *Walkthrough: Designing a Report from Multiple Tables*. These walkthrough scripts will provide additional helpful information.

Since we're going to have a page header, let's start by adding that to our layout. Right-click on the **Header** icon, and then, click on **Add Header**. Note that if we want Report Header to appear on each page, we must use the `SetData` and `GetData` functions in association with the hidden text boxes (see the **Help** article titled **How to Print Report Header Information on Multiple Pages**).

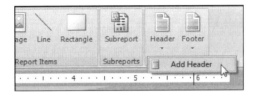

Next, we will add some fields to Page Header. First, we will expand two of the categories in the Report Data panel, which is on the left side of our layout screen. The two categories that we want to expand are **Parameters**, which contains the Captions that we checked plus any defined Labels, and **DataSets**, which contains the data elements passed from our C/SIDE RD.

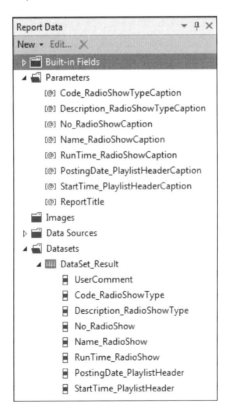

When we expand the DataSet result, we can see the importance of our data field Names being self-documenting. Having done so makes it much easier to remember what we defined in our DataSet and with which DataItems they are associated. This habit will be particularly important when we have multiple fields with the same name from different DataItems (such as Code or Description or Amount).

DataSet represents a record format in which all defined fields are present for all DataItems. This is a classic "flat file" format where the hierarchical data structure has been "flattened" out to make it easier to pass from one environment (NAV) to another (in this case, SQL Server Report Builder).

Now, we will add the report title that we defined as a label earlier in C/SIDE RD. Drag the **Report Title** field over to the Page Header workspace and position it where we want it to be. Now, expand the **Built-in Fields Section** in the **Report Data** panel. We will add some of these fields, such as **User ID**, **Execution Time**, and **Page Number** to our Page Header. We will position these fields wherever we think appropriate.

At this point in time, it would be a good idea to save our work and test to see what we have so far:

1. Click on the top-left round graphic icon or the disc icon (or *Ctrl + S*) to save the design as RDLC.

2. Click on the round graphic icon and then the **Exit Report Builder** button or the X box at the top-left of the screen (or *Alt + F4*) to return to C/SIDE RD.

3. Exit **Report Dataset Designer**.

4. Respond **Yes** to the **The layout of report id 50001 has changed...Do you want to load the changes?** Question.

5. Then, we'll see a familiar window asking us **Do you want to save Report 50001 Shows by Type?** Save and compile the report.

Now, **Run** the report. The **Preview** output should look something like the following:

Not particularly impressive, but not bad if this is our first try at creating a NAV 2015 report (By the way, the User name of ARTHUR\DAVE in the lower right corner of the image is because the authors are running tests on a computer named **Arthur** with a login of Dave.).

The wrapped report fields show us that we need to make those text boxes wider. This would be a good point to do some experimenting with positioning or adding other heading information such as "Page" in front of the page number. When we highlight a field, the properties of that field are displayed and are available for modification, in the **Properties** window. A few simple changes and our Report Heading could look like the following:

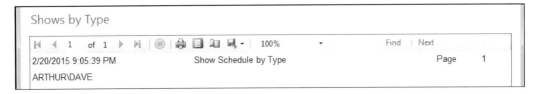

We could even experiment with various properties of the heading fields, choosing different fonts, the boldface, different colors, etc. Because we only have a small number of simple fields to display (and could recreate our report if we have to do so), this is a good time to learn more about some of the report appearance capabilities that SSRB provides.

Report building – phase 3

Finally, we are ready to layout the data display portion of our Radio Shows by Type report. The first step of this phase is to layout the fields of our controlling DataItem data in such a way that we can properly group the data of the subordinate DataItems.

Once again, **Design** the report and **View | Layout** so that the SSRB report layout screen is displayed with the **Insert** ribbon visible. We are now done with Page Heading, and from here on, all our work will be done in the body of the report design surface.

Click on the **List** icon in the **Insert** ribbon and drop a List control into the body of the report design surface. Position the control at the top left of the layout body. Since we're going to define six layout lines to hold the necessary data and header controls, we may want to expand the List control and work area (although this can be done later, as needed).

1. Click in the List control so that a shaded area appears on the top and the left of the control.

2. Right-click in the shaded area and select **Tablix Properties**.

3. Right-click on the dropdown arrow in the Dataset Name box to set the **Dataset name** value to **DataSet_Result**. This causes the List control to reference our incoming NAV data.

4. Click **OK** to save the new **Tablix** property setting.

5. Right-click again in the List control's shaded area and select **Row Group** and then **Group Properties**:

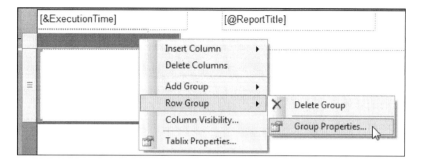

6. In the **Group Properties** screen, select the **General** tab, in the **Group expressions** area, click on **Add**, and then in **Group on:**, select **[Code-RadioShowType]**, because we want our data output grouped by the **Type** of Radio Show:

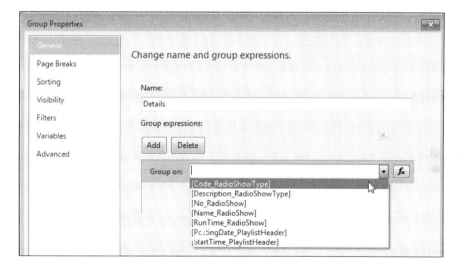

7. Click **OK** to return to the report layout design surface. Click on the **Table** control icon, choose **Insert Table**, and click in the List control to place the new Table. This will be the container for our Radio Show Type DataItem fields.

The empty control will start with two rows and three columns. Since we're only going to display two data fields (Code and Description), we only need two columns. Highlight the rightmost column (click in the body so that a shaded area appears on the left and the top of the control, then click in the shaded area above the column), right-click (in this shaded area), and chose the **Delete Columns** option.

Because this section of our report acts as a heading to subordinate sections, we will delete the Data row from the Table control and replace it with a second Header row. Once again, click in the shaded area to highlight the Data row, select the **Delete Rows** option, respond **OK** to the confirmation message, highlight the Header row, and insert a second Header row. We now have two rows and two columns of Text boxes (cells) ready for our data.

From the **Parameters** data list in the **Report Data** panel, grab the **Code_ RadioShowTypeCaption** and drop it into the top left table cell. Drag the **Description_RadioShowTypeCaption** and drop it into the top right table cell. Stretch out the cells so the data is likely to fit without wrapping.

Our next step is to place some data fields in the Table control. Click in the lower left cell of the Table control. A field list icon will be displayed. Click on the icon, and we will see all the fields in **Dataset_Result**.

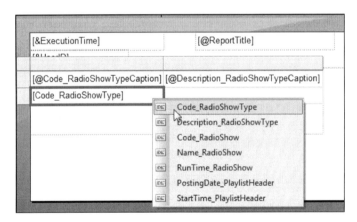

Select **Code_RadioShowType** for the bottom left cell and **Description_ RadioShowType** for the bottom right cell.

We are at another good point to save and check our work. If you are one of those people who like to do as much as possible from the keyboard, use *Ctrl + S* (to save RDLC), *Alt + F4* (to exit SSRB), *Esc* (to exit C/SIDE RD), *Enter* (to load the changed RDLC), *Enter* (to save and compile), and then *Alt + R* to **Run** the report. You'll probably have to use your mouse to respond to Request Page.

Don't worry about the vertical and horizontal layout of our output. We can fix the layout later. We should get as many instances of the Radio Show type printed from our test data as we have Types of entries selected from the Playlist Header table (based on any filters that we applied).

Assuming that our output looks pretty much as we expected (a simple list of Show Types with column headings), we can move on to the next layer of definition. This time we will define how the Radio Show data fields will be shown, including the fact that this set of data is grouped as subordinate to the Type field.

Insert another Table control in to the report design surface inside the list control. Position this control below the last Table control in a position that will show its relation to the Type data records. Usually, this will involve indenting.

Click on the control to cause the shaded outer area to display. Highlight the Header row and delete it. Highlight the Data row, right-click on it, and choose **Insert Row – Inside Group** (**Above** or **Below** doesn't matter this time). Now, to confirm that our List control is associated with the **DataSet Result**, do the following:

1. Right-click in the List control, so that a shaded area appears to the top and the left of the control.
2. Right-click in the shaded area and select **Tablix Properties**.
3. The **Dataset name** box should contain the value **DataSet_Result**.
4. Click **OK** to save the **Tablix** property setting.

In the bottom row of our second Table control, cause the field list icon to display, and then choose a field for each of the three cells (No., **Show_Description**, and Run_ Time). In the top row, we could choose **Parameter** captions as we did earlier, but perhaps, we want captions that are different to those that came across from C/SIDE RD. We could have used Labels here if we had defined them in C/SIDE RD. Or, we can just do the simple thing, type in the column headings we want (**Show No.**, **Name**, and **Run Time**), overwriting the default headings (doing this will not yield multilanguage compliant captions). Highlight the middle column (Name) and stretch it out so that a long name will display on one line rather than wrapping. Now, once again, it's time to save and test.

Our third (and final) set of data for this report will hold data from **Playlist Header DataItem**. Right-click in the grey area of the top row of the second Table control. Select **Row Group | Group Properties**. In the **Group Properties** screen, select the **General** tab, in the Group expressions area, click on **Add**, and then in **Group on:**, select **[Code-RadioShow]**, because we want the next set of data output grouped by Radio Show Code. When we return to the layout screen, we will see that the grey area next to the rows for this table will have changed from the data icon to a group brace icon that includes both of what were previously marked as data rows.

Right-click on the grey area for the bottom row, and choose **Insert Row | Inside Group – Below**. Repeat so that there are now two empty rows at the bottom of the second table area. Fill the rightmost two columns of these two rows. In the top of these two rows, insert captions from the **Parameters** list for **PostingDate** and **StartTime**. In the bottom row, use the field lists to insert data elements for **PostingDate** and **StartTime**. The final layout should look similar to the following:

[&ExecutionTime]		[@ReportTitle]		Page	[&Pa
[&UserID]					
[@Code_Radio$	[@Description_RadioShowTypeCaption]				
[Code_RadioSh	[Description_RadioShowType]				
	[@Code_Radio$	[@Name_RadioShowCapt	[@RunTime_Ra		
	[Code_RadioSh	[Name_RadioShow]	[RunTime_Radi		
		[@PostingDate_PlaylistHe	[@StartTime_Pl		
		[PostingDate_PlaylistHea	[StartTime_Play		

Finally, we save our RDLC code (*Ctrl + S*), exit SSRB (*Alt + F4*), exit CSIDE RD (*Esc*, *Enter*), and save and compile (*Enter*). Let's **Run** our report and see what we've got. While this report is not beautiful, it is serviceable, particularly for the first try. One improvement that we should make before we show it to very many people is to make its formatting more attractive.

A couple of very simple changes would be to make the heading rows bold (to stand out) and format the date and time fields, so they would show properly (not showing as SQL DateTime fields). Some easy ways to do this in the layout screen is as follows:

1. Click in a table so that the grey outline displays. Highlight the heading row. Click on the bold icon in the top ribbon. The text for the row should now show bolded.

2. Right-click in the cell for the date field. Choose **Textbox Properties**. From the list of property categories, choose **Number** and then **Date** and the preferred **Date format**. Do essentially the same thing for the time field.

After some minor formatting, the result should look similar to the following image:

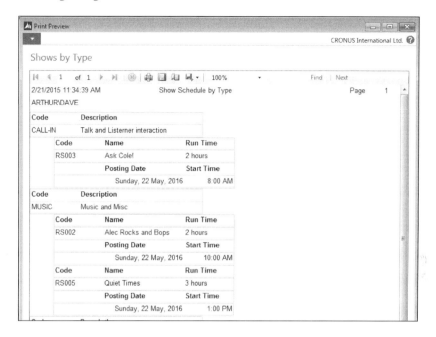

Modifying an existing report with Report Designer or Word

The basic process that we must follow to modify an existing report is the same whether the report is one of the standard reports that comes with NAV 2015 or a custom report that we are enhancing in some way. An important discipline to follow in all cases where we are modifying a report that has been in production is NOT to work on the original, but on a copy. In fact, if this is a standard report that we are customizing, we should leave the original copy alone and do all our work on a copy. Not only is this safer because we will eliminate the possibility of creating problems in the original version, but it will make upgrading easier later on. Even when working on a new custom report, it is good practice to save intermediate copies with another object number for backup. This allows for returning to a previous working step should the next development step not go as planned.

While it is certainly possible in NAV 2015 to add a new layout to an existing dataset without disturbing the original material, the potential for a mistake creating a production problem is such that best practice dictates working on a copy, and not the original.

Just like report construction, report modification requires the use of two toolsets. Any modification that is done to the processing logic or the definition of the data available for report output must be done using C/SIDE Report Designer. Modification to the layout of a report can be done using SQL Server Report Builder (SSRB – just like we've been doing), or using **Visual Studio Report Designer (VS RD)** or, when a Word layout is available, using Microsoft Word 2013. Each report can have either or both an RDLC and a Word layout, but for those reports unlikely to need modification by a nonprogrammer, a Word layout would not be very useful.

All NAV 2015 report layouts can be modified by a developer using SSRB or VS RD because all standard reports are developed with RDLC layouts. A small number of standard reports also have Word layouts available in the initial distribution of NAV 2015. These are Reports 1304, 1305, 1306, and 1307. It is quite likely that future releases of NAV will have additional report layouts available in the Word format. In the meantime, if we want other reports, standard or custom, to have the Word layout options available, we will have to create them ourselves. The primary advantage of having Word layout options for reports is to allow modifications of the layouts by a trained user/developer using only Word. Because the modifications must still conform to good (and correct) report layout practices, appropriate training, careful work, and considerable common sense are needed to make such modifications, even though the tool is Microsoft Word.

If we decided that we want to have a Word version of the layout for our report 50001 – Shows by Type, the process would be along the following lines. First, we would create a Word layout in the form of a Word document. We can either start in Word and then import the resulting template document into our report, or start in C/SIDE Report Designer and then create a blank Word document where we will build our Word format. This is done by opening **Report Designer** as before and then clicking on **Tools** | **Word Layout** | **New**. This will immediately create an empty Word layout inside our report object.

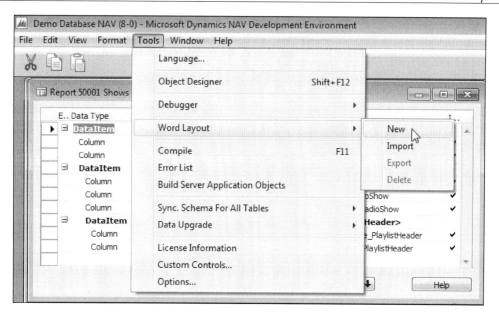

The next step is to export this Word layout so that we can work on it in Word 2013. Exporting is done in the same place as creating the new layout, this time by clicking on **Tools | Word Layout | Export**. After saving the exported Word document, we proceed to Word and open it. We must have the **Developer** tab enabled on the Word command ribbon. After opening the Word layout document, click on the **Developer** tab and then the **XML Mapping Pane** icon. As we might expect, this will open up the XML Mapping, which will show the XML data structure available from the report.

When we expand the XML groups, we can see the same type of data list that we saw earlier in SQL Server Report Builder (or would have seen had we used **Visual Studio Report Designer**). From this point, we can use standard Word capabilities combined with our report Caption, Label, and DataSet fields to create a report layout.

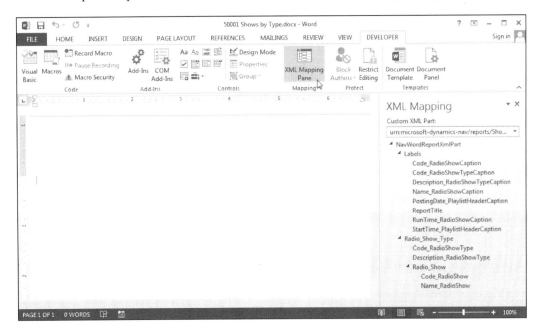

Additional information on report layout capabilities and management are available in both the system Help and online in YouTube videos. Refer to the **Help** article on **Designing Report Layouts** (accessed from the Microsoft Dynamics NAV Development Environment). For applicable YouTube videos, search using combinations of keywords such as "How do I?," NAV, Word, Report, etc. An add-on tool for creating NAV Report Word layouts, Jet Express for Word, is also available.

When our work on the report layout is complete, we save the Word document in the normal fashion. At this point, we return to C/SIDE RD and click on **Tools | Word Layout | Import to** import the Word layout template that we have just created/modified. The new layout can be tested from Role Tailored Client. First, we have to add the layout to the list of available Custom Report Layouts. From Role Tailored Client, we use the Search box in the upper-right corner, search for **Layout**, and select **Custom Report Layouts**. The following screen will be displayed:

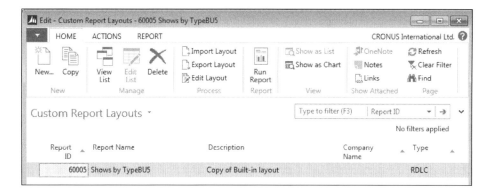

Following the guidance provided in the **Help** article titled **Managing Report Layouts** (accessed from Microsoft Dynamics NAV Client), we can maintain a list of available custom report layouts and add our new layout to the list.

Finally, we can do our testing by choosing a report layout and running the report from the **Report Layout Selection** screen. This screen is also accessed by searching for Layout and selecting **Report Layout Selection**. We can choose either a standard (built-in) layout (RDLC or Word) or Custom Layout. The choices stored in the NAV database and can be specific to individual companies and database tenants. This screen as well as the Custom Report Layouts screen can be accessed through RTC so that users with appropriate permissions can maintain and assign applicable report layouts:

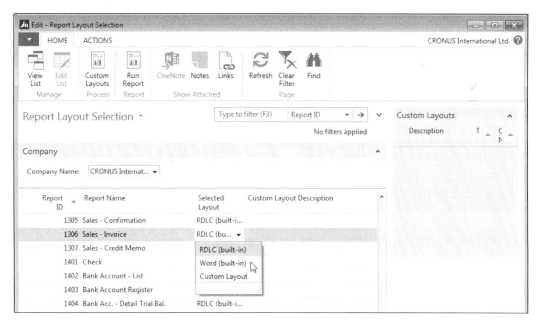

Runtime rendering

When NAV outputs a report (to screen, to hardcopy, or to PDF), NAV will render using the printer driver for the currently assigned printer. If we change the target printer for a report, the output results may change depending on the attributes of the drivers.

When we preview a report, by default, it will be displayed in an interactive preview mode. This mode will allow us to access all of the dynamic functions designed into the report, functions such as sorting and toggling for expand/collapse display, and drilling into the report. However, it may not look like the hardcopy that we get if we print it. If we click on the Print Layout button (circled in the following screenshot), then the printer layout version of the report will be displayed:

In most cases, the display on screen in the **Preview – Print Layout** mode will accurately represent how the report will appear when actually printed. In some cases though, NAV's output generation on screen differs considerably from the hardcopy version. This appears to occur most likely when the selected printer is some type of special-purpose printer (for example, a barcode label printer).

Inheritance

Inheritance operates for data displayed through report controls just as it does for page controls, but it is obviously limited to print-applicable properties. Properties, such as decimal formatting, are inherited, but as we saw with our date and time fields, not all formatting is inherited. Remember that if the property is explicitly defined in the table, it cannot be less restrictively defined elsewhere. This is one of the reasons why it's so important to focus on table design as the foundation of the system.

Interactive report capabilities

NAV 2015 reports can have interactive features enabled. Of course, these features are only available when the report is displayed in the preview mode; once the report is "printed" whether to a PDF, Word, Excel, or an output device, the interactive capabilities are no longer present.

Interactive sorting

Among the useful interactive reporting features are interactive sorting and data expand/collapse. Two standard reports that are examples of the interactive sort feature are **Customer – Top 10 List** (Report 111) and **Customer – Summary Aging** (Report 105). We'll take a look at Report 111 to see how NAV does it.

Since we're going to open **Report** in **Designer**, there is a possibility that through an unlucky combination of keystrokes, we could accidentally change this production report; therefore, the first thing that we want to do is make a copy for our inspection. Open Report 111 in C/Side Report Designer and then **Save As** Report object 50111 with a different name, such as **Customer – Top 10 List Test**. Once this is done, we can safely do almost anything that we want to Report 50111 because we can simply delete the object when we are done with it.

First, let's **Run** Report 50111 (or 111, they will look the same). At the top of four of the report columns, we will see an up/down arrowhead icon representing an interactive sort control as highlighted in the following image:

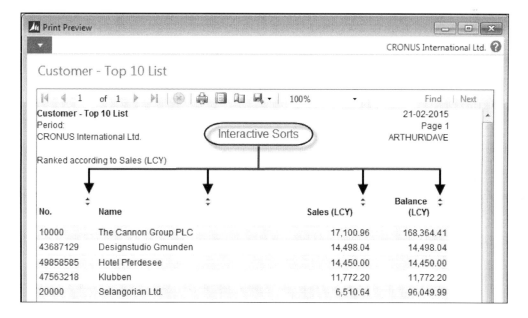

Now, open test report 50111 in C/SIDE RD and then **View | Layout** for SSRB review. Highlight the **BalanceLCY_CustomerCaption** textbox, as shown in the following image. Show the properties; choose the Interactive Sorting tab. As we can see here, interactive sort options are set for this column, to sort the details by the value of **BalanceLCY_Customer**. If we look at the properties of the other three columns that have interactive sorting enabled, we see similar setups:

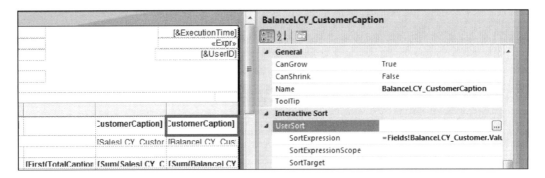

Interactive visible/not visible

As an experiment, we'll add a toggle to the rightmost column of our test report 50111 to make it visible or not visible at the user's option. In most cases, this feature would not be controlled by the user but by a parameter such as one tied to the user's login. We can set the **Visibility ToggleItem** property to the variable that we want to use as a toggle for the visibility control of the data that will be visible/hidden. This time we choose the **Customer No.** column and set the Balance column to initially be visible when the report is first run.

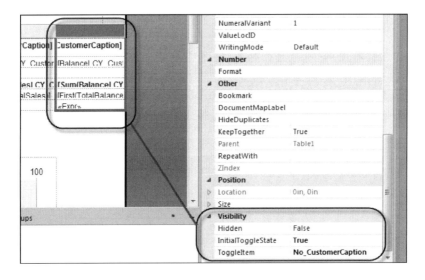

Save RDLC, exit SSRB, exit C/SIDE RD, save, compile, and **Run** the modified report. We will see an image like the top image in the following figure. If we click on the **plus** sign icon located above the **No.** column caption, **plus** will change to **minus**, and the rightmost column will be hidden, as shown in the partial image on the bottom of the following figure. If we click on **minus**, the **Balance (LCY)** column will again be visible:

Request page

Request Page is a page that is executed at the beginning of a report. Its presence or absence is under developer control. Request Page looks similar to the following screenshot based on one of the standard system reports, the **Customer – Order Detail** report, Report 108:

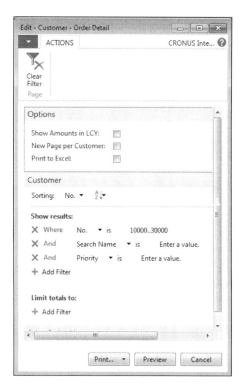

There are three FastTabs in this page. The **Customer** and **Sales Order Line** FastTabs are tied to the data tables associated with this report. These FastTabs allow the user to define both data filters and Flow Filters to control the report processing. The **Options** FastTab exists because the software developer wanted to allow some additional user options for this report.

Add a Request Page option

Because we have defined the default sort sequences (**DataItemTableView**), except for the first DataItem, and we have not defined any Requested Filters (**ReqFilterFields**), the default Request Page for our report has only one DataItem FastTab. Because we have not defined any processing options that would require user input before the report is generated, we have no Options FastTab.

Our goal now is to allow the user to optionally input text to be printed at the top of the report. This could be a secondary report heading, instructions on interpreting the report, or some other communications to the report reader.

1. Open Report 50001 in C/SIDE Report Designer.

2. Access the **C/AL Globals** screen via **View | C/AL Globals**.

3. Add a global variable named **UserComment** with **DataType** of **Text**. We will not define **Length**; this will allow the user to enter a comment of any length.

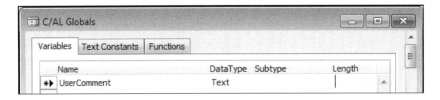

4. Add this variable as a data Column to be passed to SSRB. The Column must be subordinate to a DataItem. We do not need a caption, as we will not label this field in the report layout.

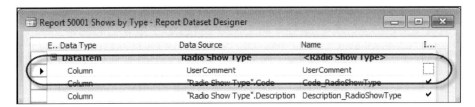

5. Access **Request Options Page Designer** via **View | Request Page**.

6. Enter three lines – a **Container**, **Group**, and **Field** with **SourceExpr** of **UserComment**.

7. Exit Page Designer.

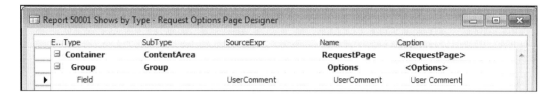

8. Access SQL Server Report Builder via **View | Layout**.

9. Add Text Box to the Layout design surface just below the **Report Title**, stretching the box out as far as the report layout allows.

10. Expand **DataSet_Result** in the **Report Data** panel.

11. Drag the **User Comment** field to the new text box.

12. Save RDLC, exit SSRB, save, compile, and exit C/SIDE RD.

13. **Run** Report 50001.

In the Request page, users can enter their comments, as shown in the following screenshot:

The report heading then shows the comment in whatever font, color, or other display attribute that the developer defined.

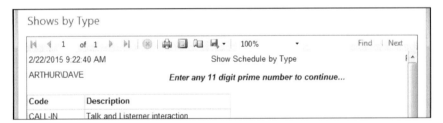

Because we did not specify the maximum length on our **UserComment** field, we can type in as much information as we want. Try it – type in a whole paragraph for a test.

Processing-Only reports

One of the report properties that we reviewed earlier was **ProcessingOnly**. If this property is set to **Yes**, then the report object will not output a dataset for display or printing, but will simply do the processing of the data that we program it to do. The beauty of this capability is that we can use the built-in processing loop of the NAV report object along with its sorting and filtering capabilities to create a variety of data updating routines with a minimum of programming. The use of report objects also gives us access to the Request Page to allow user input and guidance for the run. We could create the same functionality by using codeunit objects and by programming all of the loops, the filtering, the user-interface Request Page, and so on ourselves. However, with ProcessingOnly Report, NAV gives us a lot of help and makes it possible to create some powerful routines with minimal effort.

At the beginning of the run of a ProcessingOnly report, there is very little user interface variation compared to a "normal" printing report. The ProcessingOnly Request Page looks much as it would for a printing report, except that the **Print** and **Preview** choices are not available. Everything else looks the same. Of course, we have the big difference of no visible output at the end of processing.

Creative report plagiarism and patterns

Just as we discussed in the chapter on pages, when we want to create a new report of a certain type that we haven't done recently (or at all), it's a good idea to find another report that is similar in all important aspects, and study it. We should also check whether there is a NAV Pattern defined for an applicable category of report. At the minimum, in both of these investigations, we will learn how the developers of NAV solved a data flow or totaling or filtering challenge. In the best case scenario, we will find a model that we can follow closely, respectfully plagiarizing (copying) a working solution, thus saving ourselves much time and effort.

Often, it is useful to look at two or three of the standard NAV reports for similar functions to see how they are constructed. There is no sense in reinventing the design for a report of a particular type, when someone else has already invented a version of it. Not only this, but they have also provided us with the plans and given us the ability to examine the C/AL code as well as the complete structure of the existing report object.

When it comes to modifying a system such as NAV, plagiarism is a very effective research and design tool. In the case of reports, our search for a model may be based on any of the several key elements. We might be looking for a particular data flow approach and find that the NAV developers used the Integer table for some DataItems (as many reports do).

We may need a way to provide some creative filtering similar to what is done in an area of the standard product. We might want to provide user options to print either details or a couple of different levels of totaling, with a layout that looks good no matter which choice the user makes. We might be dealing with all three of these design needs in the same report. In such a scenario, it is likely that we will be using multiple NAV reports as our models, one for this feature, another for that feature, and so forth.

If we have a complicated, application-specific report to create, we may not be able to directly model our report on a model that already exists. However, often, we can still find ideas in standard reports that we can apply to our new design. We will almost always be better off using a model rather than inventing a totally new approach.

If our design concept is too big a leap from what has been done previously, we should consider what we might change so that we can build on the strengths of C/AL and existing NAV routines. Creating entirely new approaches may be very satisfying (when it works), but too often, the extra costs exceed the incremental benefits.

For more NAV reporting information and ideas, please refer to Claus Lundstrom's blog: `http://www.mibuso.com/blogs/clausl`.

Summary

In this chapter, we focused on the structural and layout aspects of NAV Report objects. We studied the primary structural components, data, and format, along with Request Page. We also experimented with some of the tools and modestly expanded our WDTU application.

In the next chapter, we are going to begin exploring the key tools that pull the pieces of the C/SIDE development environment, and the C/AL programming language.

Review questions

Q.1. The following are defined in C/SIDE Report Designer. Choose three.

    a. DataItems

    b. Field display editing

    c. Request Page

    d. Database updating

Q.2. Reports can be set to the ProcessingOnly status dynamically by the C/AL code. True or False?

Q.3. Reports are fixed displays of data extracted from the system, designed only for hardcopy output. True or False?

Q.4. NAV Report data flow includes a structure that provides for "child" DataItems to be fully processed for each record processed in the "parent" DataItem. What is the visible indication that this structure exists in a report Dataset Designer form? Choose one.

    a. Nesting

    b. Indentation

    c. Linking

Q.5. Queries can be designed to directly feed SQL Server Report Builder. True or False?

Q.6. Union Joins are available using a special setup parameter. True or False?

Q.7. A report that only does processing and generates no printed output can be defined. True or False?

Q.8. The following are properties of Queries. Choose two.

    a. TopNumberOfRows

    b. FormatAs

    c. OrderBy

    d. FilterReq

Q.9. NAV 2015 has four Report Designers. Reports can be created using any one of these by itself. True or False?

Q.10. NAV 2015 Queries can directly OData and CSV files and are Cloud compatible. True or False?

Q.11. The following are NAV 2015 Report Types. Choose three.

    a. List

    b. Document

    c. Invoice

    d. Posting

Q.12. Queries cannot have multiple DataItems on the same indentation level. True or False?

Q.13. Report formatting in Word has all the capabilities of report formatting in SQL Server Report Builder. True or False?

Q.14. NAV 2015 reports can be run for testing directly from SQL Server Report Builder with *Alt + R*. True or False?

Q.15. Group properties are used to control the display of data in a Parent – Child relationship in the SQL Server Report Builder layouts. True or False?

Q.16. Queries are used to support what items? Choose two.

     a.   Charts

     b.   Pages

     c.   Cues

     d.   Data Sorting

Q.17. Most reports can be initially created using Report Wizard. True or False?

Q.18. Interactive capabilities available after a report display include what? Choose two.

     a.   Font definition

     b.   Data Show/Hide

     c.   Sorting by columns

     d.   Data filtering

Q.19. DataItem parent-child relationships defined in C/Side Report Designer must also be considered in SQL Server Report Builder in order to have the data display properly in the parent-child format. True or False?

Q.20. Users can create Word report layouts based on an existing dataset and put them into production without having access to a Developer's license. True or False?

6
Introduction to C/SIDE and C/AL

"Language shapes the way we think, and determines what we can think about."

– Benjamin Lee Whorf

"Quality means doing it right when no one is looking."

– Henry Ford

So far we have reviewed the basic objects of NAV 2015: tables, data fields, pages, queries, and reports. For each of these, we also reviewed the different triggers in various areas – triggers whose purpose is to be containers for C/AL code. When triggers are "fired" (invoked), the C/AL code within is executed.

In this chapter, we're going to start learning the C/AL programming language. Many of the things you may already know from your experience of programming in other languages. Some of the basic C/AL syntax and function definitions can be found in the embedded NAV 2015 Help (as well as in the MSDN Library sections for Microsoft Dynamics NAV).

As with most of the programming languages, we have considerable flexibility for defining our own model for our code structure. However, when we insert new code within an existing code, it's always a good idea to utilize the model and follow the structure that exists in the original code. When we feel compelled to improve on the model of the existing code, we should do so in small increments and we must take into account the effect of our changes on upgradability.

The goal of this chapter is to help us productively use the C/SIDE development environment and be comfortable in C/AL. We'll focus on the tools and processes that we will use most often. We will also review concepts that we can apply in more complex tasks down the road. This chapter's topics include:

- C/SIDE Object Designers and their navigation
- C/AL Syntax, Operators, and Built-in functions
- C/AL Naming conventions
- Input/Output functions
- Creating custom functions
- Basic Process Flow structures

Understanding C/SIDE

With a few exceptions, all the development for NAV 2015 applications takes place within the C/SIDE environment. Exceptions include the use of SQL Server Report Builder (or Visual Studio) for reporting (as we saw in *Chapter 5*, *Queries and Reports*), plus work we might do in a .NET language to create compatible add-ins. While it is possible to do development using a text editor, it is only appropriate for special cases of modifications to existing objects by an advanced developer.

As an Integrated Development Environment, C/SIDE provides us with a reasonably full set of tools for our C/AL development work. While C/SIDE is not nearly as fully featured as Microsoft's Visual Studio, it is not intended to be a general purpose "one size fits all" development toolkit. Most importantly, C/SIDE and C/AL are designed for NAV compatible business applications software development with many features and functions specifically designed for business applications work.

C/SIDE includes a smart editor (it knows C/AL, though sometimes not as much as we would like), the one and only C/AL compiler, integration with the application database, and tools to export and import objects both in compiled format and as formatted text files.

We'll explore each of these C/SIDE areas in turn, starting with Object Designer.

Object Designer

All the NAV object development work starts from within the Microsoft Dynamics Development Environment in the C/SIDE Object Designer. After we have invoked the Development Environment and connected to a NAV database, **Object Designer** is accessed by selecting **Tools | Object Designer** or by pressing *Shift + F12* keys, as shown in the following screenshot:

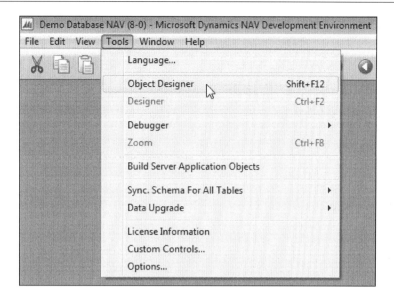

The type of object on which we're going to work is chosen by clicking on one of the buttons on the left side of the **Object Designer** screen, as shown in the following image:

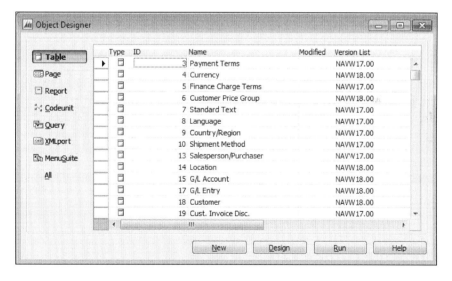

The choices match the seven object types: **Table**, **Page**, **Report**, **Codeunit**, **Query**, **XMLport**, and **MenuSuite**. When we click on one of these, the **Object Designer** screen display is filtered to show only that object type. There is also an **All** button, which allows objects of all types to be displayed on the screen.

No matter which object type has been chosen, the same four buttons appear at the bottom of the screen: **New**, **Design**, **Run**, and **Help**. But, depending on which object type is chosen, the effect of selecting one of these options changes. When we select **Design**, we open the object that is currently highlighted, in a Designer specifically tailored to work on that object type. When we select **Run**, we are requesting the execution of the currently highlighted object. The results, of course, will depend on the internal design of that particular object. When we select **Help**, the C/SIDE **Help** screen will display, positioned at the general **Object Designer** Help.

Starting a new object

When we select **New**, the screen we see will depend on what type of object has focus (the seven available object types ot Table, Page, Report, Codeunit, Query, XMLport and MenuSuite were introduced in *Chapter 1, An Introduction to NAV 2015*). In each case, we have the opportunity to create a new object in the Designer used for that object type.

Accessing the Table Designer

The **Table Designer** screen for starting a new table is shown in the following screenshot:

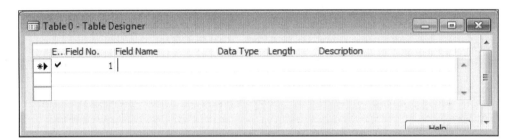

The **Table Designer** screen invites us to begin defining data fields. All the associated C/AL code will be embedded in the underlying triggers and developer-defined functions.

Accessing the Page Designer

For **Page Designer**, the first screen for a new page allows us to choose between the Wizard (for assistance) or the Page Designer (to work on our own).

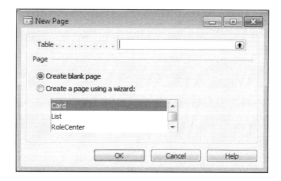

If we use the Wizard, it will walk us through defining FastTabs (collapsible/expandable groups of fields) and assigning fields to those tabs, as we saw in *Chapter 4, Pages – the User's Interactive Interface*. When we finish with the Wizard, we will be dropped into the **Page Designer** screen with our page well on the way to completion.

If we choose not to use the Wizard and want to begin designing our page totally on our own, we will select the **Create blank page** option. The empty **Page Designer** screen will display. We will do all control and field definition on our own. In either case, the C/AL code we create will be placed in triggers for the Page or its controls.

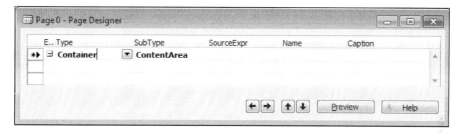

Accessing the Report Dataset Designer

For a **New Report**, the following **Report Dataset Designer** screen is initially displayed:

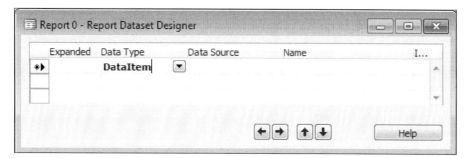

Since NAV 2015 does not have a Report Wizard, we begin Report development by defining the primary **DataItem** for our report and continuing from there as we did in *Chapter 5, Queries and Reports*. All C/AL code in a Report is tied to the Report triggers and controls.

Accessing the Codeunit Designer

When we access the Codeunit Designer using the **New** button, a Codeunit structure is opened with **C/AL Editor** active as shown in the following screenshot:

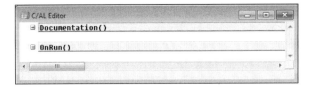

Codeunits have no superstructure or surrounding framework around the single code OnRun trigger. Codeunits are primarily a shell in which we can place our own functions and code so that it can be called from other objects.

Query Designer

For a **New Query**, the following screen is displayed:

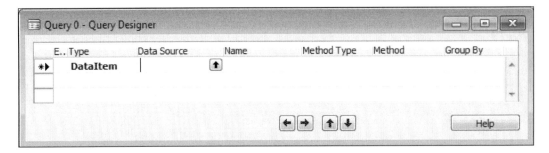

Much like a new Report, we begin Query development by defining the primary DataItem for our query and continuing from there as we did in *Chapter 5, Queries and Reports*. All C/AL code in a query is tied to the OnBeforeOpen trigger of the query (this code is often used to apply filters to the Query DataItems using the SETFILTER function).

XMLport Designer

XMLports are objects for defining and processing text-based data structures, including those which are defined in XML format. XMLports are used to import and export both the XML formatted files and the text files (particularly variations of the .csv format), but can handle many other text file formats in both delimited and fixed formats. XML is a set of somewhat standardized data formatting rules for dissimilar applications to exchange data. XML-structured files have become an essential component of business data systems.

There is no Wizard for XMLports. When we click **New**, we proceed directly to the **XMLport Designer** screen.

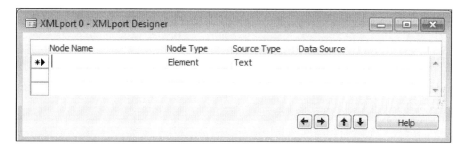

Once we become comfortable using C/SIDE and C/AL, we will learn more about XMLports for XML formatted data and other text file formats. XMLports can be run directly from menu entries as well as from within other objects. XMLport objects can also be passed as parameters to web services in a **Codeunit** function, thus supporting the easy passing of bulk information, such as a list of customers or inventory items.

MenuSuite Designer

MenuSuites are used to define the menus that are available from the **Departments** button in the **Navigation** pane and which also appear on the **Departments** page in the NAV Windows client. The initial **MenuSuite Designer** screen that comes up when we ask for a new MenuSuite, asks what MenuSuite Design Level we are preparing to create. The following screenshot shows all 15 available **Design Level** values:

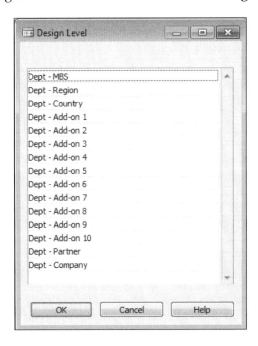

When one of the design levels has been used (created as a MenuSuite option), it will not appear in the list the next time **New** is selected for the **MenuSuite Designer**. MenuSuites can only exist at the 15 levels shown in the preceding image, and only one instance of each level is supported. Once we have chosen a level to create, NAV shifts to the **MenuSuite Designer** mode. The following screenshot shows the navigation pane in Designer mode after selection of **Create | Dept - Company**:

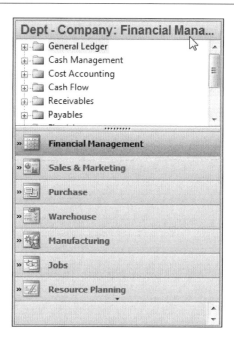

To add, change, or delete menu entries in the Navigation Pane Designer, highlight and right-click the entry. That will display the following window. The action options visible in this **MenuSuite Designer** window are dependent on the entry which is highlighted and, sometimes, on the immediate previous action taken.

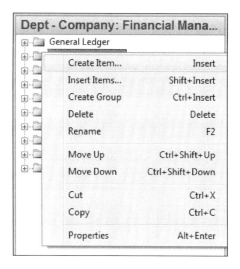

Descriptions of each of these menu maintenance action options follows:

- **Create Item...** (*Insert*): Allows the creation of a new menu action entry (Item), utilizing the same window format for Creation that is displayed when the entry **Properties** option is chosen
- **Insert Items...**(*Shift + Insert*): Allows the insertion of a new instance of a menu action entry, choosing from a list of all the existing entries
- **Create Group** (*Ctrl + Insert*): Allows the creation of a new group under which menu action entries can be organized
- **Delete** (*Delete*): For deleting either an individual entry or a whole group
- **Rename** (*F2*): To rename either an entry or a group
- **Move Up** (*Ctrl + Shift + Up*) and **Move Down** (*Ctrl + Shift + Down*): Allows moving an entry or group up or down one position in the menu structure
- **Cut** (*Ctrl + X*), Copy (*Ctrl + C*), and **Paste** (*Ctrl + V*): Provides the normal cut, copy, and paste functions for both entries and groups
- **Properties** (*Alt + Enter*): Displays the applicable property screen

A **Group Properties** screen only contains **Caption** and **CaptionML** along with the **Department Page** checkmark field. The **Item Properties** screen looks as shown in the following screenshot:

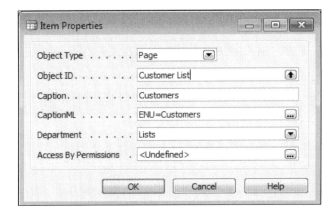

The Object Type field can be any of Report, Codeunit, XMLport, Page, or Query. The **Department** field can be Lists, Tasks, Reports and Analysis, Documents, History, or Administration, all of which are groups in the **Departments** menu.

There are a number of basic differences between the MenuSuite Designer and the other object designers including a very limited property set. One major difference is the fact that no C/AL code can be embedded within a MenuSuite entry.

To exit the **Navigation Pane Designer**, we press the *Esc* key with focus on the Navigation Pane or right-click on the **Navigation Pane Designer** heading and select the **Close Navigation Pane Designer** option as shown in the following image:

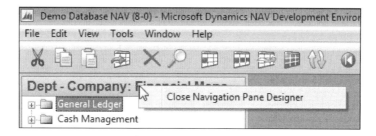

We will then be asked if we want to save our changes. We should answer **Yes** or **No** or **Cancel**, depending on what result we want.

Object Designer Navigation

In many places in the various designers within the **Object Designer**, there are standard NAV keyboard shortcuts available. For example:

- *F3* to create a new empty entry.
- *F4* to delete the highlighted entry.
- *F5* to access **C/AL Symbol Menu**, which shows us a symbol table for the object on which we are working. This isn't just any old symbol table; this is a programmer's assistant. More on this later in this chapter.
- *F9* to access the underlying C/AL code.
- *F11* to do an on-the-fly compile (very useful for error checking as we go).
- *Shift + F4* to access properties.
- *Ctrl + X, Ctrl + C,* and *Ctrl + V* in normal Windows mode for deletion (or cut), copy, and paste, respectively.

 We can cut, copy, and paste C/AL code, even functions, relatively freely within an object, from object to object, or to a text-friendly tool (for example, Word or Excel) much as if we were using a text editor. The source and target objects don't need to be of the same type.

When we are in a list of items that cannot be modified, for example, **C/AL Symbol Menu**, we can focus on a column, key a letter, and jump to the next field in the column starting with that letter. This works in a number of places where search is not supported, so it acts as a very limited search substitute, applying only to an entry's first letter.

The easiest way to copy a complete object to create a new version is as follows:

Open the object in **Design** mode. Click the **File | Save As object**, assign a new object number, and change the object name (no duplicate object names are allowed). A quick (mouseless) way to do a **Save As** is pressing *Alt + F* , then the *A* key – continuously holding down the *Alt* key while pressing first *F* and then *A*.

Don't ever delete an object or a field numbered in a range where the license doesn't allow creation of an object. If there isn't a compiled (.fob) back-up copy of the deleted object available for import, the deleted objects will be irretrievably lost.

If we must use an object or field number in the NAV reserved number range for a different purpose other than the standard system assignment (not a good idea), we must make the change in place. Don't try a delete followed by add; it won't work.

Exporting objects

Object Export from the Object Designer can be accessed for backup or distribution purposes via **File | Export**. Choosing this option, after highlighting the objects to be exported, brings up a standard Windows file-dialog screen with the file type options of .fob (NAV object) or .txt, as shown in the following screenshot:

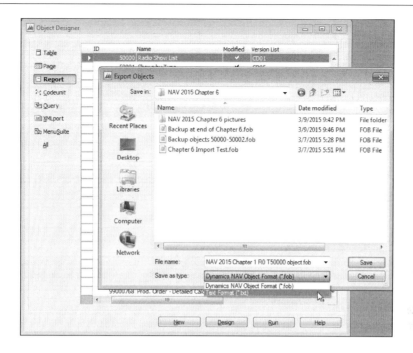

The safer, more general purpose format for exporting is as a compiled object, created with a file extension of `.fob`. But someone with a developer's license can export an object as a text file with a file extension of `.txt`. An exported text file is the only way to use a tool such as a text editor to do before and after comparisons of objects, or to search all parts of our objects for the occurrences of strings (such as finding all the places a variable name is used). An object text file can be used with a source-control tool such as Microsoft Visual Studio Online (`https://www.visualstudio.com/en-us/products/what-is-visual-studio-online-vs.aspx`), Microsoft Team Foundation, or ifacto ReVision for NAV (`http://www.ifacto.be/en/revision`).

A compiled object can be shipped to another system as a patch to be installed with little fear that it will be corrupted midstream. The system administrator at the other system has to simply import the new object following directions from the developer. Exported compiled objects also make excellent fractional backups. Before changing or importing any working production objects, it's always a good idea to export a copy of the "before" object images into a `.fob` file. These should be labeled so that they can easily be retrieved. If we want to check what objects are included in a fob, we can open the file in a text editor – the objects contained will be listed at the beginning. Any number of objects can be exported into a single `.fob` file. We can later selectively import any one or several of the individual objects from that group `.fob`.

Importing objects

Object Import is accessed through **File | Import** in the **Object Designer**. The import process is more complicated than the export process because there are more decisions to be made. When we import a compiled version of an object, the **Object Designer** allows decisions about importing and provides some information to help us make those decisions.

When we import a text version of an object, the new version is brought in immediately, regardless of what it overwrites and regardless of whether or not the incoming object can actually be compiled. The object imported from a text file is not compiled until we do so in a separate action. By importing a text-formatted object, we could actually replace a perfectly good production object with something useless.

> **Warning**: Never import a text object until there is a current backup of all the objects that might be replaced.
>
> Never send text objects to an end user for installation in their system.

When we import a compiled object from a `.fob` file, we will get one of two decision message screens, depending on what the Object Designer Import finds when it checks the existing objects. If there are no existing objects that the import logic identifies as matching and modified, then we will see the following dialog:

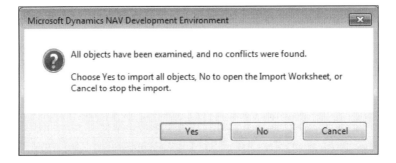

Even though you have the option to proceed without checking further, the safest thing to do is always open **Import Worksheet**, in this case by clicking on the **No** button. Examine the information displayed before proceeding with the import.

If the .fob file we are importing is found to have objects that could be in conflict with existing objects that have been previously modified, then we will see the following on our screen:

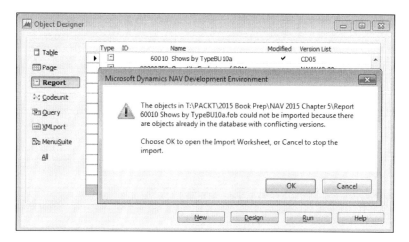

Of course, we can always click **Cancel** and simply exit the operation. Normally, we will click **OK** to open **Import Worksheet** and examine the contents.

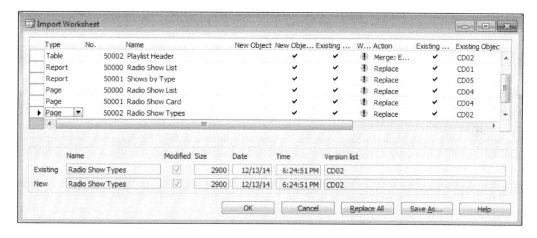

While all the information presented is useful at one time or another, usually we can focus on just a few fields. The basic question, on an object-by-object basis, is "Do I want to replace the old version of this object with this new one?"

At the bottom of the preceding screenshot, we can see the comparison of the Existing object and the **New** object information. Use this information to decide whether or not to take an action of **Create**, **Replace**, or **Skip**. More information on using Import Worksheet and the meaning of various warnings and actions can be found in the NAV **Developer and IT Pro Help** under **Import Worksheet**.

Although Import also allows us to merge the incoming and existing table versions, only very sophisticated developers should attempt to use this feature. The rest of us should always choose the **Import Action Replace** or **Skip** (or **Create**, if it is a new object).

When a .fob import completes, the system tells us the result.

Import Table object changes

When an existing table is changed as a result of a fob import, the new table definition is compared against the existing schema defined in the SQL Server database. The following message will be displayed (new in NAV 2015):

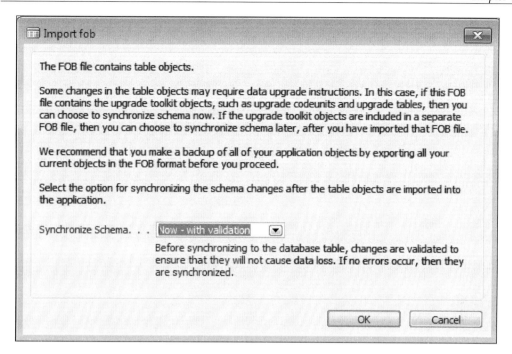

The options available for the **Synchronize Schema** choice are shown in the following screenshot:

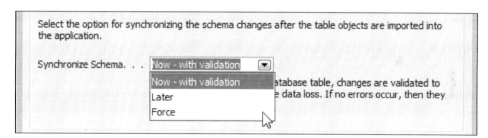

If we choose the first option, we will receive another stern warning message allowing us one last opportunity to cancel the import. If we tell the system to proceed, it will do so and, at the end of its processing, inform us of the results. More information on this process is available in the Help **Synchronizing Table Schemas**.

 Warning: Using the **Force** option may result in a corrupted database where the data structure is out of synch with the application software. This may not be recoverable except by restoring a backup. Using the Force option is especially risky in a production environment.

Text objects

A text version of an object is useful for a few specific development tasks. C/AL code or expressions can be placed in a number of different nooks and crannies of objects. In addition, sometimes object behavior is controlled by Properties. As a result, it's not always easy to figure out just how an existing object is accomplishing its tasks.

An object exported to text has all its code and properties flattened out where we can use our favorite text editor to search and view. Text copies of two versions of an object can easily be compared in a text editor. Text objects can be stored and managed in a source code library. In addition, a few tasks, such as renumbering an object, can be done more easily in the text copy than within C/SIDE.

Some useful practices

We should liberally make backups of objects on which we are working. Always make a backup of an object before changing it. Make intermediate backups regularly during the development. This allows recovery back to the last working copy.

If our project involves several developers, we may want to utilize a source control system that tracks versioning and has a check-out, check-in facility for objects. Larger projects should take advantage of the test functionality that's now part of C/AL (see **Testing the Application** in **Help**).

Compile frequently. We find errors more easily this way. Not all errors will be discovered just by compiling. Thorough and frequent testing is always a requirement.

When we are developing pages or reports, we should do test runs (or previews) of the objects relatively frequently. Whenever we reach a stage where we have made a number of changes and again have a working copy, we should save it before making more changes.

Never design a modification that places data or changes it directly in a **Ledger** table without going through the standard Posting routines. It's sometimes tempting to do so, but that's a sure path to unhappiness. If creating a new Ledger for our application, design the process with a Journal table and a Posting process consistent with the NAV standard flow.

Follow the NAV standard approach for handling Registers, Posted Document tables, and other tables normally updated during Posting. Check out what Patterns have been defined to see what applies.

If at all possible, try to avoid importing modifications into a production system when there are users logged-in to the system. If a logged-in user has an active object that is being modified, they may continue working with the old version until they exit and re-enter. Production use of the obsolete object version may possibly cause confusion or even the corruption of data.

Always test modifications in a reasonably current copy of the production system. Do the final testing by using real data (or at least realistic data) and a copy of the customer's production license. As a rule, we should never develop or test in the live production system. Always work in a copy. Otherwise, the price of a mistake, even a simple typo, can be enormous.

If we wish to check that changes to a production system are compatible with the rest of the system, we should import the changes into our test copy of the system and then recompile all of the objects in the system. We may uncover serious problems left by a previous developer with bad habits, so be prepared.

Changing data definitions

The integration of the development environment with the application database is particularly handy when we are making changes to an application that is already in production use. C/SIDE is good for not letting us make changes that are inconsistent with the existing data. For example, let's presume we have a text field that is defined as 30 characters long and there is already data in that field in the database, one instance of which is longer than 20 characters. If we attempt to change the definition of that field to 20 characters long, we will get a warning message when we try to save and compile the table object. We should not force the change until we adjust either the data in the database or we adjust the change so that it is compatible with all the existing data.

Saving and compiling

Whenever we exit the Designer for an object in which we have made a change, NAV wants to save and compile the object on which we were working. We will see a dialog similar to the following screenshot:

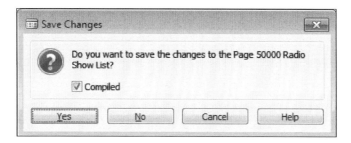

We have to be careful not to be working on two copies of the same object at once as we may lose the first set of changes when the second copy is saved. If we want to save the changed material under a new object number while retaining the original object, we must **Cancel** this **Save Changes** and instead use the **File | Save As** option to rename and renumber the new copy.

If the object under development is at one of those in-between stages where it won't compile, we can deselect the **Compiled** checkbox and save it by clicking on the **Save** button without compiling it.

[We should not complete a development session without getting an error-free compilation. Even if making big changes, make them in small increments.]

On occasion, we may make changes that we think will affect other objects. In that case, from the **Object Designer** screen, we can select a group of objects to be compiled by Marking them. Marking an object is done by putting focus on the object and pressing the *Ctrl + F1* keys. The marked object is then identified with a bullet in the left screen column for that object's row. After marking each of the objects to be compiled, use the **View | Marked Only** function to select just the marked objects.

We can then compile the Marked objects as a group. Select all the entries (using *Ctrl + A* keys is one way to do this), press *F11*, and respond **Yes** to the question Do you want to compile the selected objects? Once the compilation of all the selected objects is completed, we will get an **Error List** window indicating which objects had compilation errors of what types.

After we respond to that message, only the objects with errors will remain marked. The **Marked Only** filter will still be on, so that just those objects that need attention will be shown on the screen. In fact, anytime we do a group compilation of objects, those with errors will be marked so that we can use the **Marked Only** filter to select the objects needing attention.

Some C/AL naming conventions

In previous chapters, we discussed naming conventions for tables, pages, and reports. In general, the naming guidelines for NAV objects and C/AL encourage consistency, common sense, and readability. Use meaningful names. These make the system more intuitive to the users and more self-documenting.

When we name variables, we must try to keep the names as self-documenting as possible. We should differentiate between similar, but different, variable meanings such as **Cost** (cost from the vendor) and **Amount** (selling price to the customer). Embedded spaces, periods, or other special characters should be avoided (even though we find some violations of this in the base product). If we want to use special characters for the benefit of the user, we should put them in the caption, not in the name. If possible, we should stick to letters and numbers in our variable names. We should always avoid Hungarian naming styles; keep names simple and descriptive.

There are a number of reasons to keep variable names simple. Other software products with which we may interface may have limitations on variable names. Some special characters have special meanings to other software or in another human language. In NAV, ? and * are wildcards and must be avoided in variable names. $ has special meaning in other software. SQL Server adds its own special characters to NAV names and the resultant combinations can get quite confusing (not just to us but to the software). The same can be said for the names constructed by the internal RDLC generator, which replaces spaces and periods with underscores.

When we are defining multiple instances of a table, we should either differentiate clearly by name (for example, **Item** and **NewItem**) or by a descriptive suffix (for example, **Item**, **ItemForVarient**, **ItemForLocation**). In the very common situation where a name is a compound combination of words, begin each abbreviated word with a capital letter (for example, **NewCustBalDue**).

Avoid creating variable names that are common words and might be reserved (for example, Page, Column, Number, and Integer). C/SIDE will sometimes not warn us that we have done so and we may find our logic and the automatic logic working at very mysterious cross purposes.

Do not start variables with the prefix "x", which is used in some automatically created variables (such as xRec). We should make sure that we clearly differentiate between working storage variable names and the field names originating in tables. Sometimes C/SIDE will allow us to have a global name, local name, and/or record variable name, all with the same literal name. If we do this, we are practically guaranteeing a variable misidentification bug where the compiler uses a different variable than what we intended to be referenced.

When defining a temporary table, preface the name logically, for example with Temp. In general, use meaningful names that help in identifying the type and purpose of the item being named. When naming a new function, we should be reasonably descriptive. Don't name two functions located in different objects with the same name. It will be too easy to get confused later.

In short, be careful, be consistent, be clear, and use common sense.

Variables

As we've gone through examples showing various aspects of C/SIDE and C/AL, we've seen and referred to variables in a number of situations. Some of the following is obvious, but for clarity's sake we'll summarize here.

In *Chapter 3, Data Types and Fields*, we reviewed various data types for variables defined within objects (referred to in *Chapter 3, Data Types and Fields* as working storage data). Working Storage consists of all the variables that are defined for use within an object, but whose contents disappear when the object closes. Working Storage data types discussed in *Chapter 3, Data Types and Fields*, are those that can be defined in either the **C/AL Global Variables or C/AL Local Variables** tabs. Variables can also be defined in several other places in a NAV object.

C/AL Globals

Global variables are defined on the **C/AL Globals** form, in the **Variables** tab.

Global Text Constants are defined on the **Text Constants** tab section of the C/AL **Globals** form. The primary purpose of the Text Constants area is to allow easier translation of messages from one language to another. By putting all message text in this one place in each object, a standardized process can be defined for language translation. There is a good explanation in NAV **Developer and IT Pro Help** on *How to: Add a Text Constant to a Codeunit*. The information applies generally.

Global Functions are defined on the **Functions** tab of the **C/AL Globals** form. The following screenshot shows the **C/AL Globals** form:

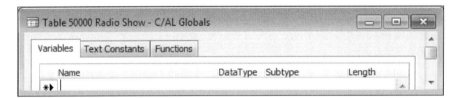

C/AL Locals

Local identifiers only exist defined within the range of a trigger. This is true whether the trigger is a developer-defined function or one of the default system triggers or standard application-supplied functions. In NAV 2015, when a new function is defined, it is set as a local function by default. This means that if we want the new function to be accessible from other objects, we must set the Local property of the function to No.

Function local identifiers

Function local identifiers are defined on one or another of the tabs on the C/AL Locals form that we use for defining a function.

Parameters and **Return Value** are defined on their respective tabs.

The **Variables** and **Text Constants** tabs for **C/AL Locals** are exactly similar in use to the C/AL Globals tabs of the same names. The tabs of the C/AL Locals form can be seen in the following screenshot:

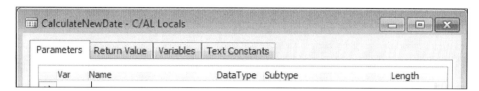

Other local identifiers

Trigger local variables (variables that are local to the scope of a trigger) are also defined on one or another of the tabs on the **C/AL Locals** form. The difference between trigger Local Variables and those for a function is that only the **Variables** and **Text Constants** tabs exist for trigger Local Variables. The use of the **Variables** and **Text Constants** tabs are exactly the same for triggers as for functions. Whether we are working within a trigger or a defined function, we can access the local variables through the menu option **View | C/AL Locals**.

Special working storage variables

Some working storage variables have additional attributes to be considered.

Temporary tables

Temporary tables were discussed in *Chapter 2, Tables*. Let's take a quick look at how one is defined. Defining a Global Temporary table begins just like any other Global Variable definition of the Record data type. With an object open in the Designer, follow these steps:

1. Select **View | C/AL Globals**.
2. Enter a variable name, data type of Record.
3. Choose the table whose definition is to be replicated for this temporary table as the Subtype.
4. With focus on the new **Record** variable, click on the **Properties** icon (or press the *Shift + F4* keys).
5. Set the **Temporary** property to **Yes**.

That's it. We've defined a temporary table similar to the one in the following image:

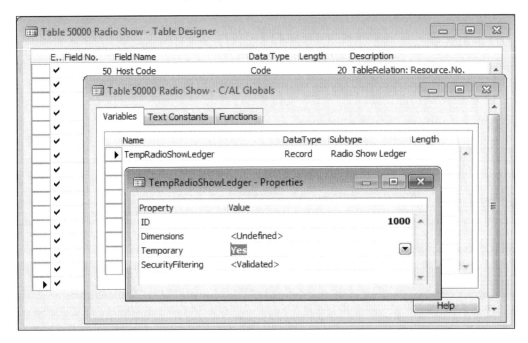

We can use a temporary table just as though it were a permanent table with some specific differences:

- The table contains only the data we add to it during this instance of the object in which it resides.

- We cannot change any aspect of the definition of the table, except by changing the permanent table (which was its template) using the Table Designer, then recompiling the object containing the associated temporary table.

- Processing for a temporary table is done wholly in the client system in a user specific instance of the business logic. It is, therefore, inherently single user.

- A properly utilized temporary table reduces network traffic and eliminates any locking issues for that table. It is often much faster than processing the same data in a permanent, database-resident table because both data transmission and physical storage I/O are significantly reduced.

In some cases, it's a good idea to copy database table data into a temporary table for repetitive processing within an object. This can give us a significant speed advantage for a particular task by updating data in the temporary table, then copying it back out to the database table at the end of processing.

When using temporary tables, we need to be very careful that references from C/AL code in the temporary table (such as data validations) don't inappropriately modify permanent data elsewhere in the database. We also must remember that if we forget to properly mark the table as temporary, we will likely corrupt production data with our processing.

Arrays

Arrays of up to 10 dimensions containing up to a total of 1,000,000 elements in a single variable can be created in a NAV object. Defining an array is done simply by setting the **Dimensions** property of a variable to something other than the default **<Undefined>**. An example is shown in the following screenshot:

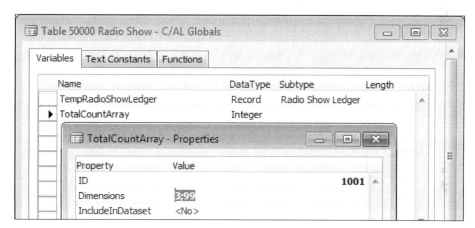

The semicolon separates the dimensions of the array. The numbers indicate the maximum number of elements of each of the dimensions. This example is a two-dimensional array which has three rows of 99 elements each. An array variable like **TotalCountArray** is referred to in C/AL as follows:

- The 15th entry in the first row is `TotalCountArray[1,15]`
- The last entry in the last row is `TotalCountArray[3,99]`

An array of a complex data type such as a record may behave differently than a single instance of the data type, especially when passed as a parameter to a function. In such a case, we must make sure the code is especially thoroughly tested so that we aren't surprised by unexpected results. NAV 2013 added the capability to also use arrays from the .NET Framework. See the **Help** titled *Using Arrays* for more information.

Initialization

When an object is initiated, the variables in that object are automatically initialized. Booleans are set to `False`. Numeric variables are set to `zero`. Text and code data types are set to the empty string. Dates are set to 0D (the undefined date) and Times are set to 0T (the undefined time). The individual components of complex variables are appropriately initialized. The system also automatically initializes all the system-defined variables.

Of course, once the object is active, through our code and property settings we can do whatever additional initialization we wish. If we wish to initialize variables at intermediate points during processing, we can use any of the several approaches. First we reset a Record variable (for example, the `TempRadioShowLedger` temporary table defined in the preceding example) with the RESET function, and then initialize with the INIT function in statements in the form:

```
TempRadioShowLedger.RESET;
TempRadioShowLedger.INIT;
```

The RESET makes sure that all previously set filters on this table are cleared. The INIT makes sure that all the fields, except those in the Primary Key, are set either to their `InitValue` property value or to their data type default value. Primary Key fields must be explicitly set by C/AL code.

For all types of data, including complex data types, we can initialize fields with the CLEAR or CLEARALL function in a statement in the following form:

```
CLEAR(TotalArray[1,1]);
CLEAR(TotalArray);
CLEAR("Shipment Code");
```

The first example would clear a single element of the array, the first element in the first row. Because this variable is an Integer data type, the element would be set to Integer zero when cleared. The second example would clear the entire array. In the third example, a variable defined as a Code data type would simply be set to an empty string.

System-defined variables

NAV also provides us with some variables automatically, such as Rec, xRec, CurrPage, CurrReport, and CurrXMLport. Which variables are provided is dependent on the object in which we are operating. Descriptions of some of these can be found in the **Help** titled *System-Defined Variables*.

C/SIDE programming

Many of the things that we do during development in C/SIDE might not be called programming by some people because it doesn't involve writing C/AL code statements. But so long as these activities contribute to the definition of the object and affect the processing that occurs, we'll include them in our broad definition of C/SIDE programming.

These activities include setting properties at the object and Data Item levels, creating Request pages in Reports, defining Controls and their properties, defining Report data structures and their properties, creating Source Expressions, defining Functions, and, of course, writing C/AL statements in all the places where we can put C/AL. We are going to primarily focus on C/SIDE programming as it relates to tables, reports, and codeunits.

We will touch on C/SIDE programming for pages and XMLports. In the case of RTC reports, C/AL statements can reside only in the components that are developed within the C/SIDE RD and not the RDLC created by the SSRB.

 Because no coding can be done within MenuSuites, we will omit those objects from the programming part of our discussions.

NAV objects are generally consistent in structure. Most have some properties and triggers. Pages and Reports have controls, though the tools that define the controls in each are specific to the individual object type. Reports have a built-in DataItem looping logic. XMLports also have DataItem looping logic but structured differently from reports (for example, Reports can have multiple DataItems at the 0 level and XMLports can only have one Node at the 0 level). All the object types that we are considering can contain C/AL code in one or more places. All of these can contain function definitions which can be called either internally or externally (if not marked as Local). Remember, good design practice says that any functions designed as "library" or reusable functions that are called from a variety of objects should be placed in a Codeunit (or, in some circumstances, in the primary table).

> Don't forget that our fundamental coding work should focus on tables and function libraries as much as possible, as these are the foundation of the NAV system.

Non-modifiable functions

A function is a defined set of logic that performs a specific task. Similar to many other programming languages, C/AL includes a set of pre-written functions that are available to us to perform a wide variety of different tasks. The underlying logic for some of these functions is hidden and not modifiable. These non-modifiable functions are supplied as part of the C/AL programming language. Following are some simple examples:

- DATE2DMY: Supply a date and, depending on a calling parameter, this will return the integer value of the day, the month, or the year of that date

- STRPOS: Supply a string variable and a string constant; the function will return the position of the first instance of that constant within the variable, or a zero if the constant is not present in the string contained in the variable

- GET: Supply a value and a table, and the function will read the record in the table with a Primary Key equal to the supplied value, if a matching record exists

- INSERT: Adds a record to a table

- MESSAGE: Supply a string and optional variables; this function will display a message to the operator

Such functions are the heart of the C/SIDE-C/AL tools. There are over 100 of them. On the whole, they are designed around the essential purpose of an NAV system: business and financial applications data processing. These functions are not modifiable; they operate according to their predefined rules. For development purposes, they act as basic language components.

Modifiable functions

In addition to the prewritten "language component" functions, there are a large number of pre-written "application component" functions as well. The difference between the two types is that the code implementing the latter is visible and modifiable, though we should be extremely cautious about making such modifications.

An example of an application component function might be one to handle the task of processing a Customer Shipping Address to eliminate empty lines and standardize the layout based on user-defined setup parameters. Such a function would logically be placed in a Codeunit and thus made available to any routine that needs this capability.

In fact, this function exists. It is called `SalesHeaderShipTo` and is located in the **Format Address** Codeunit. In the following table, we can explore the Codeunits for some functions we might find useful to use or from which to borrow logic. This is not an all-inclusive list, as there are many functions in other Codeunits which we may find useful in a future development project, either to be used directly or as templates for designing our own similar function. Many library Codeunits have the words **Management** or **Mgt.** in their name.

Object number	Name
1	ApplicationManagement
356	DateComprMgt
358	DateFilter-Calc
359	PeriodFormManagement
365	Format Address
397	Mail
5052	AttachmentManagement
5054	WordManagement
6224	XML DOM Management

The pre-written application functions have generally been provided to address the needs of the NAV developers working at Microsoft. But we can use them too. Our challenge will be to find out that they exist and to understand how they work. There is very little documentation of these "application component" functions.

One significant aspect of these application functions is the fact that they are written in C/AL and their construction is totally exposed. In theory, they can be modified, though that is not advisable. If we decide to change one of these functions, we should make sure our change is compatible with all the existing uses of that function.

A useful "trick" to find all the calls of a function is to add a dummy calling parameter to the function (temporarily) and then compile all objects in a copy of the application system. Errors will be displayed for all objects that call the changed function (we mustn't forget to remove the dummy calling parameter and recompile when we're done testing). This technique not only works for Microsoft created functions, but also for functions created as part of a customization or add-on.

Rather than changing an existing function, it is much better to clone the existing function into our own library codeunit, creating a new version, and making any modifications to the new version while leaving the original untouched.

Custom functions

We can also create our own custom functions to meet any need. The most common reason to create a new function is to provide a single, standardized instance of logic to perform a specific task. When we need to use the same logic in more than one place, we should consider creating a callable function.

We should also create a new function when we're modifying standard NAV processes. Whenever more than three or four lines of code are needed for the modification, we should consider creating the modification as a function. If we do that, the modification to the standard process can be limited to a call to the new function. It's usually not a good idea to embed a new function into an existing standard function. It's better to clone the existing function and make the modifications in-line in our copy.

Although using a function for inserting new code into the flow is a great concept, occasionally it may be difficult to implement in practice. For example, if we want to revise the way the existing logic works, sometimes it's confusing to implement the change through just a call and an external (to the mainline process) function. In such a case, we may just settle for creating an in-line modification and doing a good job of commenting the modification. This is most reasonable which this code is only required in one place and does not also need to be referenced elsewhere.

If a new function will be used in several objects, it should be housed in our library codeunit. If it is only for use in a single object, then the new function can be resident in that object. This latter option also has the advantage of allowing the new function direct access to the global variables within the object being modified, if necessary.

Create a function

Let's take a quick look at how a function can be created. We're going to add a new codeunit to our C/AL application, **Codeunit 50000**. Since this is where we will put any callable functions that we need for our WDTU application, we will simply call it **Radio Show Management**. In that Codeunit, we're going to create a function to calculate a new date based on a given date. If that seems familiar, it's the same thing we did in *Chapter 3, Data Types and Fields*, to illustrate how a DateFormula data type works. This time, our focus is going to be on the creation of a function.

Our first step is to copy **Table 50009**, which we created for testing, and then save it as table **50008**. As a reminder, we do that by opening **Table 50009** in the Table Designer, then selecting **File | Save As**, changing the object number to **50008** and **Name** to **Date Formula Test-2** (see the following screenshot), and then exiting and compiling.

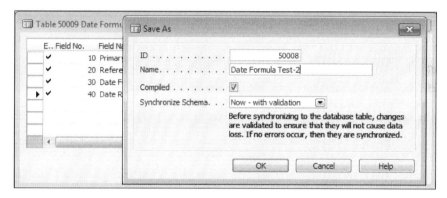

Once that's done, change the Version List to show that this table has been modified. We used CD and 03 for the original *Chapter 3, Data Types and Fields*, table Version. Now we'll add, 06 to make the new table Version read CD 03,06.

We will create our new Codeunit by simply clicking on the **Codeunit** button at the left of the **Object Designer** screen, then clicking on the **New** button and choosing File | Save As, and entering the **Object ID** of **50000** and Name as Radio Show Management.

Now comes the important part—designing and coding our new function. When we had the function operating as a local function inside the table where it was called, we didn't worry about passing the data back and forth. We simply used the data fields that were already present in the table and treated them as global variables (which they were). Now that our function will be external to the object from which it's called, we have to pass the data values back and forth. Here's the basic calling structure of our function:

```
Output := Function (Input Parameter1, Input Parameter2)
```

In other words, we need to feed two values into our new callable function and accept a return value back on completion of the function's processing.

Our first step is to click **View | C/AL Globals**, and then the **Functions** tab. Enter the name of the new function following the guidelines for good names (such as **CalculateNewDate**). Then keeping the function name in focus (highlighted), display the Properties of the function by either clicking the **Properties** icon, pressing *Shift + F4* or via **View | Properties**.

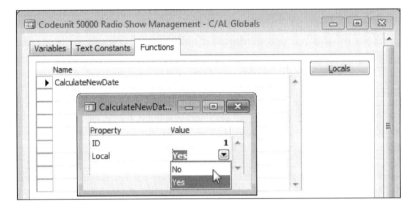

Set the **Local** property to **Yes** so that we will be able to call the function from other objects. Click on the **Locals** button. This will allow us to define all the variables that will be local to the new function. The first tab on the Locals screen is **Parameters**, our input variables.

In keeping with good naming practices, we will define two input parameters, as shown in the following screenshot:

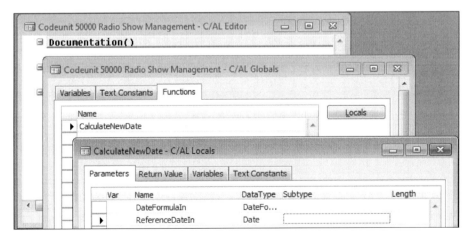

Re; Var column in the leftmost column of the Parameters tab form

If we checkmark the `Var` column, the parameter is passed by reference to the original calling routine's copy of that variable. If the parameter is passed by reference, when the called function changes the value of an input parameter, it directly changes the original variable value in the calling object.

Since we've specified the input parameter passing here with the `Var` column unchecked, changes in the value of that input parameter will be passed by value. That makes the parameter local to this function and any changes to its value will not directly affect the variable in the calling routine.

Checking the `Var` column on one or more parameters is a way to effectively have multiple results passed back to the calling routine. Parameter passing with the `Var` column checked (passing by reference) is also faster than passing by value, especially when passing complex data types (for example, records).

Select the **Return Value** tab and define our output variable as shown in the following screenshot:

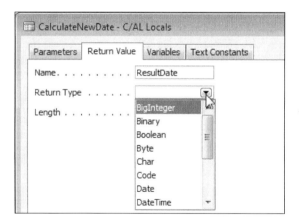

A/The name is not required for `Return Value` if the return terminates processing with an `EXIT([ReturnValue])` instruction. Choose the **Date** option for `Return Type`. Exit by using the *Esc* key and the results will be saved.

One way to view the effect of what we have just defined is to view **C/AL Symbol Menu**. From the **Codeunit Designer** screen, with our new Codeunit 50000 in view and our cursor placed in the code area for our new function, we click **View | C/AL Symbol Menu** (or just press *F5*) and see the following image:

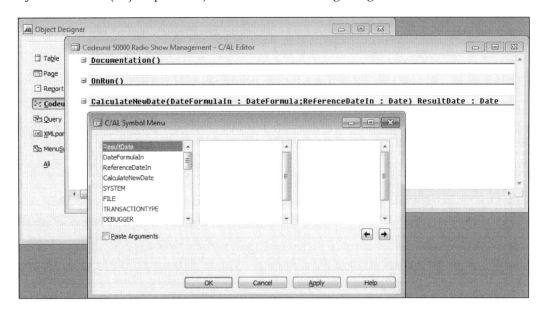

We see in the **C/AL Editor** that our CalculateNewDate function has been defined with two parameters and a result. Now press *Esc* or select **OK**, move the cursor to the OnRun trigger code area and again press *F5* to view **C/AL Symbol Menu**. We don't see the two parameters and result variables.

Why? Because Parameters and Return Value are local variables, which only exist in the context of the function and are not visible outside the function. We'll make more use of the **C/AL Symbol Menu** a little later, because it is a very valuable C/AL development tool. But right now we need to finish our new function and integrate it with our test Table 50008.

Move the cursor back to the code area for our new function. Click on the menu item **Window | Object Designer | Table** button, then click **Table 50008 | Design**, and press *F9*. That will take us to the **C/AL Code** screen for **Table 50008**. Highlight and cut the code line from the local CalculateNewDate function. Admittedly, this will not be a particularly efficient process this time, but hopefully it will make the connection between the two instances of functions easier to envision. Using the **Window** menu, move back to our Codeunit function and paste the line of code we just cut from **Table 50008**. We should see the following image:

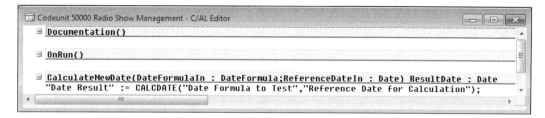

Edit the line of code just pasted into the codeunit so the variable names match those shown in our function trigger above. This will result in the following image:

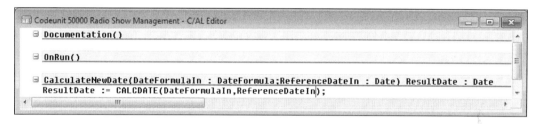

Press *F11* to check if we have a clean compile. If we get an error, we must do the traditional programmer thing. Find it, fix it, and recompile. Repeat until we get a clean compile. Then exit and **Save** our modified **Codeunit 50000**.

Finally, we will return to our test **Table 50008** to complete the changes necessary to use the external function rather than the internal function. We have two obvious choices for doing this. One is to replace the internal formula in our existing function with a call to our external function. This approach results in fewer object changes.

The other choice is to replace each of our internal function calls with a call to the external function. This approach may be more efficient at run time because when we need the external function, we invoke it in one step rather than two. We will walk through the first option here and then you should try the second option on your own.

Which is best? It depends on our criteria. Such a decision comes down to a matter of identifying the best criteria on which to judge the design options, then applying those criteria. Remember, whenever feasible, simple is best.

For the first approach (calling our new Codeunit resident function), we must add our new Radio Show Management codeunit 50000 to table 50008 as a variable. After Designing the table, **View | Globals**, click on the **Functions** tab, highlight the `CalculateNewDate` function, click on the **Locals** button, and click on the **Variables** tab. Add the Local variable as shown in the following screenshot (it's good practice to define variables as local unless global access is required):

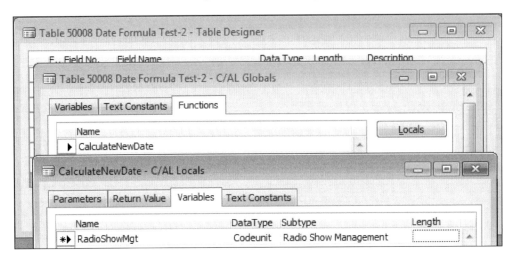

The two lines of code that called the internal function CalculateNewDate must be changed to call the external function. The syntax for that call is:

```
Global/LocalVariable := Global/LocalObjectName.FunctionName(Parameter1
,Parameter2,…).
```

Based on that, the new line of code should be:

```
"Date Result" := RadioShowMgt.CalculateNewDate("Date Formula to
Test","Reference Date for Calculation");
```

If all has gone well, we should be able to save and compile this modified table. When that step works successfully, we can Run the table and experiment with different Reference Dates and Date Formulas, just as we did back in *Chapter 3, Data Types and Fields*. We should get the same results for the same entries as we saw before.

When you try out the other approach of replacing each of the calls to the internal function by directly calling the external function, you will want to:

- Either define the Radio Show Management codeunit as a Global variable or as a Local variable for each of the triggers where you are calling the external function

- Go to the **View** | **Globals** | **Functions** tab and delete the now unused internal `CalculateNewDate` function

We should now have a better understanding of the basics of constructing both internal and external functions and some of the optional design features available to us for building functions.

C/AL syntax

C/AL syntax is relatively simple and straightforward. The basic structure of most C/AL statements is essentially similar to what we learned with other programming languages. C/AL is modeled on Pascal and tends to use many of the same special characters and syntax practices.

Assignment and punctuation

Assignment is represented with a colon followed by an equal sign, the combination being treated as a single symbol. The evaluated value of the expression, to the right of the assignment symbol, is assigned to the variable on the left-side.

```
"Phone No." := '312-555-1212';
```

All statements are terminated with a semi-colon. Multiple statements can be placed on a single program line, but that makes the code hard for others to read.

Fully qualified data fields are prefaced with the name of the record variable of which they are a part (see the preceding code line as an example where the record variable is named `ClientRec`). The same structure applies to fully qualified function references; the function name is prefaced with the name of the object in which they are defined.

Single quotes are used to surround string literals (see the phone number string in the preceding code line).

Double quotes are used to surround an identifier (for example, a variable or a function name) that contains any character other than numerals or upper and lower case letters. For example, the `Phone No.` field name in the preceding code line is constructed as "Phone No." because it contains a space and a period. Other examples would be "Post Code"(contains a space), "E-Mail" (contains a dash), and "No." (contains a period).

Parentheses are used much the same as in other languages, to indicate sets of expressions to be interpreted according to their parenthetical groupings. The expressions are interpreted in sequence - first the innermost parenthetical group, then the next level, and so forth. The expression *(A / (B + (C * (D + E))))* would be evaluated as follows:

- Summing D + E into Result1
- Multiplying Result1 times C yielding Result2
- Adding Result2 to B yielding Result3
- Dividing A by Result3

Brackets [ ] are used to indicate the presence of subscripts for indexing of array variables. A text string can be treated as an array of characters and we can use subscripts with the string name to access individual character positions within the string (but not beyond the terminating character of the string). For example, Address[1] represents the leftmost character in the Address text variable contents.

Brackets are also used for IN (In range) expressions, such as

```
Boolean := SearchValue IN[SearchTarget]
```

In this case, SearchValue and SearchTarget are text variables.

Statements can be continued on multiple lines without any special punctuation, though we can't split a variable or literal across two lines. Since the C/AL code editor limits lines to 132 characters long, this capability is often used. The following example shows two instances that are interpreted exactly in the same manner by the compiler:

```
ClientRec."Phone No." := '312' + '-' + '555' + '-' + '1212';
ClientRec."Phone No." := '312' + '-' + '555' + '-' + '1212';
```

Expressions

Expressions in C/AL are made up of four elements: **constants**, **variables**, **operators**, and **functions**. We could include a fifth element, expressions, because an expression may include a subordinate expression within it. As we become more experienced in coding C/AL, we find that the capability of nesting expressions can be both a blessing and a curse, depending on the specific use and "readability" of the result.

We can create complex statements that will conditionally perform important control actions and operate in much the same way as a person would think about the task. We can also create complex statements that are very difficult for a person to understand. These are tough to debug and sometimes almost impossible to deal with in a modification.

One of our responsibilities is to learn to tell the difference so we can write code that makes sense in operation, and is also easy to read and understand.

According to NAV **Developer and IT Pro Help**, a C/AL Expression is a group of characters (data values, variables, arrays, operators, and functions) that can be evaluated with the result having an associated data type. Following are two code statements that accomplish the same result in slightly different ways. They each assign a literal string to a text data field. In the first one, the right side is a literal data value. In the second, the right side of the := assignment symbol is an expression.

```
ClientRec."Phone No." := '312-555-1212';
ClientRec."Phone No." := '312' + '-' + '555' + '-' + '1212';
```

Operators

Now we'll review the C/AL operators grouped by category. Depending on the data types we are using with a particular operator, we may need to know the type conversion rules defining the allowed combinations of operator and data types for an expression. The NAV **Developer and IT Pro Help** provides good information on type conversion rules. Search for the phrase *Type Conversion*.

Before we review the operators that can be categorized, let's discuss some operators that don't fit well in any of the categories. These include the following:

Other Operators	
Symbol	**Evaluation**
.	Member of: Fields in Records Controls in Forms Controls in Reports Functions in Objects
()	Grouping of elements
[]	Indexing
::	Scope
..	Range
@	Case-insensitive

Following are the explanations regarding the uses of this set of symbols:

- The symbol represented by a single dot or period doesn't have a given name in the NAV documentation, so we'll call it the Member symbol or Dot operator (as it is referred to in the MSDN Visual Basic Developer documentation). It indicates that a field is a member of a table (`TableName.FieldName`), or that a control is a member of a page (`PageName.ControlName`) or report (`ReportName.ControlName`), or that a function is a member of an object (`Objectname.FunctionName`).

- Parentheses **( )** and Brackets **[ ]** could be considered operators based on the effect their use has on the results of an expression. We discussed their use in the context of parenthetical grouping and indexing using brackets, as well as with the `IN` function, earlier. Parentheses are also used to enclose the parameters in a function call:

```
Objectname.FunctionName(Param1,Param2,Param3);
```

- The Scope operator is a two character sequence consisting of two colons in a row "::" . The Scope operator is used to allow the C/AL code to refer to a specific Option value using the text descriptive value rather than the integer value that is actually stored in the database. For example, in our C/AL database Radio Show table, we have an **Option** field defined that is called Frequency with Option string values of (blank), Hourly, Daily, Weekly, and Monthly. Those values would be stored as integers 0, 1, 2, 3 or 4, but we can use the strings to refer to them in code, which makes our code more self-documenting. The Scope operator allows us to refer to `Frequency::Hourly` (rather than 1) and `Frequency::Monthly` (rather than 4). These constructs are translated by the compiler to 1 and 4, respectively. If we want to type fewer characters when entering code, we could enter just enough of the Option string value to be unique, letting the compiler automatically fill in the rest when we next save, compile, close, and reopen the object. In similar fashion, we can refer to objects in the format `[Object Type::"Object Name"]` to be translated to the object number. For example:

```
PAGE.RUN(PAGE::"Bin List"); is equivalent to  PAGE.RUN(7303);
```

- The Range operator is a two character sequence `..`, that is two dots in a row. This operator is very widely used in NAV, not only in the C/AL code (including `CASE` statements and `IN` expressions), but also in filters entered by the users. The English lower case alphabet can be represented by the range `a..z`; the set of single digit numbers by the range `-9..9` (that is, minus 9 dot dot 9); and all the entries starting with the letter "a" (lower case) by `a..a*`. Don't underestimate the power of the range operator. For more information on filtering syntax, refer to the NAV **Developer and IT Pro Help** section *Entering Criteria in Filters*.

Arithmetic operators and functions

The Arithmetic operators include the following:

Arithmetic Operators		
Symbol	**Action**	**Data Types**
+	Addition	Numeric, Date, Time, Text and Code (concatenation),
-	Subtraction	Numeric, Date, Time
*	Multiplication	Numeric
/	Division	Numeric
DIV	Integer Division (provides only the integer portion of the quotient of a division calculation)	Numeric
MOD	Modulus (provides only the integer remainder of a division calculation)	Numeric

As we can see in the **Data Types** column, these operators can be used on various data types. Numeric includes Integer, Decimal, Boolean, and Character data types. Text and Code are both String data.

Following are sample statements using DIV and MOD, where BigNumber is an integer containing 200:

```
DIVIntegerValue := BigNumber DIV 60;
```

The contents of DIVIntegerValue after executing the preceding statement would be **3**.

```
MODIntegerValue := BigNumber MOD 60;
```

The contents of MODIntegerValue after executing the preceding statement would be **20**.

The syntax for these DIV and MOD statements is:

```
IntegerQuotient := IntegerDividend DIV IntegerDivisor;
IntegerModulus := IntegerDividend MOD IntegerDivisor;
```

Boolean operators

Boolean operators only operate on expressions that can be evaluated as **Boolean**. They are as follows:

Boolean Operators	
Symbol	**Evaluation**
NOT	Logical NOT
AND	Logical AND
OR	Logical OR
XOR	Exclusive Logical OR

The result of an expression based on a Boolean operator will also be Boolean.

Relational operators and functions

The Relational operators are listed in the next screenshot. Each of these is used in an expression of the format:

```
Expression RelationalOperator Expression
```

For example: `(Variable1 + 97) > ((Variable2 * 14.5) / 57.332)`

Relational Operators	
Symbol	**Evaluation**
<	Less than
>	Greater than
<=	Less than or Equal to
>=	Greater than or Equal to
=	Equal to
<>	Not equal to
IN	IN Valueset

We will spend a little extra time on the IN operator, because this can be very handy and is not documented elsewhere. The term Valueset in the **Evaluation** column for IN refers to a list of defined values. It would be reasonable to define a Valueset as a container of a defined set of individual values, expressions, or other Valuesets. Some examples of IN as used in the standard NAV product code are as follows:

```
GLEntry."Posting Date" IN [0D,WORKDATE]

Description[I+2] IN ['0'..'9']

"Gen. Posting Type" IN ["Gen. Posting Type"::Purchase,
                 "Gen. Posting Type"::Sale]
```

```
SearchString IN ['','=><']

No[i] IN ['5'..'9']

"FA Posting Date" IN [01010001D..12312008D]
```

Here is another example of what IN used in an expression might look like:

```
TestString IN ['a'..'d','j','q','l'..'p'];
```

If the value of TestString were a or m, then this expression would evaluate to TRUE. If the value of TestString were z, then this expression would evaluate to FALSE. Note that the Data Type of the search value must be the same as the Data Type of the Valueset.

Precedence of operators

When expressions are evaluated by the C/AL compiler, the parsing routines use a predefined precedence hierarchy to determine what operators to evaluate first, what to evaluate second, and so forth. That precedence hierarchy is provided in the NAV **Developer and IT Pro Help** section *C/AL Operators – Operator Hierarchy*, but for convenience, the information is repeated here, in the following table:

C/AL Operator Precedence Hierarchy		
Sequence	**Symbols**	
1	.	Member (Fields in Records, etc)
	[]	Indexing
	()	Parenthetical Grouping
	::	Scope
	@	Case-insensitive
2		Unary instances of:
	NOT	Logical Not
	+	Positive value
	-	Negating value
3	*	Multiplication
	/	Division
	DIV	Integer division
	MOD	Modulus
	AND	Logical AND
	XOR	Logical Exclusive OR
4	+	Addition or Concatenation
	-	Subtraction
	OR	Logical OR
5	>	Greater than
	<	Less than
	>=	Greater than or equal to
	<=	Less than or equal to
	<>	Not equal to
	IN	IN Valueset
6	..	Range

For complex expressions, we should always freely use parentheses to make sure the expressions are evaluated the way we intend.

Frequently used C/AL functions

It's time to learn some more of the standard functions provided by C/SIDE. We will focus on some frequently used functions: MESSAGE, ERROR, CONFIRM, and STRMENU.

There is a group of functions in C/AL called **Dialog** functions. The purpose of these functions is to allow for communications (that is, dialog) between the system and the user. In addition, the Dialog functions can be useful for quick and simple testing / debugging. In order to make it easier for us to proceed with our next level of C/AL development work, we're going to take time now to learn about those four dialog functions. None of these functions will operate if the C/AL code is running on the NAV Application Server as it has no GUI available. To handle such situation in previous versions of NAV, the Dialog function statements had to be conditioned with the GUIALLOWED function to check whether or not the code is running in a GUI allowed environment. If the code was being used in a Web Service or NAS, it would not be GUIALLOWED. However in NAV 2015, NAS and Web Services simply ignore the Dialogue functions.

In each of these functions, data values can be inserted through use of a substitution string. The substitution string is the % (percent sign) character followed by the number 1 through 10, located within a message text string. That could look like the following (assuming the local currency was defined as USD):

```
MESSAGE('A message + a data element to display = %1', "OrderAmount");
```

If the OrderAmount value was $100.53, the output from the preceding would be:

```
A message + a data element to display = $100.53
```

We can have up to ten substitution strings in one dialog function. The use of substitution strings and their associated display values is optional. We can use any one of the Dialog functions to display a completely predefined text message with nothing variable. Use of a Text Constant (accessed through **View | C/AL Globals** in the **Text Constants** tab) for the message is recommended as it makes maintenance and multilanguage enabling easier.

The MESSAGE function

The MESSAGE function is easy to use for the display of transient data and can be placed almost anywhere in our C/AL code. All it requires of the user is acknowledgement that the message has been read. The disadvantage of messages is that they are not displayed until either the object completes its run or pauses for some other external action. Plus, if we inadvertently create a situation that generates hundreds or thousands of messages, there is no graceful way to terminate their display once they begin displaying.

It's common to use MESSAGE as the elementary trace tool. We can program the display of messages to occur only under particular circumstances and use them to view either the flow of processing (by outputting simple identifyng codes from different points in our logic) or to view the contents of particular data elements through multiple processing cycles.

MESSAGE has the following syntax: MESSAGE (String [, Value1] , ...]), where there are as many ValueX entries as there are %X substitution strings (up to ten).

Here is a sample debugging message:

```
MESSAGE('Loop %1, Item No. %2',LoopCounter,"Item No.");
```

The display would look similar to the following image (when the counter was 14 and the **Item No. was BX0925**):

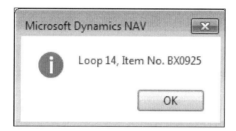

 When MESSAGE is used for debugging, make sure all the messages are removed before releasing the object to production.

The ERROR function

When an ERROR function is invoked, the execution of the current process terminates, the message is immediately displayed, and the database returns to the status it had following the last (implicit or explicit) COMMIT function as though the process calling the ERROR function had not run at all.

We can use the ERROR function in combination with the MESSAGE function to assist in repetitive testing. The MESSAGE functions can be placed in code to show what is happening with an ERROR function placed just prior to where the process would normally complete. Because the ERROR function rolls back all database changes, this technique allows us to run through multiple tests against the same data without any time-consuming backup and restoration of our test data. The enhanced Testing functionality built into NAV 2015 can accomplish the same things in a much more sophisticated fashion, but sometimes there's room for a temporary, simple approach.

An ERROR function call is formatted almost exactly like a MESSAGE call. ERROR has the syntax ERROR (String [, Value1] ,...]) where there are as many ValueX entries as there are %X substitution strings (up to ten). If the preceding MESSAGE was an ERROR function instead, the code line would be:

```
ERROR('Loop %1, Item No. %2',LoopCounter,"Item No.");
```

The display would look as shown in the following screenshot:

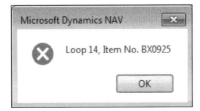

The big X in a bold red circle tells us that this is an ERROR message, but some users might not immediately realize that. We can increase the ease of ERROR message recognition by including the word ERROR in our message, as seen in the following screenshot:

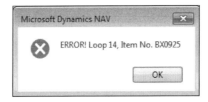

Even in the best of circumstances, it is difficult for a system to communicate clearly with the users. Sometimes our tools, in their effort to be flexible, make it too easy for developers to take the easy way out and communicate poorly or not at all. For example, an ERROR statement of the form ERROR(' ') will terminate the run and roll back all data processing without even displaying any message at all. An important part of our job as developers is to ensure that our systems communicate clearly and completely.

The CONFIRM function

The third dialog function is the CONFIRM function. A CONFIRM function call causes processing to stop until the user responds to the dialog. In CONFIRM, we would include a question in our text because the function provides **Yes** and **No** button options. The application logic can then be conditioned on the user's response.

We can also use CONFIRM as a simple debugging tool to control the path the processing will take. Display the status of data or processing flow and then allow the operator to make a choice (**Yes** or **No**) that will influence what happens next. Execution of a CONFIRM function will also cause any pending MESSAGE outputs to be displayed before the CONFIRM function displays. Combined with MESSAGE and ERROR, creative use of CONFIRM can add to our elementary debugging/diagnostic toolkit.

CONFIRM has the following syntax:

```
BooleanValue :=  CONFIRM(String [, Default]  [, Value1]  ,...)
```

When we do not specify a value for Default, the system will choose FALSE (which displays as No). We should almost always choose that option as a Default that will do no damage if accepted inadvertently by an inattentive user. The Default choice is FALSE, which is often the safest choice (but TRUE may be specified by the programmer). There are as many ValueX entries as there are %X substitution strings (up to ten).

If we just code OK := CONFIRM(String), the Default choice will be False. Note that True and False appear onscreen as the active language equivalent of **Yes** and **No** (a feature that is consistent throughout NAV for C/AL Boolean values displayed from NAV code but not for RDLC report controls displayed by the report viewer see **NAV Developer and IT Pro Helps** *How to: Change the Printed Values of Boolean Variables*).

A CONFIRM function call with similar content as the preceding examples might look as shown in the following for the code and the display:

```
Answer := CONFIRM('Loop %1, Item No. %2\OK to continue?',TRUE,LoopCoun
ter,"Item No.");
```

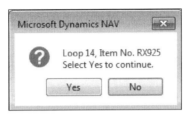

In typical usage, the CONFIRM function is part of, or is referred to, by a conditional statement that uses the Boolean value returned by the CONFIRM function.

An additional feature for on-screen dialogs is the use of the backslash (\) which forces a new line in the displayed message. This works throughout NAV screen display functions. Following are examples in **Text Constants Text063** and **Text064** in **Table 36 – Sales Header**:

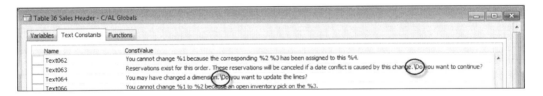

To display a backslash on-screen, we must put two of them in our message text string, \ \.

The STRMENU function

The fourth dialog function is the STRMENU function. A STRMENU function call also causes processing to pause while the user responds to the dialog. The advantage of the STRMENU function is the ability to provide several choices, rather than just two (**Yes** or **No**). A common use is to provide an option menu in response to the user pressing a command button.

STRMENU has the following syntax:

```
IntegerValue := STRMENU(StringVariable of Options separated by commas
[, OptionDefault][, Instruction])
```

Here `IntegerValue` will contain the user's selection and `OptionDefault` is an integer representing which option will be selected by default when the menu displays. If we do not provide an `OptionDefault`, the first option listed will be used as the default. `Instruction` is a text string which will display above the list of options. If the user responds *Cancel* or presses the *Esc* key, the value returned by the function is `0`.

Use of the `STRMENU` function eliminates the need to use a Page object when asking the user to select from a limited set of options. The `STRMENU` can also be utilized from within a report or Codeunit when calling a Page would restrict processing choices.

If we phrase our instruction as a question rather than simply an explanation, then we can use `STRMENU` as a multiple choice inquiry to the user.

Here is an example of `STRMENU` with the instruction phrased as a question:

```
OptionNo := STRMENU('Blue,Plaid,Yellow,Hot Pink,Orange,Unknown',6,
                    'Which of these is not like the others?');
```

Setting the default to 6 caused the sixth option (**Unknown**) to be the active selection when the menu is displayed.

Record functions

Now we will review some of the functions that we commonly use in Record processing.

The SETCURRENTKEY function

The syntax for SETCURRENTKEY is:

```
[BooleanValue :=] Record.SETCURRENTKEY(FieldName1,[FieldName2], ... )
```

The BooleanValue is optional. If we do not specify it and no matching key is found, a runtime error will occur.

Because NAV 2015 is based on the SQL Server database, SETCURRENTKEY simply determines the order in which the data will be presented for processing. The actual choice of the index to be used for the query is made by the SQL Server Query Analyzer. For this reason, it is very important that the data and resources available to the SQL Server Query Analyzer are well maintained. This includes maintaining the statistics that are used by the Query Analyzer, as well as making sure that efficient index options have been defined. Even though SQL Server picks the actual index, the developer's choice of the appropriate SETCURRENTKEY parameter can have a major affect on performance.

The indexes that are defined in SQL Server do not have to be the same as those defined in the C/AL table definition (for example, we can add additional indixes in SQL Server and not in C/AL, we can disable indixes in SQL Server but leave the matching keys enabled in C/AL, and so on). Any maintenance of the SQL Server indixes should be done through the NAV Table Designer using the NAV keys and properties, not directly in SQL Server. Even though the system may operate without problem, any mismatch between the application system and the underlying database system makes maintenance and upgrades more difficult and error prone. NAV defined keys are no longer required to support SIFT indexes because SQL Server can dynamically create the required indixes. However, depending on dynamic indixes for larger data sets can lead to bad performance. Good design is still our responsibility as developers.

The SETRANGE function

The SETRANGE function provides the ability to set a simple range filter on a field. SETRANGE syntax is as follows:

```
Record.SETRANGE(FieldName [,From-Value] [,To-Value]);
```

Prior to applying its range filter, the SETRANGE function removes any filters that were previously set for the defined field (filtering functions are defined in more detail in the next Chapter). If SETRANGE is executed with only one value, that one value will act as both the From and To values. If SETRANGE is executed without any From or To values, it will clear the filters on the field. This is a common use of SETRANGE. Some examples of the SETRANGE function in code are as follows:

- Clear the filters on Item.No.:

  ```
  Item.SETRANGE("No.");
  ```

- Filter to get only Items with a No. from 1300 through 1400:

  ```
  Item.SETRANGE("No.",'1300','1400');
  ```

- Or with the variable values from LowVal through HiVal:

  ```
  Item.SETRANGE("No.",LowVal,HiVal);
  ```

In order to be effective in a Query, SETRANGE must be called before the OPEN, SAVEASXML, and SAVEASCSV functions.

The SETFILTER function

SETFILTER is similar to, but much more flexible than, the SETRANGE function because it supports the application of any of the supported NAV filter functions to table fields. SETFILTER syntax is as follows:

```
Record.SETFILTER(FieldName, FilterExpression [Value],...);
```

The FilterExpression consists of a string (Text or Code) in standard NAV filter format including any of the operators < > * & | = in any legal combination. Replacement fields (%1, %2, …, %9) are used to represent the Values that will be inserted into FilterExpression by the compiler to create an operating filter formatted as though it were entered from the keyboard. Just as with SETRANGE, prior to applying its filter, the SETFILTER function clears any filters that were previously set for the defined field.

- Filter to get only Items with a No. from 1300 through 1400:

  ```
  Item.SETFILTER("No.",'%1..%2','1300','1400');
  ```

- Or with any of the variable values of LowVal, MedVal, or HiVal:

  ```
  Item.SETFILTER"No.",'%1|%2|%3',LowVal,MedVal,HiVal);
  ```

In order to be effective in a Query, SETFILTER must be called before the OPEN, SAVEASXML, and SAVEASCSV functions.

GET function

The GET function is the basic data retrieval function in C/AL. GET retrieves a single record, based on the Primary Key only. It has the following syntax:

```
[BooleanValue :=] Record.GET ( [KeyFieldValue1] [,KeyFieldValue2]
,...)
```

The parameter for the GET function is the Primary Key value (or all the values, if the Primary Key consists of more than one field).

Assigning the GET function result to a BooleanValue is optional. If the GET function is not successful (no record found) and the statement is not part of an IF statement, the process will terminate with a runtime error. Typically, therefore, the GET function is encased in an IF statement structured as shown in the following:

```
IF Customer.GET(NewCustNo) THEN ...
```

 GET data retrieval is not constrained by filters except for security filters (see **Help** *How to: Set Security Filters*). If there is a matching record in the table, GET will retrieve it.

FIND functions

The FIND family of functions is the general purpose data retrieval function in C/AL. It is much more flexible than GET, therefore more widely used. GET has the advantage of being faster as it operates only on an unfiltered direct access via the Primary Key, looking for a single uniquely keyed entry. There are two forms of FIND in C/AL, one a remnant from a previous database structure and the other designed specifically to work efficiently with SQL Server. Both are supported and we will find both in the standard code.

The older version of the FIND function has the following syntax:

```
[BooleanValue :=] RecordName.FIND ( [Which] ).
```

The newer SQL Server specific members of the FIND family have slightly different syntax, as we shall see shortly.

Just as with the GET function, assigning the FIND function result to a Boolean value is optional. But in almost all the cases, FIND is embedded in a condition that controls subsequent processing appropriately. Either way, it is important to structure our code to handle the instance where FIND is not successful.

Following are several important ways in which FIND differs from GET:

- FIND operates under the limits of whatever filters are applied on the subject field.

- FIND presents the data in the sequence of the key which is currently selected by default or by C/AL code.

- When FIND is used, the index used for the data reading is controlled by the SQL Server Query Analyzer.

- Different variations of the FIND function are designed specifically for use in different situations. This allows coding to be optimized for better SQL Server performance. All the FIND functions are described further in the **Help** section **C/AL Database Functions and Performance on SQL Server**.

Following are the various forms of FIND:

- FIND('-'): Finds the first record in a table that satisfies the defined filter and current key.

- FINDFIRST: Finds the first record in a table that satisfies the defined filter and defined key choice. Conceptually equivalent to FIND(' -') for a single record read but better for SQL Server when a filter or range is applied.

- FIND('+'): Finds the last record in a table that satisfies the defined filter and defined key choice. Often not an efficient option for SQL Server bcause it causes SQL Server to read a set of records when many times only a single record is needed. The exception is when a table is to be processed in reverse order. Then it is appropriate to use FIND(' +') with SQL Server.

- FINDLAST: Finds the last record in a table that satisfies the defined filter and current key. Conceptually equivalent to FIND(' +') but often much better for SQL Server as it reads a single record, not a set of records.

- FINDSET: The efficient way to read a set of records from SQL Server for sequential processing within a specified filter and range. FINDSET allows defining the standard size of the read record cache as a setup parameter, but normally defaults to reading 50 records (table rows) for the first server call. The syntax includes two optional parameters:

  ```
  FINDSET([ForUpdate][, UpdateKey]);
  ```

  The first parameter controls whether or not the read is in preparation for an update and the second parameter is TRUE when the first parameter is TRUE and the update is of key fields. FINDSET clears any FlowFields in the record read.

FIND ([Which]) options and the SQL Server alternates

Let's review the options of the FIND function using the following syntax:

```
[BooleanValue :=] RecordName.FIND ( [Which] )
```

The [Which] parameter allows the specification of which record is searched for relative to the defined key values. The defined key values are the set of values currently in the fields of the active key in the memory-resident record of table RecordName.

The following table lists the Which parameter options and prerequisites

FIND "which" parameter	FIND action	Search and primary key value prerequisite before FIND
=	Match the search key values exactly	All must be specified
>	Read the next record with key values larger than the search key values	All must be specified
<	Read the next record with key values smaller than the search key values	All must be specified
>=	Read the first record found with key values equal to or larger than the search key values	All must be specified
<=	Read the next record with key values equal to or smaller than the search key values	All must be specified
-	Read the first record in the selected set. If used with SQL Server, reads a set of records	No requirement
+	Read the last record in the selected set. If used with SQL Server, reads a set of records	No requirement

The following table lists the FIND options that are specific to SQL Server:

FINDxxxx options	FINDxxx action	Search and primary key value prerequisite before FINDxxx
FINDFIRST	Read the first record in a table based on the current key and filter. Used only for access to a single record, not in a read loop.	All must be specified
FINDLAST	Read the last record in a table based on the current key and filter. Used only for access to a single record, not in a read loop.	All must be specified
FINDSET	Read the record set specified. Syntax is `Record.FINDSET([ForUpdate][,UpdateKey])` Set `ForUpdate = True` if data to be updated Set `ForUpdate = True` and `UpdateKey = True` if a key field is to be updated If no parameter specified, both default to False	All must be specified

For all FIND options, the results always respect applied filters.

The `FIND('-')` function is sometimes used as the first step of reading a set of data, such as reading all the sales invoices for a single customer. In such a case, the `NEXT` function is used to trigger all subsequent data reads after the sequence is initiated with a `FIND('-')`. Generally `FINDSET` should be used rather than `FIND(' -' )`, however `FINDSET` only works for reading forward, not in reverse. Or use `FINDFIRST` if only the first record in the specified range is of interest.

One form of the typical C/SIDE database read loop is as follows:

```
IF MyData.FIND('-') THEN
 REPEAT
 Processing logic here
UNTIL MyData.NEXT = 0;
```

The same processing logic using the `FINDSET` function is as follows:

```
IF MyData.FINDSET THEN
 REPEAT
 Processing logic here
UNTIL MyData.NEXT = 0;
```

We will discuss the `REPEAT-UNTIL` control structure in more detail in the next chapter. Essentially, it does what it says: "repeat the following logic until the defined condition is true". For the `FIND-NEXT` read loop, the `NEXT` function provides both the definition of how the read loop will advance through the table and when the loop is to exit.

When `DataTable.NEXT = 0`, it means there are no more records to be read. We have reached the end of the available data, based on the filters and other conditions that apply to our reading process.

The specific syntax of the `NEXT` function is `DataTable.NEXT(Step)`. DataTable is the name of the table being read. Step defines the number of records NAV will move forward (or backward) per read. The default `Step` is 1, meaning NAV moves ahead one record at a time, reading every record. A `Step` of 0 works the same as a `Step` of 1. If the `Step` is set to 2, NAV will move ahead two records at a time and the process will only be presented with every other record.

Step can also be negative, in which case NAV moves backwards through the table. This would allow us to do a `FIND('+')` for the end of the table, then a `NEXT(-1)` to read backwards through the data. This is very useful if, for example, we need to read a table sorted ascending by date and want to access the most recent entries first.

Conditional statements

Conditional statements are the heart of process flow structure and control.

The BEGIN–END compound statement

In C/AL, there are instances where the syntax only allows for use of a single statement. But a design may require the execution of several (or many) code statements.

C/AL provides at least two ways to address this need. One method is to have the single statement call a function that contains multiple statements.

However, inline coding is often more efficient to run and to understand. So C/AL provides a syntax structure to define a **Compound Statement** or **Block of code**. A compound statement containing any number of statements can be used in place of a single code statement.

A compound statement is enclosed by the reserved words BEGIN and END. The compound statement structure looks like this:

```
BEGIN
  <Statement 1>;
  <Statement 2>;
  ..
  <Statement n>;
END
```

The C/AL code contained within a BEGIN – END block should be indented two characters, as shown in the preceding code, to make it obvious that it is a block of code.

The IF–THEN–ELSE statement

IF is the basic conditional statement of most programming languages. It operates in C/AL similarly to how it works in other languages. The basic structure is: IF a conditional expression is true, THEN execute Statement-1 ELSE (if condition not true) execute Statement-2. The ELSE portion is optional. The syntax is:

```
IF <Condition> THEN <Statement-1> [ ELSE <Statement-2> ]
```

Note that the statements within the IF do not have terminating semicolons unless they are contained in a BEGIN – END framework. IF statements can be nested so that conditionals are dependent on the evaluation of other conditionals. Obviously, one needs to be careful with such constructs, because it is easy to end up with convoluted code structures that are difficult to debug and difficult for the developer following us to understand. In the next chapter, we will review the CASE statement which can make some complicated conditionals much easier to format and to understand.

As we work with the NAV C/AL code, we will see that often `<Condition>` is really an expression built around a standard C/AL function. This approach is frequently used when the standard syntax for the function is "Boolean value, function expression". Some examples are as follows:

- `IF Customer.FIND('+') THEN... ELSE...`
- `IF CONFIRM(' OK to update?' ,TRUE) THEN... ELSE...`
- `IF TempData.INSERT THEN... ELSE...`
- `IF Customer.CALCFIELDS(Balance,Balance(LCY)) THEN...`

Indenting code

Since we have just discussed the `BEGIN-END` compound statements and IF conditional statements, which also are compound (that is, containing multiple expressions), this seems a good time to discuss indenting code.

In C/AL, the standard practice for indenting subordinate, contained, or continued lines is relatively simple. Always indent such lines by two characters except where there are left and right parentheses to be aligned.

 To indent a block of code by two characters at a time, select it and click on the *Tab* key. To remove the indentation one character at a time, select the code and click on *Shift + Tab*.

In the following examples, the parentheses are not required in all the instances, but they don't cause any problems and can make the code easier to read:

```
IF (A <> B) THEN
   A := A + Count1
ELSE
   B := B + Count2;
Or:
IF (A <> B) THEN
   A := A + Count1;
Or:
IF (A <> B) THEN
BEGIN
   A := A + Count1;
   B := A + Count2;
   IF (C > (A * B)) THEN
     C := A * B;
END
ELSE
   B := B + Count2;
```

Some simple coding modifications

Now we're going to add some C/AL code to objects we've created for our WDTU application.

Adding field validation to a table

In *Chapter 4, Pages – the User's Interactive Interface*, we created Table 50010 – Radio Show Fan. We've decided that we want to be able to use this list for promotional activities such as having drawings for concert tickets. Of course we want to send the tickets to the winners at their mailing addresses. We didn't originally include those fields in our table design, so must add them now. To keep our design consistent with the standard product, we will model those fields after the equivalent ones in **Table 18 – Customer**. Our updated Table 50010 will look as shown in the following screenshot:

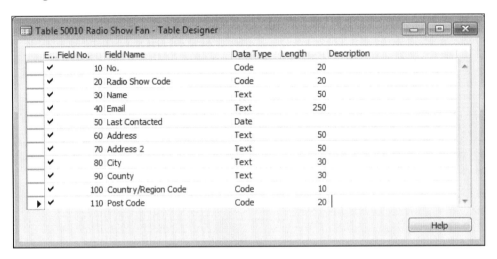

Part of modeling our **Table 50010 – Radio Show Fan** fields on those in **Table 18 – Customer** is faithfully copying the applicable properties. For example, the `TableRelation` property for the **Post Code** field in **Table 18** contains the following, which we should include for the Post Code in Table 50010:

```
IF (Country/Region Code=CONST()) "Post Code" ELSE IF (Country/Region
Code = FILTER(<>' ' ) "Post Code" WHERE (Country/Region Code = FIELD
(Country/Region Code))
```

When a **Radio Show Fan** record is added or the **Post Code** field is changed, we would like to update the appropriate address information. Let's start with some code in a Validation trigger of our table.

Since we modeled the address fields for our Fan record on the standard **Customer** table, let's look at the **Customer** table to see how Post Code validation is handled there. We can access the code through the **Table Designer** via **Object Designer** | **Table** | select **Table 18 - Customer** | **Design** | select **Field 91 - Post Code** | *F9*. We would see the following:

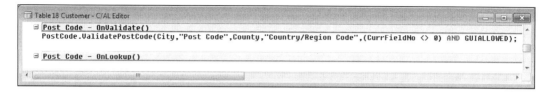

Looking at this C/AL code, we can see that the **OnValidate** trigger contains a call to a function in another object identified as **PostCode**. To find out what object **PostCode** actually is, we need to look in **C/AL Globals** (which we have sometimes referred to in this book as part of Working Storage).

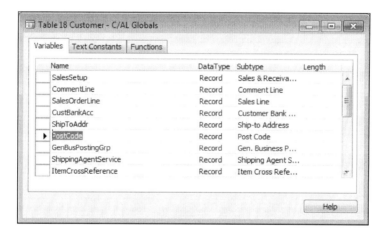

We see that PostCode is a reference to the Record (that is, table) **Post Code**. This is sort of like a treasure hunt at a birthday party. Now we follow that clue to the next stop, the Post Code table and the ValidatePostCode function that is used in the Customer Post Code validation trigger. To learn as much as we can about how this function works, how we should call it, and what information is available from the Post Code table (table 225), we will look at several things:

- The Post Code table field list
- The C/AL code for the function in which we are interested
- The list of functions available in the Post Code table
- The calling and return parameters for the ValidatePostCode function

Following are the screenshots for all these areas.

First, the field list in **Table 225 — Post Code**:

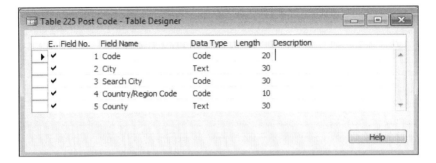

Next, the C/AL code for the `ValidatePostCode` function:

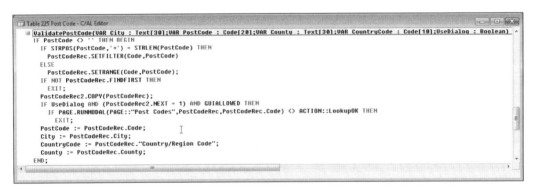

Now, the list of callable functions available within the Post Code table (this isn't critical information but helps us better understand the whole picture of the structure):

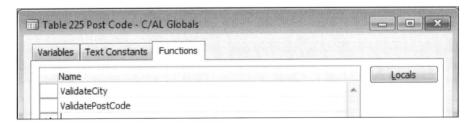

Next, a look at the calling **Parameters** for the `ValidatePostCode` function:

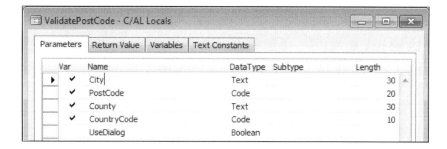

Finally, the **Return Value** for the `ValidatePostCode` function:

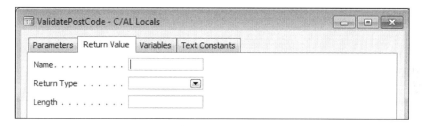

Doing some analysis of what we have dissected, we can see that the **ValidatePostCode** function call uses five calling **Parameters**. There is no Return Value. The function avoids the need for a `Return Value` by passing four of the Parameters `by Reference` (not `by Value`) as we can tell by the checkmark in the `Var` column. The function code updates the parameters that reference the data elements in the calling object. This interpretation is reinforced by studying the `ValidatePostCode` function C/AL code as well.

We conclude that we can just copy the code from the Post Code `OnValidate` trigger in the **Customer** table into the equivalent trigger in our Fan table. This will give us the Post Code maintenance we want. The result looks as shown the following screenshot (the variable `CurrFieldNo` is a System-Defined Variable leftover from previous versions retained for compatibility reasons):

If we press *F11* at this point, we will get an error message indicating that the variable **PostCode** has not been defined.

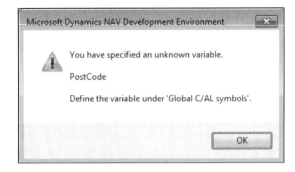

Obviously, we need to attend to this. The answer is shown in the next screenshot in the form of the **PostCode Global Variable** definition:

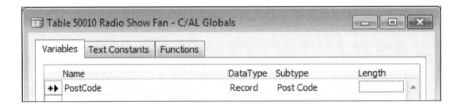

After we save this change (by simply moving focus from the new line of code to another line on the form or closing the form), press *F11* again. We should get no reaction other than a brief cursor blink when the object is compiled.

Because we haven't created a page for maintenance of Table 50010, we will test our work by Running the table. All we need to do is move to the **Post Code** field, click on it, and choose an entry from the displayed list of codes. The result should be the population of the **Post Code** field, the **Country/Region Code** field, and the **City** field. If we fill in the new data fields for some Fan records, our Radio Show Fan table would look like the following screenshot:

We've accomplished our goal. The way we've done it may seem disappointing. It didn't feel like we really designed a solution or wrote any code. What we did was find where in NAV the same problem was already solved, figured out how that solution worked, cloned it into our object, and we were done.

Each time we start this approach, first we should look at the defined Patterns (`https://community.dynamics.com/nav/w/designpatterns/105.nav-design-patterns-repository.aspx`) to see if any Patterns fit our situation. The benefit of starting with a Pattern is that the general structural definition has been defined for how this function should be done within NAV. Whether you find a matching Pattern or not, the next step is to find and study the applicable C/AL code within NAV.

Obviously, this approach doesn't work every time. But every time it does work is a small triumph of efficiency. This helps us to keep the structure of our solution consistent with the standard product, reuse existing code constructs, and minimize the debugging effort and chances of production problems. In addition, our modifications are more likely to work even if the standard base application function changes in a future version.

Adding code to a report

Most reports require some embedded logic to process user selected Options, calculate values, or access data in related tables. To illustrate some possibilities, we will extend our WDTU application to add a new report.

To support promotions giving away posters, concert tickets, and so on, we must further enhance the **Radio Show Fan** table and create a new report to generate mailing information from it. Our first step is to create a **New** report in the C/SIDE Report Designer, then define the data fields we want to include for mailings (including a Global variable of **CountryName**), and then **Save** and **Compile** the result as Report 50002 – Fan Promotion List.

Lay out the new Report Heading

Next, we will begin the design of the report layout in the SQL Server Report Builder (SSRB). From the C/SIDE RD, we click on **View | Layout** to open SSRB, ready to begin work on our layout. We'll begin by defining a report header.

Right-click in the layout work area (in the middle of the screen display), click on **Insert**, and then select Page Header. On the left-side of the menu, **ReportData** is displayed. Click on **Datasets** to display **DataSetResult**. Depending on what information we want to appear in the header, we might use fields from various parts of **ReportData**. If we had defined a **Label** to use for our Report Header, we could have done a drag-and-drop from the Label in the **Parameters** list. However, in our example, we dragged in a **Text Box** from the menu ribbon, which we placed in the upper left corner of the layout work area. We then typed a report name into that text box. Most of the other header fields were brought in from the *Report Data Built-in Fields* section. We used the **Execution Time**, **Page Number**, and **User ID** fields. We added another Text Box for the word Page in front of the Page Number.

Entering text data directly into the SSRB layout for heading labels (as we did here with the Report Header and Page label) is only appropriate for beginners or for reports that are for very short term use. Good report design practice requires that such values are defined in the C/SIDE RD, where multilanguage is supported and where such fields should be maintained. In C/SIDE RD, these values can be entered and maintained in the Report Label Designer accessed via **View | Labels**.

In the process of working on this sample report, we might want a different layout, to use Labels or add other features. Feel free to experiment and design your header to suit your own preferences. You will learn by the results of your experiments.

Fan Promotion List			Page	[&Pag
[&UserID]			[&ExecutionTime]	
To add an item to the report: on the Insert tab, click the item and drag dataset fields to the item.				

Save and test

At this point, it's time to save and test what we've done so far. Exit from the Report Builder. Save the report layout changes, exit the C/SIDE RD, and save and compile the report object.

This first test is very simple (assuming it works). **Run** Report 50002. The Report Request Page will appear in the RoleTailored client. Click **Preview** to see the Report display onscreen. The layout shown in the preceding screenshot will result in the report page seen in the following screenshot (or something similar):

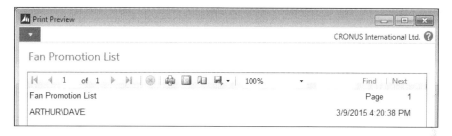

Lookup Related table data

Once we have a successful test of the report (heading only), we'll move on to laying out the body of the report. As we think through the data we want to include in a mailing address (Name, Address, Address 2, City, County (State), Country Name, Post Code), we realize that our table data includes Country Code, not Country Name. So we will look up the Country Name from the Country/Region table (Table 9). Let's take care of that now.

First we'll add a couple of Global Variables to our report. One of them will allow us to access the Country/Region table and the other will act as a holding place for the Country Name data we get from that table.

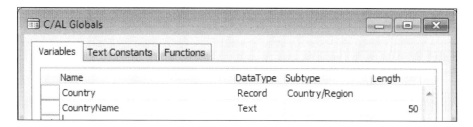

Each time we read a **Radio Show Fan** record, we'll look up the country name for that fan and store it in CountryName.

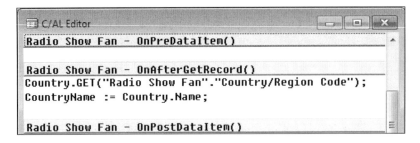

Now we can add the CountryName variable to the list of data elements attached to DataItem Radio Show Fan so it will be included in the data passed to the Report Builder and, when the report is run, to the Report Viewer.

While what we've done will probably work most of the time, how could it be made better? For one thing, shouldn't we handle the situation where there is no Country/Region Code in the fan record? And do we really need to move the country name to a Global variable instead of simply reporting it directly from the **Country/Region** record?

Both of these issues could be handled better. Look up the **GET** function in the Help to see what should be done in terms of error handling. And, after we work through the report as we're doing it here, enhance it by eliminating use of the **CountryName** Global variable. For now, let's just move on to completing an initial version of our report by creating the rest of our report layout in the SSRB.

Layout the new report body

Open the report layout in the SSRB. From the Ribbon, we'll grab a Table and drag it into the layout work area for the report body. The Table starts with only three columns. After positioning the Table to the top-left of the body, we will add four more columns to accommodate the seven data fields we want to include for each mailing address.

We will drag a data field from the `DataSet_Result` into each of the **Data Row Text Boxes** (the bottom row). In the top row, captions will appear. Where we want the displayed captions to be different than what fills in automatically, we'll either type in what we want (not very sophisticated) or delete the default captions and drag in captions from the Parameters list.

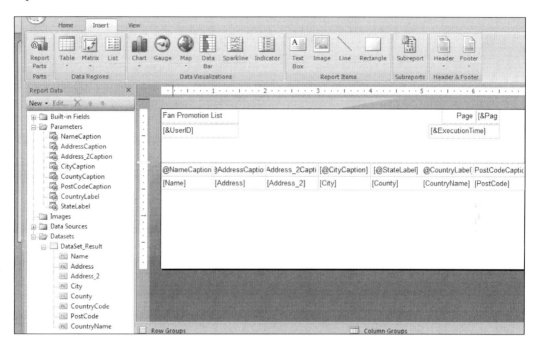

Among our caption options are the CountryLabel and StateLabel we see in the preceding and following images. These are the result of defining Labels in the C/SIDE RD Report Label Designer.

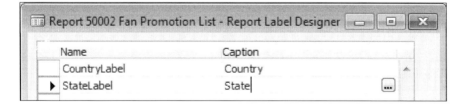

Save and test

After we lay out, **Save** and **Exit**, **Update**, and **Save** and **Compile**, it's time to do another test Run of our report in process. If we simply **Preview** without doing any filtering, we should see all of our test data address information (complete with Country Name).

Handling User-entered report options

Part of our report design includes allowing the user to choose fans based on some simple demographic data based on age and gender. We'll need to add two more fields to our Radio Show Fan table definition, one for Gender and the other for Birth Date, from which we can calculate the fan's age.

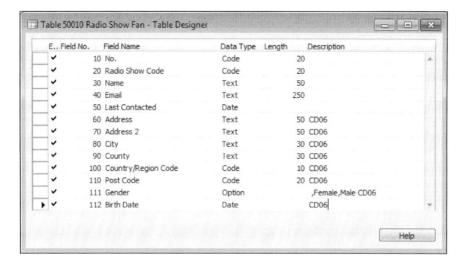

E..	Field No.	Field Name	Data Type	Length	Description
✔	10	No.	Code	20	
✔	20	Radio Show Code	Code	20	
✔	30	Name	Text	50	
✔	40	Email	Text	250	
✔	50	Last Contacted	Date		
✔	60	Address	Text	50	CD06
✔	70	Address 2	Text	50	CD06
✔	80	City	Text	30	CD06
✔	90	County	Text	30	CD06
✔	100	Country/Region Code	Code	10	CD06
✔	110	Post Code	Code	20	CD06
✔	111	Gender	Option		,Female,Male CD06
✔	112	Birth Date	Date		CD06

This back and forth process of updating first one object, then a different one, then yet another, is typical of the NAV development process much of the time. Exceptions are those cases where either the task is so simple that we think of everything the first time through or the cases where we create a completely documented, full featured design before any development starts (but nobody thinks of everything, there are always changes – our challenge is to keep the changes under control).

An advantage to the more flexible approach we are following is that it allows us to view (and share with others) intermediate versions of the application as it is developed. Design issues can be addressed as they come up and overlooked features can be considered mid-stream. Two downsides are the very real possibility of scope creep (the project growing uncontrollably) and poorly organized code. Scope creep can be controlled by good project management. If the first pass through results in poorly organized code, then a thoughtful refactoring is appropriate, cleaning up the code while retaining the design.

In order for the user to choose which Fan demographics will be used to filter the Fan data for a particular promotion, we will have to create a **Request Page** for entry of the desired criteria. This, in turn, requires the definition of a set of **Global Variables** in our Report object to support the **Request Page** data entry fields and as working variables for the age calculation and Fan selection. We've decided that if a Fan fits any of the individual criteria, we will include them. This makes our logic simpler. Our final **Global Variable** list in Report 50002 looks as shown in the following screenshot:

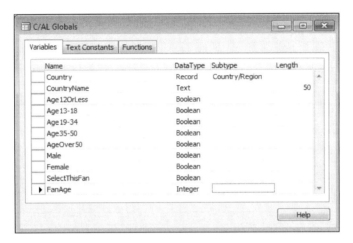

Defining the Request Page

Now, let's define the Request Page. Click **View** | **Request Page** and make the entries necessary to describe the page contents.

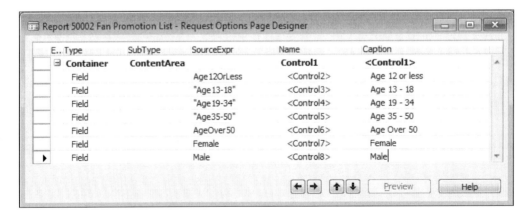

Finishing the processing code

Next, we will create the C/AL code to calculate a Fan's age (in years) based on his/her Birth Date and the current **WORKDATE**. The logic is simple: subtract the Birth Date from the **WORKDATE**. This gives a number of days. So we divide by 365 (not worrying about Leap Years) and round down to integer years (if someone is 25 years, 10 months and 2 days, we will just consider them 25). In the following code, we did the division as though the result were a decimal field. But because our math is integer, we could have used the simpler expression:

```
FanAge := ((WORKDATE - "Birth Date") DIV 365);
```

Finally, we'll write the code to check each Fan record data against our selection criteria, determining if we want to include that fan in our output data (SelectThisFan set to True). This code will select each fans who fits any of the checked criteria; there is no combination logic here. Following is our commented C/AL code for Report 50002:

```
Radio Show Fan - OnAfterGetRecord()
    //Look up the Country Name using the Country/Region Code
    Country.GET("Radio Show Fan"."Country/Region Code");
    CountryName := Country.Name;

    //Calculate the fan's age
    FanAge := ROUND(((WORKDATE - "Birth Date")/365),1.0,'<');

    //Select Fans to receive promotional material
    SelectThisFan := FALSE;
    IF Age12OrLess AND (FanAge <= 12) THEN
      SelectThisFan := TRUE;
    IF "Age13-18" AND (FanAge > 12) AND (FanAge < 19) THEN
      SelectThisFan := TRUE;
    IF "Age19-34" AND (FanAge > 18) AND (FanAge < 35) THEN
      SelectThisFan := TRUE;
    IF "Age35-50" AND (FanAge > 34) AND (FanAge < 51) THEN
      SelectThisFan := TRUE;
    IF "AgeOver50" AND (FanAge > 50) THEN
      SelectThisFan := TRUE;
    IF Male and (Gender = Gender::Male) THEN
      SelectThisFan := TRUE;
    IF Female and (Gender = Gender::Female) THEN
      SelectThisFan := TRUE;

    //If this Fan not selected, skip this Fan record on report
    IF SelectThisFan <> TRUE THEN
      CurrReport.SKIP;
```

After this version of the report is successfully tested, enhance it. Make the report support choosing any of the options (as it is now) or, at user option, choose a combination of age range plus gender. Hint: add additional checkboxes to allow the user to control which set of logic will be applied. We should also change the code to use the CASE statements (rather than IF statements). CASE statements often provide an easier to understand view of the logic.

Test the completed report

After we Save and Compile our report, we'll **Run** it again. Now we get an expanded **Request Option Page**. After we've check-marked a couple of the selection criteria.

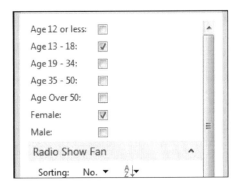

Now **Preview** our report. Using the sample data previously illustrated, our report output shows two records, one selected on the basis of Gender and the other on Age.

Output to Excel

An easy way to get the data to a mailing list is now to output it to Excel, where we can easily manipulate it into a variety of formats without further programming.

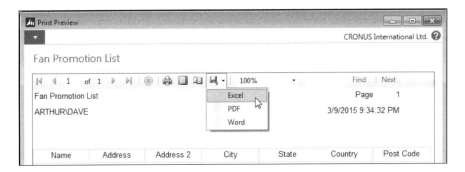

Here's what that output looks like in Excel:

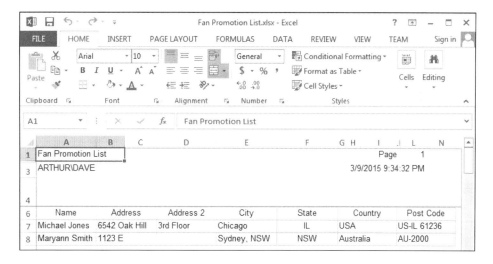

At this point we have a report that runs and is useful. It can be enhanced to support more complex selection criteria. As usual, there are a number of different ways to accomplish essentially the same result. Some of those paths would be significantly different for the developer, but nearly invisible to the user. Some might not even matter to the next developer who has to work on this report. What is important at this point is that the result works reliably, provides the desired output, operates with reasonable speed, and does not cost too much to create or maintain. If all these goals are met, most of the other differences are usually not very important.

Summary

> *"Furniture or gold can be taken away from you, but knowledge and a new language can easily be taken from one place to the other, and nobody can take them away from you."*
>
> *David Schwarzer*

In this chapter, we covered Object Designer navigation, along with navigation of the individual Designers (Table, Page, Report, and so on). We covered a number of C/AL language areas including functions and how they may be used, variables of various types (both development and system), basic C/AL syntax, expressions, and operators. Some of the essential C/AL functions that we covered included user dialogs, SETRANGE filtering, GET, variations of FIND, BEGIN-END for code structures, plus IF-THEN for basic process flow control.

Finally, we got some hands-on experience by adding validation code to a table and creating a new report that included the embedded C/AL code and a Request Page. In the next chapter, we will expand our exploration and practice in the use of C/AL. We will learn about additional C/AL functions, flow control structures, input/output functions, and filtering.

Review questions

Q.1. All NAV objects can contain C/AL code. True or False?

Q.2. What object type has a Wizard to "jump start" development?

    a.   Page

    b.   XMLport

    c.   Table

    d.   Report

Q.3. All C/AL Assignment statements include the symbol := . True or False?

Q.4. One setting defines how parameters are passed to functions, whether a parameter is passed by reference or by value. Choose that one setting's identity.

    a.   DataType

    b.   Subtype

    c.   Var

    d.   Value

Q.5. If an object type has a Wizard, we must start with the Wizard before proceeding to the object Designer form. True or False?

Q.6. C/AL code cannot be inserted into the RDLC generated by the SQL Server Report Builder (or Visual Studio Report Designer). True or False?

Q.7. When a table definition is changed, the "Force" option should always be used when saving the changes. True or False?

Q.8. Object numbers and names are so flexible that we can (and should) choose our own approach to numbering and naming. True or False?

Q.9. In what formats can objects be exported? Choose two.

      a. fob

      b. .txt

      c. .NET

      d. .XML

      e. .gif

Q.10. BEGIN – END are always required in IF statements. True or False?

Q.11. Which object export format should be used to transmit updates to client sites? Choose one.

      a. .fob

      b. .txt

      c. .NET

Q.12. All NAV development work starts from the Object Designer. True or False?

Q.13. Modifiable functions include which of the following? Choose two.

      a. Application Management

      b. DATE2MDY

      c. Mail

      d. STRLEN

Q.14. Report heading text can either be typed in manually or brought into SSRB via Label Parameters. True or False?

Q.15. Whenever possible, the controlling logic for managing data should be resident within the tables. True or False?

Q.16. Filter Wildcards include which three of the following:

      a. ?

      b. ::

      c. *

      d. ^

      e. @

Q.17. The choice of the proper version of the FIND statement can make a significant difference in processing speed. True or False?

Q.18. When we are working in the Object Designer, changing C/AL code, the Object Designer automatically backs up our work every few minutes so we don't have to do so. True or False?

Q.19. When an ERROR statement is executed, the user is given the choice to terminate processing, causing rollback, or to ignore the error and continue processing. True or False?

Q.20. Arithmetic Operators and Functions include which of the following? Choose two.

        a. *

        b. >

        c. =

        d. /

7
Intermediate C/AL

"A designer is an emerging synthesis of artist, inventor, mechanic, objective economist and evolutionary strategist."

– R. Buckminster Fuller

"Beauty of style and harmony and grace and good rhythm depend on simplicity."

– Plato

In the previous chapter, we learned enough C/AL to create a basic, operational set of code. In this chapter, we will learn about more C/AL functions and pick up a few more good habits along the way. If you are getting started as a professional NAV Developer, C/SIDE's built-in C/AL functions represent a significant portion of the knowledge that you will need on a day-to-day basis. If you are a manager or consultant needing to know what NAV can do for your business or your customer, an understanding of these functions will help you too.

Our goal is to competently manage I/O, create moderately complex program logic structures, and understand data filtering and sorting as handled in NAV and C/AL. Since the functions and features in C/AL are designed for business and financial applications, we can do a surprising amount of ERP work in NAV with a relatively small number of language constructs.

Keep in mind that anything discussed in this chapter relates only indirectly to those portions of NAV objects which contain no C/AL (for example, MenuSuites, **SQL Server Report Builder** (**SSRB**), and **Visual Studio Report Designer** (**VSRD**) report layouts). This chapter's goals are to:

- Review some C/AL development basics
- Learn about a variety of useful (and widely used) C/AL functions

- Better understand filtering
- Apply some of what we've learned to expand our WDTU applicationSome C/AL development tools

All internal NAV logic development is done in C/AL and all C/AL development is done in C/SIDE. Some user interface design is done by means of the SSRB/VSRD. And it is possible to have integrated .NET objects for a variety of purposes.

C/AL Symbol Menu

As an Integrated Development Environment (**IDE**), C/SIDE contains a number of tools designed to make our C/AL development effort easier. One of these is the C/AL Symbol Menu. When we are in one of the Object Designers where C/AL code is supported, C/AL Symbol Menu can be accessed via either the menu option **View** | **C/AL Symbol Menu** or by pressing *F5*.

The three-column display has variables and object categories in the left column. If the entry in the left column is an object or a variable of function type, then the center column contains subcategories for the highlighted left-column entry. The right column contains the set of functions that are a part of the highlighted center-column entry. In a few cases (such as BLOB fields), additional information is displayed in the columns further to the right. These columns are accessed through the arrows displayed just below the rightmost display column, as shown in the following screenshot:

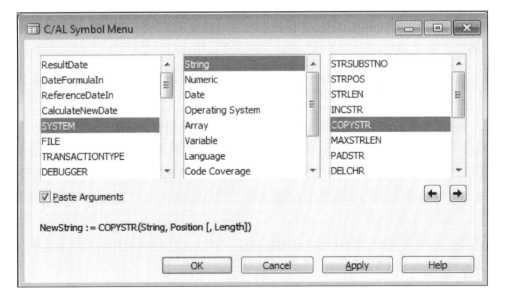

The **C/AL Symbol Menu** is a very useful multi-purpose tool for the developer. We can use it as a quick reference to see what C/AL functions are available to us, see the syntax of those functions, access **Help** on those functions, and view what other systems would refer to as the **Symbol Table**. We can also use the **C/AL Symbol Menu** as a source of variable names or function structures to paste into our code.

Use of the **C/AL Symbol Menu** for reference purposes is not only very helpful when we are a novice C/AL developer but also after we become experienced developers. It is a guide to the inventory of available code tools with some very handy built-in programming aids.

The **C/AL Symbol Menu** displays the highlighted function's syntax at the bottom left of the screen. It also provides quick access to **Developer and IT Pro Help** to further study the highlighted function and its syntax. Pressing *F1* may bring up the general **Developer and IT Pro Help** rather than a specific entry (or it may bring up an entry only somewhat related to the focus location.

The second use of the **C/AL Symbol Menu** is as a symbol table. The symbol table for our object is visible in the left column of the **C/AL Symbol Menu** display. The displayed symbol set (that is, variable set) is context sensitive. It will include all system-defined symbols, all our **Global** symbols, and the **Local** symbols from the function that had focus at the time we accessed the **C/AL Symbol Menu**. Though it would be useful, there is no way within the Symbol Menu to see all Local variables in one view. The Local symbols will be at the top of the list, but we have to know the name of the first Global symbol to determine the scope of a particular variable (that is, if an entry appears in the symbol list before the first Global, it is a Local variable, otherwise it's Global).

The third use for the C/AL Symbol Menu is as a code template with a paste function option available. This function will be enabled if we have accessed **C/AL Symbol Menu** from **C/AL Editor**. Paste is initiated by pressing either the **Apply** button or the **OK** button, or highlighting and double-clicking. In each of these cases, the element with focus will be pasted into our code. Apply will leave the **Symbol Menu** open and **OK** will close it (double-clicking on the element has the same effect as clicking on **OK**).

If the element with focus is a simple variable, then that variable will be pasted into our code. If the element is a function whose syntax appears at the lower left of the screen, the result of the paste action (that is, Apply or **OK** or double-click) depends on whether **Paste Arguments** (just below the leftmost column) is checked or not. If the **Paste Arguments** checkbox is not selected, then only the function itself will be pasted into our code. If the **Paste Arguments** checkbox is selected (as shown in the preceding screenshot), then the complete syntax string, as shown, will be pasted into our code. This can be a very convenient way to create a template to help us enter the correct parameters with the correct syntactical structure and punctuation more quickly.

When we are in the C/AL Symbol Menu, we can focus on a column, click on a letter, and jump to the next column field in sequence that starts with that letter. This acts as a limited Search substitute, like an assisted browse.

Internal documentation

When we are creating or modifying software, we should always document what we have done. It is often difficult for developers to spend much time (or, money) on documentation because many don't enjoy doing it and the benefits are uncertain. A reasonable goal is to provide enough documentation so that a knowledgeable person following us can understand what we have done as well as the reasons why.

If we choose good variable names, the C/AL code will tend to be self-documenting. If we lay out our code neatly, use indentation consistently, and localize logical elements in functions, then the flow of our code should be easy to read. We should also include comments which describe the functional reason for the change. This will help the next person in this code to not only be able to follow the logic of the code, but to understand the business reasons for it as well.

In case of a brand-new function, a simple statement of purpose is often all that is necessary. In case of a modification, it is extremely useful to have comments providing a functional definition of what the change is intended to accomplish, as well as a description of what has been changed. If there is external documentation of the change, including a design specification, the comments in the code should refer to this external documentation.

In any case, the primary focus should be on the functional reason for the change, not just the technical reason. Any good programmer can study the code and understand what was changed, but without the documentation describing why the change was made, the task of the next person to maintain or upgrade that code will be made much more difficult.

In the following example, the documentation is for a brand-new report. The comments are in the **Documentation** section, where there are no format rules, except for those we impose. This is a new report, which we created in *Chapter 6, Introduction to C/SIDE and C/AL*. The comment is coded to indicate the organization making the change (in this case **CD**) and a sequence number for this change. In this case, we are using a two digit number (**06**) for the change, plus the version number of the change, **00**; hence, we start with **CD.06.00**, followed by the date of the change. Some organizations also include an identifier for the developer in the **Documentation** section comments.

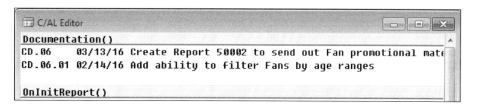

We can make up our own standard format that will identify the source and date of the work, but we should have a standard and use it. When we add a new data element to an existing table, the **Description** property should receive the same modification identifier that we would place in the code comments.

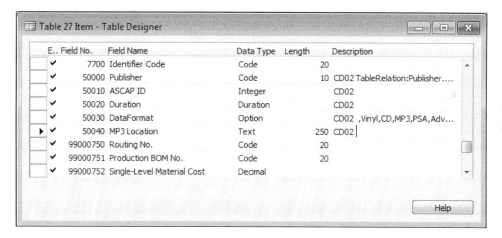

When we make a subsequent change to an object, we should document that change in the Documentation trigger and also in the code, as described earlier.

Inline comments can be made in two ways. The most visible way is to use a //
character sequence (two forward slashes). The text that follows the slashes on that
line will be treated as a comment by the compiler; it will be ignored. If the comment
spans multiple physical lines, each line of the comment must also be preceded by
two forward slashes.

In the following image we have used // to place comments inline to identify a change:

Here we have made the modification version number **01**, resulting in a change
version code of **CD.07.01**. In the following code, modifications are highlighted by
bracketing the additional code with comment lines containing the modification
identifier, and start and end text indicators. Published standards do not include
the dashed lines shown here, but doing something that makes comments stand out
makes it easier to spot modifications when we are visually scanning the code.

A second way to place a comment within the code is to surround the comment with
a matched pair of braces { }. Because braces are less visible than the slashes, we
should use // when our comment is relatively short. If we decide to use { }, it's a
good idea to insert a // comment at least at the beginning and end of the material
inside the braces, to make the comments more visible. Some experienced developers
recommend using // on all removed code lines, to make the deletions easier to spot
later. Evolving standards recommend against any use of the braces for commenting
out code.

For example:

```
{//CD.07.02 start deletion ------------
//CD.07.02 Replace validation with a call to an external function
...miscellaneous C/AL validation code
//CD.07.02 end deletion ------------ }
```

When we delete code that is part of the original Microsoft distribution, we should leave the original statements in place but commented out, so the old code is inoperative (an exception to this may apply if a source code control system is in use which tracks all the changes). The same concept applies when we change the existing code; leave the original code in place, but commented out, with the new version being inserted as shown in the following screenshot. This approach does not necessarily apply to code that we ourselves created originally.

```
SetStyle() : Text
  IF Open THEN BEGIN
    IF WORKDATE > "Due Date" THEN
      EXIT('Unfavorable')
  END ELSE
  //CD07.11 ----start----
  //   IF "Closed at Date" > "Due Date" THEN
    IF "Closed at Date" >= "Due Date" THEN
  //CD07.11 ---- end ----|
      EXIT('Attention');
  EXIT('');
```

Comment Selection and **Uncomment Selection** options have been added to the Edit menu option list in NAV 2015. When we are commenting or uncommenting large chunks of code, these can be useful. See the Help **C/AL Comments**.

When we make changes such as these, we don't want to forget to also update the object version numbers located in the Version List field on the **Object Designer** screen. It's also a good idea to take advantage of one of the previously mentioned source code management tools to track modifications.

From our previous experience, we know that the format of the internal documentation is not what's critical. What is critical is that the documentation exists, is consistent in format, and accurately describes the changes that have occurred. The internal documentation should be a complement to external documentation which defines the original functional requirements, validation specifications, and recommended operating procedures.

Yet another approach, one that is especially suitable for modifications that exceed a small number of lines of code or which will be called from multiple places, is to create a new function for the modification, name the function so that its purpose is obvious, then call the function from the point of use. In this case, that function might be named something like CheckDatePrizeLastWon and would contain the C/AL code shown earlier, specifically IF (WORKDATE - "Last Prize Date") < 30 THEN CurrReport.SKIP. In this case, the function would only have one line of code (not a good example), we would pass in the Last Prize Date value and the function would return a Boolean value telling us whether or not the individual was eligible for a new prize.

Validation functions

C/AL includes a number of utility functions designed to facilitate data validation or initialization. Some of these functions are:

- TESTFIELD
- FIELDERROR
- INIT
- VALIDATE

TESTFIELD

The TESTFIELD function is widely used in standard NAV code. With TESTFIELD, we can test a variable value and generate an error message in a single statement if the test fails. The syntax is:

```
Record.TESTFIELD (Field, [Value] )
```

If a Value is specified and the field does not contain that value, the process terminates with an error condition and the error message is issued.

If no Value is specified, the field contents are checked for values of zero or blank. If the field is zero or blank, then that an error message is issued.

The advantage of TESTFIELD is the ease of use and consistency in the code and the message displayed. The disadvantage is that the error message is not as informative as we might provide as a careful developer.

The following screenshot of TESTFIELD usage is from **Table 18 – Customer**. This code checks to make sure that the Sales Order field Status is equal to the option value Open before allowing the value of the field "Sell-to Customer No." to be entered.

```
TESTFIELD(State,Status::Open);
```

An example of the error message generated when attempting to change the "Sell-to Customer No." when Status is not equal to the option value Open, is as follows:

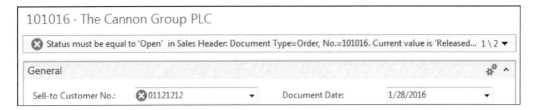

FIELDERROR

Another function very similar to the TESTFIELD function is FIELDERROR. But where TESTFIELD performs a test and terminates with either an error or an **OK** result, FIELDERROR presumes that the test was already performed and the field failed the test. FIELDERROR is designed to display an error message, then terminate the process. This approach is followed in much of the NAV logic, especially in the Posting Codeunits (for example, Codeunits 12, 80, 90). The syntax is as follows:

```
TableName.FIELDERROR(FieldName[,OptionalMsgText]);
```

If we include our own message text by defining a Text Constant in the **C/AL Globals | Text Constants** tab (so the code can be multilingual), we will have:

```
Text001    must be greater than Start Time
```

Then we can reference the Text Constant in code:

```
IF Rec."End Time" <= "Start Time" THEN
  Rec.FIELDERROR("End Time",Text001);
```

The result is an error message from FIELDERROR like that shown in the following screenshot:

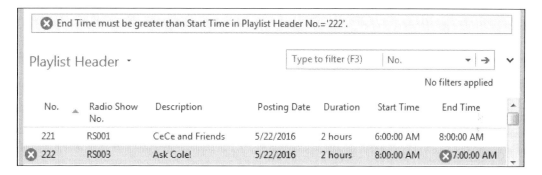

An error message that simply identifies the data field, but does not reference a message text, looks like the following screenshot, with the record key information displayed:

Because the error message begins with the name of the field, we need to be careful that our Text Constant is structured to make the resulting error message easy to read.

If we don't include our own message text, the default message comes in two flavors. The first instance is the case where the referenced field is not empty. Then the error message presumes that the error is due to a wrong value, as shown in the previous image. In the case where the referenced data field is empty, the error message logic presumes the field should not be empty, as shown in the following image:

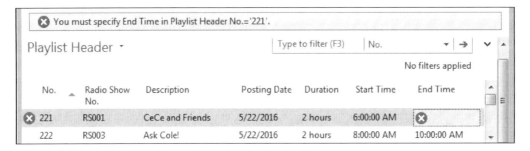

INIT

The INIT function initializes a record in preparation for its use, typically in the course of building a record entry to insert in a table. The syntax is:

```
Record.INIT;
```

All the data fields in the record are initialized as follows:

- Fields which have a defined InitValue property are initialized to the specified value.

- Fields which do not have a defined `InitValue` are initialized to the default value for their data type.

- Primary key fields and timestamps are not automatically initialized. If they contain values, those will remain. If new values are desired, they must be assigned in code.

VALIDATE

The syntax of the `VALIDATE` function is as follows:

```
Record.VALIDATE ( Field [, Value] )
```

`VALIDATE` will fire the `OnValidate` trigger of `Record.Field`. If we have specified a `Value`, that `Value` is assigned to the field and the field validations are invoked.

If we don't specify a `Value`, then the field validations are invoked using the field value that already exists in the field. This function allows us to easily centralize our code design around the table, which is one of NAV's strengths.

For example, if we were to code changing `Item."Base Unit of Measure"` to another unit of measure, the code should make sure the change is valid. We should get an error if the new unit of measure has any quantity other than 1 (because that is a requirement of the **Base Unit of Measurement** field). Making the unit of measure change with a simple assignment statement would not catch a quantity error.

Following are the two forms of using `VALIDATE` which give the same end result:

- `Item.VALIDATE("Base Unit of Measure",'Box');`

- `Item."Base Unit of Measure" := 'Box';`

  `Item.VALIDATE("Base Unit of Measure");`

Date and Time functions

NAV provides a considerable number of Date and Time functions. We will cover those in the following list. They are are more commonly used, especially in the context of accounting date sensitive activity.

- `TODAY`, `TIME`, and `CURRENTDATETIME` functions

- `WORKDATE` functions

- `DATE2DMY`, `DATE2DWY`, `DMY2DATE`, `DWY2DATE`, and `CALCDATE` functions

TODAY, TIME, and CURRENTDATETIME functions

TODAY retrieves the current system date as set in the operating system. TIME retrieves the current system time as set in the operating system. CURRENTDATETIME retrieves the current date and time in the DATETIME format, which is stored in UTC international time (formerly referenced as GMT or Greenwich Mean Time) and then displayed in local time. If we are using the Windows client, this uses the time in the NAV Client. If the system operates in multiple time zones at one time, search **Microsoft Dynamics NAV Help** on time zone for several references on how to deal with multiple time zones.

The syntax for each of these is as follows:

```
DateField := TODAY;
TimeField := TIME;
DateTimeField := CURRENTDATETIME;
```

These are often used for date- and time-stamping transactions or for filling in default values in fields of the appropriate data type. For data entry purposes, the current system date can be entered by simply typing the letter **T** or the word **TODAY** in the date entry field (this is not a case-sensitive entry). NAV will automatically convert this entry to the current system date.

The undefined date in NAV 2015 is represented by the earliest valid DATETIME in SQL Server, which is January 1, 1753 00:00:00:000. The undefined date in NAV is represented as 0D (zero D, as in Days), with subsequent dates handled through December 31, 9999. A date outside this range will result in a run-time error.

The Microsoft Dynamics NAV undefined time (0T) is represented by the same value as an undefined date (0D). If a two digit year is entered or stored, and has a value of 30 to 99, it is assumed to be in the 1900s. If the two digit date is in the range of 00 to 29, then it is treated as a 2000s date.

WORKDATE function

Many standard NAV routines default dates to **Work Date** rather than to the system date. When a user logs into the system, the Work Date is initially set equal to the System Date. But at any time, the operator can set the Work Date to any date by accessing the Application Menu, clicking on **Set Work Date...,** and then entering the new Work Date.

The user can also click on the **Work Date** displayed in the status bar at the bottom of the RTC. The following screenshot shows the **Set Work Date** screen:

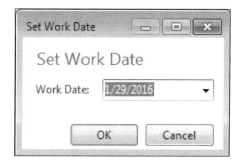

For data entry purposes, the current Work Date can be entered by the operator by simply typing the letter w or W, or the word WORKDATE, in the date entry field. NAV will automatically convert that entry to the current Work Date.

The syntax for getting the current WorkDate value from within the C/AL code is as follows:

```
DateField := WORKDATE;
```

The syntax for setting the WorkDate to a new date from within the C/AL code is as follows:

```
WORKDATE(newdate);
```

DATE2DMY function

DATE2DMY allows us to extract the sections of a date (Day of the month, Month, and Year) from a Date field. The syntax is as follows:

```
IntegerVariable := DATE2DMY ( DateField, ExtractionChoice )
```

The `IntegerVariable` and `DateField` fields are just what their names imply. The `ExtractionChoice` parameter allows us to choose which value (Day, Month, or Year) will be assigned to the `IntegerVariable`. The following table provides the `DATE2DMY` extraction choices:

DATE2DMY extraction choice	Integer value result
1	2 digit day (1 – 31)
2	2 digit month (1 – 12)
3	4 digit year

DATE2DWY function

`DATE2DWY` allows us to extract the sections of a date (Day of the week, Week of the year, and Year) from a Date field in exactly the same fashion as `DATE2DMY`. The `ExtractionChoice` parameter allows us to choose which value (Day, Week, or Year) will be assigned to the `IntegerVariable`, as shown in the following table:

DATE2DWY extraction choice	Integer value result
1	2 digit day (1 – 7 for Monday – Sunday)
2	2 digit week (1 – 53)
3	4 digit year

DMY2DATE and DWY2DATE functions

`DMY2DATE` allows us to create a date from integer values (or defaults) representing the day of the month, month of the year, and the four-digit year. If an optional parameter (`MonthValue` or `YearValue`) is not specified, the corresponding value from the **System Date** is used. The syntax is as follows:

```
DateVariable := DMY2DATE ( DayValue [, MonthValue] [, YearValue] )
```

The only way to have the function use the **Work Date** values for Month and Year is to extract those values and then use them explicitly. An example is as follows:

```
DateVariable := DMY2DATE(22,DATE2MDY(WORKDATE,2),DATE2MDY(WORKDATE,3))
```

 This example also illustrates how expressions can be built up of nested expressions and functions. We have WORKDATE within DATE2MDY within DMY2DATE.

`DWY2DATE` operates similarly to `DMY2DATE`; allowing us to create a date from integer values representing the day of the week (from 1 to 7 representing Monday to Sunday), week of the year (from 1 to 53) followed by the four-digit year. The syntax is as follows:

```
DateVariable := DWY2DATE ( DayValue [, WeekValue] [, YearValue] )
```

An interesting result can occur for week 53 because it can span two years. By default, such a week is assigned to the year in which it has four or more days. In that case, the year of the result will vary depending on the day of the week in the parameters (in other words, the year of the result may be one year greater than the year specified in the parameters). This is a perfect example of why thorough testing of our code is always appropriate.

CALCDATE function

`CALCDATE` allows us to calculate a date value assigned to a Date data type variable. The calculation is based on a Date Expression applied to a Base Date (Reference Date). If we don't specify a `BaseDateValue`, the current system date is used as the default date. We can specify the `BaseDateValue` either in the form of a variable of data type Date or as a Date constant.

The syntax for `CALCDATE` is as follows:

```
DateVariable := CALCDATE ( DateExpression [, BaseDateValue])
```

There are a number of ways in which we can build a `DateExpression`. The rules for the `CALCDATE` function `DateExpression` are similar to the rules for **DateFormula** described in *Chapter 3*, *Data Types and Fields*.

If there is a `CW`, `CM`, `CP`, `CQ`, or `CY` (Current Week, Current Month, Current Period, Current Quarter, or Current Year) parameter in an expression, then the result will be evaluated based on the `BaseDateValue`. If we have more than one of these in our expression, the results are unpredictable. Any such expression should be thoroughly tested before releasing to the users.

If our Date Expression is stored in a `DateFormula` variable (or a Text or Code variable with the **DateFormula** property set to **Yes**), then the Date Expression will be language independent. Also, if we create our own Date Expression in the form of a string constant within our inline C/AL code, surrounding the constant with < > delimiters as part of the string, it will make the constant language independent. Otherwise, the Date Expression constant will be language dependent.

Regardless of how we have constructed our `DateExpression`, it is important to test it carefully and thoroughly before moving on. Incorrect syntax will result in a runtime error. One easy way to test is by using a Report whose sole task is to evaluate our expression and display the result. If we want to try different Base Dates, we can use the Request Page, accept the Base Date as input, then calculate and display the `DateVariable` in the `OnValidate` trigger.

Some sample `CALCDATE` expression evaluations are as follows:

- `('<CM>',031016D)` will yield 03/31/2016; that is, the last day of the Current Month for the date 3/10/2016
- `('<-WD2>',031216D)` will yield 03/08/2016; that is, the WeekDay #2 (the previous Tuesday) before the date 3/12/2016
- `('<CM+1D>',BaseDate)`, where `BaseDate` equals 03/10/16, will yield 04/01/2016; that is, the last day of the month of the Base Date plus one day (the first day of the month following the Base Date)

Data conversion and formatting functions

Some data type conversions are handled in the normal process flow by NAV without any particular attention on part of the Developer (for example, Code to Text, Char to Text). Some data type conversions can only be handled through C/AL functions. Formatting is included because it can also include a data type conversion. Rounding does not do a data type conversion, but does result in a change in format (the number of decimal places).

- ROUND function
- FORMAT function
- EVALUATE function

ROUND

The ROUND function allows us to control the rounding precision for a decimal expression. The syntax for the ROUND function is as follows:

```
DecimalResult := ROUND (Number [, Precision] [, Direction] )
```

Here, `Number` is what is being rounded, `Precision` spells out the number of digits of decimal precision, and `Direction` indicates whether to round up, round down, or round to the nearest number. Some examples of `Precision` values are as follows:

Precision value	Rounding effect
100	To a multiple of 100
1	To an integer format
.01	To two decimal places (the US default)
0.01	Same as for .01
.0001	To four decimal places

If no `Precision` value is specified, the Rounding default is controlled by a value set in **General Ledger Setup** in the **Appln. Rounding Precision** field on the **Application** tab. If no value is specified, Rounding will default to two decimal places. If the precision value is (for example) .04 rather than .01, the rounding will be done to multiples of 4 at the number of decimal places specified.

The options available for the Direction value are shown in the following table:

Direction value (a text value)	Rounding effect
'='	Round to the nearest (mathematically correct and the default)
'>'	Round up
'<'	Round down

Refer to the following statement:

```
DecimalValue := ROUND (1234.56789,0.001,'<')
```

This would result in a `DecimalValue` containing 1234.567. However, refer now to the following statements:

```
DecimalValue := ROUND (1234.56789,0.001,'=')
DecimalValue := ROUND (1234.56789,0.001,'>')
```

These would each result in a `DecimalValue` containing 1234.568.

FORMAT function

The FORMAT function converts of an expression of any data type (for example, integer, decimal, date, option, time, Boolean) into a formatted string. The syntax is as follows:

```
StringField := FORMAT( ExpressionToFormat [, OutputLength]
    [, FormatString or FormatNumber])
```

The formatted output of `ExpressionToFormat` will be assigned to the output `StringField`. The optional parameters control the conversion according to a complex set of rules. These rules can be found in the **Developer and IT Pro Help** file for the `FORMAT` function and `FORMAT` Property. Whenever possible, we should always apply `FORMAT` in its simplest form. The best way to determine the likely results of a `FORMAT` expression is to test it through a range of the values to be formatted. We should make sure that we include the extremes of the range of possible values in our testing.

The optional `OutputLength` parameter can be zero (which is the default), a positive integer, or a negative integer. The typical `OutputLength` value is either zero, in which case the defined format is fully applied, or it is a figure designed to control the maximum character length and padding of the formatted string result.

The last optional parameter has two mutually exclusive sets of choices. One set, represented by integer `FormatNumber`, allows the choice of a particular predefined (standard) format, of which there are four to nine choices depending on the `ExpressionToFormat` data type. The format parameter of number 9 is used for XMLport data exporting. Use of the optional number 9 parameter will convert C/SIDE format data types into XML standard data types. The other set of choices allows us to build our own format expression.

The **Developer and IT Pro Help** information for the `FORMAT` property provides a relatively complete description of the available tools from which we can build our own format expression. The `FORMAT` property Help also provides a complete list of the predefined format choices as well as a good list of example formats and formatted data results.

Note that a `FORMAT` function which cannot be executed will result in a run-time error that will terminate execution of the process. Thus, to avoid production crashes, we will want to place high importance on thoroughly testing any code where `FORMAT` is used.

EVALUATE function

The `EVALUATE` function is essentially the reverse of the `FORMAT` function, allowing conversion of a string value into the defined data type. The syntax of the `EVALUATE` function is as follows:

```
[ BooleanVariable := ] EVALUATE ( ResultVariable,
                                   StringToBeConverted [, 9]
```

The handling of a run-time error can be done by specifying the `BooleanVariable` or including `EVALUATE` in an expression to deal with an error (such as an `IF` statement). The `ResultVariable` data type will determine which data conversion the `EVALUATE` function will attempt. The format of the data in `StringToBeConverted` must be compatible with the data type of `ResultVariable` otherwise a run-time error will occur.

The optional parameter, number 9, only is used for XMLport data exporting. Using the optional number 9 parameter will convert the C/SIDE format data types into XML standard data types. This deals with the fact that several equivalent C/SIDE-XML data types are represented differently at the base system level (that is, "under the covers"). The C/SIDE data types for an Evaluate result can include decimal, Boolean, datetime, date, time, integer, and duration.

FlowField and SumIndexField functions

In *Chapter 3, Data Types and Fields*, we discussed SumIndexFields and FlowFields in the context of table, field, and key definition. To recap briefly, SumIndexFields are defined in the screen where table keys are defined. They allow very rapid calculation of values in filtered data. In most ERP and accounting software systems, the calculation of group totals, periodic totals, and such, require reading of all the data to be totaled.

SIFT allows a NAV system to respond almost instantly with totals in any area where the SumIndexField was defined and is maintained. In fact, use of SIFT totals combined with NAV's retention of detailed data supports totally flexible ad hoc queries in similar form to: "What were our sales for red widgets between the dates of November 15th and December 24th?" And the answer is returned almost instantly! `SumIndexFields` are the basis of FlowFields which have a **Method** of `Sum` or `Average`; such a FlowField must refer to a data element that is defined as a `SumIndexField`.

When we access a record that has a SumIndexField defined, there is no visible evidence of the data sum that the SumIndexField represents. When we access a record that contains FlowFields, the FlowFields are empty virtual data elements until they are calculated. When a FlowField is displayed on a page or report, it is automatically calculated by NAV; the developer doesn't need to do so. But in any other scenario, the developer is responsible for calculating FlowFields (using the `CALCFIELDS` function).

FlowFields are one of the key areas where NAV systems are subject to significant processing bottlenecks. Even with the improved NAV 2015 design, it is still critical that the Table Keys used for SumIndexField definition are designed with efficient processing in mind. Sometimes, as part of a performance-tuning effort, it's necessary to revise existing keys or add new keys to improve FlowField performance.

 Although we can manage indexes in SQL Server independent of the NAV key definition, having two different definitions of keys for a table may make our system more difficult to support. This is because the SQL Server resident changes aren't always readily visible to the NAV developer.

In addition to being careful about the SIFT-key structure design, it is also important not to define any SumIndexFields that are not necessary. Each additional SumIndexField adds additional processing requirements and thus adds to the processing load of the system.

 Including SumIndexFields in a List page display is almost always a bad idea, because each SumIndexField instance will be calculated as it is displayed. Applicable functions include CALCFIELDS, CALCSUMS, and SETAUTOCALCFIELDS.

CALCFIELDS function

The syntax for CALCFIELDS is as follows:

```
[BooleanField := ] Record.CALCFIELDS ( FlowField1 [, FlowField2] ,…)
```

Executing the CALCFIELDS function will cause all the specified FlowFields to be calculated. Specification of the BooleanField allows us to handle any run-time error that may occur. Any runtime errors for CALCFIELDS usually result from a coding error or a change in a table key structure.

The FlowField calculation takes into account the filters (including FlowFilters) that are currently applied to the Record (we need to be careful not to overlook this). After the CALCFIELDS execution, the included FlowFields can be used similarly to any other data fields. CALCFIELDS must be executed for each cycle through the subject table.

Whenever the contents of a BLOB field are to be used, CALCFIELDS is used to load the contents of the BLOB field from the database into memory.

When the following conditions are true, CALCFIELDS uses dynamically maintained SIFT data:

- The NAV key contains the fields used in the filters defined for the FlowField
- The SumIndexFields on the operative key contain the fields provided as parameters for calculation
- The **MaintainSIFTIndex** property on the key is set to Yes (this is the default setting)

If all these conditions are not true and a CALCFIELDS is invoked, we will not get a run-time error as in the previous NAV version, but SQL Server will calculate the requested total(s) the hard way, by reading all the necessary records. This could be very slow and inefficient, and should not be used for frequently processed routines or large data sets. On the other hand, if the table does not contain a lot of data or if the SIFT data will not be used very often, it may be better to have the **MaintainSIFTIndex** property set to No.

SETAUTOCALCFIELDS function

The syntax for SETAUTOCALCFIELDS is as follows:

```
[BooleanField := ] Record.SETAUTOCALCFIELDS
                ( FlowField1 [, FlowField2] [, FlowField3]...)
```

When SETAUTOCALCFIELDS is inserted in to the code in front of the record retrieval, the specified FlowFields are automatically calculated as the record is read. This is more efficient than performing a CALCFIELDS on the FlowFields after the record has been read.

If we want to end the automatic FlowField calculation on a record, call the function without any parameters:

```
[BooleanField := ] Record.SETAUTOCALCFIELDS()
```

Automatic FlowField calculation equivalent to SETAUTOCALCFIELDS is automatically set on for the system record variables Rec and xRec.

CALCSUMS function

The CALCSUMS function is conceptually similar to CALCFIELDS for the calculation of Sums only. But CALCFIELDS operates on FlowFields and CALCSUMS operates directly on the record where the SumIndexFields are defined for the keys. This difference means that we must specify the proper key plus any filters to apply when using CALCSUMS (the applicable key and filters to apply are already defined in the properties for the FlowFields).

The syntax for CALCSUMS is as follows:

```
[ BooleanField := ] Record.CALCSUMS ( SumIndexField1
                     [,SumIndexField2] ,…)
```

Prior to such a statement, to maximize the probability of good performance, we should specify a key that has SumIndexFields defined. Before executing the CALCSUMS function, we also need to specify any filters that we want to apply to the Record from which the sums are to be calculated. The SumIndexField calculations take into account the filters that are currently applied to the Record.

Executing the CALCSUMS function will cause the specified SumIndexField totals to be calculated. Specification of the BooleanField allows us to handle any runtime errors that may occur. Runtime errors for CALCSUMS usually result from a coding error or a change in a table key structure. If possible, CALCSUMS uses the defined SIFT. Otherwise, SQL Server creates a temporary SIFT on the fly.

Before the execution of CALCSUMS, SumIndexFields contain only the data from the individual record that was read. After the CALCSUMS execution, the included SumIndexFields contain the totals that were calculated by the CALCSUMS function (these totals are only in memory, not in the database). These totals can then be used the same as data in any field, but if we want to access the individual record's original data for that field, we must either save a copy of the record before executing the CALCSUMS or we must reread the record. The CALCSUMS must be executed for each read cycle through the subject table.

CALCFIELDS and CALCSUMS comparison

In the Sales Header record, there are FlowFields defined for Amount and "Amount Including VAT". These FlowFields are all based on Sums of entries in the Sales Line table. The CalcFormula for Amount is Sum("Sales Line".Amount WHERE (Document Type=FIELD(Document Type),Document No.=FIELD(No.))). Remember, Amount must be a SumIndexField assigned to a Sales Line key that contains the fields on which we will filter (in this case by Document Type and Document No.). To calculate a TotalOrderAmount value while referencing the Sales Header table, the code can be as simple as:

```
"Sales Header".CALCFIELDS (Amount);
TotalOrderAmount := "Sales Header".Amount;
```

To calculate the same value from code directly referencing the Sales Line table, the required code would be similar to the following (assuming a Sales Header record has already been read):

```
"Sales Line".SETRANGE("Document Type","Sales Header"."Document Type");
"Sales Line".SETRANGE("Document No.","Sales Header"."No.");
"Sales Line".CALCSUMS(Amount);
TotalOrderAmount := "Sales Line".Amount;
```

Flow control

Process flow control functions are the functions that execute the decision making and resultant logic branches in executable code. IF-THEN-ELSE, discussed in *Chapter 6, Introduction to C/SIDE and C/AL*, is also a member of this class of functions. Here we will discuss the following:

- REPEAT-UNTIL
- WHILE-DO
- FOR-TO and FOR-DOWNTO
- CASE-ELSE
- WITH-DO
- QUIT, BREAK, EXIT, and SKIP

REPEAT-UNTIL

REPEAT-UNTIL allows us to create a repetitive code loop which REPEATs a block of code UNTIL a specific conditional expression evaluates to TRUE. In that sense, REPEAT-UNTIL defines a block of code, operating somewhat like the BEGIN-END compound statement structure which we covered in *Chapter 6, Introduction to C/SIDE and C/AL*. REPEAT tells the system to keep reprocessing the block of code, while UNTIL serves as the exit doorman, checking if the conditions for ending the processing are true. Because the exit condition is not evaluated until the end of the loop, a REPEAT-UNTIL structure will always process at least once through the contained code.

REPEAT-UNTIL is very important in NAV because it is often part of the data input cycle along with the FIND-NEXT structure, which will be covered shortly.

Here is an example of the REPEAT-UNTIL structure to process and sum data in the 10-element array CustSales:

```
LoopCount := 0;
REPEAT
 LoopCount := LoopCount + 1;
 TotCustSales := TotCustSales + CustSales[LoopCount];
UNTIL LoopCount = 10;
```

WHILE-DO

A WHILE-DO control structure allows us to create a repetitive code loop which will DO (execute) a block of code WHILE a specific conditional expression evaluates to TRUE. WHILE-DO is different from REPEAT-UNTIL, both because it may need a BEGIN-END structure to define the block of code to be executed repetitively (REPEAT-UNTIL does not) and it has different timing for the evaluation of the exit condition.

The syntax of the WHILE-DO control structure is as follows:

```
WHILE <Condition> DO <Statement>
```

Condition can be any Boolean expression which evaluates to TRUE or FALSE. Statement can be simple or the most complex compound BEGIN-END statement. Most WHILE-DO loops will be based on a BEGIN-END block of code. Condition will be evaluated at the beginning of the loop. When it evaluates to FALSE, the loop will terminate. Thus, a WHILE-DO loop can be exited without processing.

A WHILE-DO structure to process data in the 10-element array CustSales is as follows:

```
LoopCount := 0;
WHILE LoopCount < 10
DO BEGIN
 LoopCount := LoopCount + 1;
 TotCustSales := TotCustSales + CustSales[LoopCount];
END;
```

In NAV, REPEAT-UNTIL is much more frequently used than WHILE-DO.

FOR-TO or FOR-DOWNTO

The syntax for a FOR-TO or FOR-DOWNTO control statement is as follows:

```
FOR <Control Variable> := <Start Number> TO <End Number> DO
<Statement>
```

or

```
FOR <Control Variable> := <Start Number> DOWNTO <End Number> DO
<Statement>
```

A FOR control structure is used when we wish to execute a block of code a specific number of times.

The Control Variable is an Integer variable. Start Number is the beginning count for the FOR loop and End Number is the final count for the loop. If we wrote the statement: FOR LoopCount := 5 TO 7 DO [block of code] then [block of code] would be executed 3 times.

FOR-TO increments the Control Variable. FOR-DOWNTO decrements the Control Variable.

We must be careful not to manipulate the Control Variable in the middle of our loop. Doing so will likely yield unpredictable results.

CASE-ELSE statement

The CASE-ELSE statement is a conditional expression very similar to IF-THEN-ELSE, except that it allows for more than two choices of outcomes for the evaluation of the controlling expression. The syntax of the CASE-ELSE statement is as follows:

```
CASE <ExpressionToBeEvaluated> OF
  <Value Set 1> : <Action Statement 1>;
  <Value Set 2> : <Action Statement 2>;
  <Value Set 3> : <Action Statement 3>;
  . . .
  . . .
  <Value Set n> : <Action Statement n>;
 [ELSE <Action Statement n + 1>;
END;
```

The ExpressionToBeEvaluated must not be a record. The data type of the Value Set must be capable of being automatically converted to the data type of the ExpressionToBeEvaluated. Each Value Set must be an expression, a set of values, or a range of values. The following example illustrates a typical instance of a CASE-ELSE statement:

```
CASE Customer."Salesperson Code" OF
   '2','5','9': Customer."Territory Code" := 'EAST';
   '16'..'20': Customer."Territory Code" := 'WEST';
   'N': Customer."Territory Code" := 'NORTH';
```

```
    '27'..'38': Customer."Territory Code" := 'SOUTH';
  ELSE Customer."Territory Code" := 'FOREIGN';
END;
```

In the preceding example, we see several alternatives for the Value Set. The first line (EAST) Value Set contains the list of values. If Salesperson Code is equal to '2', '5', or '9', the value EAST will be assigned to Customer."Territory Code". The second line (WEST) Value Set is a range, any value from '16' through '20'. The third line (NORTH) Value Set is just a single value ('N'). If we look through standard NAV code, we will see that a single value is the most frequently used CASE structure in NAV. In the fourth line of our example (SOUTH), the Value Set is again a range ('27'..'38'). If nothing in any Value Set matches ExpressionToBeEvaluated, the ELSE clause will be executed.

An example of an IF-THEN-ELSE statement equivalent to the preceding CASE-ELSE statement is as follows:

```
IF Customer."Salesperson Code" IN ['2','5','9'] THEN
  Customer."Territory Code" := 'EAST'
    ELSE IF Customer."Salesperson Code" IN ['16'..'20'] THEN
      Customer."Territory Code" := 'WEST'
    ELSE IF Customer."Salesperson Code" = 'N' THEN
      Customer."Territory Code" := 'NORTH'
    ELSE IF Customer."Salesperson Code" IN ['27'..'38'] THEN
      Customer."Territory Code" := 'SOUTH'
      ELSE Customer."Territory Code" := 'FOREIGN';
```

The following is a slightly less intuitive example of the CASE-ELSE statement. In this instance, ExpressionToBeEvaluated is a simple TRUE and the Value Set statements are all conditional expressions. The first line containing a Value Set expression that evaluates to TRUE will be the line whose Action Statement is executed. The rules of execution and flow in this instance are same as in the previous example.

```
CASE TRUE OF Salesline.Quantity < 0:
 BEGIN
  CLEAR(Salesline."Line Discount %");
  CredTot := CredTot - Salesline.Quantity;
 END;
  Salesline.Quantity > QtyBreak[1]:
   Salesline."Line Discount %" := DiscLevel[1];
  Salesline.Quantity > QtyBreak[2]:
   Salesline."Line Discount %" := DiscLevel[2];
  Salesline.Quantity > QtyBreak[3]:
   Salesline."Line Discount %" := DiscLevel[3];
  Salesline.Quantity > QtyBreak[4]:
```

```
    Salesline."Line Discount %" := DiscLevel[4];
  ELSE
    CLEAR(Salesline."Line Discount %");
END;
```

WITH-DO statement

When we are writing code referring to fields within a record, the most specific syntax for field references is the fully qualified reference [RecordName.FieldName]. When referring to the field **City** in the record **Customer**, use the reference Customer.City.

In many C/AL instances, the record name qualifier is implicit, because the compiler assumes a default record qualifier based on the code context. This happens automatically for variables within a page bounded to a table. The bound table becomes the implicit record qualifier for fields referenced in the Page object. In a Table object, the table is the implicit record qualifier for fields referenced in the C/AL in that object. In Report and XMLport objects, the Data Item record is the implicit record qualifier for the fields referenced within the triggers of that Data Item such as OnAfterGetRecord and OnAfterImportRecord.

In all other C/AL code, the only way to have an implicit record qualifier is to use the WITH-DO statement. WITH-DO is widely used in the base product in Codeunits and processing Reports. The WITH-DO syntax is:

```
WITH <RecordQualifier> DO <Statement>
```

Typically, the DO portion of this statement will be followed by a BEGIN-END code block, allowing for a compound statement. The scope of the WITH-DO statement is terminated by the end of the DO statement.

When we execute a WITH-DO statement, RecordQualifier becomes the implicit record qualifier used by the compiler until the end of that statement or until that qualifier is overridden by a nested WITH-DO statement. Where fully qualified, syntax would requires the following form:

```
Customer.Address := '189 Maple Avenue';
Customer.City := 'Chicago';
```

The WITH-DO syntax takes advantage of the implicit record qualification making the code easier to write, and hopefully easier to read. For example:

```
WITH Customer DO
BEGIN
 Address := '189 Maple Avenue';
 City := 'Chicago';
END;
```

Best practice says that WITH-DO statements should only be used in functions within a Codeunit or a Report.

WITH-DO statements nested one within another are legal code, but are not used in standard NAV. They are also not recommended because they can easily confuse the developer, resulting in bugs. The same comments apply to nesting a WITH-DO statement within a function where there is an automatic implicit record qualifier, such as in a table, Report, or XMLport.

Of course, wherever the references to record variables other than the implicit one occur within the scope of a WITH-DO statement, we must include the specific qualifiers. This is particularly important when there are variables with the same name (for example, City) in multiple tables that might be referenced in the same set of C/AL logic.

Some developers maintain that it is always better to use fully qualified variable names to reduce the possibility of inadvertent reference errors. This approach also eliminates any possible misinterpretation of variable references by a maintenance developer who works on this code later.

QUIT, BREAK, EXIT, and SKIP functions

This group of C/AL functions also control process flow. Each acts to interrupt flow in different places and with different results. To get a full appreciation for how these functions are used, we need to review them in the correct place in code in NAV 2015.

QUIT function

The QUIT function is the ultimate processing interrupt for Report or XMLport objects. When a QUIT is executed, processing immediately terminates even for the OnPostObject triggers. No database changes are committed. QUIT is often used in reports to terminate processing when the report logic determines that no useful output will be generated by further processing.

The syntax of the QUIT function is as follows:

```
CurrReport.QUIT;
CurrXMLport.QUIT;
```

BREAK function

The BREAK function terminates the DataItem in which it occurs. BREAK can only be used in Data Item triggers in Reports and XMLports. It can be used to terminate the sequence of processing one DataItem segment of a report while allowing subsequent DataItem processing to continue.

The BREAK syntax is one of the following:

```
CurrReport.BREAK;
CurrXMLport.BREAK;
```

EXIT function

EXIT is used to end the processing within a C/AL trigger. EXIT works the same whether it is executed within a loop or not. It can be used to end the processing of the trigger or to pass a return value from a local function. A return value cannot be used for system defined triggers or local functions that don't have a return value defined. If EXIT is used without a return value, a default return value of zero is returned. The syntax for EXIT is:

```
EXIT([<ReturnValue>])
```

SKIP function

When executed, the SKIP function will skip the remainder of the processing in the current record cycle of the current trigger. Unlike BREAK, it does not terminate the DataItem processing completely. It can be used only in the OnAfterGetRecord trigger of a Report or XMLport object. In reports, when the results of processing in the OnAfterGetRecord trigger are determined not to be useful for the output, the SKIP function is used to terminate that single iteration of the trigger without interfering with any subsequent processing.

The SKIP syntax is one of the following:

```
CurrReport.SKIP;
CurrXMLport.SKIP;
```

Input and Output functions

In the previous chapter, we learned about the basics of the FIND function. We learned about FIND('-') to read from the beginning of a selected set of records, FINDSET to read a selected set of records, and FIND('+') to begin reading at the far end of the selected set of records. Now we will review additional functions that are generally used with the FIND functions in typical production code. While we are designing code which uses the MODIFY and DELETE record functions, we need to consider possible interactions with other users on the system. There might be someone else modifying and deleting records in the same table which our application is updating.

We may want to use the LOCKTABLE function to briefly gain total control of the data, while updating the data. We can find more information on LOCKTABLE in the online **C/AL Reference Guide Help**. The SQL Server database supports Record Level Locking. There are a number of factors that we should consider when coding data locking in our processes. It is worthwhile reading all of the **C/AL Reference Guide** material found by a Search on LOCKTABLE, particularly **Locking in Microsoft SQL Server**.

NEXT function with FIND or FINDSET

The syntax defined for the NEXT function is:

```
IntegerValue := Record.NEXT ( ReadStepSize )
```

The full assignment statement format is rarely used to set an IntegerValue. In addition, there is no documentation for the usage of a non-zero IntegerValue. When IntegerValue goes to zero, it means that a NEXT record was not found. In early versions of NAV 2015, the Help text for NEXT does not properly explain the use of or value setting for IntegerValue.

If the ReadStepSize value is negative, the table will be read in reverse; if ReadStepSize is positive (the default), then the table will be read forward. The size of the value in ReadStepSize controls which records should be read. For example, if ReadStepSize is 2 or -2, then every second record will be read. If ReadStepSize is 10 or -10, then every tenth record will be read. The default value is 1, in which case every record will be read and the read direction will be forward.

In a typical data read loop, the first read is a FIND or FINDSET function followed by a REPEAT-UNTIL loop. The exit condition is the expression UNTIL Record.NEXT = 0;. The C/AL for FINDSET and FIND('-') are structured alike.

The full C/AL syntax for this typical loop looks like the following:

```
IF CustRec.FIND('-') THEN
REPEAT
 Block of C/AL logic
UNTIL CustRec.NEXT = 0;
```

INSERT function

The purpose of the INSERT function is to add new records to a table. The syntax for the INSERT function is as follows:

```
[BooleanValue :=] Record.INSERT ( [ TriggerControlBoolean ] )
```

If `BooleanValue` is not used and the `INSERT` function fails (for example, if the insertion would result in a duplicate Primary Key), the process will terminate with an error. Generally, we should handle a detected error in code by using the `BooleanValue` and supplying our own error handling logic rather than allowing a default termination.

The `TriggerControlBoolean` value controls whether or not the table's `OnInsert` trigger fires when the `INSERT` occurs. The default value is `FALSE`. If we let the default `FALSE` control, we run the risk of not performing error checking that the table's designer assumed would be run when a new record was added.

When we are reading a table and we also need to `INSERT` records into that same table, the `INSERT` should be done to a separate instance of the table. We can use either a global or local variable for that second instance. If we `INSERT` into the same table we are reading, we run the risk of reading the new records as part of our processing (likely a very confusing action). We also run the risk of changing the sequence of our processing unexpectedly due to the introduction of new records into our data set. While the database access methods are continually improved by Microsoft and this warning may be overcautious, it is better to be safe than sorry.

MODIFY function

The purpose of the `MODIFY` function is to modify (update) the existing data records. The syntax for `MODIFY` is:

```
[BooleanValue :=] Record.MODIFY ( [ TriggerControlBoolean ] )
```

If `BooleanValue` is not used and `MODIFY` fails (for example, if another process changes the record after it was read by this process), then the process will terminate with an error statement. The code should either handle a detected error or gracefully terminate the process. The `TriggerControlBoolean` value controls whether or not the table's `OnModify` trigger fires when this `MODIFY` occurs. The default value is `FALSE`, which would not perform any `OnModify` processing. `MODIFY` cannot be used to cause a change in a Primary Key field. In that case, the `RENAME` function must be used.

There is system based checking to make sure that a `MODIFY` is done using the current version of the data record by making sure that another process hasn't modified and committed the record after it was read by this process. Our logic should refresh the record using the `GET` function, then change any values, and then call the `MODIFY` function.

Rec and xRec

In Table and Page objects, the system automatically provides us with the system variables Rec and xRec. Until a record has been updated by MODIFY, Rec represents the current record data in process and xRec represents the record data before it was modified. By comparing field values in Rec and xRec, we can determine if changes have been made to the record in the current process cycle. Rec and xRec records have all the same fields in the same structure as the table to which they relate.

DELETE function

The purpose of the DELETE function is to delete existing data records. The syntax for DELETE is as follows:

```
[BooleanValue :=] Record.DELETE ( [ TriggerControlBoolean ] )
```

When DELETE fails and the BooleanValue is not used, the process will terminate with an error statement. Our code should handle any detected error or terminate the process, as appropriate.

The TriggerControlBoolean value is TRUE or FALSE, and it controls whether or not the table's OnDelete trigger fires when this DELETE occurs. The default value is FALSE. If we let the default FALSE value in place, we run the risk of not performing error checking that the table's designer assumed would be run when a record was deleted.

In NAV 2015, there is improved checking to make sure a DELETE is using the current version of the record, which making sure another process hasn't modified and committed the record after it was read by this process. Therefore, before the DELETE function is called, the program should refresh the record using the GET function.

MODIFYALL function

MODIFYALL is the high-volume version of the MODIFY function. If we have a group of records for which we wish to modify one field in all of them to the same new value, we should use MODIFYALL. MODIFYALL is controlled by the filters that apply at the time of invoking. The other choice for doing a mass modification would be to have a FIND–NEXT loop in which we modify each record, one at a time. The advantage of MODIFYALL is that it allows the developer and the system to optimize the code for the volume update. Any system optimization will be a function of the SQL statements are generated by the C/AL compiler.

The syntax for MODIFYALL is as follows:

```
Record.MODIFYALL (FieldToBeModified,NewValue
    [,TriggerControlBoolean ] )
```

The `TriggerControlBoolean` value, a `TRUE` or `FALSE` entry, controls whether or not the table's `OnModify` trigger fires when this `MODIFY` occurs. The default value is `FALSE` which would result in the field `OnValidate` trigger not being executed. In a typical situation, a filter or a series of filters would be applied to a table followed by the `MODIFYALL` function. A simple example where we are going to reassign all the `Territory Codes` for a particular `Salesperson` to `NORTH`, is as follows:

```
Customer.RESET;
Customer.SETRANGE("Salesperson Code",'DAS');
Customer.MODIFYALL("Territory Code",'NORTH',TRUE);
```

DELETEALL function

`DELETEALL` is the high volume version of the `DELETE` function. If we have a group of records that we wish to delete, use `DELETEALL`. The other choice would be a `FIND-NEXT` loop in which we delete each record one at a time. The advantage of `DELETEALL` is that it allows the developer and the system to optimize the code for the volume deletion. Any system optimization will be a function of what SQL statements are generated by the C/AL compiler.

The syntax for `DELETEALL` is as follows:

```
Record.DELETEALL ( [,TriggerControlBoolean] )
```

The `TriggerControlBoolean` value, a `TRUE` or `FALSE` entry, controls whether or not the table's `OnDelete` trigger fires when this `DELETE` occurs. The default value is `FALSE`. If the `TriggerControlBoolean` value is `TRUE`, then the `OnDelete` trigger will fire for each record deleted. In that case, there is little or no speed advantage for `DELETEALL` versus the use of a `FIND-DELETE-NEXT` loop.

In a typical situation, a filter or a series of filters would be applied to a table followed by the `DELETEALL` function, similar to the preceding example. Like `MODIFYALL`, `DELETEALL` respects the filters that have been set and does not do any referential integrity error checking.

Filtering

Few other systems have filtering implemented as comprehensively as NAV, nor do they have it tied so neatly to the detailed retention of historical data. The result of NAV's features is that even the most basic implementation of NAV includes very powerful data analysis capabilities available to the end user.

As developers, we should appreciate the fact that we cannot anticipate every need of any user, let alone anticipate all the needs of all the users. We know we should give the users as much freedom as possible to allow them to selectively extract and review data from their system. Wherever feasible, users should be given the opportunity to apply their own filters so that they can determine the optimum selection of data for their particular situation. On the other hand, freedom, here as everywhere, is a double-edged sword. With the freedom to decide just how to segment one's data, comes the responsibility for figuring out what constitutes a good segmentation to address the problem at hand.

As experienced application software designers and developers, presumably we have considerable insight into good ways to analyze and present the data. On that basis, it may be appropriate for us to provide some predefined selections. In some cases, constraints of the data structure allow only a limited set of options to make sense. In such a case, we should provide specific accesses to data (through pages and/or reports). But we should allow more sophisticated users to access and manipulate the data flexibly on their own.

When applying filters by using any of the options, be very conscious of the table key that will be active when the filter takes effect. In a table containing a lot of data, filtering on a field that is not very high in (near the front of) the currently active key may result in poor (or very poor) response time for the users. In the same context, in a system suffering from a poor response time during processing, we should first investigate the relationships of active keys to applied filters, as well as how the keys are maintained. This may require SQL Server expertise in addition to NAV 2015 expertise.

Both SETCURRENTKEY and SETRANGE functions are important in the context of data filtering. These were reviewed in *Chapter 6, Introduction to C/SIDE and C/AL*, so we won't review them again here.

SETFILTER function

SETFILTER allows us to define and apply any Filter expression that could be created manually, including various combinations of ranges, C/AL operators, and even wild cards. SETFILTER syntax is as follows:

```
Record.SETFILTER ( Field, FilterString [, FilterValue1], . . . ] );
```

SETFILTER can also be applied to Query objects with similar syntax:

```
Query.SETFILTER ( ColumnName, FilterString
                  [, FilterValue1], . . . ] );
```

`FilterString` can be a literal such as `'1000..20000'` or `'A*|B*|C*'`, but this is not good practice. Optionally, we can use variable tokens in the form of `%1`, `%2`, `%3`, and so forth, representing variables (but not operators) `FilterValue1`, `FilterValue2`, and so forth to be substituted in the filter string at runtime. This construct allows us to create filters whose data values can be defined dynamically at runtime. A new `SETFILTER` replaces any previous filtering in the same filtergroup (this will be discussed in more detail shortly) on that field or column prior to setting the new filter.

A pair of `SETFILTER` examples follow:

```
Customer.SETFILTER("Salesperson Code",'KKS'|'RAM'|'CDS');
Customer.SETFILTER("Salesperson Code",'%1|%2|%3',SPC1,SPC2,SPC3);
```

If `SPC1` equals `'KKS'`, `SPC2` equals `'RAM'`, and `SPC3` equals `'CDS'`, these two examples would have the same result. Obviously, the second option allows flexibility not provided by the first option because the variables could be assigned other values.

COPYFILTER and COPYFILTERS functions

These functions allow copying the filters of a single field or all the filters on a record (table) and applying those filters to another record. The syntaxes follow:

```
FromRecord.COPYFILTER(FromField, ToRecord.ToField)
```

The From and To fields must be of the same data type. The From and To tables do not have to be the same.

```
ToRecord.COPYFILTERS(FromRecord)
```

Note that the `COPYFILTER` field based function begins with the `FromRecord` variable while that of the `COPYFILTERS` record based function begins with the `ToRecord` variable. ToRecord and From Record must be different instances of the same table.

GETFILTER and GETFILTERS functions

These functions allow us to retrieve the filters on a single field or all the filters on a record (table), and assign the result to a text variable. The syntaxes are as follows:

- `ResultString := FilteredRecord.GETFILTER(FilteredField)`
- `ResultString := FilteredRecord.GETFILTERS`

Similar functions exist for Query Objects. Those syntaxes are:

- `ResultString := FilteredQuery.GETFILTER(FilteredColumn)`
- `ResultString := FilteredQuery.GETFILTERS`

The text contents of the `ResultString` will contain an identifier for each filtered field and the currently applied value of the filter. `GETFILTERS` is often used to retrieve the filters on a table and print them as part of a report heading. The `ResultString` will look similar to the following: **Customer:.No.: 10000..999999, Balance: >0**

FILTERGROUP function

The `FILTERGROUP` function can change or retrieve the filtergroup that is applied to a table. A filtergroup contains a set of filters that have been applied to the table previously by `SETFILTER` or `SETRANGE` functions or as table properties defined in an object. The `FILTERGROUP` syntax is:

```
[CurrentGroupInteger ] := Record.FILTERGROUP ([NewGroupInteger])
```

Using just the `Record.FILTERGROUP([NewFilterGroupInteger])` portion sets the active Filter Group.

Filtergroups can also be used to filter Query Data Items. All the currently defined filtergroups are active and apply in combination (they are logically ANDed, that is, they result in a logical intersection of the sets). The only way to eliminate the effect of a filtergroup is to remove the filters in a group.

The default filtergroup for NAV is 0 (zero). Users have access to the filters in this filtergroup. Other filtergroups, numbered up to 6, have assigned NAV uses. We should not redefine the use of any of these filtergroups but use higher numbers for any custom filtergroups in our code.

See the **Developer and IT Pro Help** for `FILTERGROUP function` and `Understanding Query Filters` for more information.

One use of a filtergroup would be to assign a filter which the user cannot see is present or change. Our code could change the filtergroup, set a special filter, and then return the active filtergroup to its original state. An example:

```
Rec.FILTERGROUP(42);
Rec.SETFILTER(Customer."Salesperson Code",MySalespersonID);
Rec.FILTERGROUP(0);
```

This could be used to apply special application-specific permissions to a particular system function, such as filtering out access to customers by a salesperson so that each salesperson can only examine data for his/her own customers.

MARK function

A mark on a record is an indicator that disappears when the current session ends and which is only visible to the process that is setting the mark. The MARK function sets the mark. The syntax is as follows:

```
[BooleanValue := ] Record.MARK ( [SetMarkBoolean] )
```

If the optional BooleanValue and assignment operator (:=) are present, the MARK function will give us the current Mark status (TRUE or FALSE) of the Record. If the optional SetMarkBoolean parameter is present, the Record will be Marked (or unmarked) according to that value (TRUE or FALSE). The default value for SetMarkBoolean is FALSE. The MARK functions should be used carefully and only when a simpler solution is not readily available. Marking records can cause significant performance problems on large data sets.

CLEARMARKS function

CLEARMARKS clears all the marks from the specified record (that is, from the particular instance of the table in this instance of the object). The syntax is as follows:

```
Record.CLEARMARKS
```

MARKEDONLY function

MARKEDONLY is a special filtering function that can apply a mark-based filter.

The syntax for MARKEDONLY is as follows:

```
[BooleanValue := ] Record.MARKEDONLY
    ( [SeeMarkedRecordsOnlyBoolean] )
```

If the optional BooleanValue parameter is defined, it will be assigned a value TRUE or FALSE to tell us whether or not the special MARKEDONLY filter is active. Omitting the BooleanValue parameter, MARKEDONLY will set the special filter depending on the value of SeeMarkedRecordsOnlyBoolean. If that value is TRUE, it will filter to show only marked records; if that value is FALSE, it will remove the marked filter and show all records. The default value for SeeMarkedRecordsOnlyBoolean is FALSE.

Though it may not seem logical, there is no option to see only the unmarked records.

For additional information, refer to Mark Brummel's blog at https://markbrummel.wordpress.com/2014/03/07/tip-36-using-mark-and-markedonly-in-the-role-tailored-client/.

RESET function

This function allows us to RESET (that is, clear) all filters that are currently applied to a record. RESET also sets the current key back to the Primary Key, removes any marks, and clears all internal variables in the current instance of the record. Filters in FILTERGROUP 1 are not reset. The syntax is as follows:

```
FilteredRecord.RESET;
```

InterObject communication

There are several ways for communicating between objects during NAV processing.

Communication via data

The most widely used and simplest communication method is through data tables. For example, the table No. Series is the central control for all document numbers. Each object that assigns numbers to a document (for example, Order, Invoice, Shipment, and so on) uses Codeunit 396, **NoSeriesManagement**, to access the **No. Series** table for the next number to use, and then updates the **No. Series** table so that the next object needing to assign a number to the same type of document will have the updated information.

Communication through function parameters

When an object calls a function in another object, information is generally passed through the calling and return parameters. The calling and return parameter specifications were defined when the function was originally developed. The generic syntax for a function call is as follows:

```
[ReturnValue := ] FunctionName ( [ Parameter1 ] [ ,Parameter2 ] ,…)
```

The rules for including or omitting the various optional fields are specific to the local variables defined for each individual function. As developers, when we design the function, we define the rules and thereby determine just how communications with the function will be handled. It is obviously important to define complete and consistent parameter passing rules, prior to beginning a development project.

Communication via object calls

Sometimes we need to create an object which in turn calls other objects. We may simply want to allow the user to be able to run a series of processes and reports but only enter the controlling parameters once. Our user interface object will be responsible for invoking the subordinate objects after having communicated setup and filter parameters.

There is a significant set of standard functions designed for various modes and circumstances of invoking other objects. Examples of these functions are SETTABLEVIEW, SETRECORD, and GETRECORD (there are others as well). There are also instances where we will need to build our own data passing function.

In order to properly manage these relatively complex processes, we need to be familiar with the various versions of RUN and RUNMODAL functions. We will also need to understand the meaning and effect of a single instance or multiple instances of an object. Briefly, key differences between invoking a page or report object from within another object via RUN versus RUNMODAL are as follows:

- RUN will clear the instance of the invoked object every time the object completes, which means that all of the internal variables are initialized. This clearing behavior does not apply to a codeunit object; state will be maintained across multiple calls to RUN.

- RUNMODAL does not clear the instance of the invoked object, so internal global variables are not reinitialized each time the object is called. The object can be reinitialized by using CLEAR(Object).

- RUNMODAL does not allow any other object to be active in the same user session while it is running, whereas RUN allows another object instance to run in parallel with the RUN initiated object instance.

Covering these topics in more detail is too advanced for this book, but once you have mastered the material covered here, you should study the information in the **Developer and IT Pro Help** relative to this topic. There is also a Pattern on this topic defined at:

```
https://community.dynamics.com/nav/w/designpatterns/108.posting-
routine-select-behaviour.
```

Enhancing the WDTU application

Now that we have some more tools with which to work, let's enhance our WDTU application. This time our goal is to implement functionality to allow the Program Manager to plan the Playlist schedules for Radio Shows. The process, from the user's point of view, will be essentially as follows:

- Call up the Playlist document page which displays Header, Details, and Factbox workspaces.

- Enter the Playlist Header, using the Radio Show table data.

- Enter Playlist Lines, using the Resource table DJ data, the Radio Show table for News, Weather, or Sports shows, and the Item table for Music, PSAs, and Advertisements.

- The Factbox will display the Required program element fields from Radio Show/Playlist Header. These will include News (Yes or No), Weather (Yes or No), Sports (Yes or No), Number of required PSAs, and Advertisements.

- The Factbox will also track each of the five possible required elements.

Since this development effort is an exercise to learn more about developing NAV applications, we also have some specific NAV C/AL components we want to use so we can learn more about them. Among those are the following:

- Create a CASE statement as well as a multipart IF statement for contrast

- Add code to the `OnValidate` trigger of fields in a table

- Implement a lookup into a related table to access the needed data

- Cause FlowFields to be processed for display

- Implement a FactBox (to display Radio Show requirements for News, Sports, Weather, PSAs, and Ads)

- Create a new function, passing a parameter in and getting results passed back

As with any application enhancement, there will be a number of auxiliary tasks we'll have to accomplish to get the job done. These include adding some new fields to one or more tables. Not surprisingly, adding new data fields often leads to adding the new fields to one or more pages for maintenance or display. We'll have to create some test data in order to test our modifications. It's not unusual in the course of an enhancement to also find that other changes are needed to support the new functionality.

Modifying Table Fields

Because we want the NAV tables to be the core of the design and to host as much of the processing as makes sense, we will start our enhancement work with table modifications.

The first table modification is to add the data fields to the Playlist Header to support the definition and tracking of various program segment requirements. In the Radio Show table, each show has requirements defined for specific numbers of PSAs and Advertisements, and for the presence of News, Sports, and Weather spots. The Playlist Header needs this requirements information stored along with the associated counts for this show instance for PSAs and Ads. We are going to obtain the News, Sports, and Weather line counts by means of a function call.

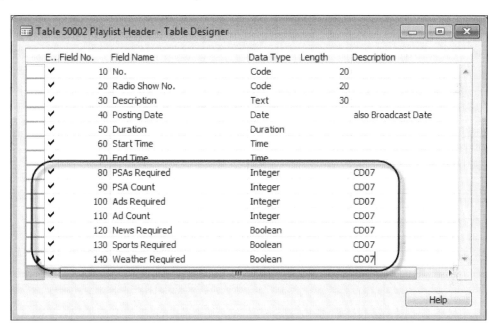

Since the Playlist Line includes an **Option** field which identifies the PSA and Advertisement records, we use a **FlowField** to calculate the counts for each of those line types. We construct the **FlowField** definition starting in the **Properties** form of the field.

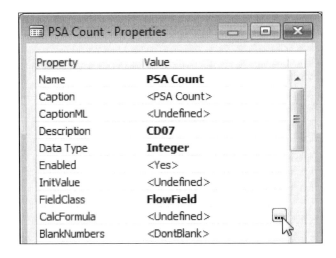

When we click on the **CalcFormula** line ellipsis, the **Calculation Formula** screen appears, as shown in the following screenshot:

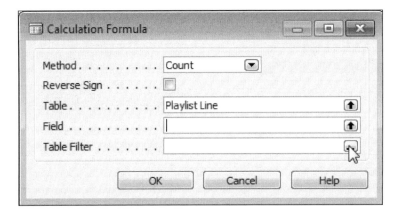

In this case, the **Method** we want to use is Count. Then, when we click on the **Table Filter** ellipsis, we will have the opportunity to enter the components defining the filters that should be applied to the Playlist Line to isolate the records that we want to count.

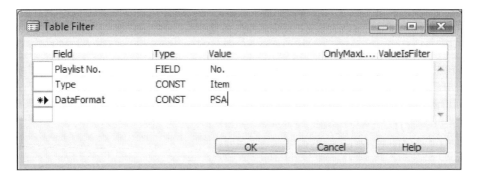

When we complete the **Table Filter** definition and click on the **OK** button, we will return to the **Calculation Formula** screen with the **Table Filter** field filled in (if we just click on *Esc*, the data we entered will not be saved).

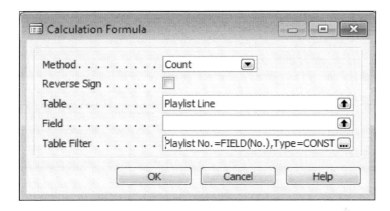

Again, click on the **OK** button to return to the **Properties** screen.

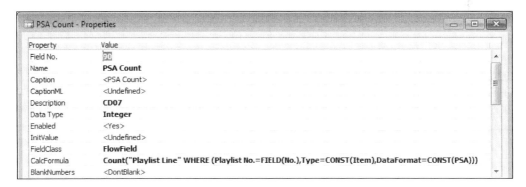

Go through the same sequence for the Ad Count field.

The only change we now want to make to the Playlist Line table now is to be sure the Duration field is not editable. We do this so that the Start Time and End Time scheduling defines Duration rather than the other way around. Making the Duration field non-editable is done by simply setting the field's **Editable** property to No, as shown in the following screenshot:

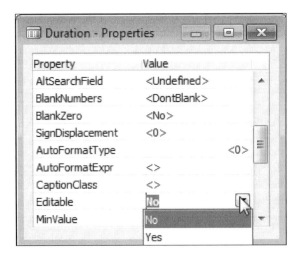

Add Validation logic

We need Validation logic for both our Playlist tables, Header and Line.

Playlist Header Validations

The Playlist Header data fields are:

- **No.**: The ID number for this instance of a radio show; user defined
- **Radio Show No.**: Chosen from the Radio Show table
- **Description**: Displayed via a FlowField from the Radio Show table
- **Posting Date**: This show's scheduled broadcast date
- **Start Time**: This show's scheduled broadcast start time
- **End Time**: This show's scheduled broadcast end time
- **Duration**: The length of the show; displayed via a FlowField from the Radio Show table

- **PSAs Required and Ads Required**: How many PSAs and Ads are planned during the show; copied from the Radio Show table, but editable by the user

- **News Required, Sports Required, and Weather Required**: Whether or not each of these program segments are required during the show; copied from the Radio Show table, but editable by the user

When the user chooses the Radio Show to be scheduled, we want the five different feature requirements fields in the Playlist Header to be filled in.

```
Table 50002 Playlist Header - C/AL Editor

  No. - OnLookup()

  Radio Show No. - OnValidate()
    IF RadioShow.GET("Radio Show No.") THEN
      BEGIN
        "PSAs Required" := RadioShow."PSA Planned Quantity";
        "Ads Required" := RadioShow."Ads Planned Quanity";
        "News Required" := RadioShow."News Required";
        "Sports Required" := RadioShow."Sports Required";
        "Weather Required" := RadioShow."Weather Required";
      END ELSE
      BEGIN
        CLEAR("PSAs Required");
        CLEAR("Ads Required");
        CLEAR("News Required");
        CLEAR("Sports Required");
        CLEAR("Weather Required");
      END;
```

Even though the `Radio Show No.` was entered in the data field, our validation code needs to read the Radio Show record (here, defined as the Global variable `RadioShow`). Once we have read the Radio Show record, we can assign all five show feature requirements fields from the Radio Show record into the Playlist Header record.

Then, because two fields in the Playlist Header record are Lookup FlowFields, we need to Update the page after the entry of the `Radio Show No.` value The Update is done via a `CurrPage.UPDATE` command, as shown in the following image:

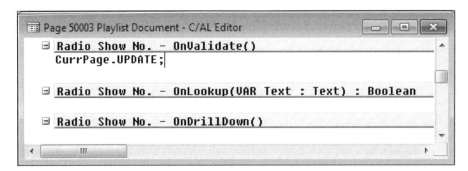

The next Validation we need is to calculate the show's `End Time` as soon as the `Start Time` has been entered. The calculation is simple—add the length of the show to the `Start Time`. Because we have defined the `Duration` field in the Playlist Header to be a Lookup reference to the source field in the Radio Show record, to calculate with that field would require using a `CALCFIELDS` function first, so, instead, we'll obtain the show length from the Radio Show record.

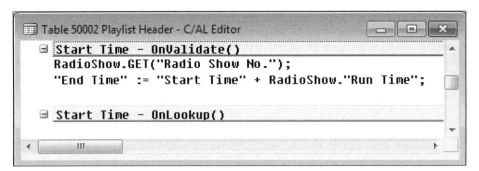

Now we see that we have one of those situations we sometimes encounter when developing a modification. It might have been better to have the Playlist Header `Duration` field as a **Normal** data field rather than a **FlowField**. If this is the only place where we will use `Duration` from the Playlist Header for calculation or assignment, then the current design is fine. Otherwise, perhaps we should change the `Duration` field to be a **Normal** field and assign `Run Time` from Radio Show to it at the same time the several requirements fields are assigned. At this point though, for the purposes of our WDTU scenario, we will stick with what we already have.

Creating the Playlist Subform page

In *Chapter 2*, *Tables*, a homework assignment was to create Page 50003 Playlist Document. We should have used the Page Wizard to create that page, giving us something like this following screenshot:

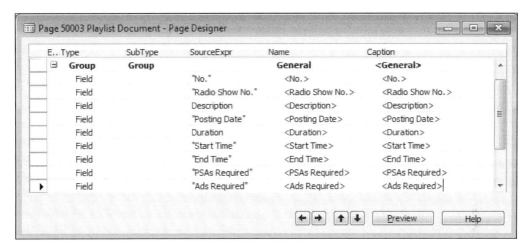

Another necessary part of a Document page is the Subform (someday to be known as a Subpage) page. Our Subform page can be created using the Page Wizard to create a ListPart based on Table **50003 Playlist Line**. After we **Finish** the Wizard, we'll save and compile the page as **50004 Playlist Subform**. The result will look like the following image:

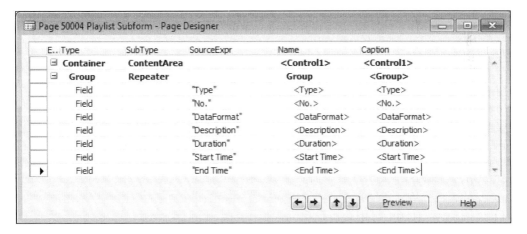

To make the Document work the way we are used to having NAV Document forms work, we need to set some properties for this new page. See the bolded properties circled in the following image:

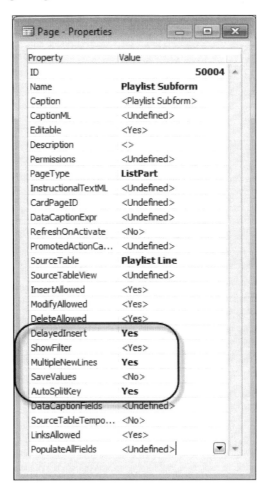

We have set the **DelayedInsert, MultipleNewLines**, and **AutoSplitKey** properties to Yes. These settings will allow the Playlist Lines to not be saved until the primary key fields are all entered (**DelayedInsert**), will support simple sequential entry of data lines (**MultipleNewLines**), and will support the easy insertion of new entries between two existing lines (**AutoSplitKey**).

Finally, we need to connect our new Playlist Subform Listpart Page 50004 to the Playlist Document Page 50003 to give us a basic, complete Document page. All we need to do to accomplish that is add a new `Part` line to **Page 50003** with as is shown in the following:

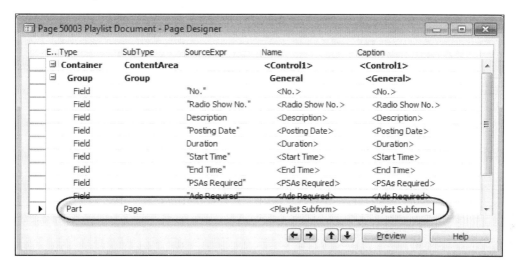

Entering the **PagePartID** in the `Part` line properties (as shown in the following image) will populate the **Name** and **Caption** fields (as shown in the preceding image).

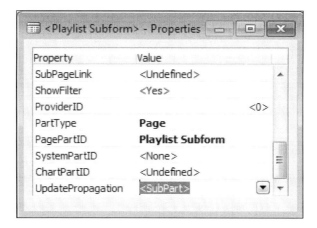

Note that the highlighted property, **UpdatePropagation**, in the preceding image. This property can be set to either SubPart (the default) or Both. This controls how the parent and child page are updated when a change is made to the data displayed by the child page (the SubPart). If the property value is SubPart, only the child page information display is updated. If the property value is Both, both the child and parent page displays are updated. This is useful when data in the SubPage is updated and the change affects data displayed in the parent page.

The last step in this phase of our development is to set the Page Part property SubPageLink to automatically filter the contents of the Subform page to only be the lines that are children of the parent record showing in the card-like portion of the Document page (at the top) of the page).

Playlist Line Validations

The Playlist Line data fields are:

- **Playlist No.**: The automatically assigned link to the No. field in the parent Playlist record (the automatic assignment is based on the Playlist Subform page properties, which we'll take care of when working on the Playlist pages)

- **Line No.**: An automatically assigned number (based on page properties); the rightmost field in the Playlist Line primary key

- **Type**: A user selected option defining if this entry is a Resource (such as an announcer), a Show (such as a News show), or an Item (such as a recording to play on the air)

- **No.**: The ID number of the selected entry in its parent table

- **DataFormat**: Information from the Item table for a show or recording

- **Description**: Assigned from the parent table, but can be edited by the user

- **Duration**, **Start Time**, and **End Time**: Information about a show or recording indicating its length and its position within the schedule of this Radio Show

The source of contents of the **No.**, **DataFormat**, **Description**, and time related fields of the record depend on the Type field. If the **Type** is **Resource**, the fields are filled in from the Resource table; for Item, from the Item table; and for Show, from the Radio Show table. To support this, our **OnValidate** code looks at the Type entry and uses a CASE statement to choose which set of actions to take.

First, we will build the basic CASE statement, as shown in the following image, and compile it. That way we make sure we've got all the components of the structure in place and only need to fill in the logic for each of the option choices.

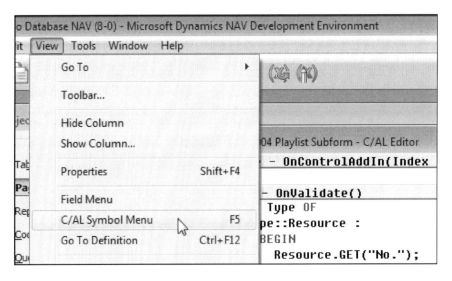

Next we must add a Global Variable for each of the tables from which we are going to pull data: **Resource, Item,** and **Radio Show**. That done, using the **C/AL Symbol Menu** makes it much easier to find the correct field names for each of the variables we want to select to assign to the Playlist Line record fields.

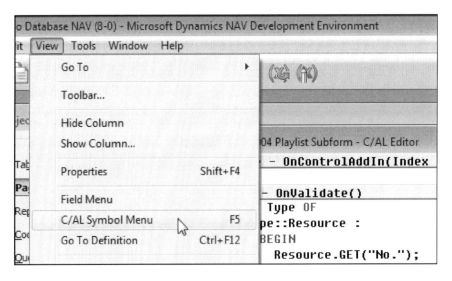

Once the C/AL Symbol Menu is displayed, we first select the source object or variable in the left column. In this case, that's the **Resource** table. Then select the subcategory in the middle column. We want a list of the fields in the **Resource** table, so we select **FieldName**. Then, in the third column, a list of **Resource FieldNames** is displayed. We select Name to assign to the **Playlist Line Description** field. When we double-click on the desired **FieldName**, it will be inserted at the point of focus in the C/AL Editor.

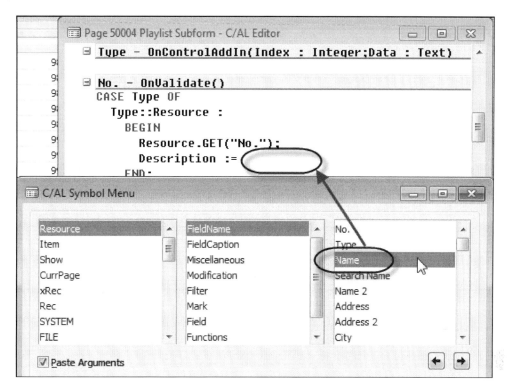

When we are all done constructing the CASE Statement, it should look like the following screenshot:

```
No. - OnValidate()
CASE Type OF
  Type::Resource :
    BEGIN
      Resource.GET("No.");
      Description := Resource.Name
    END;
  Type::Item :
    BEGIN
      Item.GET("No.");
      DataFormat := Item.DataFormat;
      Description := Item.Description;
      Duration := Item.Duration;
    END;
  Type::Show :
    BEGIN
      Show.GET("No.");
      Description := Show.Name;
    END;
END;
```

The last set of **OnValidate** code we need to add is to calculate End Time from the supplied Start Time and Duration (or Start Time from the End Time and Duration).

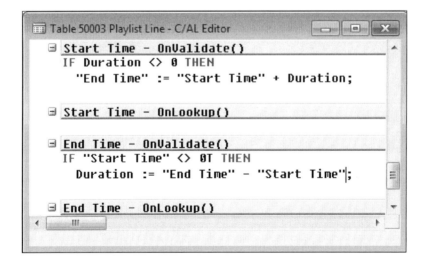

```
Table 50003 Playlist Line - C/AL Editor
Start Time - OnValidate()
 IF Duration <> 0 THEN
   "End Time" := "Start Time" + Duration;

Start Time - OnLookup()

End Time - OnValidate()
 IF "Start Time" <> 0T THEN
   Duration := "End Time" - "Start Time";

End Time - OnLookup()
```

Obviously, the design could be expanded to have the Duration value be user editable along with an appropriate change in the C/AL logic. After our initial work on the Playlist functionality is completed, making that change would be a good exercise for you as would be the addition of "housekeeping" commands to clear out fields that are not used by the assigned record **Type** (such as clearing the **DataFormat** field for a Show record).

Creating a function for our Factbox

For this application, we want our FactBox to display information relating to the specific Radio Show we are scheduling. The information to be displayed includes the five show segment requirements and the status of fulfillment (counts) of those requirements by the data entered to date. The requirements come from Playlist Header fields: PSAs Required, Ads Required, News Required, Sports Required, and Weather Required. The counts come from summing up data in the Playline Line records for a show. We can use the Playlist Header fields PSA Count and Ad Count for those two counts. These counts can be obtained through the FlowField property definitions we defined earlier for these two fields.

For the other three counts, we must read through the Playlist Lines and total up each of the counts. To accomplish that, we'll create a Function which we can call from the FactBox page. Since our new function is local to the Playlist Header and Playlist Lines tables, we will define the function in the Playlist Header (table 50002).

The first step in defining the function is to enter its name in to the **Functions** tab of the **Globals** screen for the object. Open the object, Table 50002, by clicking **Table | Design**, then **View | C/AL Globals**, and then click the **Functions** tab. Enter the name of the new function, access its **Properties** (through the Properties icon or *Shift + F4*) and set the **Local** property to No so the function can be called from the Factbox Page.

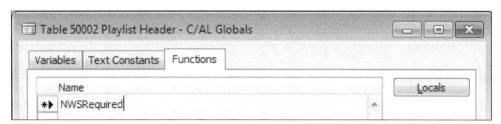

Then, after clicking on the **Locals** button and viewing the **Parameters** tab, we can enter the parameters we want to pass to the function. In this case, we want the parameter to be passed by value, not by reference, so we do not check the **Var** checkbox on the **Parameter** line. For more information about parameter passing, look at **Help** sections *C/AL Function Calls* and *How to: Add a Function to a Codeunit,* as well as the Create a Function section in *Chapter 6, Introduction to C/SIDE and C/AL.* The name of the Parameter is local to the function.

Since we want a single function that will serve to count Playlist Lines that are News, Weather, or Sports, the parameter we pass in will be an Option code of News, Weather, or Sports. The **Option Subtype** sequence must be the same as those in the field **Type** in the table **Playlist Lines**, otherwise we will have **Options** mismatching.

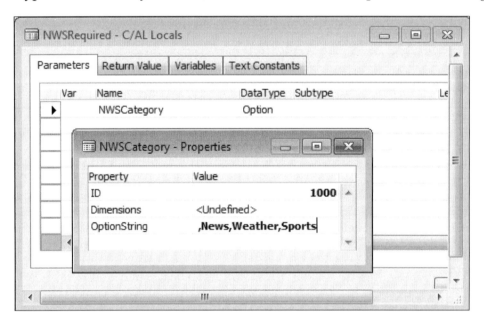

The return value we want back from this function is an Integer count. Again, the variable name is local.

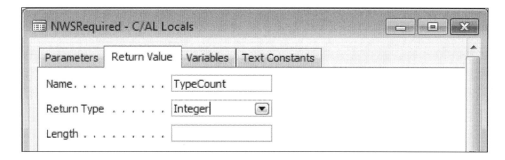

The logic of our counting process is described in the following pseudocode:

1. Filter the Playlist Line table for the Radio Show we are scheduling and for the segment entries (Playlist Line) that represent shows.
2. Look up the Radio Show record for each of those records.
3. Using the data from the Radio Show record, look up the Radio Show Type code.
4. In the Radio Show Type record, use the News, Weather, and Sports fields to determine which Playlist Line counter should be incremented.

Based on this logic, we must have **Local Variables** defined for the three tables Playlist Line, Radio Show and Radio Show Type. The following image shows those **Local Variables**:

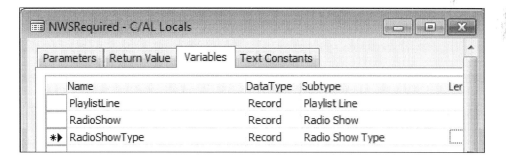

Translating our pseudocode into executable C/AL, our function looks like the following:

```
Table 50002 Playlist Header - C/AL Editor                              [_][□][X]

NWSRequired(NWSCategory : ' ,News,Weather,Sports') TypeCount : Integer
PlaylistLine.RESET;
PlaylistLine.SETRANGE("Playlist No.",Rec."No.");
PlaylistlINE.SETRANGE(Type,PlaylistLine.Type::Show);
IF PlaylistLine.FINDSET(FALSE,FALSE) THEN REPEAT
  IF RadioShow.GET(PlaylistLine."No.") THEN BEGIN
    CASE NWSCategory OF
      NWSCategory::News :
       BEGIN
         IF RadioShowType.Code ='News' THEN
           TypeCount += 1;
       END;
      NWSCategory::Weather :
       BEGIN
         IF RadioShowType.Code ='Weather' THEN
           TypeCount += 1;
       END;
      NWSCategory::Sports :
       BEGIN
         IF RadioShowType.Code ='Sports' THEN
           TypeCount += 1;
       END;
    END;
  END;
UNTIL PlaylistLine.NEXT = 0;
```

In the process of writing this code, we notice another design flaw. We defined the type of Radio Show with a code which allows users to enter their choice of text strings. We just wrote some code that depends on the contents of that text string being specific values. A better design would have been to have the critical field be an Option data type so we could depend on the choices are members of a predefined set. However, the Code field is our Primary Key field and we probably shouldn't use an Option field as the Primary Key. We will continue with our example with the design as is, but you should consider how to improve it. Making that improvement would be excellent practice with C/AL.

Creating a Factbox page

All the hard work is now done. We just have to define a Factbox page and add it to the Playlist page. We can create a Factbox page using the **New Page** Wizard to define a CardPart.

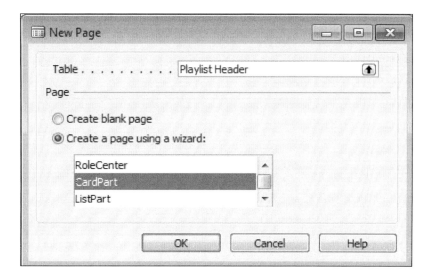

Our Factbox will contain the fields from the Playlist Header that relate to two of the five required show segments, the PSA Count and Ad Count fields.

Once we exit the Page Wizard into the Page Designer, we will have a page layout that looks like the following image:

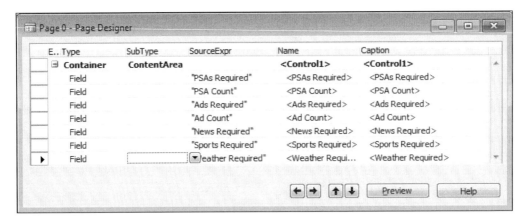

At this point we need to put in place the logic to take advantage of the **NWSRequired** function that we created earlier. That function is designed to return the count of the segment type identified in the calling parameter. Since a line on a page can be an expression, we can simply code the function calls right on the page lines, with an appropriate caption defined, as we can see in the following image. The only other task has been to define a Global variable, **NWSCategory**, which is defined as an **Option** with the choices of **News**, **Weather**, and **Sports**. This variable is used for the calling parameter. We intersperse the Count lines for a consistent appearance on the Page.

We save the new FactBox page as **Page 50010**, named `Playlist FactBox`.

One final development step is required. We must connect the new **FactBox CardPart** to the **Playlist Document**. All that is required is to define the **FactBox Area** and add our FactBox as an element in that area.

Properties for the **Playlist Subform** Pagepart are as shown in the following screenshot:

Properties for the FactBox Pagepart are as shown in the following image:

Multiple FactBoxes can be part of a primary page. If we look at **Page 21 – Customer Card**, we will see a FactBox Area with eight FactBoxes, of which two are System Parts.

The end result of our development effort is shown when we **Run** Page 50000 – Playlist with some sample test data (which we entered by Running the various tables).

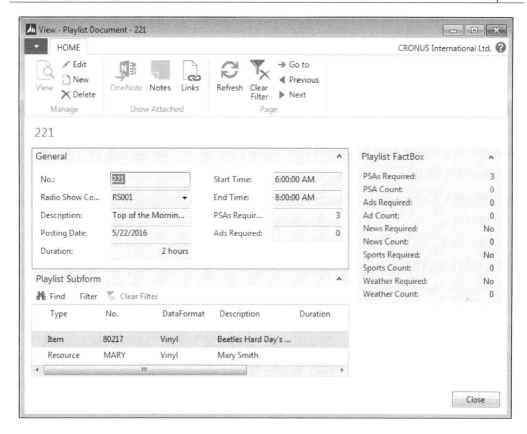

Summary

In this chapter, we have covered a number of practical tools and topics regarding C/AL coding and development. We started with reviewing methods and then we dived into a long list of functions that we will need on a frequent basis.

We have covered a variety of selected data-centric functions, including some for computation and validation, some for data conversion, and others for date handling. Next we reviewed functions that affect the flow of logic and the flow of data, including FlowFields and SIFT, Processing Flow Control, Input and Output, and Filtering. Finally, we put a number of these to work in an enhancement for our WDTU application.

In the next chapter, we will move from the details of the functions to the broader view of C/AL development integration into the standard NAV code, and debugging techniques.

Review questions

Q1. Which three of the following are valid date related NAV functions?

    a.   `DATE2DWY`

    b. `CALCDATE`

    c. `DMY2DATE`

    d. `DATE2NUM`

Q2. RESET is used to clear the current sort key setting from a record. True or False?

Q3. Which functions can be used to cause FlowFields to be calculated? Choose two.

    a.   `CALCSUMS`

    b. `CALCFIELDS`

    c. `SETAUTOCALCFIELDS`

    d. `SUMFLOWFIELD`

Q4. Which of the following functions should be used within a report `OnAfterGetRecord` trigger to end processing just for a single iteration of the trigger? Choose one.

    a. EXIT

    b. BREAK

    c. QUIT

    d. SKIP

Q5. The WORKDATE value can be set to a different value from the System Date. True or False?

Q6. Only one FactBox is allowed on a page. True or False?

Q7. Braces {} are used as a special form of a repeating CASE statement. True or False?

Q8. Which of the following is not a valid C/AL flow control combination? Choose one.

    a. REPEAT-UNTIL

    b. DO-UNTIL

    c. CASE-ELSE

    d. IF-THEN

Q9. A FILTERGROUP function should not be used in custom code. True or False?

Q10. The REPEAT-UNTIL looping structure is most often used to control data reading processes. True or False?

Q11. Which of the following formats of MODIFY will cause the table's OnModify trigger to fire? Choose one.

    a. MODIFY

    b. MODIFY(TRUE)

    c. MODIFY(RUN)

    d. MODIFY(READY)

Q12. MARKing a group of records creates a special index, therefore MARKing is especially efficient. True or False?

Q13. A CASE statement structure should never be used in place of a nested IF statement structure. True or False?

Q14. An Average FlowField requires which one of the following?

    a. A record key

    b. SQL Server database

    c. An Integer variable

    d. A Decimal variable

Q15. The TESTFIELD function can be used to assign new values to a variable. True or False?

Q16. The VALIDATE function can be used to assign new values to a variable. True or False?

Q17. The C/AL Symbol Menu can be used for several of the following purposes. Choose two.

    a. Find applicable functions

    b. Test coded functions

    c. Use entries as a template for function syntax and arguments

    d. Translate text constants into a support language

Q18. Documentation cannot be integrated into in-line C/AL code. True or False?

Q19. If MAINTAINSIFTINDEX is set to NO and CALCFIELDS is invoked, the process will terminate with an error. True or False?

Q20. SETRANGE is often used to clear all filtering from a single field. True or False?

8

Advanced NAV Development Tools

"Beauty is more important in computing than anywhere else in technology because software is so complicated. Beauty is the ultimate defense against complexity."

– David Gelernter

"Often when you think you're at the end of something, you're at the beginning of something else."

– Fred Rogers

Because NAV is extremely flexible and suitable for addressing many problem types, there are a lot of choices for advanced NAV topics. We'll try to cover those which will be most helpful in the effort of putting together a complete implementation.

First, we will review the overall structure of NAV as an application software system, aiming for a basic understanding of the process flow of the system along with some of the utility functions built into the standard product. Before designing modifications for NAV, it is important to have a good understanding of the structural "style" of the software, so that our enhancements are designed for a better fit.

Second, we will review some special components of the NAV system that allow us to accomplish more at less cost. These resources include features such as XMLPorts and Web Services that we can build on, and which help us to use standard interface structures to connect with the world outside of NAV system. Fortunately, NAV has a good supply of such features.

NAV process flow

Primary data such as sales orders, purchase orders, production orders, and financial transactions flow through the NAV system as follows:

- **Initial Setup**: The Essential Master data, reference data, and control and setup data is entered. Most of this preparation is done when the system (or a new application) is prepared for production use.

- **Transaction Entry**: The transactions are entered into Documents and then transferred as part of a Posting sequence into a `Journal` table, or data may be entered directly into a Journal table. Data is preliminarily validated as it is entered with master and auxiliary data tables being referenced as appropriate. Entry can be via manual keying, an automated transaction generation process, or an import function that brings in transaction data from another system.

- **Validate**: This provides for additional data validation processing of a set of one or more transactions, often in batches, prior to submitting it to Posting.

- **Post**: This posts a Journal Batch, which includes completing transaction data validation, adding entries to one or more Ledgers, and perhaps also updating a register and document history.

- **Utilize**: Access the data via Pages, Queries, and/or Reports including those that feed Web Services and other consumers of data. At this point, total flexibility exists. Whatever tools are appropriate for users' needs should be used, whether internal to NAV or external (external tools are often referred to as **Business Intelligence (BI)** tools). NAV's built-in capabilities for data manipulation, extraction, and presentation should not be overlooked.

- **Maintenance**: The continued maintenance of all NAV data as appropriate.

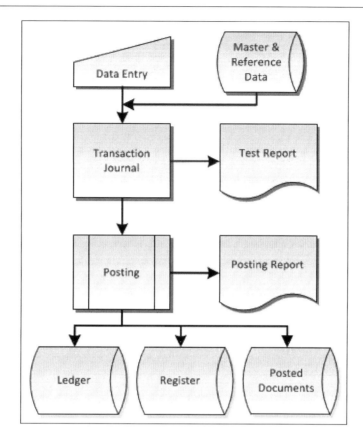

The preceding image provides a simplified picture of the flow of application data through a NAV system. Many of the transaction types have additional reporting, multiple ledgers to update, and even auxiliary processing. But this represents the basic data flow in NAV whenever a Journal and a Ledger table are involved.

When we enhance an existing NAV functional area (such as Jobs or Service Management), we may need to enhance related process flow elements by adding new fields to journals, ledgers, posted documents, and so on. It's always a good idea to add new fields rather than change the use of standard fields. It makes debugging, maintenance, and upgrading all easier.

When we create a new functional area, we will likely want to replicate the standard NAV process flow in some form for the new application's data. For example, for our WDTU application, we handle the entry of Playlists in the same fashion as a Journal is entered. A day's Playlists would be similar to a Journal Batch in another application. When a day's shows have been broadcast, the Playlist will be posted into the Radio Show Ledger as a permanent record of the broadcasts.

Initial setup and data preparation

Data must be maintained as new Master data becomes available, as various system operating parameters change, and so on. The standard approach for NAV data entry allows records to be entered that have just enough information to define the primary key fields, but not necessarily enough to support processing. This allows a great deal of flexibility in the timing and responsibility for entry and completeness of new data. This approach applies to both setup data entry and ongoing production transaction data entry.

This system design philosophy allows initial and incomplete data entry by one person, with validation and completion to be handled later by someone else. This works because often data comes into an organization on a piecemeal basis.

For example, a sales person might initialize a new customer entry with name, address, and phone number, entering just that data to which they have easy access. At this point, there is not enough information recorded to process orders for this new customer. At a later time, someone in the accounting department can set up posting groups, payment terms, and other control data that should not be controlled by the sales department. With this additional data, the new customer record is ready for production use.

The NAV data entry approach allows the system to be updated on an incremental basis as the data arrives, providing an operational flexibility that many systems lack. The other side of this flexibility is added responsibility for the users to ensure that partially updated information is completed on a timely fashion. For the customer who can't deal with that responsibility, it may be necessary to create special procedures or even system customizations which enforce the necessary discipline.

Transaction entry

Transactions are entered into a Journal table. Data is preliminarily validated as it is entered; master and auxiliary data tables are referenced as appropriate. Validations are based on the evaluation of the individual transaction data plus the related Master records and associated reference tables (for example, lookups being satisfied, application or system setup parameter constraints being met, and so on).

Testing and posting the Journal batch

Any additional validations that need to be done to ensure the integrity and completeness of the transaction data prior to being Posted, are done either in pre-Post routines or directly in the course of the Posting processes. The actual Posting of a Journal batch occurs when the transaction data has been completely validated. Depending on the specific application, when Journal transactions don't pass muster during this final validation stage, either the individual transaction is bypassed while acceptable transactions are Posted, or the entire Journal Batch is rejected until the identified problem is resolved.

The Posting process adds entries to one or more Ledgers, and sometimes to a document history table. When a Journal Entry is Posted to a Ledger, it becomes a part of the permanent accounting record. Most data cannot be changed or deleted once it resides in a Ledger.

Register tables may also be updated during Posting, recording the ID number ranges of ledger entries posted, when posted, and in what batches. This adds to the transparency of the NAV application system for audits and analysis.

In general, NAV follows the standard accounting practice of requiring Ledger revisions to be made by Posting reversing entries, rather than by deletion of problem entries. The overall result is that NAV is a very auditable system, a key requirement for a variety of government, legal, and certification requirements for information systems.

Utilizing and maintaining the data

The data in a NAV system can be accessed via Pages, Queries, and/or Reports, providing total flexibility. Whatever tools are available to the developer or the user, which are appropriate, should be used. There are some very good tools in NAV for data manipulation, extraction, and presentation. Among other things, these include the SIFT/Flowfield functionality, the pervasive filtering capability (including the ability to apply filters to subordinate data structures), and the Navigate function. NAV includes the ability to create page parts for graphing, with a wide variety of predefined chart page parts included as part of the standard distribution. We can also create our own chart parts using tools that were delivered with the system or available from Web blogs.

The NAV database design approach could be referred to as a "rational normalization". NAV isn't constrained by a rigid normalized data structure, where every data element appears only once. The NAV data structure is normalized so long as that principle doesn't get in the way of processing speed. Where processing speed or ease of use for the user is improved by duplicating data across tables, NAV does so. In addition, the duplication of master file data into transactions allows for one-time modification of that data when appropriate (such as a ship-to address in a Sales Order). That data duplication also often greatly simplifies data access for analysis.

Data maintenance

As with any database-oriented application software, ongoing maintenance of Master data, reference data, and setup and control data is required. In NAV, maintenance of data uses many of the same data preparation tools as were initially used to set up the system.

Role Center pages

One of the key features of NAV 2015 is the Role Tailored user experience centered on Role Centers tied to user work roles. The Role Tailored approach provides a single point of entry and access into the system for each user through their assigned Role Center. The user's Role Center acts as their home page. Each Role Center focuses on the tasks needed to support its users' jobs throughout the day. Primary tasks are front and center, while the Action Ribbon and Departments Menu provide easy access to other functions only a click or two away.

The standard NAV 2015 distribution from Microsoft includes 23 different Role Center pages, identified for user roles such as Bookkeeper, Sales Manager, Shop Supervisor, Purchasing Agent, and so on (Page 9011 is identified as a **Foundation** rather than as a **Role Center** or **RC**). Some localized NAV distributions may have additional Role Center pages included. It is critical to realize that the Role Centers supplied out of the box are not generally intended to be used directly out of the box. Only a portion of the 23 supplied Role Center pages have been fully configured. Three of those are:

- 9004 – Bookkeeper
- 9005 – Sales Manager
- 9006 – Order Processor

The 23 Role Center pages should be used as templates for custom Role Centers tailored to the specific work role requirements of the individual customer implementation.

One of the very critical tasks of implementing a new system is to analyze the work flow and responsibilities of the system's intended users and configure Role Centers to fit the users. In some cases, the supplied Role Centers can be used with minimal tailoring. Sometimes, it will be necessary to create complete new Role Centers. Even then, we will often be able to start with a copy of an existing Role Center Page, which we will modify as required. In any case, it is important to understand the structure of the Role Center Page and how it is built.

The Role Center structure

The following screenshot shows Page 9006 – Order Processor Role Center:

The components of the Role Center highlighted in the preceding image are:

1. Action Ribbon.
2. Navigation Pane.
3. Activity Pane.
4. Cue Group Actions (in Cue Groups).
5. Cues (in Cue Groups).
6. Page Parts.
7. System Part.

A general representation of the structure of a Role Center Page is shown in the following outline:

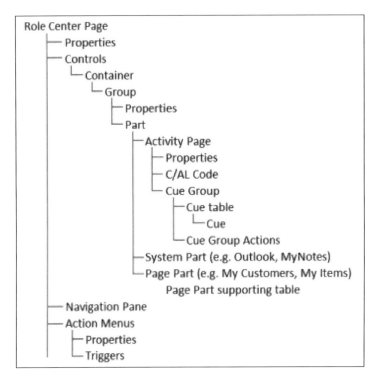

We need to understand the construction of a Role Center Page so that we are prepared to modify an existing Role Center or create a new one. First, we'll take a look at Page 9006 – Order Processor Role Center in the Page Designer.

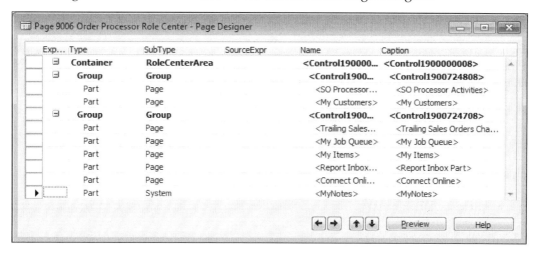

The Role Center page layout should look familiar, because it's very similar in structure to the pages we've designed previously. What's specific to a Role Center page? There is a Container control of **SubType RoleCenterArea**. This is required for a Role Center page. There are two Group Controls, which represent the two columns (left and right) of the Role Center page display. Each group contains several parts, which show up individually in the Role Center display.

Role Center page properties are accessed by highlighting the first blank line on the Page Designer form (the line below all the defined controls), then clicking on the **Properties** icon, or we could right-click and choose the **Properties** option, or click on **View | Properties** or press *Shift + F4*. Note that **PageType** is RolieCenter, and there is no **Source Table**. The page properties not shown in this image are all default values:

The Role Center activities page

Since the Group Control has no underlying code or settings, we'll take a quick look at the first Part Control's Properties. The **PagePartId** property is Page SO Processor Activities.

Cue Groups and Cues

Now we'll focus on Page **9060 – SO Processor Activities**. Designing that page, we see the layout shown in the next screenshot. Comparing the controls we see here to those of the Role Center, we can see this Page Part is the source of the **Activities** section of the Role Center Page. There are three **CueGroup** Controls – **For Release, Sales Orders Released Not Shipped**, and **Returns**. In each **CueGroup**, there are **Field Controls** for the individual **Cues**.

An individual Cue is displayed as an iconic shortcut to a filtered list through a FlowField, or to a Query or other data source through a Normal field. The stack of papers in the Cue icon resulting from a filtered value represents an idea of the number of records in that list. The actual number of entries is also displayed next to the icon (see the **Sales Orders - Open** example in the following screenshot). The purpose of this type of Cue is to provide a focus and single click access to a specific user task. The set of these Cues is intended to represent the full set of primary activities for a user, based on their work Role:

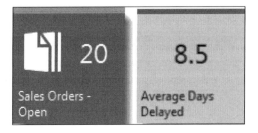

NAV 2015 provides another Cue format, like the **Average Days Delayed** Cue in the preceding image, which is based on a calculated value stored in a Normal field.

Cue source table

In the Properties of the SO Processor Activities page, we see this is a **PageType** of `CardPart` tied to **SourceTable** Sales Cue.

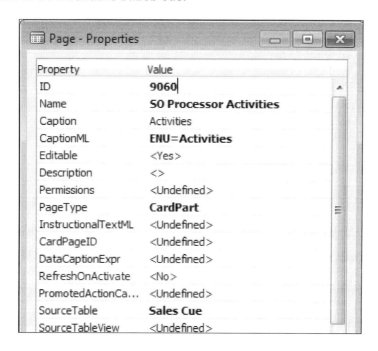

Next, we want to **Design** the referenced table, **Sales Cue**, to see how it is constructed.

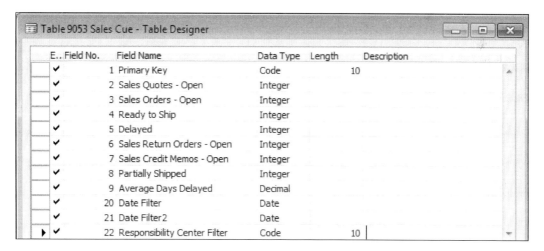

As we see in the preceding image, there is a simply structured table, with an integer field for each of the action Cues and a decimal field for the information Cue, all of which were displayed in the Role Center we are analyzing. There is also a key field, two fields identified as Date Filters, and a field identified as a Responsibility Center Filter.

When we display the properties of one of these integer fields, **Sales Orders - Open**, we find it is a `FlowField` providing a Count of the `Sales Orders` with a `Status` of `Open`.

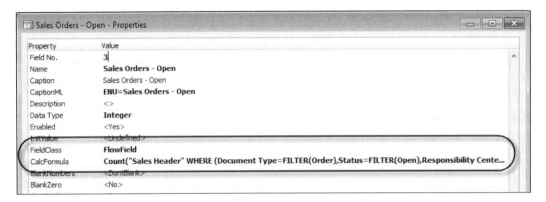

If we inspect each of the other integer fields in this table, we will find a similar FlowField setup. Each is defined to fit the specific Cue to which it's tied. If we think about what the Cues show (a count) and how FlowFields work (a calculation based on a range of data records), we can see this is a simple, direct method of providing the information necessary to support the Cue displays. Clicking on the action Cue (the count) then opens up the list of records being counted. The information Cue is tied to a decimal field which is computed by means of a function (shown in the following image) in the Cue table which is invoked from the Role Center page when the Cue is displayed:

```
Table 9053 Sales Cue - C/AL Editor

  CalculateAverageDaysDelayed() AverageDays : Decimal
  FilterOrders(SalesHeader,FIELDNO(Delayed));
  IF SalesHeader.FINDSET THEN BEGIN
    REPEAT
      SumDelayDays += WORKDATE - SalesHeader."Shipment Date";
      CountDelayedInvoices += 1;
    UNTIL SalesHeader.NEXT = 0;
    AverageDays := SumDelayDays / CountDelayedInvoices;
  END;


  CountOrders(FieldNumber : Integer) : Integer
```

The following screenshot shows the list of Cue tables. Each of the Cue tables contains a series of FlowFields and other fields that support a set of Cues. Some Cue tables service more than one of the Role Center pages:

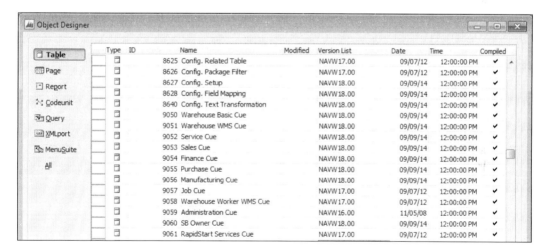

Type	ID	Name	Modified	Version List	Date	Time	Compiled
	8625	Config. Related Table		NAVW17.00	09/07/12	12:00:00 PM	✔
	8626	Config. Package Filter		NAVW17.00	09/07/12	12:00:00 PM	✔
	8627	Config. Setup		NAVW18.00	09/09/14	12:00:00 PM	✔
	8628	Config. Field Mapping		NAVW18.00	09/09/14	12:00:00 PM	✔
	8640	Config. Text Transformation		NAVW18.00	09/09/14	12:00:00 PM	✔
	9050	Warehouse Basic Cue		NAVW18.00	09/09/14	12:00:00 PM	✔
	9051	Warehouse WMS Cue		NAVW18.00	09/09/14	12:00:00 PM	✔
	9052	Service Cue		NAVW18.00	09/09/14	12:00:00 PM	✔
	9053	Sales Cue		NAVW18.00	09/09/14	12:00:00 PM	✔
	9054	Finance Cue		NAVW18.00	09/09/14	12:00:00 PM	✔
	9055	Purchase Cue		NAVW18.00	09/09/14	12:00:00 PM	✔
	9056	Manufacturing Cue		NAVW18.00	09/09/14	12:00:00 PM	✔
	9057	Job Cue		NAVW17.00	09/07/12	12:00:00 PM	✔
	9058	Warehouse Worker WMS Cue		NAVW17.00	09/07/12	12:00:00 PM	✔
	9059	Administration Cue		NAVW16.00	11/05/08	12:00:00 PM	✔
	9060	SB Owner Cue		NAVW18.00	09/09/14	12:00:00 PM	✔
	9061	RapidStart Services Cue		NAVW17.00	09/07/12	12:00:00 PM	✔

Cue Group Actions

Another set of Role Center page components to analyze are **Cue Group Actions**. While the Cues are the primary tasks that are presented to the user, the Cue Group Actions are a related secondary set of tasks displayed to the right of the Cues.

Cue Group Actions are defined in the Role Center in essentially the same way as Actions are defined in other page types. As the name implies, Cue Group Actions are associated with a Control with the **SubType** CueGroup. If we right-click on the CueGroup Control, one of the options available is **Control Actions** (as shown in the following screenshot):

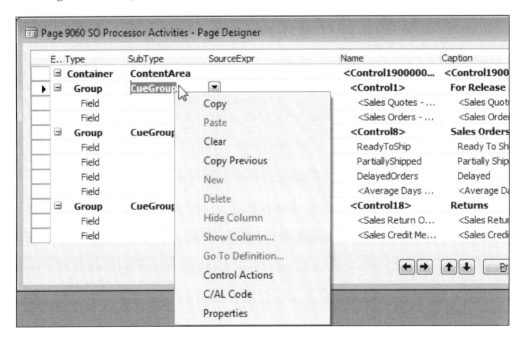

When we choose **Control Actions**, the **Action Designer** form will be displayed showing the two CueGroup actions in the For Release CueGroup in the SO Processor Role Center page. If we open **Properties,** we will see the "New" functionality is accomplished by setting the **RunPageMode** property to Create.

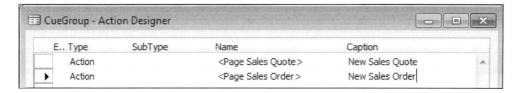

System Part

Now that we have covered the components of the **Activities** portion of the Role Center page, let's take a look at the other components.

Returning to Page 9006 in **Page Designer**, we examine **Properties** of the System Part Control. This Page Part is the one that incorporates a view of the user's Notes data into the Role Center. Looking at this control's properties, we see a **PartType** of System and a **SystemPartID** of MyNotes (which displays as **My Notifications**).

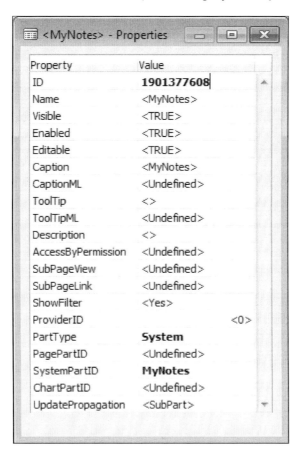

Page Parts

Let's look at the second Group in Page 9006, the Group that defines the right hand column appearing in the Role Center page. There are five Page Parts and a System Part defined.

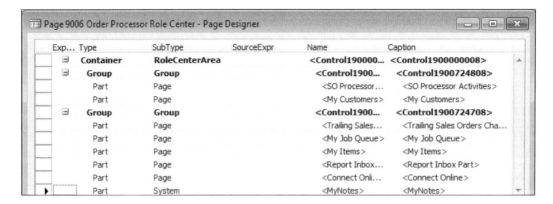

Page Parts not visible

If we look again at the display of the Role Center page generated by this layout, we will see a chart (**Trailing Sales Orders**), followed by two ListParts (**My Items** and **Report InBox**), and in turn followed by the System Part (**My Notifications**). The two Page Parts, **My Job Queue** and **Connect Online**, do not appear. These two Page Parts have been defined by the developer with the **Visible** property equal to FALSE, which causes them not to display unless the Role Center Page is customized by the user (or an administrator or developer) and the part added to the visible part list.

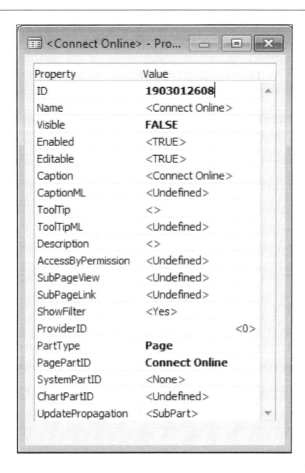

Page Part Charts

The first Page **Part** in the second **Group** provides for a Chart to display using the Chart Control Add-in included in NAV 2015. The Chart Control Add-in is documented in the **Developer and IT Pro Help** in *Displaying Charts Using the Chart Control Add-in*. In the Page 9006, the Page Part **Trailing Sales Orders Chart** invokes Page 760 of the same name. Looking at Page 760 in the Page Designer, we see the following layout:

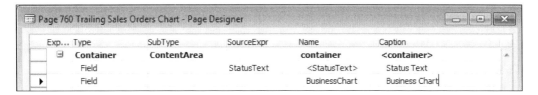

The properties of the **Field** named **Business Chart** look like the following:

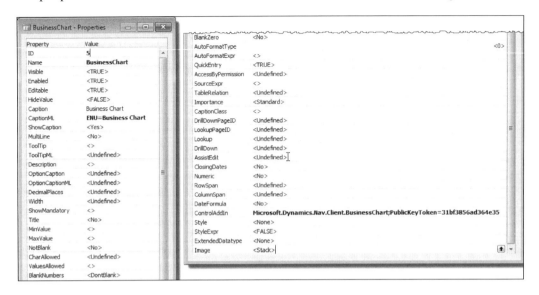

Note that the property **ControlAddIn** contains the necessary information to access the Chart Control Add-in. This property provides access to the screen, shown in the following screenshot, where the Client Add-ins are listed that are available for use in our NAV system. An Add-in is a Microsoft .NET Framework assembly (a module external to NAV but registered with the system) that lets us add customer functionality to a NAV Windows Client. The **Client Add-in** screen shown next displays after clicking on the lookup arrow at the right end of the **ControlAddIn** property:

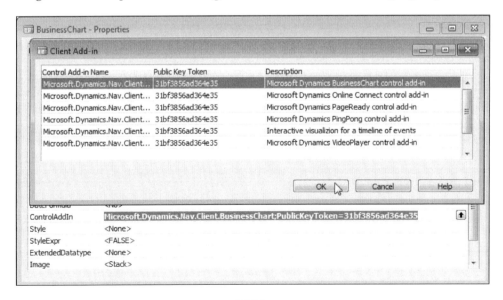

Page Parts for user data

Three of the Page Parts in Role Center Page 9006 provide data that is specific to the individual user. They track "My" data, information important to the user who is logged in. If we Design any one of the pages, we can open the page properties to find out what table the page is tied to. Then viewing any of those tables in the Table Designer, we will see that a highly ranked field is User ID. An example is the My Item table:

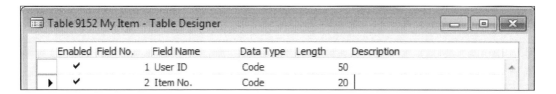

The User ID allows the data to be filtered to present user specific information to each user. In some cases, this data can be updated directly in the Role Center Page Part; for example, in My Customers and My Items. In other cases, such as My Job Queue, the data is updated elsewhere and is only viewed in the Role Center Page Part. If our users needed to track other information in a similar manner, such as My Service Contracts, we could readily plagiarize the approach used in the standard Page Parts.

The Navigation Pane and Action menus

The last major Role Center Page components we're going to review are the **Navigation Pane** and the **Action Ribbon**. Even though there are two major parts of the Role Center Page that provide access to action choices, they both are defined in **Action Designer** section of **Page Designer**.

The display of Action Controls in a Role Center page is dependent on a combination of the definition of the controls in the Action Designer, certain properties of the page, and configuration/personalization of the page. Many of the default Role Centers provided with the product are configured as examples of possibilities of what can be done. Even if one of the default Role Centers seems to fit our customer's requirements exactly, we should create a copy of that Role Center page as another page object and reconfigure it. That way we can document how that page was set up and make any necessary tweaks.

We're going to start with Role Center Page 9006, because it is used as the default Role Center and is used in many other examples. Copy Page 9006 into Page **50020 – WDTU Role Center** using the sequence **Object Designer | Page | Design | File |Save As...** , with a new page object ID of 50020 and object Name of WDTU Role Center.

Once we have the new page saved, in order to use this page as a Role Center we must create a Profile for the page. This is done within the Role Tailored Client (RTC) and is typically a System Administrator task. Invoke the RTC and click on the **Departments** menu button in the Navigator Pane. Then click on **Administrator: Application Setup | Role Tailored Client | Lists: Profiles**. Click on the **New** icon and create a new profile like the following one:

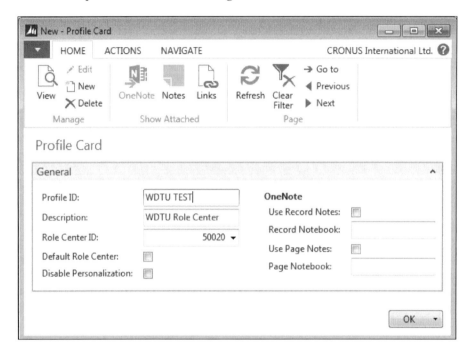

For the purpose of easy access to this Role Center for testing, we could also checkmark the **Default Role Center** box. Then, when we invoke the RTC, our test Role Center will be the one that displays (if no other profile is assigned to this user). Another approach to testing is to assign our User ID to use this Profile.

When we are doing development work on a Role Center, we can run the Role Center as a page from the C/SIDE Object Designer in the same way as other pages. However, the Role Center page will launch as a task page on top of whatever Role Center is configured for the active user. The Navigation Pane of the Role Center being modified will not be active and can't be tested with this approach. In order to test all the aspects of the Role Center page, we must launch it as the assigned Role Center for the active user.

A major area where action choices are presented in a Role Center (and also in other page types) is in the ribbon. The ribbon for the standard Page 9006 – Order Processor Role Center, as delivered from Microsoft, looks like the following:

After we have created our Role Center copy, the ribbon for Page 50020 – Order Processor RC WDTU looks like the following:

When we compare the available actions in the two ribbon images, we see most of the same actions, but displayed quite a bit differently. Two of the report actions available in the standard ribbon don't show up in the Page 50020 ribbon, but if we take a look at the report tab on the ribbon, we'll see that they are available there.

If we made the same kind of analysis of some of the other default Role Centers, we would find similar results. When the page is copied to another object number, the appearance of the ribbon changes, losing detail. As it turns out, many of the default Role Centers have been manually configured by Microsoft as part of the effort to show good examples of Role Center ribbon design. Thus, we should start with a fresh copy of our Role Centers when designing for our customer, so that we know what tailoring has been done and are in control of the design.

Action Designer

The actions for a page are defined and maintained in **Action Designer**. **Action Designer** is accessed from within the **Page Designer**. Open our new Page **50020 - WDTU Role Center** in the **Page Designer**, then either press *Ctrl + Alt + F4* or **View | Page Actions** to open the **Action Designer** to view the current set of actions defined for this page.

For our newly created Page 50020, cloned from Page 9006, the Action Designer contents look like the following:

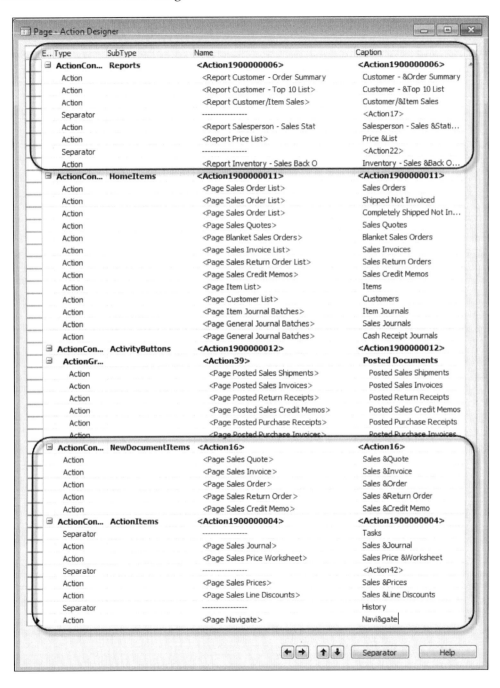

The actions enclosed in rectangles are the ones that are assigned to the ribbon. Whether or not they are actually displayed, how they are displayed, and where they are displayed are all controlled by a combination of the following factors:

- The structure of the controls within the action list
- The properties of the individual actions
- The customizations/personalizations that have been applied by the developer, administrator, or the user

The first column of each action control is the **Type.** In hierarchical order, the action control entries can be ActionContainer, Action Group, Action, or Separator. The specific **SubType** of each **ActionContainer** entry determines the area, Ribbon, or Navigation Pane, in which the subordinate groups of actions will appear.

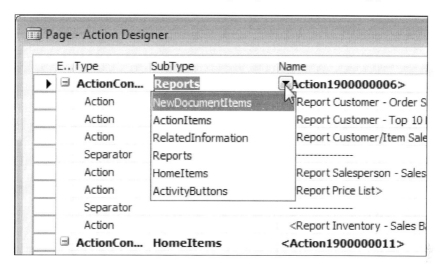

If the **SubType** is HomeItems or ActivityButtons (Page Control SubTypes that can only be used in Role Center pages), the indented subordinate actions will appear in the Navigation Pane. All the other SubTypes (NewDocumentItems, ActionItems, and Reports) will cause their subordinate actions to appear in the Role Center Ribbon. These three SubTypes are not limited to use in Role Center pages. The **SubType** RelatedInformation is not intended for use in Role Center pages, but only in other page types.

An ActionGroup control provides a grouping of actions, which will appear as a category in the Ribbon. This is one way of defining a category to display in the ribbon. For actions to appear within the category on the ribbon, those Action controls must follow the ActionGroup and be indented. If an ActionGroup is indented within a parent ActionGroup, it will generate a drop-down list of actions.

The other type of action control is the `Separator`. In the NAV 2015 Action Ribbon, the separator controls don't appear to do anything.

If we compare the control entries in the preceding Action Designer screenshot to the action icons that display in the screenshot of the unmodified Page 50020 ribbon, we see the following:

- The action control entries of the `NewDocumentItems` and `ActionItems` `ActionContainers` appear on the Actions tab of the ribbon. ActionItems is intended for task related functions while NewDocumentItems is intended for those actions that cause a new document to be opened.
- All the control entries in the `NewDocumentItems ActionContainer` appear in the New Document Category in the Action Ribbon.
- The control entries in the `ActionItems ActionContainer` appear in the **General** Category of the ribbon.
- One action, **Refresh**, is a default action that is automatically generated and assigned to the **Page** Category.
- All the control entries in the `Reports ActionContainer` are in the General Category on the Reports tab of the Action Ribbon.

Create a WDTU Role Center Ribbon

If we were creating a Role Center to be used in a real production environment, we are likely to be defining a new Activities Page, new Cues, a new or modified Cue table, new FactBoxes, and so on. But since our primary purpose here is learning, we're going to take the shortcut of piggybacking on the existing role center and simply add our WDTU actions to the foundation of that existing role center.

There are several steps to be taken to define our WDTU Role Center Ribbon. The same end result, from the user's point of view, can be achieved using different approaches. We can also perform the development steps in different sequences. For the WDTU ribbon work, we will use the Developer tools.

The steps we need to do for our WDTU actions are:

- Define one or more new ribbon categories for the WDTU actions
- Create the WDTU action controls in the Action Designer
- Assign the WDTU action controls to the appropriate ribbon categories
- Finalize any look and feel items

Because some of the original Order Processor Role Center ribbon layout disappeared when we cloned Page 9006 to Page 50020, we will also want to recreate that layout. For this part of our ribbon definition effort, because we want to learn more ways to accomplish implementation goals, we will use the Configuration/Personalization tools.

The steps needed to replicate the Page 9006 ribbon layout are:

- Define the needed ribbon categories
- Assign the action controls to the appropriate categories
- Finalize any look and feel items

The normal sequence of defining an Action Ribbon is to complete the work that utilizes development tools, then proceed with the work that can be done by an implementer or system administrator (or even an authorized user). So we will work on the WDTU portion of the Action Ribbon first, and then follow with the work of replicating the original layout.

Let's add the following functions to the WDTU portion of the Action Ribbon:

- Radio Show List page
- Playlist page
- Radio Show Types page
- Playlist Item Rates page
- Item List (filtered for Playlist Items) page
- Record Labels page

We'll put the first two items in a category named WDTU Operations and the other four items in a category named WDTU Data Maintenance.

Promoted Actions Categories

There are at least two ways available to set up the categories. One involves assigning values to the Page Property **PromotedActionCategoriesML** (which appears to be originally intended to support NAV's MultiLanguage capabilities rather than Ribbon layout customization, simply because it is using a ML property).

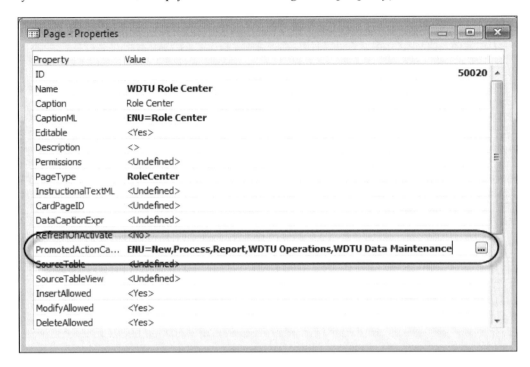

To enter the **PromotedActionCategoriesML** data shown in the preceding screenshot, first we click on the ellipsis on the property and enter the desired headings, as shown in the following image:

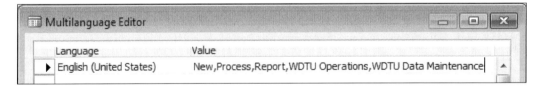

There are 10 **PromotedActionCategoriesML** slots available. The first three are assigned by default categories of New, Process, and Report, but can be renamed (the default names are retained in this example). The category slots must be referred to by their default names (New, Process, Report, Category4, Category5, ..., Category10) when referred to in code. In the standard product, the CategoryN names are used in a number of pages. Category4 up through as high as Category7 are used in Pages **88 Job Card**, **950 Time Sheet**, **5900 Service Order**, **1027 Job WIP Cockpit, 8629 Config. Wizard,** and **9500 Debugger**.

To add an action, access the **Page – Action Designer** screen, go to the bottom of the list of existing actions, add a line of **Type** Action, and then open the **Properties** screen for that line. Click on the **RunObject** property **Value** field and select the object to be run, in this case it is Page Radio Show List. Next, define the target ribbon menu category, caption, icon display size, and icon to represent this menu option.

Individual actions are assigned to appear in a specific category through the action's properties. **Promoted** is set to Yes and the **PromotedCategory** is (in this case) set to Category4 which has been assigned to display as **WDTU Operations**. Note that the **Image** property was also assigned; as a general rule, an image should be assigned for all action controls to indicate functionality to the user.

Let's do the same thing for one of our WDTU Maintenance actions, the Radio Show Types page. We'll set **Promoted** to `Yes`, the **PromotedCategory** to `Category5`, the **Caption** to `Radio Show Types`, and the **Image** to `Entry`. The Ribbon resulting from the two actions being **Promoted** and assigned looks like the following image. Using this method of defining and assigning Categories causes a new **Home** tab to be added to the ribbon.

Action Groups

Another way of defining Categories and assigning actions to them is through the use of ActionGroups. This approach seems quite a bit simpler. We need to make the proper `ActionGroup` entries in the **Action Designer** with the appropriate `Action` entries indented under them, as shown in the following image. We should also choose appropriate images and decide which entries should be promoted so that they stand out.

To get all our actions on the **Actions** tab, we must remove the Category references from the properties. The resulting Ribbon looks like the following image. Note that this time the WDTU categories and actions appear on the Actions tab and there are no entries on the **Home** tab:

Configuration/Personalization

The procedures and interface tools we use to do Configuration are also used by users to do Personalization. Both terms refer to revising the display contents and format of a Role Center as it appears to one or more users. As it says in the Help *Walkthrough: Configuring the Order Processor Role Center*:

> The difference between configuration and personalization is that Configuring a Role Center changes the user interface for all the users who have that profile, whereas Personalizing a Role Center only changes the user interface for a single user.

We could replace the WDTU Category assignments we just made using ActionGroups by defining Categories and assigning actions using Configuration. The result would look exactly the same to our users. But instead, let's use Configuration to quickly restore the layout of the actions that were in Role Center Page 9006. We can run page 9006 to see what that layout is (or reference the earlier snapshot of the Page 9006 ribbon).

A couple of important points:

- Configuration is tied to a specific profile. Other profiles using the same Role Center page do not see the same Configuration layout.

- Configuration can only be done by the Owner of a Profile. When we created our WDTU Test Profile, we did not assign an owner so that will have to be done now.

- Profile setup can be accessed in the RTC in **Departments | Administration | Application Setup | Role Tailored Client | Profiles**. This can also be found by entering the word Profile in the RTC Search box. The Owner ID for a Profile can be updated there by an Administrator with sufficient Permissions.

A Role Center ribbon is configured by opening the Role Tailored Client in Configuration mode with the focus on the Profile we want to configure. Personalization doesn't require this step. This is done from the DOS Command prompt using a command line essentially similar to:

```
"C:\Program Files (x86)\Microsoft Dynamics NAV\80\
RoleTailored Client\Microsoft.Dynamics.Nav.Client.exe"
 -configure -profile:"WDTU Test"
```

For additional information, refer to the Developer Help (either resident or in MSDN) *How to: Open the Microsoft Dynamics NAV Windows Client in Configuration Mode.*

 In NAV 2015, there is an option field called the **UI Elements Removal Tool** in the NAV Server Administration tool. Depending on the setting, the system administrator can limit the accessible **User Interface** (**UI**) elements to be either only those on objects available in the license or to which the user has access permission. For more information on this feature, see the Help **How to Specify When UI Elements are Removed**.

Once the Role Center displays, click on the arrowhead to the right of the Microsoft Dynamics icon (*1* in the following screenshot image), then on **Customize** option (*2* in the following image), followed by the **Customize Ribbon** option (*3* in the following image).

This will take us to the following screen:

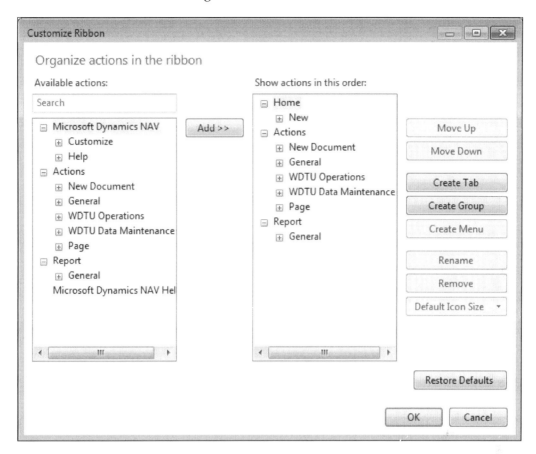

As we can see, using the Customize Ribbon screen we can Create Groups (referred to as Categories elsewhere), add new actions to those available on the ribbon, remove actions (that is, make them not visible), reorganize ribbon entries, and even create new tabs or rename existing items. In sum, everything that we've done so far to customize the Role Center Ribbon can be done through this screen. The big difference is that Customization (a general term encompassing both Configuration and Personalization) is specific to a single profile, while the other modifications will apply to all the profiles.

As part of our Personalizing, we might use the **Create Tab**, **Move Up,** and **Move Down** options to rearrange the actions on the ribbon, moving the WDTU actions to their own ribbon tab. When we are done configuring the ribbon for the WDTU Test Profile, the WDTU portion might look like the following image:

The Navigation Pane

The Navigation Pane is the menu list that makes up the leftmost column on a Role Center. A Navigation Pane can have two or more buttons. The required two buttons are Home and Departments.

The Navigation Home Button

The basic contents of the Home button for a Role Center are defined in the **Action Designer** in the `ActionContainer` of **SubType** `HomeItems`.

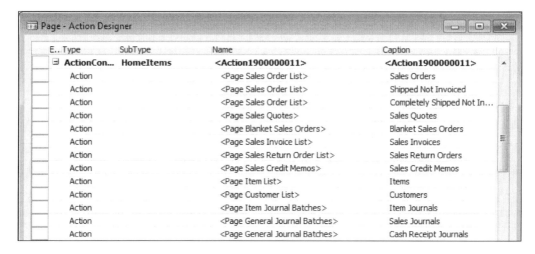

In addition to the action controls defined in the Action Designer, the Navigation Pane Home menu list includes all the Cue entries that appear in the Activities Pane of the Role Center. We can see the combined sets of action options in the following screenshot. Note that there are a number of indented (nested) options within groups such as **Sales Orders**, **Sales Quotes**, and **Sales Credit Memos**. These groups have been set up using the same type of Configuration tools that we just used for the ribbon:

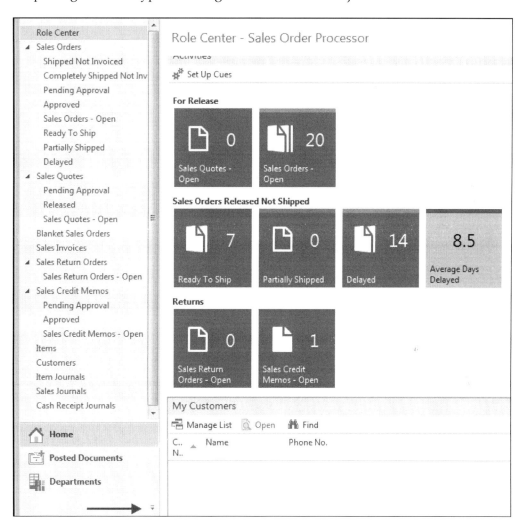

We can access the Configuration/Personalization tools either through the arrow next to the drop down arrowhead to the left of the ribbon (as shown earlier) or through the very tiny icon at the bottom right of the Navigation Pane (highlighted by an arrow in the preceding image).

The Navigation Departments Button

The other required Navigation Pane button, the **Departments** button, has its menu entries generated based on the contents of the MenuSuite object. If we click on the **Departments** button, a screen like the following will be displayed:

Other Navigation Buttons

Other Navigation Pane buttons can be defined and populated by means of `ActionGroup` entries with the `ActionContainer ActivityButtons` in the **Action Designer**, as shown in the following screenshot:

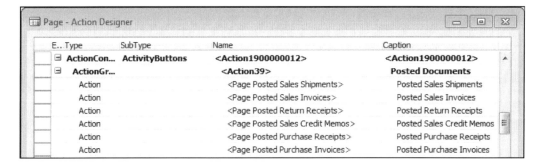

Navigation Pane buttons can also be added, renamed, repopulated, and made not visible through the **Customize Navigation Pane...** option in the page **Customization** submenu.

XMLports

XML is **eXtensible Markup Language**, a structured text format developed to describe data to be shared by dissimilar systems. XML has become a default standard for communications between systems. To make handling XML-formatted data simpler and more error resistant, NAV provides XMLports, a data import/export object. In addition to processing XML-formatted data, XMLports can also handle a wide variety of other text file formats (including CSV files, generic flat files, and so on). XML formatted data is text based, with each piece of information structured in one of two basic formats, Elements or Attributes. An Element is the overall logical unit of information while an Attribute is a property of an Element. They are formatted as follows:

- `<Tag>element value</Tag>` (an Element format)
- `<Tag AttribName = "attribute data value">` (an Attribute format)

Elements can be nested, but must not overlap. Element and Attribute names are case-sensitive. Names cannot start with a number, punctuation character, or the letters "xml" (or XML, and such). Also, they cannot contain spaces.

An Attribute value must always be enclosed in single or double quotation marks. Some references suggest that Elements should be used for data and Attributes for metadata. Complex data structures are built up of combinations of these two formats.

For example:

```
<Table Name='Sample XML format'>
   <Record>
      <DataItem1>12345</DataItem1>
      <DataItem2>23456</DataItem2>
   </Record>
   <Record>
      <DataItem1>987</DataItem1>
   </Record>
   <Record>
      <DataItem1>22233</DataItem1>
      <DataItem2>7766</DataItem2>
   </Record>
</Table>
```

In this case, we have a set of data identified as a `Table` with an attribute of Name equal to `'Sample XML format'`, which contains three `Records`, each `Record` containing data in one or two fields named `DataItem1` and `DataItem2`. The data is in a clearly structured text format so it can be read and processed by any system prepared to read this particular XML format. If the field tags are well designed, the data is easily interpretable by humans as well. The key to successful exchange of data using XML is the sharing and common interpretation of the format between the transmitter and the recipient.

XML is a standard format in the sense that the data structure options are clearly defined. But it is very flexible in the sense that the identifying tag names in < > brackets and the related data structures that can be defined and handled are totally open-ended. The specific structure and the labels are whatever the communicating parties decide they should be. The "rules" of XML only determine how the basic syntax shall operate.

XML data structures can be as simple as a flat file consisting of a set of identically formatted records or as complex as a sales order structure with headers containing a variety of data items, combined with associated detail lines containing their own variety of data items. An XML data structure can be as complicated as the application requires.

XML standards are maintained by the W3C whose web site is `http://www.w3.org/`. There are many other useful web sites for basic XML information.

XMLport components

Although in theory XMLports can operate in both an import and an export mode, in practice, individual XMLport objects tend to be dedicated to either import or export. This allows the internal logic to be simpler. XMLports utilize a process of looping through and processing data similar to that of Report objects.

The components of XMLports are:

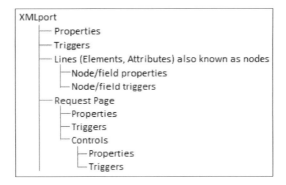

XMLport properties

XMLport properties are shown in the following screenshot of the **Properties** of the XMLport object **9170**:

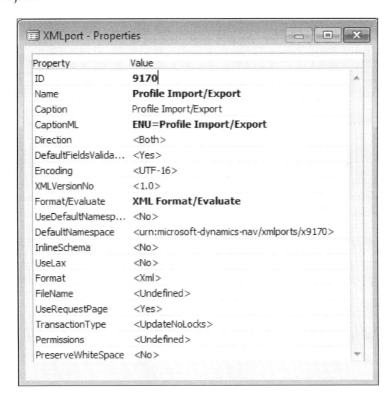

Descriptions of the individual properties follow:

- **ID**: The unique XMLport object number.
- **Name**: The name by which this XMLport is referred to within the C/AL code.
- **Caption**: The name that is displayed for the XMLport; it defaults to the contents of the **Name** property.
- **CaptionML**: The **Caption** translation for a defined alternative language.
- **Direction**: This defines whether this XMLport can only **Import**, **Export**, or **<Both>**; the default is **<Both>**.
- **DefaultFieldsValidation**: This defines the default value (**Yes** or **No**) for the **FieldValidate** property for individual XMLport data fields. The default for this field is **Yes**, which would in turn set the default for individual field **FieldValidate** properties to **Yes**.
- **Encoding (or TextEncoding)**: This defines the character encoding option to be used – **UTF-8** (ASCII compatible), **UTF-16** (not ASCII compatible), or ISO-8859-2 (for certain European languages written in Latin characters). **UTF-16** is the default. This is inserted into the heading of the XML document.

  The **TextEncoding** option is only available if the **Format** property is Fixed Text or Variable Text. In this case, a character coding option of **MS-DOS** is available and is the default.

- **XMLVersionNo**: This defines to which version of XML the document conforms, **Version 1.0** or **1.1**. The default is **Version 1.0**. This is inserted into the heading of the XML document.
- **Format/Evaluate**: This can be **C/SIDE Format/Evaluate** (the default) or **XML Format Evaluate**. This property defines whether the external text data is (for imports) or will be (for exports) XML data types or C/SIDE data types. Default processing for all fields in each case will be appropriate to the defined data type. If the external data does not fit in either of these categories, then the XML data fields must be processed through a temporary table. First, a temporary table is defined with a suitable number and size text data fields. Second, the external data is read into those text data fields. Finally, data conversion logic converts the data to C/AL compatible data types which can be stored in the NAV database. Very limited additional information on this is available in the online **Help** in Temporary Property (XMLports).

- **UseDefaultNamespace** and **DefaultNamespace**: These properties are provided to support compatibility with other systems that require the XML document to be in a specific namespace, such as use of a web service as a reference within Visual Studio. **UseDefaultNamespace** defaults to **No**. A default namespace in the form of **URN** (**Uniform Resource Name** or, in this case, a **Namespace Identifier**) concluding with the object number of the XMLport is supplied for the **DefaultNamespace** property. This property is only active if the **Format** property is XML.

- **InlineSchema**: This property defaults to **No**. An inline schema allows the XML schema document (an XSD) to be embedded within the XML document. This can be used by setting the property to **Yes** when exporting an XML document, which will add the schema to that exported document. This property is only active if the **Format** property is XML.

- **UseLax**: This property defaults to **No**. Some systems may add information to the XML document, which is not defined in the XSD schema used by the XMLport. When this property is set to **Yes**, that extraneous material will be ignored, rather than resulting in an error. This property is only active if the **Format** property is XML.

- **Format**: This property has the options of XML, Variable Text, or Fixed Text. It defaults to XML. This property controls the import/export data format that the XMLport will process. Choosing **XML** means that the processing will only deal with a properly formatted XML file. Choosing **Variable Text** means that the processing will only deal with a file formatted with delimiters set up as defined in the **FieldDelimiter**, **FieldSeparator**, **RecordSeparator**, and **TableSeparator** properties (such as **CSV** files). Choosing **Fixed Text** means that each individual element and attribute must have its Width property set to a value greater than 0 (zero) and the data to be processed must be formatted accordingly. If enabled, these four fields can also be changed programmatically from within the C/AL code.

- **FileName**: This can be filled with the predefined path and name of a specific external text data file to be either the source (for **Import**) or target (for **Export**) for the run of the XMLport, or this property can be set dynamically. Only one file at a time can be opened, but the file in use can be changed during the execution of the XMLport (not often done).

- **FieldDelimiter**: This applies to the **Variable Text** format external files only. It defaults to **<">** — double quote, the standard for so-called "comma-delimited" text files. This property supplies the string that will be used as the starting delimiter for each data field in the text file. If this is an **Import**, then the XMLport will look for this string, and then use the following string as data until the next **FieldDelimiter** string is found, terminating the data string. If this is an **Export**, the XMLport will insert this string at the beginning and end of each data field contents string.

- **FieldSeparator**: This applies to the **VariableText** format external files only. Defaults to **<,>** — a comma, the standard for so-called "comma delimited" text files. This property supplies the string that will be used as the delimiter between each data field in the text file (looked for on **Imports** and inserted on **Exports**). See the Help for this property for more information.

- **RecordSeparator**: This applies to the **VariableText** or **FixedText** format external files only. This defines the string that will be used as the delimiter at the end of each data record in the text file. If this is an **Import**, the XMLport will look for this string to mark the end of each data record. If this is an **Export**, the XMLport will append this string at the end of each data record output. The default is **<<NewLine>>**, which represents any combination of CR (carriage return — ASCII value 13) and LF (line feed — ASCII value 10) characters. See the Help for this property for more information.

- **TableSeparator**: This applies to the **VariableText** or **FixedText** format external files only. This defines the string that will be used as the delimiter at the end of each Data Item (for example, each text file). The default is **<<NewLine><NewLine>>**. See the Help for this property for more information.

- **UseRequestForm**: This determines whether a Request Page should be displayed to allow the user choice of Sort Sequence, entry of filters, and other requested control information. The options are **Yes** and **No**. The default is **<Yes>**. An XMLport Request Page has only the **OK** and **Cancel** options.

- **TransactionType**: This property identifies the XMLport processing Server Transaction Type as **Browse**, **Snapshot**, **UpdateNoLocks**, or **Update**. This is an advanced and seldom-used property. For more information, we can refer to the Help files and SQL Server documentation.

- **Permissions**: This property provides report-specific setting of permissions, which are rights to access data, subdivided into **Read**, **Insert**, **Modify**, and **Delete**. This allows the developer to define permissions that override the user-by-user permissions security setup.

XMLport triggers

The XMLport has a very limited set of triggers, which are listed next:

- **Documentation()** is for documentation comment
- **OnInitXMLport()** is executed once when the XMLport is loaded before the table views and filters have been set
- **OnPreXMLport()** is executed once after the table views and filters have been set. Those can be reset here
- **OnPostXMLport()** is executed once after all the data is processed, if the XMLport completes normally

XMLport data lines

An XMLport can contain any number of data lines. The data lines are laid out in a strict hierarchical structure, with the elements and attributes mapping exactly, one for one, in the order of the data fields in the external text file, the XML document.

XMLports should not be run directly from a Navigation Pane action command (due to conflicts with NAV UX standards), but can be run either from ribbon actions on a Role Center or other page, or by means of an object containing the necessary C/AL code. When running from another object (as opposed to running from an action menu entry), the C/AL code calls the XMLport to stream data either to or from an appropriately formatted file (XML document or other text format). This calling code is typically written in a Codeunit, but can be placed in any object that can contain the C/AL code.

The following example code executes an exporting XMLport and saves the resulting file from the NAV service tier to the client machine:

```
XMLfile.CREATE(TEMPORARYPATH + 'RadioShowExport.xml');
XMLfile.CREATEOUTSTREAM(OutStreamObj);
XMLPORT.EXPORT(50000,OutStreamObj);
FromFileName := XMLfile.NAME;
ToFileName := 'RadioShowExport.xml';
XMLfile.CLOSE;

//Need to call DOWNLOAD to move the xml file
//from the service tier to the client machine
DOWNLOAD(FromFileName,'Downloading File...','C:','Xml file(*.xml)|*.
xml',ToFileName);
```

```
//Make sure to clean up the temporary file from the
//service tier
ERASE(FromFileName);
```

Two text variables (the "from" file name and "to" file name), a file variable, and an OutStream object variable are required to support the preceding code. The data variables are defined as shown in the following screenshot:

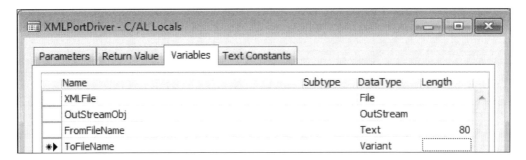

XMLport line properties

The XMLport line properties which are active on a line depend on the contents of the **SourceType** property. The first four properties listed are common to all three **SourceType** values (**Text**, **Table**, and **Field**) and the other properties specific to each are listed below the screenshots showing all the properties for each **SourceType**.

- **Indentation**: This indicates at what subordinate level in the hierarchy of the XMLport this entry exists. Indentation **0** is the primary level, parent to all higher numbered levels. Indentation **1** is a child of indentation **0**, indentation **2** is a child of **1**, and so forth. Only one Indentation **0** is allowed in an XMLport, so often we will want to define the Level 0 line to be a simple text element line. This allows the definition of multiple Tables at Indentation level 1.

- **NodeName**: This defines the Node Name that will be used in the XML document to identify the data associated with this position in the XML document. No spaces are allowed in a **NodeName**; we can use underscores, dashes, and periods but no other special characters.

- **NodeType**: This defines if this data item is an **Element** or an **Attribute**.
- **SourceType**: This defines the type of data this field corresponds to in the NAV database. The choices are **Text**, **Table**, and **Field**. Text means that the value in the **SourceField** property will act as a Global variable and, typically must be dealt with by embedded C/AL code. Table means that the value in the **SourceField** property will refer to a NAV table. Field means that the value in the **SourceField** property will refer to a NAV field within the parent table previously defined as an element.

SourceType as Text

The following screenshot shows the properties for **SourceType** as **Text**:

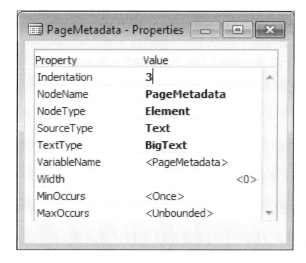

The description of the Text-specific properties is as follows:

- **TextType**: This defines the NAV Data Type as **Text** or **BigText**. **Text** is the default.
- **VariableName**: This contains the name of the Global variable, which can be referenced by the C/AL code.

The **Width**, **MinOccurs**, and **MaxOccurs** properties are discussed later in this chapter.

SourceType as Table

The following screenshot shows the properties for **SourceType** as **Table**:

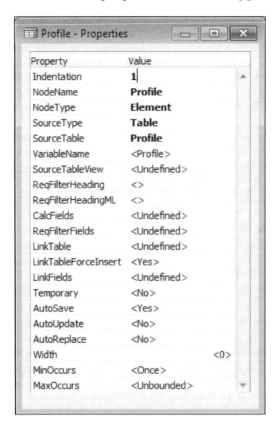

The descriptions of the table-specific properties are as follows:

- **SourceTable**: This defines the NAV table being referenced.

- **VariableName**: This defines the name to be used in the C/AL code for the NAV table. This is the functional equivalent to definition of a Global variable.

- **SourceTableView**: This enables the developer to define a view by choosing a key and sort order or by applying filters on the table.

- **ReqFilterHeading** and **ReqFilterHeadingML**: These fields allow the definition of the name of the Request Page filter definition tab that applies to this table.

- **CalcFields**: This lists the FlowFields in the table that are to be automatically calculated.

- **ReqFilterFields**: This lists the fields that will initially display on the Request page filter definition tab.

- **LinkTable**: This allows the linking of a field in a higher-level item to a key field in a lower-level item. If, for example, we were exporting all the Purchase Orders for a Vendor, we might Link the **Buy-From Vendor No.** in a Purchase Header to the **No.** in a Vendor record. The **LinkTable** in this case would be Vendor and **LinkField** would be No.; therefore **LinkTable** and **LinkFields** work together. Use of the **LinkTable** and **LinkFields** operates the same as applying a filter on the higher-level table data so that only records relating to the defined lower-level table and field are processed. See the Help for more detail.

- **LinkTableForceInsert**: This can be set to force the insertion of the linked table data and execution of the related **OnAfterInitRecord()** trigger. This property is tied to the **LinkTable** and **LinkFields** properties. It also applies to **Import**.

- **LinkFields**: This defines the fields involved in a table + field linkage.

- **Temporary**: This defaults to No. If this property is set to Yes, it allows the creation of a Temporary table in working storage. Data imported into this table can then be evaluated, edited, and manipulated before being written out to the database. This Temporary table has the same capabilities and limitations as a Temporary table defined as a Global variable.

- **AutoSave**: If set to Yes (the default), an imported record will be automatically saved to the table. Either **AutoUpdate** or **AutoReplace** must also be set to Yes.

- **AutoUpdate**: If a record exists in the table with a matching primary key, all the data fields are initialized, and then all the data from the incoming record is copied into the table record.

- **AutoReplace**: If a record exists in the table with a matching primary key, the populated data fields in the incoming record are copied into the table record; all the other fields in the target record are left undisturbed. This provides a means to update a table by importing records with a limited number of data fields filled in.

The **Width**, **MinOccurs**, and **MaxOccurs** properties are discussed later in this chapter.

SourceType as Field

The following screenshot shows the properties for **SourceType** as **Field**:

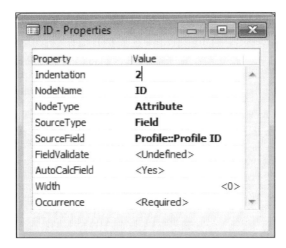

The description of the Field-specific properties is as follows:

- **SourceField**: This defines the data field being referenced. It may be a field in any defined table.
- **FieldValidate**: This applies to Import only. If this property is Yes, then whenever the field is imported into the database, the **OnValidate()** trigger of the field will be executed.
- **AutoCalcField**: This applies to Export and FlowField Data fields only. If this property is set to Yes, the field will be calculated before it is retrieved from the database. Otherwise, a FlowField would export as an empty field.

The details of the **Width**, **MinOccurs**, and **MaxOccurs** properties follow in the next section.

The Element or Attribute

An **Element** data item may appear many times but an **Attribute** data item may only appear at most once; the occurrence control properties differ based on the **NodeType**.

NodeType of Element

The Element-specific properties are as follows:

- **Width**: When the XMLport **Format** property is `Fixed Text`, then this field is used to define the fixed width of this element's field.

- **MinOccurs**: This defines the minimum number of times this data item can occur in the XML document. This property can be `Zero` or `Once` (the default).

- **MaxOccurs**: This defines the maximum number of times this data item can occur in the XML document. This property can be `Once` or `Unbounded`. `Unbounded` (the default) means any number of times.

NodeType of Attribute

The Attribute-specific property is as follows:

- **Occurrence**: This is either `Required` (the default) or `Optional`, depending on the text file being imported

XMLport line triggers

The XMLport line triggers are shown in the following screenshot for the three line Source types: **Profiles** (Text), **Profile** (Table), and **ID** (Field):

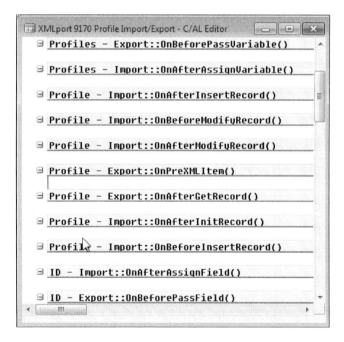

As we can see in the preceding screenshot, there are different XMLport triggers depending on whether **DataType** is Text, Table, or Field.

DataType as Text

The triggers for DataType as Text are:

- **Export::onBeforePassVariable()**, for **Export** only: This trigger is typically used for manipulation of the text variable.

- **Import::OnAfterAssignVariable()**, for **Import** only: This trigger gives us access to the imported value in text format.

DataType as Table

The triggers for DataType as Table are as follows:

- **Import::OnAfterInsertRecord()**, for **Import** only: This trigger is typically used when the data is being imported into Temporary tables. This is where we would put the C/AL code to build and insert records for the permanent database table(s).

- **Import::OnBeforeModifyRecord()**, for **Import** only: This trigger is for use when AutoSave is Yes, to update the imported data before saving it.

- **Import::OnAfterModifyRecord()**, for **Import** only: This trigger is for use when AutoSave is Yes, to update the data after updating.

- **Export::OnPreXMLItem()**, for **Export** only: This trigger is typically used for setting filters and initializing before finding and processing the first database record.

- **Export::OnAfterGetRecord()**, for **Export** only: This trigger allows access to the data after the record is retrieved from the NAV database. It is typically used to allow manipulation of table fields being exported.

- **Import::OnAfterInitRecord()**, for **Import** only: This trigger is typically used to check whether or not a record should be processed further or to manipulate the data.

- **Import::OnBeforeInsertRecord()**, for **Import** only: This is another place where we can manipulate data before it is inserted into the target table. This trigger is executed after the **OnAfterInitRecord()** trigger.

DataType as Field

The triggers for DataType as Field are as follows:

- **Import::OnAfterAssignField()**, for **Import** only: This trigger provides access to the imported data value for evaluation or manipulation before outputting to the database.

- **Export::OnBeforePassField()**, for **Export** only: This trigger provides access to the data field value just before the data is exported.

XMLport Request Page

XMLports can also have a Request Page to allow the user to enter Option control information and filter the data being processed. Default filter fields that will appear on the Request Page are defined in the Properties form for the table XMLport Line.

Any desired options that are to be available to the user as part of the Request Page must be defined in the **Request Options Page Designer**. This Designer is accessed from the XMLport Designer through **View | Request Page**. The definition of the contents and layout of the Request Options Page is done in essentially the same way as other pages are done. As with any other filter setup screen, the user has complete control of what fields are used for filtering and what filters are applied.

Web services

Web services are an industry standard software interface that allows software applications to interoperate using standard interface specifications along with standard communications services and protocols. When NAV publishes some web services, these functions can be accessed and utilized by properly programmed software residing anywhere on the Web. This software does not need to be directly compatible with C/SIDE or even .NET; it just needs to obey web services conventions and have security access to the NAV Web Services.

Some benefits of NAV Web Services are:

- Very simple to publish (that is, to expose a web service to a consuming program outside of NAV)

- Provides managed access to NAV data while respecting and enforcing NAV rules, logic, and design that already exists

- Uses Windows Authentication and respects NAV data constraints

- Supports SSL — Secure Socket Layer

- Supports both the SOAP interface (cannot access Query objects) and the OData interface (cannot access Codeunit objects)

Disadvantages of NAV Web Services include:

- Allowing access to a system from the Web requires a much higher level of security

- The NAV objects that are published generally need to be designed (or at least customized) to properly interface with this very different user interface

- Access from the Web complicates the system administrator's job of managing loads on the system

There are several factors that should be considered in judging the appropriateness of an application being considered for web services integration. Some of these are:

- What is the degree to which the functionality of the standard RTC interface is needed? A web services application should not try to replicate what would normally be done with a full client, but should be used for limited, focused functionality.

- What is the amount of data to be exchanged? Generally, web services are used remotely. Even if it is used locally, there are additional levels of security handshaking and inter-system communications required. These involve additional processing overhead. Web services should be used for low data volume applications.

- How public is the user set? For security reasons, the user set for direct connection to our NAV system should generally be limited to known users, not the general public. Web services should not be used to provide Internet exposure to the customer's NAV system, but rather for **intranet** access.

Because web services are intended for use by low-intensity users, there are separate license options available with lower costs per user than the full client license. This can make the cost of providing web services-based access quite reasonable, especially if by doing so, we increase the ability of our customer to provide a better service to their customers and to realize increased profits.

Exposing a web service

Three types of NAV objects can be published as Web Services: Pages, Queries, and Codeunits. The essential purposes are:

- Pages provide access to the associated primary table. Use Card Pages for table access unless there is a specific reason for using another page type.
- Codeunits provide access to the functions contained within each Codeunit.
- Queries provide rapid, efficient access to data in a format that is especially compatible with a variety of other Microsoft products as well as products from other vendors.

An XMLPort can be exposed indirectly as a Codeunit parameter. This provides a very structured way of exposing NAV data through a Web Service. (See AJ Kauffmann's blog series on XMLPorts in Web Services at `http://kauffmann.nl/index.php/2011/01/15/how-to-use-xmlports-in-web-services-1/`). There is an example later in this chapter.

When a Page has no special constraints, either via properties or permissions, there will normally be eleven methods available. They are:

- `Create`: Create a single record (similar to a NAV INSERT).
- `CreateMultiple`: Create a set of records (passed argument must be an array).
- `Read`: Read a single record (similar to a NAV GET).
- `ReadMultiple`: Read a filtered set of records, paged. Page size is a parameter.
- `Update`: Update a single record (similar to a NAV MODIFY).
- `UpdateMultiple`: Update a set of records (passed argument must be an array).
- `Delete`: Delete a single record.
- `IsUpdated`: Check if the record has been updated since it was read.
- `ReadBiyRecID`: Read a record based on the record ID.
- `GetReciIDFromKey`: Get a record ID based on the record key.
- `Delete_<PagePartName> (PagePartRecordKey)`: Delete a single record that is exposed by a page part of **Type** `Page` such as the **Sales Order Subform** Page Part of the **Sales Order** page.

Whatever constraints have been set in the page that we have published will be inherited by the associated web services. For example, if we publish a page that has the **Editable** property set to No, then only the Read, ReadMultiple, and IsUpdated methods will be available as web services. The other five methods will have been suppressed by virtue of the Editable = No property.

A codeunit that has been published as a web service has its functions made available to for access. A query published as a web service provides access to a service metadata (EDMX) document or an AtomPub Document. To learn more about using queries published as web services, refer to the information published in the **Developer and IT Pro Help** in the system or in MSDN.

Publishing a web service

Publishing a web service is one of the easiest things we will ever do in NAV. But, as stated earlier, that doesn't mean we will be able to simply publish existing objects without creating versions specifically tailored for use with Web Services. However, for the moment, let's just go through the basic publishing process.

The point of access is the Departments menu through **Navigation Pane | Departments | Administration | IT Administration | General | Web Services**. The Web Services page displays as shown in the following screenshot.

The first column allows us to specify whether the object is a Page, Codeunit, or Query. That is followed by the Object ID and then the **Service Name**. Finally, the **Published** flag must be checked. At that point, the web services for that object have been published.

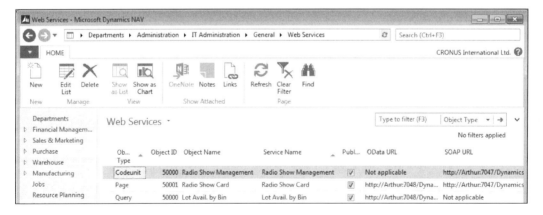

Enabling web services

Prior to using web services, we must enable them from the NAV Administration application. In NAV Administration, we can see the checkboxes for enabling. We can enable either SOAP Services, OData Services, or both, as shown in the following screenshot:

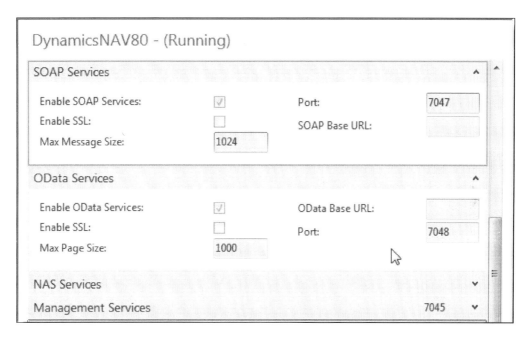

Determining what was published

Once an object has been published, we may want to see exactly what is available as a web service. Since web services are intended to be accessed from the Web, in the address bar of our browser, we will enter the following (all as one string):

```
http://<Server>:<WebServicePort>/<ServerInstance>/WS/
<CompanyName>/services
```

Example URL addresses are:

```
http://localhost:7047/DynamicsNAV/WS/Services
http://Arthur:7047/DynamicsNAV/WS/CRONUS International Ltd/Services
```

 The company name is optional and case-sensitive.

When the correct address string is entered, our browser will display a screen similar to the following image. This image is in an XML format of a data structure called **WSDL, Web Services Description Language**:

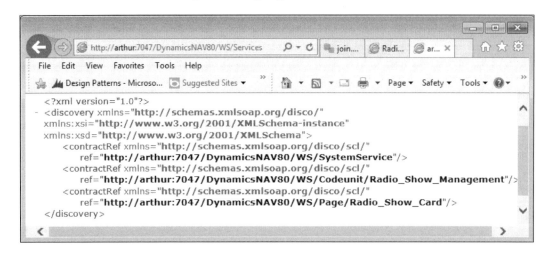

In this case, we can see that we have two NAV SOAP Services available: `Codeunit/ Radio_Show_Management` and `Page/Radio_Show_Card`.

To see the methods (that is, NAV functions) that have been exposed as web services by publishing these two objects, we can enter other similar URLs in our browser address bar. To see the web services exposed by our codeunit, we change the URL used earlier to replace the word `Services` with `Codeunit/Radio_Show_Management`. We must also include the company name in the URL that lists the methods WSDL.

To see the OData services, change the URL to the following form:

```
http://<Server>:<WebServicePort>/<ServerInstance>/OData
```

From that entry in our browser, we get information about what's available as OData. OData is structured like XML, but it provides the full metadata (structural definition) of the associated data in the same file as the data. This allows OData to be consumed without the requirement of a lot of back and forth technical pre-planning communications.

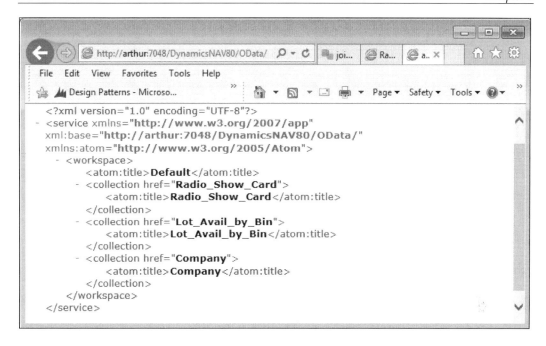

```
<?xml version="1.0" encoding="UTF-8"?>
- <service xmlns="http://www.w3.org/2007/app"
  xml:base="http://arthur:7048/DynamicsNAV80/OData/"
  xmlns:atom="http://www.w3.org/2005/Atom">
    - <workspace>
          <atom:title>Default</atom:title>
        - <collection href="Radio_Show_Card">
              <atom:title>Radio_Show_Card</atom:title>
          </collection>
        - <collection href="Lot_Avail_by_Bin">
              <atom:title>Lot_Avail_by_Bin</atom:title>
          </collection>
        - <collection href="Company">
              <atom:title>Company</atom:title>
          </collection>
      </workspace>
  </service>
```

The actual consumption (meaning "use of") of a web service is also fairly simple, but that process occurs outside of NAV in any of a wide variety of off-the-shelf or custom applications, not part of this book's focus. Examples are readily available in Help, the MSDN library, the NAV forums, and elsewhere.

Tools that can be used to consume NAV Web Services include, among others, Microsoft InfoPath, Microsoft Excel, Microsoft Sharepoint, applications written in C#, other .NET languages, open source PHP, and a myriad of other application development tools. Remember, web services are a standard interface for dissimilar systems.

As with any other enhancement to the system functionality, serious thought needs to be given to the design of what data is to be exchanged and what functions within NAV 2015 should be invoked for the application to work properly. In many cases, we will want to provide some simple routines to perform standard NAV processing or validation tasks without exposing the full complexity of NAV internals as web services.

Perhaps we want to provide just two or three functions from a Codeunit that contains many additional functions. Or we want to expose a function that is contained within a Report object. In each of these instances and others, it will be necessary to create a basic library of C/AL functions, perhaps in a codeunit that can be published as web services (generally recognized as a best practice).

Use of web services carries with it issues that must be dealt with in any production environment. In addition to delivering the required application functionality, there are security, access, and communications issues that need to be addressed. It is recommended that a NAV Web Service not be directly exposed to external users, but NAV data be secured by limiting access through the use of custom, functionally limited, external software interfaces. While beyond the scope of this text, proper attention to data security is critical to the implementation of a good quality solution.

XMLport – a web services integration example for WDTU

WDTU subscribes to a service that compiles listenership data. That data is provided to subscribers in the form of XML files. The agency that provides the service has agreed to push that XML data directly to a web service exposed by our NAV 2015 system. This approach will allow WDTU to have access to the latest listenership data as soon as it is released by the agency.

WDTU must provide access to the XMLport that fits the incoming XML file format. The handshaking response expected by the agency computer from our web service is a fixed XML file with one element (Station ID) and an attribute of the said element (Frequency).

The first step is to build our XMLport. We access the XMLport designer through **Object Designer | XMLport button | New button**. Define the new XMLport lines as shown in the following screenshot:

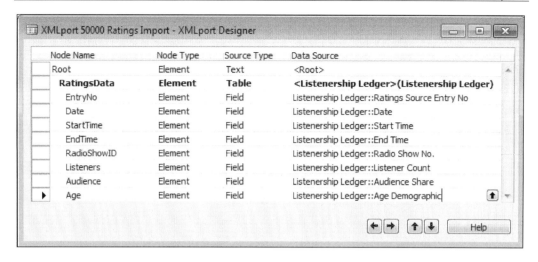

After we have the lines entered, we will click on *Alt + F* | **Save As…**. Fill in the **Save As** screen, as shown in the next image, and click **OK** to save and compile the XMLport without exiting the XMLport Designer:

Highlight the blank line at the bottom of the XMLport Designer screen and click *Shift + F4* (or the **Properties** icon, or right-click then click **Properties**) to display the XMLport properties screen.

Set the **Format/Evaluate** property to XML Format/Evaluate. This allows Visual Studio to automatically understand the data types (integer, decimal, and so on) involved. Set **UseDefaultNamespace** to Yes, and **DefaultNamespace** to urn:Microsoft-dynamics-nav/xmlports/x50000 (which is the default format) or urn:Microsoft-dynamics-nav/xmlports/RatingsImport.

Even though we are using the XMLport as an import only object, make sure the **Direction** property stays at <Both>. When the value is set to either Import or Export, it is not possible to use the XMLport as a **Var** (by reference) parameter in the codeunit function which we will expose as a web service.

Following is the XMLport 50000 Properties screen with these changes in place:

After we close the **Properties** screen for the XMLport, we can highlight the **Root Element** line and display its properties. Set the property **MaxOccurs** to Once, as shown in the following image:

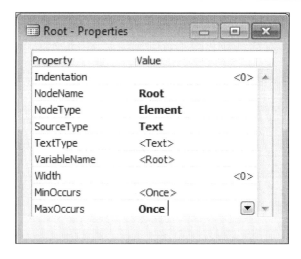

Close **Root Properties**, highlight **RatingsData Table Element**, and access its **Properties** screen. Set **MinOccurs** to `Zero` and make sure **MaxOccurs** remains at the default value of <Unbounded> as shown in the following screenshot. Once this is done, close the **RatingsData – Properties** screen. Because our XMLport matches the incoming data format from the listenership ratings agency, no C/AL code is necessary in this XMLport. Exit **XMLport Designer** and save and compile **XMLport 50000**.

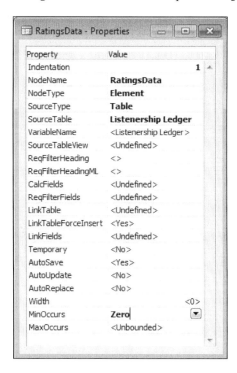

Now that we have our XMLport constructed, it's time to build the codeunit that will be published as a web service. Go to the **Object Designer | Codeunit button | New** button. Then click on the menu option **View | C/AL Globals | Functions** tab. Enter the new **Function** name of ImportRatings and click on the **Locals** button.

In the **C/AL Locals** screen, enter the single parameter RatingsXML, **Type** XMLport, and a **SubType** of Ratings Import. Make sure the **Var** column on the left is checked. The **C/AL Locals** screen should then look like the following screenshot:

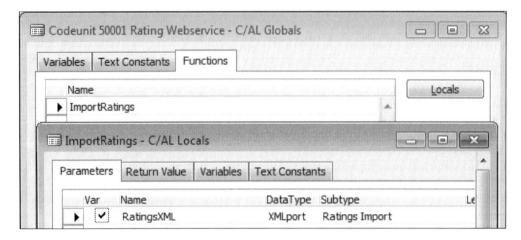

Now click on the **Return Value** tab and set **Return Type** to Text and **Length** to 250. Exit the **C/AL Locals** and **C/AL Globals** screens, returning to the **Codeunit C/AL Editor** screen. Finally, we will highlight our new Function in the **Functions** tab, and set the **Local** property to No so that we can access this function from Web Services.

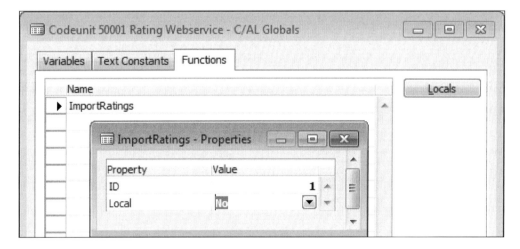

Before proceeding any further, let's save our work. Just as in **XMLport Designer**, we can save our work without exiting the Designer by clicking on **File | Save As...** , then entering the designer object number (**50001**) and name (**Ratings Webservice**).

We only need two lines of C/AL code in the codeunit. The first line's task is to import the XML utilizing the XMLport parameter to cause the XMLport to process. The second line of code's purpose is to send the required text response back to the external system, with the response formatted as XML data. That code looks like the following image in **C/AL Editor**:

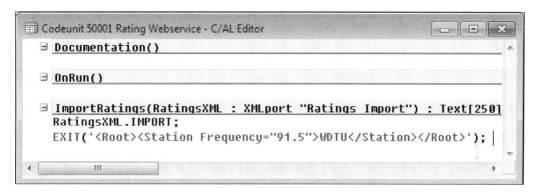

Exit **Codeunit 50001**, compile and save it. Now we want to publish the codeunit that we have just created.

Open the Role Tailored Client, navigate to **Departments/Administration/IT Administration/General/Web Services** (or just search for Web Services using the **Search** box) and invoke the **Web Services** page. Fill in **Object Type** of Codeunit, **Object ID** of 50001, **Service Name** of WDTU Ratings, and check **Published**.

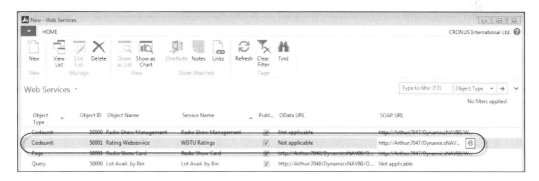

Now, to test what we've done, we need to open a browser and enter a URL in the following format:

```
http://<Server>:<SOAPWebServicePort>/<ServerInstance>/WS/
<CompanyName>/services
```

For example, more specifically:

```
http://localhost:7047/DynamicsNAV70/WS/CRONUS International Ltd/
Codeunit/WDTU_Ratings
```

Or, for testing purposes, we could just click on the Web icon on the right hand end of our new entry in the web services screen (as shown in the preceding image). The result in our browser screen should look like the following screenshot, showing that we can connect with our web service and that our XMLport contains all the fields for the data that we plan to import:

Summary

In this chapter, we reviewed some of the more advanced NAV 2015 tools and techniques. By now, we should have a strong admiration for the power and flexibility of NAV 2015. Many of these subject areas require more study and hands-on practice by you. We spent a lot of time on Role Center construction because that is the heart of the Role Tailored Experience. Much of what you learn about Role Center design and construction can be applied across the board in role tailoring other components. We went through XMLports and Web Services, then showed how the two capabilities can be combined to provide a simple, but powerful method of interfacing with external systems. By now, you should be almost ready to begin your own development project. In the next chapter, we will cover the debugger, extensibility (adding non-C/AL controls to pages), and additional topics.

Review questions

Q.1. Users cannot delete or modify database data through Web Services. True or False?

Q.2. The Action items for the Departments button come from what source? Choose one.

    a.   Action Menu entries

    b.   Cue Group definitions

    c.   MenuSuite objects

    d.   Navigation Pane objects

Q.3. Software external to NAV that accesses NAV Web Services must be dot NET compatible. True or False?

Q.4. Action Ribbons can be modified in which of the following ways. Choose three.

    a.   C/Side changes in the Action Designer

    b.   Dynamic C/AL code Configuration

    c.   Implementer/Administrator Configuration

    d.   User Personalization

    e.   Application of a profile template

Q.5. XMLports cannot contain C/AL code. All data manipulation must occur outside of the XMLport object. True or False?

Q.6. The default PromotedActionCategoriesML includes which two of the following?

a. Page
b. Report
c. Standard
d. New

Q.7. Web services are an industry standard interface defined by the World Wide Web Consortium. True or False?

Q.8. Role Centers can have several components. Choose two.

a. Activity Pane
b. Browser Part
c. Cues
d. Report Review Pane

Q.9. Web Services are a good tool for publishing NAV to be used as a public retail sales system on the web. True or False?

Q.10. An action can appear in multiple places in a Role Center, for example, in the Home button of the Navigation Pane, in the Action Ribbon, and in a Cue Group. True or False?

Q.11. Which of the following object types can be published as Web Services? Choose two.

a. Reports
b. Queries
c. XMLPorts
d. Pages

Q.12. A Cue may be a shortcut to a filtered list supported by a field in a Cue table. True or False?

Q.13. New System Parts can be created by a NAV developer using C/SIDE tools. True or False?

Q.14. All new implementations should create new Role Centers based on the results of detailed analysis of the intended users' work roles, only using the standard Role Centers as templates. True or false?

Q.15. All Web Service data interfaces require the use of XML data files. True or false?

Q.16. Role Center Cues can be tied to FlowFields, Normal fields, or Queries. True or false?

Q.17. Actions in a ribbon are Promoted so they can be displayed in color. True or false?

Q.18. Role Center components include which of the following? Choose two.

    a.   Cues

    b.   Microsoft Office parts

    c.   Web Services

    d.   Page parts

Q.19. Once a Role Center layout has been defined by the Developer, it cannot be changed by the users. True or false?

Q.20. In the Role Tailored Client, XMLports can only be used to process XML formatted files and cannot process other text file formats. True or false?

9
Successful Conclusions

"The most powerful designs are always the result of a continuous process of simplification and refinement."

– Kevin Mullet

"All the good ideas never lie under one hat."

– Dale Turner

Each new version of NAV includes new features and capabilities. NAV 2015 is no exception. It is our responsibility to understand how to apply these new features, to use them intelligently in our designs, and to develop with both their strengths and limitations in mind. The new features in NAV 2015 include new ways to debug our work and new ways to deliver information to our users. Our goal in the end is not only to provide workmanlike results but, if possible, to delight our users with the quality of the experience and the ease of use of our products.

In this chapter, we will:

- Review NAV objects that contain functions we can use directly or as templates in our solutions
- Review some of the primary NAV C/SIDE tools that help us debug our solutions
- Learn about the way we can enhance our solutions using external controls integrated into NAV
- Discuss design, development, and delivery issues that should be addressed in our projects.

Creating new C/AL routines

Now that we have a good overall picture of how we enable users to access the tools that we have created, we are ready to start creating our own NAV C/AL routines. It is important that we learn our way around the NAV C/AL code in the standard product first. You may recall the advice in a previous chapter that the new code we create should be visually and logically compatible with what already exists. If we think of our new code as a guest being hosted by the original system, we will be doing what any thoughtful guest does – fitting smoothly into the host's environment.

An equally important aspect of becoming familiar with the existing code is to increase the likelihood we can take advantage of the features and components of the standard product to address some of our application requirements. There are at least two types of existing NAV C/AL code, of which we should make use whenever appropriate.

One group is the callable functions that are used liberally throughout NAV. Once we know about these, we can use them in our logic whenever they fit. There is no documentation for most of these functions, so we must either learn about them here or by doing our homework, studying the NAV code. The second group includes the many code snippets we can copy when we face a problem similar to something the NAV developers have already addressed.

The code snippets differ from the callable functions in two ways. First, they are not structured as coherent and callable entities. Second, they are likely to serve as models - code that must be modified to fit the situation (for example, changing variable names, adding or removing constraints, and so on).

In addition to the directly usable C/AL code, we should also make liberal use of the NAV Design Patterns Repository located at: `https://community.dynamics.com/nav/w/designpatterns/105.nav-design-patterns-repository.aspx`

NAV Design Patterns provide common definitions of how certain types of functions are implemented in NAV. Pattern examples include:

- Copy Document
- Create Data from Templates
- No. Series
- Single-Record (Setup) Table
- Master Data

There are many others and new pattern definitions are added often.

Callable functions

Most of the callable functions in NAV are designed to handle a very specific set of data or conditions and have no general-purpose use (for example, the routines for updating Check Ledger entries during a posting process are likely to apply only to that specific function). If we are making modifications to a particular application area within NAV, we may find functions that we can utilize, either as is or as models for our new functions.

There are quite a few functions within NAV that are relatively general purpose. They either act on data that is common in many different situations (such as dates) or they perform processing tasks that are common to many situations (such as providing access to an external file). We will review a few such functions in detail, then list a number of others worth studying. If nothing else, these functions are useful as guides for "here is how NAV does it". The various parameters in these explanations are named to assist with our learning and not named the same as in the NAV code (though all structures, data types, and other technical specs match the NAV code).

If we are going to use one of these functions, we must take care to clearly understand how it operates. In each case, we should study the function and test with it before assuming that we understand how it works. There is little or no documentation for most of these functions, so understanding their proper use is totally up to us. If we need a customization, that must be done by making a copy of the target function and then modifying the copy.

Codeunit 358 – Date FilterCalc

This codeunit is a good example of how a well designed and well written code has long term utility. If we look at the Object Designer information for this codeunit, we will see that it originated in NAV (Navision) V3.00 in 2001. That doesn't mean it is out of date; it means that it was well thought out and complete.

Codeunit 358 contains two functions we can use in our code to create filters based on the Accounting Period Calendar. The first is `CreateFiscalYearFilter`. If we are calling this from an object that has Codeunit 358 defined as a Global variable named DateFilterCalc, our call would use the following syntax:

```
DateFilterCalc,CreateFiscalYearFilter
        (Filter,Name,BaseDate,NextStep)
```

The calling parameters are `Filter` (text, length 30), `Name` (text, length 30), `BaseDate` (date), and `NextStep` (integer).

The second such function is `CreateAccountingPeriodFilter` that has the following syntax:

```
DateFilterCalc.CreateAccountingPeriodFilter
          (Filter,Name,BaseDate,NextStep)
```

The calling parameters are `Filter` (text, length 30), `Name` (text, length 30), `BaseDate` (date), and `NextStep` (integer).

In the following code screenshot from Page 151 – Customer Statistics, we can see how NAV calls these functions. Page 152 – Vendor Statistics, Page 223 – Resource Statistics, and a number of other Master table statistics forms also use this set of functions:

```
OnAfterGetRecord()
  IF CurrentDate <> WORKDATE THEN BEGIN
    CurrentDate := WORKDATE;
    DateFilterCalc.CreateAccountingPeriodFilter(CustDateFilter[1],CustDateName[1],CurrentDate,0);
    DateFilterCalc.CreateFiscalYearFilter(CustDateFilter[2],CustDateName[2],CurrentDate,0);
    DateFilterCalc.CreateFiscalYearFilter(CustDateFilter[3],CustDateName[3],CurrentDate,-1);
  END;
```

In the next code screenshot, NAV uses the filters stored in the `CustDateFilter` array to constrain the calculation of a series of FlowFields for the Customer Statistics page:

```
FOR i := 1 TO 4 DO BEGIN
  SETFILTER("Date Filter",CustDateFilter[i]);
  CALCFIELDS(
    "Sales (LCY)","Profit (LCY)","Inv. Discounts (LCY)","Inv. Amounts (LCY)","Pmt. Discounts (LCY)",
    "Pmt. Disc. Tolerance (LCY)","Pmt. Tolerance (LCY)",
    "Fin. Charge Memo Amounts (LCY)","Cr. Memo Amounts (LCY)","Payments (LCY)",
    "Reminder Amounts (LCY)","Refunds (LCY)","Other Amounts (LCY)");
```

When one of these functions is called, the `Filter` and `Name` parameters are updated within the function, so we can use them as return parameters, allowing the function to return a workable filter and a name for that filter. The filter is calculated from the `BaseDate` and `NextStep` we supply.

The returned filter is supplied back in the format of a range filter string, `'startdate..enddate'` (for example, 01/01/16..12/31/16). If we call `CreateFiscalYear`, the `Filter` will be for the range of a fiscal year, as defined by the system's `Accounting Period` table. If we call `CreateAccountingPeriodFilter`, the `Filter` will be for the range of a fiscal period, as defined by the same table.

The dates of the Period or Year filter returned are tied to the `BaseDate` parameter, which can be any legal date. The `NextStep` parameter tells which period or year to use, depending on which function is called. A `NextStep = 0` says use the period or year containing the `BaseDate`, `NextStep = 1` says use the next period or year into the future, and `NextStep = -2` says use the period or year before last (go back two periods or years).

The `Name` value returned is also derived from the `Accounting Period` table. If the call is to `CreateAccountingPeriodFilter`, then `Name` will contain the appropriate Accounting Period Name. If the call is to `CreateFiscalYearFilter`, then `Name` will contain `'Fiscal Year yyyy'`, where `yyyy` will be the four-digit numeric year.

Codeunit 359 – Period Form Management

This codeunit contains three functions that can be used for date handling. They are `FindDate`, `NextDate`, and `CreatePeriodFormat`.

- `FindDate` function
    - Calling Parameters (`SearchString` (text, length 3), `Calendar` (Date table), `PeriodType` (Option, integer))
    - Returns `DateFound` Boolean

```
FindDate(SearchString,CalendarRec,PeriodType)
```

This function is often used in pages to assist with the date calculation. The purpose of this function is to find a date in the virtual Date table based on the parameters passed in. The search starts with an initial record in the Calendar table. If we pass in a record that has already been initialized by positioning the table at a date, then that will be the base date, otherwise the Work Date will be used.

`PeriodType` is an Option field with the option value choices of day, week, month, quarter, year, and accounting period. For ease of coding, we could call the function with the integer equivalent (0, 1, 2, 3, 4, 5) or set up our own equivalent Option variable. In general, it's a much better practice to set up an Option variable because the Option strings make the code self-documenting.

`SearchString` allows us to pass in a logical control string containing =, >, <, <=, >=, and so on. `FindDate` will find the first date starting with the initialized `Calendar` date that satisfies the `SearchString` logic instruction and fits the `PeriodType` defined. For example, if the `PeriodType` is day and the date 01/25/16 is used along with the `SearchString` of >, then the date 01/26/16 will be returned in `Calendar`.

- `NextDate` function

    ○ Calling Parameters (`NextStep` (integer), `Calendar` (Date table), `PeriodType` (Option, integer))

    ○ Returns Integer:

    ```
    IntegerVariable := NextDate(NextStep,CalendarRec,PeriodType)
    ```

`NextDate` will find the next date record in the `Calendar` table that satisfies the calling parameters. The `Calendar` and `PeriodType` calling parameters for `FindDate` have the same definition as they do for the `FindDate` function. However, for this function to be really useful, `Calendar` must be initialized before calling `NextDate` – otherwise, the function will calculate the appropriate next date from day 0. The `NextStep` parameter allows us to define the number of periods of `PeriodType` to move, so as to obtain the desired next date. For example, if we start with a `Calendar` table positioned on 01/25/16, `PeriodType` of quarter (that is 3), and `NextStep` of 2, then `NextDate` will move forward two quarters and return with `Calendar` focused on Quarter 7/1/16 to 9/30/16.

- `CreatePeriodFormat` function

    ○ Calling Parameters (`PeriodType` (Option, integer), `Date` (date))

    ○ Returns Text, length 10

    ```
    FormattedDate := CreatePeriodFormat(PeriodType,DateData)
    ```

`CreatePeriodFormat` allows us to supply a date and specify which of its format options we want via `PeriodType`. The function's return value is a ten-character formatted text value; for example, mm/dd/yy, ww/yyyy, mon/yyyy, qtr/yyyy, or yyyy.

Codeunit 365 – Format Address

The functions in the `Format Address` codeunit do the obvious, they format addresses in a variety of situations. The address data in any master record (Customer, Vendor, Sales Order Sell-to, Sales Order Ship-to, Employee, and so on) may contain embedded blank lines. For example, the Address 2 line may be empty. When we print out the address information on a document or report, it will look better if there are no blank lines. These functions take care of such tasks.

In addition, NAV provides setup options for multiple formats of City – Post Code – County – Country combinations. The `Format Address` functions format addresses according to what was chosen in the setup or was been defined in the Countries/ Regions page for different postal areas.

There are over 60 data-specific functions in the `Format Address` codeunit. Each data-specific function allows us to pass a record parameter for the record containing the raw address data (such as a Customer record, a Vendor Record, a Sales Order, and so on) plus a parameter of a one-dimensional Text array with 8 elements of length up to 90 characters. Each function extracts the address data from its specific master record format and stores it in the array. The function then passes that data to a general-purpose function, which does the actual work of re-sequencing according to the various setup rules and compressing the data by removing blank lines.

The following are examples of function call format for the functions for `Company` and the `Sales Ship-to` addresses. In each case, `AddressArray` is Text, Length 90, and one-dimensional with 8 elements.

```
"Format Address".Company(AddressArray,CompanyRec);
"Format Address".SalesHeaderShipTo(AddressArray,SalesHeaderRec);
```

The function's processed result is returned in the `AddressArray` parameter.

In addition to the data-specific functions in the `Format Address` codeunit, we can also directly utilize the more general-purpose functions contained there. If we add a new address structure as part of an enhancement, we may want to create our own data-specific address formatting function in our custom codeunit. But we should design our function to call the general purpose functions that already exist (and are already debugged).

The primary general-purpose address formatting function (the one we are most likely to call directly) is `FormatAddr`. This is the function that does most of the work in this codeunit. The syntax for the `FormatAddr` function is as follows:

```
FormatAddr(AddressArray,Name,Name2,ContactName,Address1,Address2,
        City,PostCode,County,CountryCode)
```

The calling parameters of `AddressArray`, `Name`, `Name2`, and `ContactName` are all Text, length 90. `Address1`, `Address2`, `City`, and `County` are all Text, length 50. `PostCode` and `CountryCode` are data type Code, length 20 and length 10, respectively.

Our data is passed into the function in the individual `Address` fields. The results are passed back in the `AddressArray` parameter for us to use.

There are two other functions in the `Format Address` codeunit that are often called directly. They are `FormatPostCodeCity` and `GeneratePostCodeCity`. The `FormatPostCodeCity` function serves the purpose of finding the applicable setup rule for `PostCode` + `City` + `County` + `Country` formatting. It then calls the `GeneratePostCodeCity` function, which does the actual formatting.

Accompanying the defined NAV Patterns (on the same website as the Patterns), there is a section entitled "Recipes – The NAV C/AL Cookbook". One of those recipes, "Address Integration", applies to the preceding section on address formatting and provides a presentation on this topic at `https://community.dynamics.com/nav/w/designpatterns/234.address-integration.aspx`.

Codeunit 396 – NoSeriesManagement

Throughout NAV, master records (for example Customer, Vendor, Item, and so on) and activity documents (Sales Order, Purchase Order, Warehouse Transfer Orders, and so on) are controlled by the unique identification number assigned to each one. This unique identification number is assigned through a call to a function within the `NoSeriesManagement` codeunit. That function is `InitSeries`. The calling format for `InitSeries` is as follows:

```
NoSeriesManagement.InitSeries(WhichNumberSeriesToUse,
LastDataRecNumberSeriesCode, SeriesDateToApply, NumberToUse,
NumberSeriesUsed)
```

The parameter `WhichNumberSeriesToUse` is generally defined on a **Numbers** Tab in the Setup record for the applicable application area. `LastDataRecNumberSeriesCode` tells the function what Number Series was used for the previous record in this table. The `SeriesDateToApply` parameter allows the function to assign ID numbers in a date-dependent fashion. `NumberToUse` and the `NumberSeriesUsed` are return parameters.

The following screenshot shows an example for Table 18 – Customer:

```
Table 18 Customer - C/AL Editor
OnInsert()
  IF "No." = '' THEN BEGIN
    SalesSetup.GET;
    SalesSetup.TESTFIELD("Customer Nos.");
    NoSeriesMgt.InitSeries(SalesSetup."Customer Nos.",xRec."No. Series",0D,"No.","No. Series");
  END;
```

The next screenshot shows a second example for Table 36 – Sales Header. In this case, the call to `NoSeresMgt` has been placed in a local function:

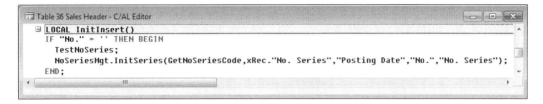

```
Table 36 Sales Header - C/AL Editor

LOCAL InitInsert()
  IF "No." = '' THEN BEGIN
    TestNoSeries;
    NoSeriesMgt.InitSeries(GetNoSeriesCode,xRec."No. Series","Posting Date","No.","No. Series");
  END;
```

With the exception of `GetNextNo` (used in assigning unique identifying numbers to each of a series of transactions) and possibly `TestManual` (used to test if manual numbering is allowed), we are not likely to use other functions in the `NoSeriesManagement` codeunit. The other functions are principally used either by the `InitSeries` function or other NAV routines whose job it is to maintain Number Series control information and data.

There is also a NAV Pattern defined describing the use of number series in NAV. It is titled "No. Series".

Function models to review and use

It is very helpful when we're creating new code to have a model that works which we can study (or clone). This is especially true in NAV where there is little or no development "how to" documentation available for many of the different functions we would like to use. One of the more challenging aspects of learning to develop in the NAV environment is learning how to handle issues in the "NAV way". Learning the "NAV way" is very beneficial because then our code works better, is easier to maintain, and is easier to upgrade. There is no better place to learn the strengths and subtle features of the product than to study the code written by the developers who are part of the inner circle of NAV creation.

If there is a choice, don't add custom functions to the standard NAV Codeunits. Well segregated customizations in clearly identified custom objects make both maintenance and upgrades easier. When we build functions modeled on NAV functions, the new code should be in a customer licensed codeunit.

A list of objects follows which contain functions we may find useful for use in our code or as models. We find these useful for studying how "it's" done in NAV ("it" obviously varies depending on the function's purpose).

- Codeunit 1 – Application Management: A library of utility functions widely used in the system
- Codeunits 11, 12, 13, 21, 22, 23, 80, 81, 82, 90, 91, 92 – the Posting sequences for Sales, Purchases, General Ledger, Item Ledger; these control the posting of journal data into the various ledgers
- Codeunit 228 – Test Report-Print: Functions for printing Test Reports for user review prior to Posting data
- Codeunit 229 – Print Documents: Functions for printing Document formatted reports.
- Codeunits 397, 400 – Mail: Functions for interfacing with Outlook and SMTP mail
- Codeunit 408 – Dimension Management: Don't write your own; use these
- Codeunit 419 – 3-tier File Management: Functions including BLOB tasks, file uploading, and downloading
- Codeunits 802 – Online Map interfacing
- Codeunit 5054 – Word Management: Interfaces to Microsoft Word
- Codeunit 5063 – Archive Management: Storing copies of processed documents
- Codeunits 5300 thru 5313 – More Outlook interfacing
- Codeunits 5813 thru 5819 – Undo functions
- Codeunit 6224 – XML DOM Management for XML structure handling
- Table 330 – Currency Exchange Rate: Contains some of the key currency conversion functions
- Table 370 – Excel Buffer: Excel interfacing
- Page 344 – Navigate: Home of the unique and powerful Navigate feature

Management codeunits

There are over 150 codeunits with the word "Management" or "Mgt" as part of their description name (filter the codeunits using `*Management*` | `*Mgt*`). Each of these codeunits contains functions in which the purpose is the management of some specific aspect of NAV data. Many are very specific to a narrow range of data. Some are more general, because they contain functions we can reuse in another application area (for example, Codeunit 396 – NoSeriesManagement).

When we are working on an enhancement in a particular functional area, it is extremely important to check the Management codeunits utilized in that area. We may be able to use some existing standard functions directly. This will have the benefit of reducing the code we have to create and debug. Of course, when a new version is released, we will have to check to see if the functions on which we relied have changed in a way that affects our code.

If we can't use the existing material as is, we may find functions we can use as models for tasks in the area of our enhancement. And, even if that is not true, by researching and studying the existing code, we will learn more about how data is structured and processes flow in the standard NAV system.

Multi-language system

The NAV system is designed as a multi-language system, meaning it can interface with users in many languages. The base product is distributed with American English as the primary language, but each local version comes with one or more other languages ready for use. Since the system can be set up to operate from a single database displaying user interfaces in several different languages, NAV is particularly suitable for firms operating from a central system, serving users in multiple countries. NAV is used by businesses all over the world, operating in dozens of different languages. It is important to note that when the application language is changed, it has no effect on the data in the database. The data is not multi-language unless we provide that functionality by means of our own enhancements or data structure. There is a NAV Pattern, known as Multilanguage Application Data, which describes how data and UI elements can be multilanguage enabled.

The basic elements that support the multi-language feature include:

- Multi-language Captioning properties (for example, **CaptionML**) supporting definitions of alternative language captions for all fields, action labels, titles, and so on

- Application Management codeunit logic that allows language choice at login

- `fin.stx` files supplied by NAV, which are language specific and contain texts used by C/SIDE for various menus such as File, Edit, View, Tools, and so on (`fin.stx` cannot be modified except by Microsoft)

- The Text Constants property **ConstantValueML** supporting definition of alternative language messages

Before embarking on an effort to create multi-language enabled modifications, review all the available documentation on the topic (search Help on the word **language**). It's wise to do some small scale testing to ensure we understand what is required, and that our approach will work (such testing is required for any significant enhancement).

Multi-currency system

NAV was one of the first ERP systems to fully implement a multi-currency system. Transactions can start in one currency and finish in another. For example, we can create the order in US dollars and accept payment for the invoice in Euros. For this reason, where there are money values, they are generally stored in the local currency (referenced as **LCY**) as defined in the setup. There is a set of currency conversion tools built into the applications and there are standard (by practice) code structures to support and utilize these tools. Two examples of code segments from the `Sales Line` table illustrating handling of money fields follow:

```
GetSalesHeader;
IF SalesHeader."Currency Code" <> '' THEN BEGIN
  Currency.TESTFIELD("Unit-Amount Rounding Precision");
  "Unit Cost" :=
    ROUND(
      CurrExchRate.ExchangeAmtLCYToFCY(
        GetDate,SalesHeader."Currency Code",
        "Unit Cost (LCY)",SalesHeader."Currency Factor"),
      Currency."Unit-Amount Rounding Precision")
END ELSE
  "Unit Cost" := "Unit Cost (LCY)";
```

In both cases, there's a function call to ROUND and use of the currency specific **Currency**. **Amount Rounding Precision** control value.

```
"Line Discount Amount" :=
  ROUND(
    ROUND(Quantity * "Unit Price",Currency."Amount Rounding Precision") *
    "Line Discount %" / 100,Currency."Amount Rounding Precision");
```

As we can see, before creating any modification that has money fields, we must familiarize ourselves with the NAV currency conversion feature, the code that supports it, and the related setups. A good place to start is the C/AL code in Table 37 – Sales Line, Table 39 – Purchase Line, and Table 330 – Currency Exchange Rate.

Navigate

Navigate is an under-appreciated tool for both the user and for the developer. Our focus here is on its value to the developer. Navigate (Page 344) finds and displays the counts and types of all the associated entries for a particular posting transaction. The term "associated", in this case, is defined as those entries having the same **Document Number** and **Posting Date**. This is a handy tool for the developer as it can show the results of posting activity and provide the tools to drill into the detail of all those results. If we add new transactions and Ledgers as part of an enhancement, our Navigate function should cover them too.

Navigate can be called from the **Navigate** action, which appears in a number of places in the Departments Tasks menu and Role Center ribbons. From anywhere within NAV, the easiest way to find Navigate is to type the word into the Search box (see the following image):

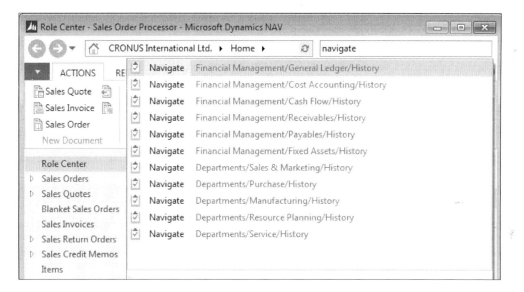

If we invoke the Navigate page using the menu action item, we must enter **Posting Date** and **Document Number** for the entries we wish to find. Alternately, we can enter **Business Contact Type** (Vendor or Customer), **Business Contact No.** (Vendor No. or Customer No.), and optionally, **External Document No**. There are occasions when this option is useful, but the **Posting Date + Document No.** option is more frequently useful.

Instead of seeking out a Navigate page and entering the critical data fields, it is much easier to call Navigate from a **Navigate** action on a page showing data. In this case, we just highlight a record and click on **Navigate** to search for all the related entries. In the following example, **Posted Invoice** is highlighted:

After clicking the **Navigate** action, the page will pop up, filled in like the following screenshot:

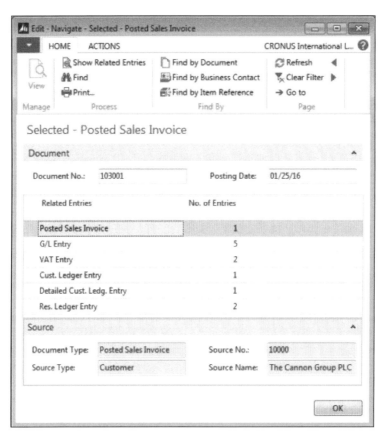

Had we accessed the **Navigate** page through one of the menu entries we found via **Search** (*Ctrl + F3*), we would have filled in the **Document No.** and **Posting Date** fields and clicked on **Find**. As we can see here, the **Navigate** page shows a list of related, posted entries (one of which will include the entry we highlighted when we invoked the Navigate function). If we highlight one of the lines in the **Related Entries** list and then click on the **Show Related Entries** icon at the top of the page, we will see an appropriately formatted display of the chosen entries.

If we highlight the **G/L Entry** table entries and click on **Show**, we will see a result like the following screenshot. Note that all **G/L Entry** are displayed for same **Posting Date** and **Document No.**, matching those specified at the top of the **Navigate** page:

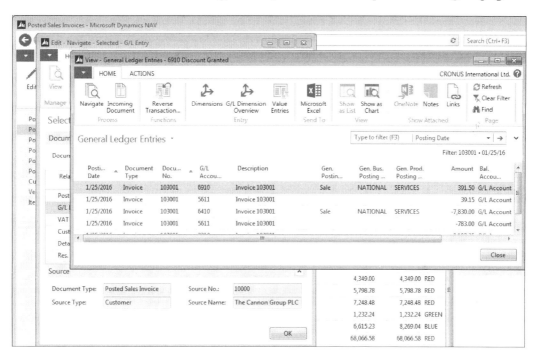

Modifying for Navigate

If our modification creates a new table that will contain posted data and the records contain both Document No. and Posting Date fields, we can include this new table in the **Navigate** function.

The C/AL Code for **Posting Date + Document No**. Navigate functionality is found in the FindRecords and FindExtRecords functions of Page 344 – Navigate. The following screenshot shows the segment of the Navigate CASE statement code for the Check Ledger Entry table:

```
IF SalesInvHeader.READPERMISSION THEN BEGIN
  SalesInvHeader.RESET;
  SalesInvHeader.SETCURRENTKEY("Sell-to Customer No.","External Document No.");
  SalesInvHeader.SETFILTER("Sell-to Customer No.",ContactNo);
  SalesInvHeader.SETFILTER("External Document No.",ExtDocNo);
  InsertIntoDocEntry(
    DATABASE::"Sales Invoice Header",0,Text003,SalesInvHeader.COUNT);
END;
```

The code checks READPERMISSION. If that permission is enabled for this table, then the appropriate filtering is applied. Next, there is a call to the InsertIntoDocEntry function, which fills the temporary table that is displayed in the **Navigate** page. If we wish to add a new table to the Navigate function, we must replicate this functionality for our new table.

In addition, we must add the code that will call up the appropriate page to display the records that Navigate finds. This code should be inserted in the ShowRecords function trigger of the **Navigate** page, modeling on the applicable section of code in this function (that is, choose the code set that best fits our new tables). Making a change like this, when appropriate, will not only provide a powerful tool for our users, but also provide a powerful tool for us as developers.

Debugging in NAV 2015

In general, the processes and tools we use for debugging can serve multiple purposes. The most immediate purpose is always that of identifying the causes of errors and then resolving those errors. There are two categories of production errors (which may also occur during development) and NAV 2015's Debugger module is very well suited to addressing both of these. The NAV debugger smoothly integrates developing in the Development Environment and testing in the Role Tailored Client.

The first category is the type that causes an error condition which terminates processing. In this case, the immediate goal is to find the cause and fix it as quickly as possible. The new debugger is an excellent tool for this purpose. The second category is the type that, while running to completion successfully, gives erroneous results.

We often find that debugging techniques can be used to help us better understand how NAV processes work. We may be working on the design of (or determination of the need for) a modification or we may simply want to learn more about how a particular function is used or outcome is accomplished in the standard NAV routines. It would be more appropriate to refer to these efforts as analysis or self-education, rather than debugging, even though the processes we use to dissect the code and view what it's doing are very similar. In the course of these efforts, less sophisticated approaches are sometimes useful in understanding what's going on. We'll quickly review some of these alternate approaches before studying use of the NAV 2015 Debugger.

Text Exports of Objects

Using a developer license, we are allowed to export objects into text files, where we can use a text editor to examine or even manipulate the result. Let us take a look at an object that has been exported into text and imported into your favorite text editor. We will use one of the tables that is part of our WDTU development, the `Playlist Item Rate` table, **50004** as shown in the following screenshot:

```
OBJECT Table 50004 Playlist Item Rate
{
  OBJECT-PROPERTIES
  {
    Date=04/18/15;
    Time=11:46:50 AM;
    Modified=Yes;
    Version List=CD02;
  }
  PROPERTIES
  {
    LookupPageID=Page50005;
    DrillDownPageID=Page50005;
  }
  FIELDS
  {
    { 10  ;  ;Type              ;Option      ;TableRelation=IF (Type=CONST(Vendor)) Vendor.No.
                                                            ELSE IF (Type=CONST(Customer)) Customer.No.;
                                              OptionCaptionML=ENU=Vendor,Customer;
                                              OptionString=Vendor,Customer;
                                              Description=Vendor,Customer }
    { 20  ;  ;No.               ;Code20      }
    { 30  ;  ;Item No.          ;Code20      }
    { 40  ;  ;Start Date        ;Date        }
    { 50  ;  ;End Date          ;Date        }
    { 60  ;  ;Rate Amount       ;Decimal     }
    { 70  ;  ;Publisher Code    ;Code20      ;Description=TableRelation:Publisher.Code }
  }
  KEYS
  {
    {  ;Type                                 ;Clustered=Yes }
  }
  FIELDGROUPS
  {
  }
  CODE
  {

    BEGIN
    END.
  }
}
```

The general structure of all the exported objects is similar, with just those differences that we would expect for the different objects. This particular table contains no C/AL-coded logic, as those statements would be visible in the text listing. We can see by looking at this table object that we could easily search for instances of the string Code throughout the text export of the entire system, but it would be more difficult to look for references to **Playlist Item Rates** because it is only referenced by page ID, Page50005. While we can find the instances of Code with our text editor, it would be quite difficult to differentiate those instances that relate to the **Playlist Item Rate** table from those in any other table. This includes those that have nothing to do with our WDTU system enhancement, as well as those simply defined in an object as Global Variables.

If we are determined to use a text editor to find all instances of "Playlist Item Rate"."Rate Amount", we can do the following:

- Rename the field in question to something unique. C/SIDE will rename all the references to this field to this new name.

- Export all the sources to text followed by using our text editor (or even Microsoft Word) to find the new, unique name.

- Either return the field in the database to the original name or work in a temporary copy of the database, which we will then discard. Otherwise, we will have quite a mess.

One task that needs to be done occasionally is to renumber an object or to change an internal object reference that refers to a no longer existing element. The C/SIDE editor may not let us do that easily or, in some cases, not at all. In such a case, the best answer may be to export the object into text, make the change there, and then import it back in as modified. Be careful. When we import a text object, C/SIDE does not check to see if the incoming object is valid. C/SIDE makes that check when we import a compiled fob object. If we must do object renumbering, we should use the functionality built into Mergetool (available at http://www.mergetool.com/default.html). Many years ago, Mergetool was the recommended Upgrade support tool for Navision and once again it's the best answer.

There are occasions when it is very helpful to simply view an object "flattened out" in text format. In a report or XMLport where we may have combinations of logic and properties, the only way to see everything at once is in text format. We can use any text editor we like, Notepad or Word, or one of the visual programming editors; the exported object is just text. We need to cope with the fact that when we export a large number of objects in one pass, they all end up in the same text file. This makes the exported file relatively difficult to use. The solution is to split that file into individual text files, named logically, one for each NAV object. There are several freeware tools to do just that, available from the NAV forums on the Internet.

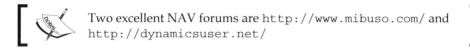

Two excellent NAV forums are `http://www.mibuso.com/` and `http://dynamicsuser.net/`

Dialog function debugging techniques

Sometimes the simpler methods are more productive than the more sophisticated tools, because we can set up and test quickly, resolve the issue (or answer a question), and move on. All the simpler methods involve using one of the C/AL `DIALOG` functions such as `MESSAGE`, `CONFIRM`, `DIALOG`, or `ERROR`. All of these have the advantage of working well in the RTC environment. However, we should remember that none of these techniques conform to **Testing Best Practices** in the **Testing the Application** Help. These should only be used when a quick, one-time approach is needed or when recommended testing practices won't easily provide the information needed and one of these techniques will do so.

Debugging with MESSAGE and CONFIRM

The simplest debug method is to insert the `MESSAGE` statements at key points in our logic. It is very simple and, if structured properly, provides us a simple "trace" of the code logic path. We can number our messages to differentiate them and display any data (in small amounts) as part of a message such as the one shown following.

```
MESSAGE('This is Test 4 for %1',Customer."No.");
```

A big disadvantage is that the `MESSAGE` statements do not display until processing either terminates or is interrupted for user interaction. If we force a user interaction at some point, then our accumulated messages will appear prior to the interaction. The simplest way to force user interaction is to issue a `CONFIRM` message in the format as follows:

```
IF CONFIRM ('Test 1',TRUE) THEN;
```

If we want to do a simple trace but want every message to be displayed as it is generated (that is, have the tracking process move at a very measured pace), we could use the `CONFIRM` statements for all the messages. The operator must then respond to each one before our program will move on, but sometimes that is what we want. However, if we make the mistake of creating the situation where hundreds of messages are generated, the operator will have to respond to each one individually in what could be a very time consuming and inefficient process.

Debugging with DIALOG

Another tool that is useful for progress tracking is the DIALOG function. DIALOG is usually set up to display a window with a small number of variable values. As processing progresses, the values are displayed in real time. Some ways we might use this are listed next:

- Simply tracking progress of processing through a volume of data. This is the same reason we would provide a DIALOG display for the benefit of the user. The act of displaying slows down the processing somewhat, so we may want to update the DIALOG display occasionally, not on every record.

- Displaying indicators when processing reaches certain stages. This can be used as a very basic trace with the indicators showing the path taken so we may gauge the relative speed of progress through several steps.

- We might have a six-step process to analyze. We could define six tracking variables and display all of them in DIALOG. We would initialize each variable with values dependent on what we are tracking, such as A1, B2000, C300000, and so on. At each process step, update and display the current state of one or all the variables. This can be a very helpful guide for how our process is operating. To slow things down, we could put a SLEEP(100) or SLEEP(500) after the DIALOG statement (the number is milliseconds of delay).

Debugging with text output

We can build a very handy debugging tool by outputting the values of critical variables or other informative indicators of progress to either an external text file or to a table created for this purpose. We need to either do this in single user mode or make it multiuser by including the USER ID on every entry.

This technique allows us to run a considerable volume of test data through the system, tracking some important elements while collecting data on the variable values, progress through various sections of code, and so on. We can even timestamp our output records so that we can use this method to look for processing speed problems.

Following the test run, we can analyze the results of our test more quickly than if we were using displayed information. We can focus on just the items that appear most informative and ignore the rest. This type of debugging is fairly easy to set up and to refine, as we identify the variables or code segments of most interest. We can combine the approach of using text output to track activity with the ERROR statement approach (described following). To do so, we output to an external text file, and then close it before invoking the ERROR statement, so that its contents are retained following the termination of the test run.

Debugging with ERROR

One of the challenges of testing is maintaining repeatability. Quite often, we need to test several times using the same data, but the test changes the data. If we have a small database, we can always back up the database and start with a fresh copy each time. But that can be inefficient and, if the database is large. If we are using the built-in NAV Test functions, we can roll back any database changes so the tests are totally repeatable. Another alternative is to conclude our test with an ERROR function to test and retest with exactly the same data.

The ERROR function forces a run-time error status, which means that the database is not updated (it is rolled back to the status at the beginning of the process). This works well when our debugging information is provided by using the Debugger or by use of any of the DIALOG functions just mentioned prior to the execution of the ERROR function. If we are using MESSAGE to generate debugging information, we could execute CONFIRM immediately prior to the ERROR statement and be assured that all the messages are displayed. Obviously, this method won't work well when our testing validation is dependent on checking results using Navigate or our test is a multi-step process such as order entry, review, and posting. In this latter case, only use of the built-in Test functions (creating Test Runner Codeunits, and such) will be adequate. But in some situations, use of the ERROR function is a very handy technique for repeating a test with minimal effort.

When testing just the posting of an item, it often works well to place the test-concluding ERROR function just before the point in the applicable Posting codeunit where the process would otherwise be completed successfully. In order for the Rollback function to be effective, we must make sure that there aren't any COMMIT statements included in the range of the code being tested.

The NAV 2015 Debugger

As defined in the Help **Debugging** (which should be studied), debugging is the process of finding and correcting errors. NAV 2015 has a powerful built-in debugger. The user interface for the NAV 2015 Debugger is written in C/AL. The Debugger objects can be identified by filtering in the Object Designer, **All** objects, on *Debug*. Reviewing the structure of the Debugger objects in C/SIDE may help better understand its inner workings.

The new Debugger can be activated in multiple different ways including from within the Development Environment, from within the RTC, from a command line, and by means of a C/AL function. The latter two options attach to a session at the same time as they activate. The best choice for activation method depends on the specific situation and the debugging technique being utilized by the developer.

Only a user who has SUPER permissions for all companies is allowed to activate the debugger. The user permissions setup should have an empty Company field as we can see in the circled space in the following image:

Activating the Debugger

Activating the Debugger from the Development Environment is a simple matter of clicking on **Tools | Debugger | Debug Sessions...** (or *Shift + Ctrl + F11*). The initial page that displays when the Debugger is activated will look like the following screenshot (typically with each session having a different User ID). Multiple sessions can be debugged in parallel:

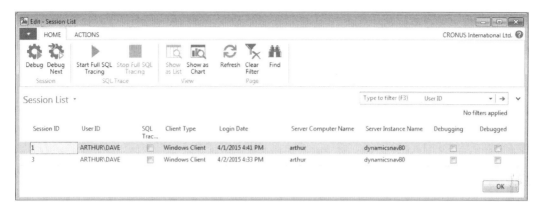

If we activate the Debugger by means of any method that does not specify a session, this same screen will appear. The Debugger can also be activated from within the RTC as follows:

1. Enter Sessions in the Search box.

2. Select the link displayed (**Administration/IT Administration/General**).

3. In the **General** section, click on **Sessions**.

We can also get to this same point by clicking on the **Departments** button in the Navigation pane, then **IT Administration | General**, followed by **Sessions** in the **Tasks** section.

However we activate it, the Debugger runs as a separate independent session, which can be attached to an operating session. The Help **Activating the Debugger** describes activating the Debugger to debug a Web Service. The Help **Configuring NAS Services** has information about using the Debugger with a NAS Service.

Attaching the Debugger to a Session

From the **Edit – Session** list screen, we have two options for attaching the Debugger session to a session. One way is to highlight a Session and then click on the **Debug** icon:

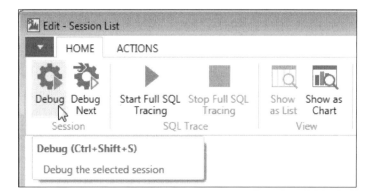

The other way is to click on the **Debug Next** icon, then initiate a new Session. The Debugger will be attached to the new Session:

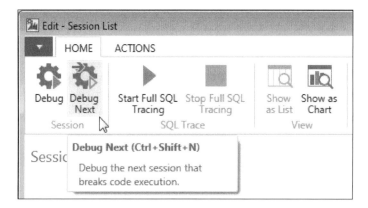

When we click on **Debug Next**, an empty View – Debugger page will open, awaiting the event that will cause a break in processing and the subsequent display of Code detail, Watched variables, and the Call Stack.

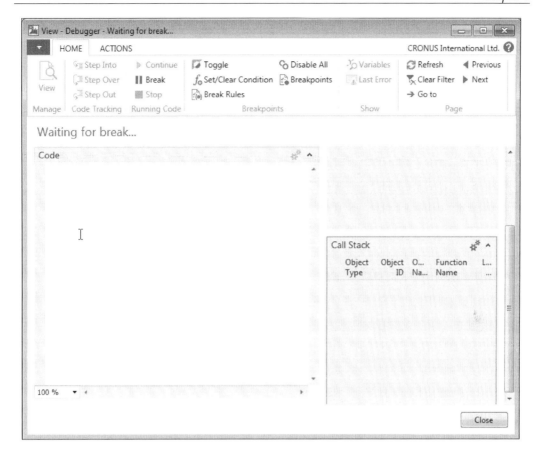

Creating Break Events

Once the Debugger is activated and attached to a session, some break event must occur to cause the debug trace and associated data display to begin. Break events include (but are not limited to) the following occurences:

- An error occurs that would cause object execution to be terminated

- A previously set **Breakpoint** is reached during processing

- The record is read when **Break on Record Changes Break Rule** is active

- The Break icon in the Running Code group is clicked in the ribbon of the **View – Debugger** page

- A Breakpoint Condition, which has been set in the Breakpoints group in the ribbon of the **View – Debugger** page, is satisfied during processing

Of the preceding events, the two most common methods of starting up a debug trace are the first two, an error or reaching a previously set breakpoint. If, for example, an error condition is discovered in an operating object, the debugging process can be initiated by:

1. Activating the debugger.
2. Attaching the debugger session to the session where the error will occur.
3. Running the process where the error occurs.

When the error occurs, the page parts (Code, Watches, and Call Stack) in the debug window will be populated and we can proceed to investigate variable values, review code, and so forth.

Breakpoints are stopping points in an object which have been set by the developer. Breakpoints can be set in a variety of ways including in the Development Environment, in the **View – Debugger Code** page, and in the **Edit – Debugger Breakpoint List**.

While the latter two locations for setting breakpoints may be very useful while we are in the middle of a debugging session, those breakpoints only display while the Debugger is active. Once we exit the debugging session, those breakpoints that were set in the Debugger will disappear from view, while the breakpoints that were set from within the applicable C/SIDE Designer will remain visible and available for use until removed.

The result may be somewhat confusing because when we can only see all of the breakpoints when we are in the Debugger. If we try to set a breakpoint in the Development Environment and a breakpoint has already been set on that line of code while in the Debugger, we will get an error message:

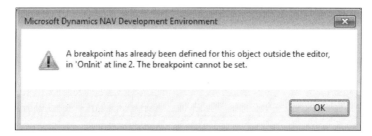

For this reason, it may be better practice to set all our planned testing breakpoints in the Development Environment. When we set breakpoints within the Debugger, we should clear them before ending our test session. Otherwise we may later run into breakpoints we didn't remember existed and which we can't see in the Designers.

Active breakpoints are represented in code by a filled in circle. Disabled breakpoints are represented by an empty circle. Examples are shown in the following code:

```
⊟ OnInsert()
●    IF "No." = '' THEN BEGIN
        PurchSetup.GET;
        PurchSetup.TESTFIELD("Vendor Nos.");
        NoSeriesMgt.InitSeries(PurchSetup."Vendor No
     END;
○    IF "Invoice Disc. Code" = '' THEN|
        "Invoice Disc. Code" := "No.";
```

When viewing the C/AL code in a Designer, breakpoints can be set, disabled, or removed by pressing the *F9* key. When viewing the C/AL code in the Code window of the Debugger, breakpoints can only be set or removed by pressing the *F9* key or clicking on the **Toggle** icon. Other Debugger breakpoint controls are shown in the following image.

The Debugger window

The following screenshot shows the debugger window:

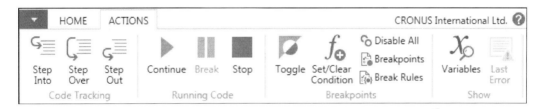

The ribbon actions in the Debugger window are as follows:

- **Step Into**: Designed to trace into a function.
- **Step Over**: Designed to execute a function without stopping, and then break.
- **Step Out**: Designed to complete the current function without stopping, and then break.
- **Continue**: Continue until the next break.
- **Break**: Break at the next statement.
- **Stop**: Stop the current activity but leave the debugging session active.
- **Toggle**: Set or clear a breakpoint at the current line.
- **Set/Clear Condition**: Set or clear a conditional (based on C/AL expression) breakpoint at the current line.

- **Disable All**: Disables all checkpoints in the attached session.
- **Break Rules**: Displays the following screen:

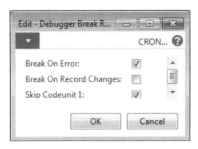

- ○ **Break On Error** default is on
- ○ If **Break On Record Changes** is on when a debug session is attached to an operating session, the debugging will start immediately
- ○ **Skip Codeunit 1** default is on, allowing all the Codeunit 1 processing to normally be processed without tracing

- **Breakpoints** displays a list of the active breakpoints and provides action options to enable, disable, or delete breakpoints individually or in total.

- **Variables** displays the Debugger Variable List where we can examine the status of all variables that are in scope. Additional variables can be added to the Watch list here.

- **Last Error** displays the last error message shown by the session being debugged.

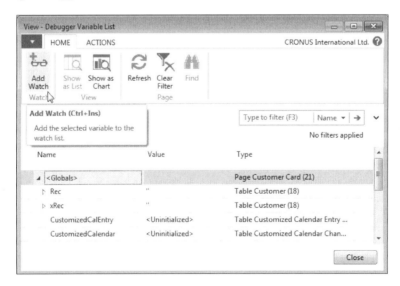

Variables can be removed from the Watch list in the Debugger **Watches** page part.

There are quite a number of valuable Help sections on use of the Debugger including the following (and many others):

- *Debugging*
- *Debugger Keyboard Shortcuts*
- *Breakpoints* (this one is especially good)
- *Closing the Debugger*
- *How to: Add Variables to the Watches FactBox*
- *How to: Debug a Background Session*
- *How to: Manage Breakpoints from the Development Environment*
- *How to: Set Conditional Breakpoints*
- *Walkthrough: Debugging the Microsoft Dynamics NAV Windows Client*

Changing code while debugging

While a debugger session is active, we can open the object being debugged in an appropriate Designer, change the object, save, and recompile it. The revised object will immediately be available to other sessions on the system. However, the version of the object that is being executed and in view in the debugger is the old version of the object, not the changed one. Furthermore, if we refresh the view of the code in the Debugger **Code** window, the new version will be displayed while the old version continues to be executed, leaving potential for significant confusion. Therefore, it's best not to change an object and continue to debug it without starting a new session.

C/SIDE Test-driven development

NAV 2015 includes the enhanced C/AL Testability feature set designed to support C/AL test-driven development. **Test-driven development** is an approach where the application tests are defined prior to the development of the application code. In an ideal situation, the code supporting application tests is written prior to, or at least at the same time as, the code implementing the target application function written.

Advantages of test-driven development include:

- Design testing processes in conjunction with functional design
- Find bugs early
- Prevent bugs reaching production
- Enable regression testing, preventing changes introducing bugs into previously validated routines

The C/AL Testability feature provides test specific types of Codeunits—Test Codeunits and Test Running Codeunits. Test Codeunits contain Test methods, UI handlers, and the C/AL code to support Test methods including the **AssertError** function. Test Runner Codeunits are used to invoke Test Codeunits, for test execution management, automation, and integration. Test Runner Codeunits have two special triggers, each of which run in separate transactions, so that the test execution state and results can be tracked. The TestRunner trigger descriptions follow:

- **OnBeforeTestRun** is called before each test. It allows defining, via a Boolean, to determine whether or not the test should be executed.

- **OnAfterTestRun** is called when each test completes and the test results are available. This allows the test results to be logged, or otherwise processed via the C/AL code.

Among the ultimate goals of the C/AL Testability feature are:

- The ability to run suites of application tests both in automated mode and in regression tests:
    - **Automated** means that a defined series of tests could be run and the results recorded, all without user intervention
    - **Regression testing** means that the test can be run repeatedly as part of a new testing pass to make sure that features previously tested are still in working order

- The ability to design tests in an "atomic" way, matching the granularity of the application code. In this way, the test functions can be focused and simplified. This allows for relatively easy construction of a suite of tests and, in some cases, reuse of test codeunits (or at least reuse of the structure of previously created Test Codeunits).

- The ability to develop and run the Test and Test Runner Codeunits within the familiar C/SIDE environment. The code for developing these testing codeunits is C/AL.

The **TestIsolation** property of TestRunner Codeunits allow tests to be run, then all database changes are rolled back so that no changes are Committed. After a test series in this mode, the database after the test is the same as it was before the test.

Once the testing Codeunits have been developed, the actual testing process should be simple and fast in order to run and evaluate the results.

Both positive and negative testing are supported. **Positive testing** looks for a specific result, a correct answer. **Negative testing** checks that errors are presented when expected, especially when data or parameters are out of range. The testing structure is designed to support the logging of the test results, both failures and success, to tables for review, reporting, and analysis.

A function property defines functions within Test Codeunits to be either `Test`, `TestHandler`, or `Normal`. Another function property, **TestMethodType**, allows the definition of a variety of Test Function types to be defined. The **TestMethodType** property options include the following which are designed to handle User Interface events without the need for a user to intervene:

- **MessageHandler**: Handles the `MESSAGE` statement
- **ConfirmHandler**: Handles the `CONFIRM` dialogs
- **StrMenuHandler**: Handles the `STRMENU` menu dialogs
- **PageHandler**: Handles Pages that are not run modally
- **ModalPageHandler**: Handles Pages that are run modally
- **ReportHandler**: Handles Reports
- **RequestPagetHandler**: Handles the Request Page of a specific Report

C/SIDE Test Driven Development approach should proceed along the following lines:

- Define an application function specification
- Define the application technical specification
- Define the testing technical specification including both Positive and Negative tests
- Develop Test and Test Running codeunits (frequently only one or a few Test Running codeunits will be required)
- Develop Application objects
- As soon as feasible, begin running Application object tests by means of the Test Running codeunits, and logging test results for historical and analytical purposes
- Continue the development — testing cycle, and updating the tests and the application as appropriate throughout the process
- At the end of the successful completion of development and testing, retain all the Test and TestRunning codeunits for use in regression testing the next time the application must be modified or upgraded

On PartnerSource, there is a full set of 7,000 to 9,000 regression tests available that were written by Microsoft for NAV 2013 using the NAV Testability tools. These are the tests that the NAV product developers used to validate their work. The number of tests that applies to a specific situation depends on the local version and specific features involved. At the time of writing this, the tools for NAV 2015 have not been released by Microsoft. To access the download for the NAV 2013 tools, search on **testability** and download **Application Test Toolset for Microsoft Dynamics NAV 2013**. Make sure your license is updated too.

 Even if we can't use the older version of the tests for full regression testing, we can use them as models for creating regression tests for our own customizations.

Included in the supplement are the regression tests and various tools for managing and executing tests built on top of the testability features released for Microsoft Dynamics NAV. Also included is a coverage tool and guidance documentation for creating our own tests and integrating those with the Microsoft provided tests. This allows us to do full regression testing for large modifications and ISV solutions.

Other Interfaces

Some NAV systems must communicate with other software or even with hardware. Sometimes that communication is *Inside-Out* (that is, initiated by NAV), and sometimes it is *Outside-In* (that is, initiated by the outside connection). It's not unusual for system-to-system communications to be a two-way street, a meeting of peers. To supply, receive, or exchange information with other systems (hardware or software), we need at least a basic understanding of the interface tools that are part of NAV.

 Because of NAV's unique data structures and the critical business logic embedded therein, it is very risky for an external system to access NAV data directly via SQL Server without using C/AL based routines as an intermediary.

NAV has a number of methods of interfacing with the world outside its database. We will review those very briefly here. To learn more about these, we should begin by reviewing the applicable material in the online **Developer and IT Pro Help** material plus any documentation available with the software distribution. We should also study sample code, especially that in the standard system as represented by the Cronus Demonstration Database. And, of course, we should take advantage of any other resources available including the NAV-oriented Internet forums and blogs.

Automation Controller

One option for NAV interfacing is by connection to COM Automation servers. A key group of Automation servers are the Microsoft Office products. Automation components can be instantiated, accessed, and manipulated from within NAV objects using the C/AL code. Data can be transferred back and forth between the NAV database and COM Automation components.

Only non-visual controls are supported via this interface (that doesn't mean we couldn't figure out a work-around, just that they aren't supported by Microsoft). The Client Add-in feature, discussed later in this chapter, provides visual interface capability through another integration approach.

We cannot use an Automation Controller defined COM component as a control on a NAV Page object. Only client side automation objects are supported. This is because the NAV server tier operates in 64-bit mode and many COM objects are not compatible with 64-bit operating systems. Instead of server side automation objects, use Microsoft .NET interoperability functionality (for more information, search Help on interoperability).

Some common uses of Automation Controller interfaces are to:

- Populate Word template documents to create more attractive communications with customers, vendors, and prospects (for example, past due notices, purchase orders, promotional letters, and so on)

- Move data to Excel spreadsheets for manipulation (for example, last year's sales data to create this year's projections)

- Move data to and from Excel spreadsheets for manipulation (for example, last year's financial results out and next year's budgets back in)

- Use Excel's graphing capabilities to enhance management reports

- Access to and use of ActiveX Data Objects (ADO) Library objects to support access to and from external databases and their associated systems

It will also be helpful to review the information on this topic in the following Help sections:

- *COM Overview*

- *Best Practices for Using Automation With the Microsoft Dynamics NAV Windows Client*

- *Automation Data Type*

- *Using COM Technologies in Microsoft Dynamics NAV*

Linked Data Sources

The two table properties, **LinkedObject** and **LinkedInTransaction**, are available for NAV tables. Use of these properties in the prescribed fashion allows data access, including views, in linked server data sources such as Excel, Access, other instances of SQL Server, and even an Oracle database. For additional information, see the Help sections **Using Linked Objects** and **Accessing Objects in Other Databases or on Linked Servers**. This is one way to integrate NAV with external applications in a way that is seamless for the users.

NAV Application Server (NAS)

Microsoft Dynamics NAV Application Server (NAS) is a middle-tier server component that executes business logic without a user interface or user interaction. In NAV 2015, NAS is one of the client services that runs in the Microsoft Dynamics NAV Server.

NAS is essentially an automated user client. Because NAS is effectively a non-UI version of the standard NAV client module, it can access all of NAV's business rules.

Error messages that are generated by a NAS process are logged in the Event Viewer.

NAS operates essentially the same as any other NAV Windows client. If setup to run the JobQueue, it processes requests in the queue one at a time, in the same manner as the GUI client. Therefore, as developers, we need to limit the number of concurrent calls to a NAS instance as the queue should remain short to allow timely communications between interfaces. In NAV 2015, multiple background sessions can be started from client sessions. This provides opportunities for NAV automation for the creative designer/developer.

Client Add-ins

The NAV 2015 Client Add-in API (also known as Client Extensibility) provides the capability to extend the Role Tailored Client for Windows, Web, or Tablet through the integration of external, non-NAV controls. The Client Add-in API uses .NET interfaces as the binding mechanism between a control add-in and the NAV framework. Different interfaces and base classes are available to use, or a custom interface can be created. Controls can be designed to raise events that call on the **OnControlAddin** trigger on the page field control that hosts the add-in. They can also add events and methods that can be called from within C/AL.

Contrary to the limitations on other integration options, Client Add-ins can be graphical and appear on the RTC display as part of, or mingled with, native NAV controls. Following are a few simple examples of how Client Add-ins might be used to extend RTC UI behavior:

- A NAV text control that looks normal but offers a special behavior. When the user double-clicks on it, the field's contents would display in a popup screen accompanied by other related information or even a graphical display.

- A dashboard made up of several dials or gauges showing the percentage of chosen resources relative to target limits or goals. The dials are defined to support click and drill into the underlying NAV detail data.

- An integrated sales call mapping function displays customer locations on a map and creating a sequenced call list with pertinent sales data from the NAV database.

- Interactive visualization of a workflow or flow of goods in a process, showing the number of entries at each stage, supporting filtering to display selected sets of entries.

- Entry and storage of a written document signature on a touch screen.

Client Add-in construction

Some Client Add-ins will be created, packaged, and distributed by ISV Partners who specialize in an application area. When enhancing a system for a customer's specific application, we may decide to create a special purpose add-in.

As with any API, there is a defined approach that we must use to create a Client Add-in to interface with the NAV Windows RTC. So long as the code within the add-in is a well-behaved .NET code, we have a great deal of flexibility in the structure of the code within the add-in. The control can be one we create, a standard WinForms control, or one that we've acquired from a third party.

Once we have the .NET control we're going to use for our application, we need to build the add-in structure which envelopes the control. The most logical toolsets for building add-ins are the current versions of Visual Studio or one of the free downloadable tools such as Visual Studio Express for C#. When building an add-in, we must make sure that we are using a compatible version of .NET framework. The Developer and IT Pro Help in NAV 2015 contain many Help sections covering a wide variety of topics relating to Client Add-ins. Here's a partial list:

- *Binding a Windows Client Control Add-in to the Database*
- *Client Extensibility API Overview*
- *Developing Windows Client Control Add-ins*

- *Exposing Events and Calling the Respective C/AL Triggers from a Windows Client Control Add-in*

- *Exposing Methods and Properties in a Windows Client Control Add-in*

- *Extending the Windows Client Using Control Add-ins*

- *How to: Create a Window Client Control Add-in*

- *How to: Determine the Public Key Token of the Windows Client Control Add-in*

- *How to: Install a Windows Client Control Add-in Assembly*

- *How to: Register a Windows Client Control Add-in*

- *Installing and Configuring Windows Client Control Add-ins on Pages*

- *Walkthrough: Creating and Using a Window Client Control Add-in*

- *Windows Client Control Add-in Overview*

WDTU Client Add-in

Let's create a Client Add-in for WDTU. We want to add an MP3 player to the Playlist page to allow the user to preview songs on the Playlist. The following screenshot shows what it will look like when we're done (our MP3 player FactBox is circled):

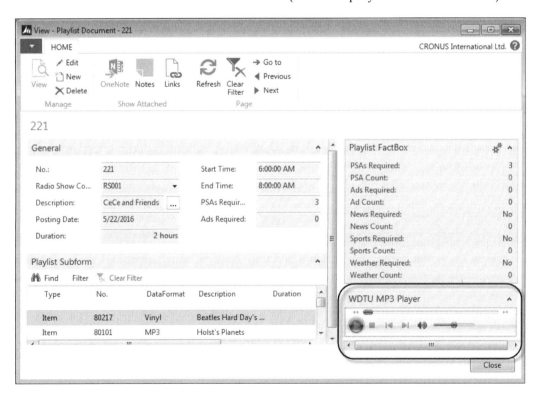

To accomplish this, we will create a Visual Studio 2012 or higher .NET assembly (.dll) utilizing the Windows Media Player.

To start, we are going to open Visual Studio 2013 and create a New Project. For a template, select **Visual C# - Windows Class Library**. Make sure the .NET Framework selected is 4.5 or higher. Name the solution **WDTUplayer**, and place in a directory we can access later (we'll use **C:\Temp**). Check the **Create directory for solution** option.

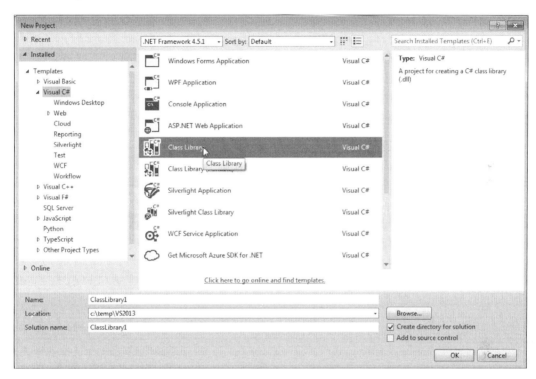

In order to access the `.dll` in NAV, we need to create a **Strong Key Name (SNK)**. To do this in Visual Studio, go to the menu for **Project** and select **WDTUPlayer Properties**.

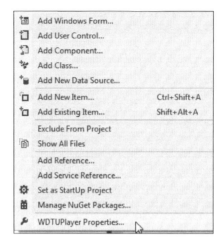

Select the **Signing** option on the left:

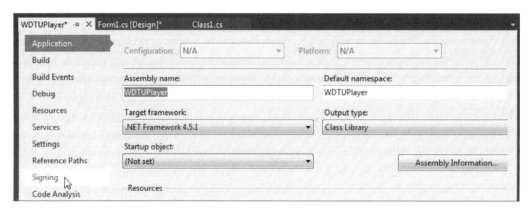

Then Checkmark the **Sign the Assembly** option:

Select **<New...>** from the dropdown for the box **Choose a strong name key file**, and fill in a file name such as WDTUplayer.snk. Creating the SNK before adding any controls or other objects to the project allows the additional elements to inherit the SNK.

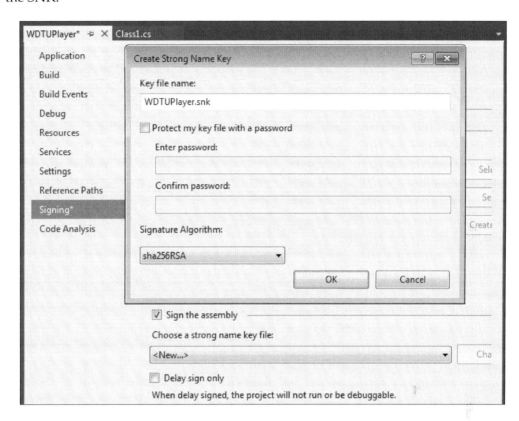

Go to the **Project** menu option and select **Add New Item** (*Ctrl + Shift + A*) and select **Windows Form**. The new Windows Form object will be added to our Form design layout screen. Right-click on the form and select **Properties** (or **View | Properties**). Review the form properties and set the ones defined in the following table:

Property	Value
AutoScaleMode	None
AutoSize	True
FormBorderStyle	None
Locked	True
Padding	0,0,0,0
MaximizeBox	False

Property	Value
MaximumSize	0,0
MinimizeBox	False
MinimumSize	0,0
Size	276,47
Text	WDTU MP3 Player

Next, we need to make the Windows Media Player (a COM object) available in the Toolbox. Windows Media Player must be installed on our machine (it typically already is). Click on **View | Toolbox** (or *Ctrl + W, X*) and scroll to the **General** group:

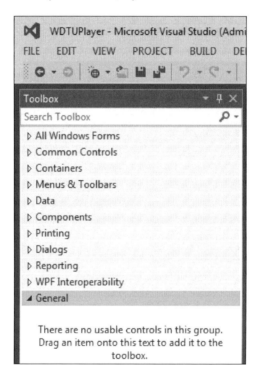

Right-click on **General** and select the **Choose Items** option. In the **Choose Toolbox Items** form, select the **COM Components** tab and scroll down to **Windows Media Player**. Check the box and click **OK**:

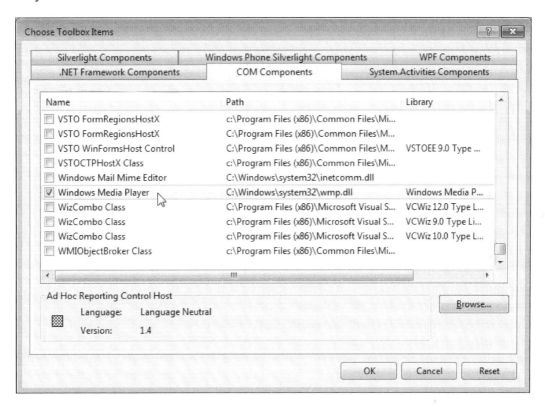

The **Windows Media Player** control will now be available in the **Toolbox | General** tab.

Select the **Windows Media Player** control and drop it into the form that we added earlier. Right-click on the **Windows Media Player** control and then click on **Properties**. Uncheck **Auto Start** and check **Stretch to Fit**:

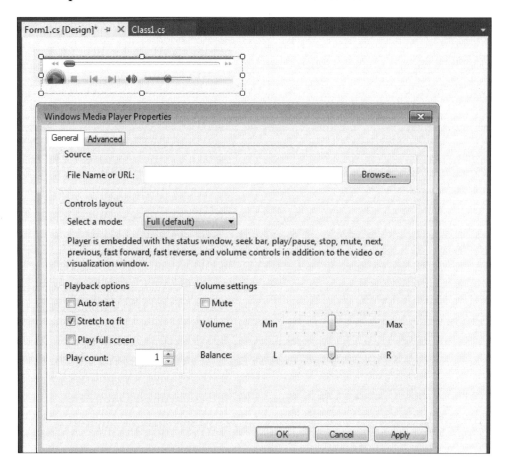

Close the **Windows Media Player Properties** window, click on **View | Properties Window** (or *Ctrl + W, P*), and set properties as shown in the following table:

PROPERTY	VALUE
Name	WDTU_MP3_Player
Anchor	Top, Bottom, Left, Right
fullScreen	False
Location	0,0
Margin	0,0,0,0
Locked	True

PROPERTY	VALUE
Size	275, 45
stretchToFit	False
windowlessVideo	False

In the Quick Launch box at the top right of the screen, type in Add Reference to search for that function (in the following image, only "add ref" was typed before the **Project – Add Reference** link was displayed):

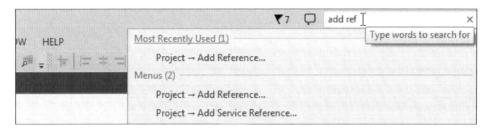

Click on **Project – Add Reference** to display the following screen:

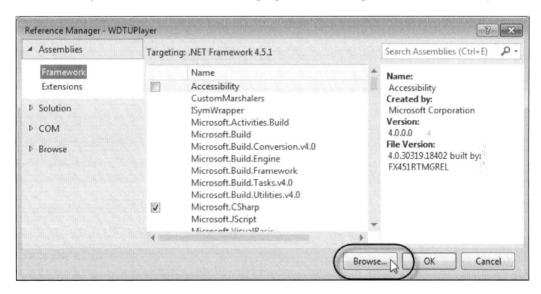

Click on the **Browse** button. Find **Microsoft.Dynamics.Framework.UI.Extensiblity**, usually found in `C:\Program Files (x86)\Microsoft Dynamics NAV\70\ RoleTailored Client\`, as shown in the following image:

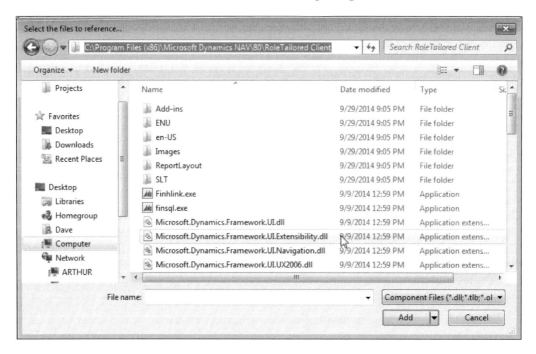

Then add it as a Reference, and click **OK**:

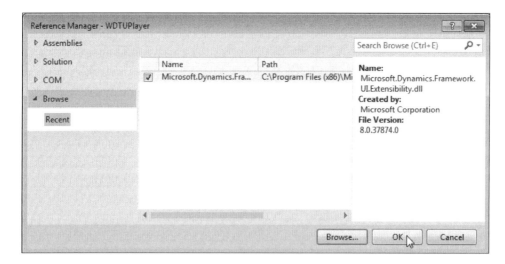

To get to the code behind the `Form1.cs`, in the **Solution Designer** window, right-click to select **View Code** or double-click on the form image in the main window. Once we are viewing the code, we should make it look like the following:

```
using System;
using System.Collections.Generic;
using System.ComponentModel;
using System.Data;
using System.Drawing;
using System.Linq;
using System.Threading.Tasks;
using System.Text;
using System.Windows.Forms;

namespace WDTUplayer
{
    public partial class Form1 : Form
    {
        //string to put value from NAV into
        string MoviePath;

        public Form1()
        {
            //Make sure not a null string -
            //will error if not initalized
            MoviePath = "";
            InitializeComponent();
        }

        //Function called from Class to set URL path string
        public void SetMoviePath(string pMoviePath)
        {
            MoviePath = pMoviePath;
        }

        //Default function for NAVMediaPlayer control on form
        //where the URL can be dynamically set from NAV
        private void WDTU_MP3_Player_Enter(object sender,
          EventArgs e)
        {
            WDTU_MP3_Player.settings.autoStart = false;
            WDTU_MP3_Player.URL = MoviePath;
        }

    }
}
```

In the `Class1.cs` object, the code needs to be created as follows:

```
using System;
using System.Collections.Generic;
using System.ComponentModel;
using System.Linq;
using System.Text;
using System.Threading.Tasks;
using Microsoft.Dynamics.Framework.UI.Extensibility;
using Microsoft.Dynamics.Framework.UI.Extensibility.WinForms;
using System.Windows.Forms;
using System.Drawing;

namespace WDTUplayer
{
    [ControlAddInExport("Cronus.DynamicsNAV.WDTU_MP3")]
    [Description("WDTU MP3 Player")]

    public class WDTU : StringControlAddInBase
    {
        //Create form instance to pass value from NAV
        WDTUPlayer.Form1 WMPForm = new WDTUPlayer.Form1();

        //Initialize the form
        protected override Control CreateControl()
        {
            WMPForm.TopLevel = false;
            WMPForm.Visible = true;
            return WMPForm;
        }

        // This is the function that receives from NAV (set)
        // and sends back to NAV (get) the string value from
        // the SourceExp property on the NAV page field with
        // the ControlAddIn assigned to it
        public override string Value
        {
            get
            {
                return base.Value;
            }
            set
            {
                base.Value = value;
```

```
            WMPForm.SetMoviePath(base.Value);
            //Function in form
        }

    }
  }
}
```

Note the statement defining `public override string` Value. This is the override of the `Value` property in the `Class1.cs` object that retrieves the value passed from NAV (`set`) and passes the value from the .NET assembly back to NAV (`get`). Because we defined the **WMPForm** variable as the Form object, we can pass the value retrieved from NAV (the field value linked in the CardPart page we will create to hold our Client Add-in).

Save all the objects and go to the **Build** menu and select **Build WDTUPlayer**. Locate and copy the following files from our Visual Studio Project folder:

- `WDTUplayer.dll`
- `Interop.WMPLib.dll`
- `AxInterop.WMPLib.dll`

Client Add-ins are each placed in their own directory within the directory `C:\Program Files (x86)\Microsoft Dynamics NAV\80\RoleTailored Client\ Add-ins` (this is the default location).

We'll create directory `WDTU_mp3` in that location and place our three files there. Depending on the development computer's setup, additional files may also have to be copied to the `WDTU_mp3` directory.

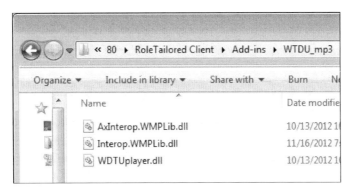

From **Start Menu | All Programs | Visual Studio 2013 | Visual Studio Tools**, run **Developer Command Prompt for VS2013**. When the **Visual Studio Command Prompt** screen displays, enter the following:

```
sn -T "C:\Temp\WDTUplayer\WDTUplayer\bin\Debug\WDTUplayer.dll"
```

Public key token in this image is **4fd8f2011abd9509** (yours is likely to be different).

Exit the Visual Studio Command screen and open the NAV 2015 Development Environment. Click on the **Object Designer** button **Tables**, find **Table 2000000069 - Client Add-in,** then **Run** the table. Enter the control add-in name, public key token, a version (you decide which version), and a description.

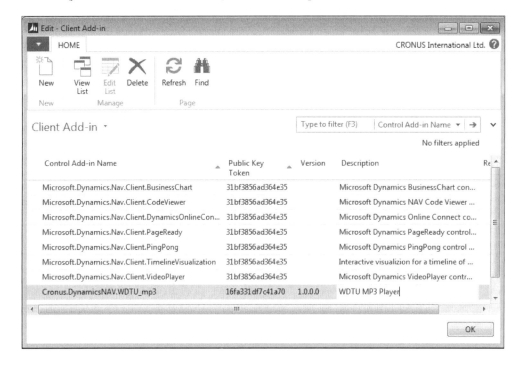

Now that our client add-in is registered in NAV, we will create a CardPart to display a control containing our new Media Player Add-in control (which links the .NET .dll element to a field in NAV).

Click on **Page | New** in the Development Environment, enter Item for the table, **Create a page using a wizard:** and **CardPart** for the page type:

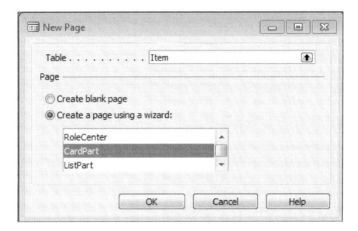

On the next tab, only select a single field, **MP3 Location**. This is the value we wish to pass to the .NET assembly:

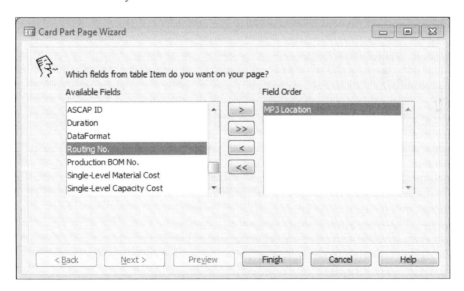

Click **Finish** and save the Page as `50011 - WDTU MP3 Player`. Click on the field **MP3 Location** and view the properties. Scroll down to **ControlAddIn** and perform a lookup to select **Cronus.DynamicsNAV.WDTU_MP3**. The public key token will also be populated. Set the **ShowCaption** property to `No`.

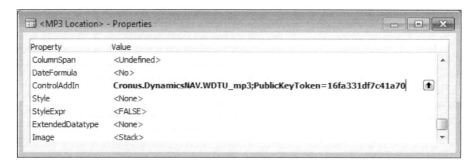

Save and close the page. Design **Page 50003 - Playlist**. Open the properties of the subform control for the Playlist Subform and copy the control ID.

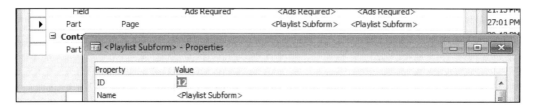

We need to assign this to the WDTU MP3 Player CardPart to link the CardPart to the SubForm lines. In the Page Designer for Playlist page, add the CardPart as a FactBox under the PlaylistFactbox.

Display the properties for this new Page Part control and fill in the properties as shown in the following screenshot:

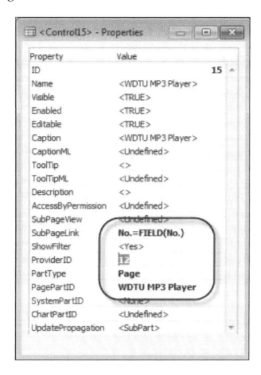

Now we will test our work. Of course, in order to test, we have to have test data set up to match what we've designed in our software. We must have Items that represent MP3 files and which contain the location of those MP3 files. Plus, the MP3 files must exist in the defined location. We should set up at least a couple of test items and associated MP3 files so we can enjoy the results of our work.

Once we have a minimal amount of test data set up, **Run** the **Playlist** page (**50003**). If all is well, the WDTU MP3 player should play the MP3 from the defined file location for each item in the playlist subpage. If it doesn't work, then this will be an opportunity to experiment some more with the NAV 2015 Debugger.

Client Add-in comments

In order to take advantage of the Client Add-in capabilities, we need to develop some minimal Visual Studio development skills and probably some .NET programming skills. Care will have to be taken when designing add-ins that their User Interface style complements, rather than clashes with, the UI standards of the NAV RTC.

Client Add-ins are a major extension of the Dynamics NAV system. This feature allows ISVs to create and sell libraries of new controls and new control-based micro-applications. It allows vertically focused Partners to create versions of NAV that are much more tailored to their specific industries. This feature allows the integration of third-party products, software, and hardware, at an entirely new level.

The Client Add-in feature is very powerful. If we learn to use it, we will have another flexible tool in our kit and our users will benefit.

Customizing Help

NAV 2015 comes with a Help Server component. When installing NAV 2015, we need to make sure that we are also installing the NAV Help Server on a Web server system to which all clients have access. Review the following Developer and IT Pro Help entries along with other entries that relate to modifying and maintaining Help data:

- Configuring Microsoft Dynamics NAV Help Server
- Microsoft Dynamics NAV Help Server
- Adding Help to Your Microsoft Dynamics NAV Tablet Client
- Upgrading You Existing Help Content

All the NAV Help files are now HTML files, accessible for whatever type of changes are appropriate for the installed system. That includes adding information to existing helps, having multiple language Helps, adding new Helps associated with customized or tailored applications, and whatever changes will make the software work better for the customer.

The process for developing customized Help is similar in many ways to developing customizations to the application software. The top-level style of new material should be essentially similar to the original product material. If the customizations are too different from the base material, it will create operational challenges for the users as well as training and support challenges for the Partner.

Help customizations should be designed to make it as easy as possible to port them to new versions of the product when upgrading occurs. Similar to software development, whenever possible, Help revisions should be done on a copy of the original Help topic, leaving the original unchanged. For example, if the Customer Card is modified, make the Help changes in a copy of the Customer Card Help.

NAV development projects – general guidance

Now that we understand the basic workings of the NAV C/SIDE development environment and C/AL, we'll review the process of software design for NAV enhancements and modifications.

When we start a new project, the goals and constraints for the project must be defined. The degree to which we meet these will determine our successes. Following are some examples:

- What are the functional requirements and what flexibility exists within these?
- What are the user interface standards?
- What are the coding standards?
- What are the calendar and financial budgets?
- What existing capabilities within NAV will be used?

Knowledge is the key

Designing for NAV requires more forethought and knowledge of the operating details of the application than was needed with traditional models of ERP systems. As we have seen, NAV has unique data structure tools (SIFT and FlowFields), quite a number of NAV-specific functions that make it easier to program business applications, and a software data structure (journal, ledger, and so on) which is inherently an accounting data structure. The learning curve to become expert in the way NAV works is not easy. NAV has a unique structure and the primary documentation from Microsoft is limited to the embedded Help (which improves with every release of the product). The NAV books published by PACKT Publishing are of great help as are the NAV Development Team blogs, the blogs from various NAV experts around the world, and the NAV forums that were mentioned earlier.

Data-focused design

Any new application design must begin with certain basic analysis and design tasks. That is just as applicable whether our design is for new functionality to be integrated into NAV or for an enhancement/expansion of existing NAV capabilities.

First, determine what underlying data is required. What will it take to construct the information the users need to see? What level of detail and in what structural format must the data be stored so that it may be quickly and completely retrieved? Once we have defined the inputs that are required, we must identify the sources of this material. Some may be input manually, some may be forwarded from other systems, some may be derived from historical accumulations of data, and some may be derived from combinations of all these, and more. In any case, every component of the information needed must have a clearly defined point of origin, schedule of arrival, and format.

Defining the needed data views

Define how the data should be presented. How does it need to be "sliced and diced"? What levels of detail and summary? What sequences and segmentations? What visual formats? What media will be used? Will the users be local or remote? Ultimately, many other issues also need to be considered in the full design, including user interface specifications, data and access security, accounting standards and controls, and so on. Because there are a wide variety of tools available to extract and manipulate NAV data, we can start relatively simply and expand as appropriate later. The most important thing is to ensure that we have all the critical data elements identified and then captured.

Designing the data tables

Data table definition includes the data fields, the keys to control the sequence of data access and to ensure rapid processing, frequently used totals (which are likely to be set up as **SumIndex Fields**), references to lookup tables for allowed values, and relationships to other primary data tables. We not only need to do a good job of designing the primary tables, but also all those supporting tables containing the "lookup" and "setup" data. When integrating a customization, we must consider the effects of the new components on the existing processing as well as how the existing processing ties into our new work. These connections are often the finishing touch that makes the new functionality operate in a truly seamlessly integrated fashion with the original system.

Designing the user data access interface

Design the pages and reports to be used to display or interrogate the data. Define what keys are to be used or are available to the users (though the SQL Server database supports sorting data without predefined NAV C/AL keys). Define what fields will be allowed to be visible, what are the totaling fields, how the totaling will be accomplished (for example, FlowFields or on-the-fly processing), and what dynamic display options will be available. Define what type of filtering will be needed. Some filtering needs may be beyond the ability of the built-in filtering function and may require auxiliary code functions. Determine whether external data analysis tools will be needed and will therefore need to be interfaced. Design considerations at this stage often result in returning to the previous data structure definition stage to add additional data fields, keys, SIFT fields, or references to other tables.

Designing the data validation

Define exactly how the data must be validated before it is accepted upon entry into a table. There are likely to be multiple levels of validation. There will be a minimum level, which defines the minimum set of information required before a new record is accepted.

Subsequent levels of validation may exist for particular subsets of data, which are in turn tied to specific optional uses of the table. For example, in the base NAV system, if the manufacturing functionality is not being used, the manufacturing-related fields in the Item Master table do not need to be filled in. But if they are filled in, they must satisfy certain validation criteria.

As mentioned earlier, the sum total of all the validations that are applied to data when it is entered into a table may not be sufficient to completely validate the data. Depending on the use of the data, there may be additional validations performed during processing, reporting, or inquiries.

Data design review and revision

Perform these three steps: table design, user access, and data validation for the permanent data (Masters and Ledgers) and then for the transactions (Journals). Once all the supporting tables and references have been defined for the permanent data tables, there are not likely to be many new definitions required for the Journal tables. If any significant new supporting tables or new table relationships are identified during the design of Journal tables, we should go back and re-examine the earlier definitions. Why? Because there is a high likelihood that this new requirement should have been defined for the permanent data and was overlooked.

Designing the posting processes

First define the final data validations, then define and design all the ledger and auxiliary tables (for example, Registers, Posted Document tables, and so on). At this point, we are determining what the permanent content of the Posted data will be. If we identify any new supporting table or table reference requirements at this point, we should go back to the first step to make sure that this requirement didn't need to be in the design definition.

Whatever variations in data are permitted to be Posted must be acceptable in the final, permanent instance of the data. Any information or relationships that are necessary in the final Posted data must be ensured to be present before Posting is allowed to proceed.

Part of the Posting design is to determine whether data records will be accepted or rejected individually or in complete batches. If the latter, we must define what constitutes a Batch; if the former, it is likely that the makeup of a Posting Batch will be flexible.

Designing the supporting processes

Design the processes necessary to validate, process, extract, and format data for the desired output. In earlier steps, these processes can be defined as "black boxes" with specified inputs and required outputs, but without overdue regard for the details of the internal processes. This allows us to work on the several preceding definition and design steps without being sidetracked into the inner workings of the output related processes.

These processes are the cogs and gears of the functional application. They are necessary, but often not pretty. By leaving design of these processes in the application design as late as possible, we increase the likelihood that we will be able to create common routines and standardize how similar tasks are handled across a variety of parent processes. At this point, we may identify opportunities or requirements for improvement in material defined in one of the previous design steps. In that case, we should return to that step relative to the newly identified issue. In turn, we should also review the effect of such changes for each subsequent step's area of focus.

Double-check everything

Do one last review of all the defined reference, setup, and other control tables to make sure that the primary tables and all defined processes have all the information available when needed. This is a final design quality control step.

It is important to realize that returning to a previous step to address a previously unidentified issue is not a failure of the process, it is a success. An appropriate quote used in one form or another by construction people the world over is *Measure twice, cut once*. It is much cheaper and more efficient (and less painful) to find and fix design issues during the design phase rather than after the system is in testing or, worse yet, in production.

Design for efficiency

Whenever we are designing a new modification, we not only need to design to address the defined needs, but also to provide a solution that processes efficiently. An inefficient solution carries unnecessary ongoing costs. Many of the things that we can do to design an efficient solution are relatively simple. Some of the areas to address include:

- Properly configure system and workstation software (often overlooked)
- Make sure networks can handle the expected load (and more)
- Have enough server memory to avoid using virtual memory (that is, disk)
- Most of all, do everything reasonable to minimize disk I/O

Disk I/O

The slowest thing in any computer system is the disk I/O. Disk I/O almost always takes more time than any other system processing activity. When we begin concentrating our design efforts on efficiency, focus first on minimizing disk I/O.

The most critical elements are the design of the keys, the number of keys, the design of the SIFT fields, the number of SIFT fields, the design of the filters, and the frequency of accesses of data (especially FlowFields). If our system is going to have five or ten users processing a few thousand order lines per day, and if our system is not heavily modified, we probably won't have much trouble. But if we are installing a system with one or more of the following attributes, any of which can have a significant effect on the amount of disk I/O, we will need to be very careful with our design and implementation:

- Large concurrent user count
- High transaction volumes, especially in data being Posted
- Large stored data volumes, especially that resulting from customizations or setup option choices
- Significant modifications
- Very complex business rules

Locking

One important aspect of the design of an integrated system such as NAV, that is often overlooked until it rears its ugly head after the system goes into production, is the issue of "**Locking**". Locking occurs when one process has control of a data element, record, or group of records (in other words, part or all of a table) for the purpose of updating the data within the range of the locked data and, at the same time, another process requests the use of some portion of that data but finds it to be locked by the first process.

In the worst case, which is a "**deadlock**", there is a design flaw; each process has data locked that the other process needs and neither process can proceed. As developers or implementers, one of our jobs is to minimize the locking problems and eliminate any deadlocks.

Locking interference between processes in an asynchronous processing environment is inevitable. There are always going to be points in the system where one process instance locks out another one momentarily. The secret to success is to minimize the frequency of these and the time length of each lock. Locking becomes a problem when the locks are held too long and the other locked-out processes are unreasonably delayed.

One might ask *What is an unreasonable delay?* For most of the part, a delay becomes unreasonable when the users can tell that it's happening. If the users see stopped processes or experience counter-intuitive processing time lengths (that is, a process that seems like it should take 10 seconds actually takes two minutes), then the delays will seem unreasonable. Of course, the ultimate unreasonable delay is the one that does not allow the required work to get done in the available time.

The obvious question is how to avoid locking problems. The best solution is to simply speed up the processing. This will reduce the number of lock conflicts that arise. Important recommendations for speed include the following:

- Restrict the number of active keys, especially on the SQL Server
- Restrict the number of active SIFT fields, eliminating them when feasible
- Carefully review the keys, not necessarily using the "factory default" options
- Make sure that all the disk access code is SQL Server optimized

Following are some additional steps that can be taken to minimize locking problems:

- Always process tables in the same relative order
- When a common set of tables will be accessed and updated, lock a "standard" master table first (for example, when working on Orders, always lock the Order Header table first)
- Shift long-running processes to off-hours or even separate databases

In special cases, the following techniques can be used (if done very, very carefully):

- Process data in small quantities (for example, process 10 records or one order, then COMMIT, which releases the lock). This approach should be very cautiously.
- In long process loops, process a SLEEP command in combination with an appropriate COMMIT command to allow other processes to gain control (see the preceding caution).

Refer to the documentation with the system distribution and in the NAV forums.

Updating and upgrading

One must differentiate between "updating" a system and "upgrading" a system. In general, most of the NAV development work we will do is modifying individual NAV systems to provide tailored functions for end-user firms. Some of these modifications will be created by developers as part of an initial system configuration and implementation before the NAV system is in production use. Other such modifications will be targeted at a system that is in day to day production, to bring the system up to date with changes in business process or external requirements. We'll refer to these system changes as "Updating".

"Upgrading" is when we implement a new version of the base C/AL application code distributed by Microsoft and port all the previously existing modifications into that new version. First we'll discuss updating, and then we'll discuss upgrading.

Design for updating

Any time we are updating a production system by applying modifications to it, a considerable amount of care is required. Many of the disciplines that should be followed in such an instance are the same for a NAV system as for any other production application system. But some disciplines are specific to NAV and the C/SIDE environment.

Increasing the importance of designing for ease of updating is Microsoft's process of providing NAV updates on a frequent basis so that systems can be kept more up to date with fixes and minor feature enhancements. Keeping up with these Microsoft provided updates is especially important for multi-tenant systems running in the cloud (that is, systems serving multiple unrelated customers with the software and databases being resident on Internet based server systems). Fortunately, in support of the pressure to apply updates more frequently, Microsoft has also provided a set of tools to help us. Many of these tools are based on Windows Powershell scripts, also referred to as **cmdlets**. For additional information, refer to the Help topics on *Deployment and Upgrading*.

Customization project recommendations

Even though there are new tools to help us update our NAV systems, we should still follow good practices in our modification designs and the processes of applying updates. Some of these recommendations may seem obvious. That would be a measure of our personal store of experience and our own common sense. Even so, it is surprising the number of projects that go sour because one (or many) of the following are not considered in the process of developing modifications:

- One modification at a time
- Design thoroughly before coding
- Design the testing in parallel with the modification
- Use the C/AL Testability feature extensively
- Multi-stage testing:
    - Cronus for individual objects
    - Special test database for functional tests
    - Copy of production database for final testing as appropriate
    - Setups and implementation
- Testing full features:
    - User interface tests
    - System load tests
    - User Training
- Document and deliver in a predefined, organized manner
- Follow up, wrap up, and move on

One change at a time

It is important to make changes to objects in a very well organized and tightly controlled manner. In most situations, only one developer at a time will make changes to an object. If an object needs to be changed for multiple purposes, the first set of changes should be fully tested (at least through development testing stage) before the object is released to be modified for a second purpose.

If the project is so large and complex or deadlines are so tight that this "one modification at a time" approach is not feasible, we should consider using a software development version control system. Because most version control systems don't interface smoothly with C/SIDE, some significant effort will be required. One notable exception is the iFacto ReVision Source Code Control system, specifically designed to work with Dynamics NAV (see `http://www.ifacto.be/en/solutions/revision`).

Similarly, we should only be working on one functional change at a time. As developers, we might be working on changes in two different systems in parallel, but we shouldn't be working on multiple changes in a single system simultaneously. It's challenging enough to keep all the aspects of a single modification to a system under control without having incomplete pieces of several tasks all floating around in the same system.

If multiple changes need to be made simultaneously to a single system, one approach is to assign multiple developers, each with their own components to address. Another approach is for each developer to work on their own copy of the development database, with a project librarian assigned to resolve overlapping updates. We should learn from the past. In mainframe development environments, having multiple developers working on the same system at the same time was common. Coordination issues were addressed as a standard part of the project management process. Applicable techniques are well-documented in professional literature. Similar solutions still apply.

Testing

As we all know, there is no substitute for complete and thorough testing. Fortunately, NAV provides some very useful tools, such as those previously discussed earlier in this chapter in the sections C/SIDE Test-driven development and Debugging in NAV 2015, to help us to be more efficient than we might be in some other environment. In addition to the built-in testing tools, there are also some testing techniques that are NAV-specific.

Database testing approaches

If modifications are not tied to previous modifications and specific customer data, then we may be able to use the Cronus database as a test platform. This works well when our target is a database that is not heavily modified in the area on which we are currently working. As the Cronus database is small, we will not get lost in large data volumes. Most of the master tables in Cronus are populated, so we don't have to create and populate this information. Setups are done and generally contain reasonably generic information.

If we are operating with an unmodified version of Cronus, we have the advantage that our test is not affected by other pre-existing modifications. The disadvantage, of course, is that we are not testing in a wholly realistic situation. Because the data volume in Cronus is so small, we are not likely to detect a potential performance problem.

Even when our modification is targeted at a highly modified system where those other modifications will affect what we are doing, it's often useful to test a version of our modification initially in Cronus. This may allow us to determine if our change has internal integrity before we move on to testing in the context of the fully modified copy of the production system.

If the target database for our modifications is an active customer database, then there is no substitute for doing complete and final testing in a copy of the production database using a copy of the customer's license. This way, we will be testing the compatibility of our work with the production setup, the full set of existing modifications, and of course, live data content and volumes. The only way to get a good feeling for possible performance issues is to test in a recent copy of the production database.

 Final testing should always be done using the customer's license.

Testing in production

While it is always a good idea to thoroughly test before adding our changes to the production system, sometimes we can safely do our testing inside the production environment. If the modifications consist of functions that do not change any data and can be tested without affecting any ongoing production activity, it may be feasible to test within the production system.

Examples of modifications that could be tested in the live production system can range from a simple inquiry page or a new analysis report or export of data that is to be processed outside the system to a completely new subsystem that does not change any existing data. There are also situations where the only changes to the existing system are the addition of fields to existing tables. In such a case, we may be able to test just a part of the modification outside the production, and then implement the table changes to complete the rest of the testing in the context of the production system.

Finally, we can use the Testing functions to control tests so that any changes to the database are rolled back at the conclusion of the testing. This approach allows for testing inside a production database with less fear of corrupting live data.

Using a testing database

From a testing point of view, the most realistic testing environment is a current copy of the actual production database. There are often apparently good excuses about why it is just too difficult to test using a copy of the actual production database.

 Don't give in to excuses — use a testing copy of the production database!

Remember, when we implement our modifications, they are going to receive the "test by fire" in the environment of production. We need to do everything within reason to assure success. Let's review some of the potential problems involved in testing with a copy of the production database and how to cope with them:

- *It's too big* — this is not a good argument relative to disk space. Disk space is so inexpensive that we can almost always afford plenty of disk space for testing. We should also make every possible useful intermediate stage backup. Staying organized and making lots of backups may be time consuming, but done well and done correctly, it is less expensive to restore from a backup than recovering from being disorganized or having to redo a major testing process. This is one of the many places where appropriate use of the C/AL Testability tools can be very helpful by allowing various approaches to repetitive testing.

- *It's too big* — this is a meaningful argument if we are doing file processing of some of the larger files (for example, Item Ledger, Value Entry, and so on). But NAV's filtering capabilities are so strong that we should relatively easy to carve out manageable size test data groups with which to work.

- *There's no data that's useful* — this might be true. But it would be just as true for a test database unless it were created expressly for this set of tests. By definition, whatever data is in a copy of the production database is what we will encounter when we eventually implement the enhancements on which we are working. If we build useful test data within the context of a copy of the production database, our tests will be much more realistic and, therefore, of better quality. In addition, the act of building workable test data will help to define what will be needed to set up the production system to utilize the new enhancements.

- *Production data will get in the way* — may be true. If this is especially true, then perhaps the database must be preprocessed in some way to begin testing, or testing must begin with some other database such as Cronus or a special testing-only mockup. As stated earlier, all the issues that exist in the production database must be dealt with when we put the enhancements into production. Therefore, we should test in that environment. Overcoming such challenges will prepare us to do a better job at the critical time of going live with the newly modified objects.

- *We need to test repeatedly from the same baseline.* or *We must do regression testing* — both are good points, but don't have much to do with the type of database we're using for the testing. Both the cases are addressed by properly managing the setup of our test data and keeping incremental backups of our pre-test and post-test data at every step of the way. SQL Server tools can assist in this effort. In addition, the C/AL Testability Tools are explicitly designed to support regression testing.

Remember, doing the testing job well is much less expensive than implementing a buggy modification and repairing the problems during production.

Testing techniques

As experienced developers, we will already be familiar with good testing practices. Even so, it never hurts to be reminded about some of the more critical habits to maintain.

Any modification greater than trivial should be tested in one way or another by at least two people. The people assigned should not be a part of the team who created the design or code of the modification. It would be best if one of the testers is an experienced user because users seem to have a knack (for obvious reasons) of understanding how the modification operates compared to how the rest of the system acts in the course of day-to-day work. This helps us to obtain meaningful feedback on the user interface before going into production.

One of the testing goals is to supply unexpected data and make sure that the modification can deal with it properly. Unfortunately, those who were involved in creating the design will have a very difficult time being creative in supplying the unexpected. Users often enter data that the designer or programmer didn't expect. For that reason, testing by experienced users is beneficial.

The C/AL Testability Tools provide features to support testing how system functions deal with problem data. If possible, it would be good to have the users' help to define test data, and then use the Testability Tools to ensure that the modifications properly handle the data.

After we cover the mainstream issues (whatever it is that the modification is intended to accomplish), we need to make sure that our testing covers all boundary conditions. Boundary conditions are the data items that are exactly equal to the maximum, minimum, or other range limit. More specifically, boundaries are the points at which input data values change from valid to invalid. Boundary condition checking in the code is where programmer logic often goes astray. Testing at these points is very effective for uncovering data-related errors.

Deliverables

Create useful documentation and keep good records of testing processes and results. Testing scripts, both human-oriented and C/AL Testability Tool-based, should be retained for future reference. Document the purpose of the modifications from a business point of view. Add a brief, but complete, technical explanation of what must be done from a functional design and coding point of view to accomplish the business purpose. Record briefly the testing that was done. The scope of the record keeping should be directly proportional to the business value of the modification being made and the potential cost of not having good records. All such investments are a form of insurance and preventative medicine. We hope they won't be needed but we have to allow for the possibility that they may be needed.

More complex modifications will be delivered and installed by experienced implementers, maybe even by the developers themselves. Small NAV modifications may be transmitted electronically to the customer site for installation by a skilled super-user. Whenever this is done, all the proper and normal actions must occur, including those actions regarding backup before importing changes, user instruction (preferably written) on what to expect from the change, and written instruction on how to correctly apply the change. There must also be a plan and a clearly defined process for restoring the system to its state prior to the change, in case the modification doesn't work correctly. As responsible developers, whenever we supply objects for installation by others, we must make sure that we always supply .fob format files (compiled objects), not text objects. This is because the import process for text objects simply does not have the same safeguards as the import process for compiled objects.

Finishing the project

Bring projects to conclusion, don't let them drag on through inaction and inattention—open issues get forgotten and then don't get addressed. Get it done, wrap it up, and then review what went well and what didn't go well, both for remediation and for application to future projects.

Set up ongoing support services as appropriate, and then move on to the next project. With the flexibility of the Role Tailored Client allowing page layout changes by both super users (configuration) and users (personalization), the challenge of user support has increased. The person offering support can no longer expect to know what display the user is viewing today.

Consequently, support services will almost certainly require the capability for the support person to view the user's display. Without that, it will be much more difficult, time consuming, and frustrating for the two way support personnel – user communication to take place. If it doesn't already exist, this capability will have to be added to the Partner's support organization tool set and practices. There may be communications and security issues that need to be addressed at both the support service and the user site.

Plan for upgrading

The ability to upgrade a customized system is a very important feature of NAV. Most other complex business application systems are very difficult to customize at the database-structure and process-flow levels. NAV readily offers this capability. This is a significant difference between NAV and the competitive products in the market.

Complementing the ability to be customized is the ability to upgrade a customized NAV system. While not a trivial task, at least it is possible with NAV. In many other systems, the only reasonable path to an upgrade is often to discard the old version and re-implement with the new version, recreating all customizations. Not only is NAV unusually accommodating to being upgraded, but with each new version of the system, Microsoft has enhanced the power and flexibility of the tools it provides to help us do upgrades. In the Microsoft Dynamics NAV 2015 Development Shell, among other useful cmdlets, there is **Merge-NAVApplicationObject cmdlet**. Refer to the **Developer and IT Pro Help** files for details on starting and using a Development Shell session (hint: use the **Search** box to find information on the Development Shell).

We may say, *Why should a developer care about upgrades?* There are at least two good reasons we should care about upgrades. First, because our design and coding of our modifications can have a considerable impact on the amount of effort required to upgrade a system. Second, because as skilled developers doing NAV customizations, we might well be asked to be involved in an upgrade project. Since the ability to upgrade is important and because we are likely to be involved in one way or another, we will review a number of factors that relate to upgrades.

Benefits of upgrading

Just so we are on common ground about why upgrading is important to both the client and the NAV Partner, following is a brief list of some of the benefits that an upgrade can give:

- Easier support of a more current version
- Access to new features and capabilities
- Continued access to fixes and regulatory updates
- Improvements in speed, security, reliability, and user interface
- Assured continuation of support availability
- Compatibility with necessary infrastructure changes, such as new operating system versions
- An opportunity to do any necessary training, data cleaning, and process improvement
- An opportunity to resolve old problems, to do postponed "housekeeping", and create a known system reference point

This list is not complete and not every benefit will be realized in any one situation.

Coding considerations

The most challenging and most important part of an upgrade is porting the code and data modifications from the older version of a system to the new version. When the new version has major design or data structure changes in an area that we have customized, it is quite possible that our modification structure will have to be re-designed and perhaps even be recoded from scratch.

On the other hand, often the changes in the new product version of NAV don't affect much existing code, at least in terms of the base logic. If our modifications are done properly, it's often not difficult to port custom code from the older version into the new version. By applying what some refer to as "low-impact coding" techniques, we can make the upgrade job easier and thereby less costly.

Good documentation

In the earlier chapters, we discussed some documentation practices that are good to follow when making C/AL modifications. Here is a brief list of practices that should be followed:

- Identify every project with its own unique project tag
- Use the project tag in all documentation relating to the modification
- Include a brief but complete description of the functional purpose of the modification in a related `Documentation()` trigger
- Include a description of the modifications to each object in the `Documentation()` trigger of that object, including changes to properties, Global and Local variables, functions, and so on
- Add the project tag to the version code of all modified objects
- As much as possible, make all code self-documenting, using meaningful names for all data elements and functions, and breaking code segments into logical functions so that process flow is self-evident
- Bracket all C/AL code changes with inline comments so that they can be easily identified
- Retain all replaced code within comments, using // or { }
- Identify all new table fields with the project tag

Low-impact coding

We have already discussed most of these practices in other chapters, but we will review them here in the context of coding to make it easier to upgrade. We won't be able to follow each of the following listed options, but we will have to choose the degree to which we can implement low-impact code and which options to choose:

- Separate and isolate new code
- Create functions for significant amounts of new code that can be accessed using single code line function calls
- Either add independent Codeunits as repositories of modification functions or, if that is overkill, place the modification functions within the modified objects
- Add new data fields; don't change the usage of existing fields
- When the functionality is new, add new tables rather than modifying existing tables

- For minor changes, modify the existing pages, otherwise copy and change the clone pages

- Copy, then modify the copies of reports and XMLports, rather than modifying the original versions in place

- Don't change field names in objects, just change captions and labels as necessary

In any modification, we will have conflicting priorities regarding doing today's job in the easiest and least expensive way versus doing the best we can do to plan for future maintenance, enhancements, updates, and upgrades. The right decision is never a black and white choice, but must be guided by subjective guidelines as to which choice is really in the customer's best interest.

Supporting material

With every NAV system distribution there have been some reference guides. These are minimal in NAV 2015. There are previously published guides available, but sometimes we have to search for them. Some were distributed with previous versions of the product but not with the latest version. Some are posted at various locations on PartnerSource or another Microsoft websites. Some may be available on one of the forums or from a blog.

Be a regular visitor to websites for more information and advice on C/AL, NAV, and other related topics. The websites `dynamicsuser.net` and `http://www.mibuso.com/` are especially comprehensive and well attended. Other smaller or more specialized sites also exist. Some of those available at the time of writing this book are:

- Microsoft Dynamics NAV Team Blog: `http://blogs.msdn.com/b/nav/`

- Mark Brummel's Blog: `http://nav-skills.com/blog/`

- Clausl's Dynamics NAV Blog: `http://www.mibuso.com/blogs/clausl`

- Waldo's Blog: `http://www.waldo.be/`

- Vjekoslav Babic's Blog: `http://vjeko.com/`

- Alain Krikilion's Blog: `http://mibuso.com/blogs/kriki/`

- Soren Klemmensen's Blog: `http://www.klemmensen.ca/`

There are a number of other good blogs available. Look for them and review them regularly. The good ideas posted by the members of the NAV community in their blogs and on the NAV forums are generously shared freely and often.

Finally, there are a number of books focusing on various aspects of Dynamics NAV published by PACKT Publishing (`https://www.packtpub.com/`). Even the books that are about older versions of NAV have a lot of good information about developing with the NAV tools and applying NAV's functionality in a wide variety of application environments.

Summary

We have covered many topics in this book with the goal of helping you to become productive in C/AL development with Dynamics NAV 2015. Hopefully, you've found your time spent with us to be a good investment. From this point on, your assignments are to continue exploring and learning, enjoy working with NAV, C/SIDE, and C/AL, and to treat others as you would have them treat you.

> *"We live in a world in which we need to share responsibility. It's easy to say "It's not my child, not my community, not my world, not my problem." There are those who see the need and respond. Those people my heroes."*

> *– Fred Rogers*

Review questions

Q.1. Which one of the following provides access to several libraries of functions for various purposes widely used throughout the NAV system?

    a.   Codeunit 412 – Common Dialog Management

    b.   Codeunit 408 – Dimension Management

    c.   Codeunit 396 – NoSeriesManagement

    d.   Codeunit 1 – Application Management

Q.2. The Help files for NAV cannot be customized by Partner or ISV developers. True or False?

Q.3. Which of the following are good coding practices? Choose three.

      a.   Careful naming

      b.   Good documentation

      c.   Liberal use of wildcards

      d.   Design for ease of upgrading

Q.4. Custom C/AL code is not allowed to call functions that exist in the base Microsoft created NAV objects. True or False?

Q.5. NAV's multi-language capability allows for an installation to have multiple languages active at any one time. True or False?

Q.6. Designing to minimize disk I/O in NAV is not important because SQL Server takes care of everything. True or False?

Q.7. Which of the following defines the Client Add-in feature? Choose one.

      a.   The ability to add a new client of your own design to NAV 2015

      b.   A tool to provide for extending the Role Tailored Client User Interface behavior

      c.   A special calculator feature for the RTC client

      d.   A new method for mapping Customers to Contacts

Q.8. When planning a new NAV development project, it is good to focus the design on the data structure, required data accesses, validation, and maintenance. True or False?

Q.9. The Navigate feature can be used for which of the following? Choose three.

      a.   Auditing by a professional accountant

      b.   User analysis of data processing

      c.   Reversing posting errors

      d.   Debugging

Q.10. NAV 2015 modifications should always be delivered to customers in the form of text files. True or False?

Q.11. Both source code changes and setting Debugger Breaks can only be done in the C/AL Editor. True or False?

Q.12. You can enhance the Navigate function to include new tables that have been added to the system as part of an enhancement. True or False?

Q.13. The C/SIDE Testing tools allow the implementation of regression tests. True or False?

Q.14. Client Add-ins must be written in what language? Choose one.

      a.   C#

      b.   VB.NET

      c.   A suitable .NET language

      d.   C/AL.NET

Q.15. The NAV 2015 Debugger allows the value of Watched Variables to be changed in the middle of a debugging session. True or False?

Q.16. The NAV 2015 Debugger runs as a separate session. True or False?

Q.17. The C/SIDE Testing tools support which of the following? Choose four.

      a.   Positive testing

      b.   Negative testing

      c.   Automated testing

      d.   C# test viewing

      e.   TestIsolation (roll-back) testing

Q.18. NAV 2015 includes a flexible multi-currency feature which allows transactions to begin in one currency and conclude in a different currency. True or False?

Q.19. NAV does not support linked SQL Server databases. True or False?

Q.20. Simple debugging can be done without use of the Debugger. True or False?

Review Answers

Chapter 1, An Introduction to NAV 2015

Q.1. a, b, c, e

Q.2. a, c, e

Q.3. True

Q.4. a-4, b-5, c-1, d-3, e-2

Q.5. True

Q.6. a, d

Q.7. Table, Page, Report, Codeunit, Query, XMLPort, MenuSuite

Q.8. False

Q.9. True

Q.10. d

Q.11. False

Q.12. b

Q.13. False

Q.14. True, but through use of a temporary table

Q.15. True

Q.16. b, d

Q.17. False

Q.18. False

Q.19. a, c

Q.20. False

Chapter 2, Tables

Q.1. a, d

Q.2. False

Q.3. c

Q.4. False

Q.5. a, d

Q.6. False

Q.7. False

Q.8. False – 50000 – 99999

Q.9. a, c, d

Q.10. True

Q.11. False

Q.12. a, c

Q.13. True

Q.14. a, c, d

Q.15. True

Q.16. False – except with a very advanced technical method

Q.17. False

Q.18. False

Q.19.c

Q.20. False

Chapter 3, Data Types and Fields

Q.1. False

Q.2. c

Q.3. 1 – c

Q.4. c

Q.5. a

Q.6. True

Q.7. False

Q.8. b

Q.9. b, d

Q.10. a, c, e

Q.11. False

Q.12.

a.   False

b.   False

Q.13. True

Q.14. True

Q.15. True

Q.16. False

Q.17. b, d

Q.18. False

Q.19. False

Q.20. a, b

Q.21. b, c

Chapter 4, Pages – The Interactive Interface

Q1. False

Q2. b, d

Q3. False

Q4. False

Q5. a, d

Q6. False

Q7. False

Q8. b, d

Q9. True

Q10. True

Q11. True

Q12. b, c

Q13. False

Q14. c

Q15. False

Q16. a, b, c

Q17. c

Q18. False

Q19. False

Q20. True

Chapter 5, Queries and Reports

Q1. a, c, d

Q2. False

Q3. False

Q4. b

Q5. False

Q6. False

Q7. True

Q8. a, c

Q9. False

Q10. False

Q11. a, b, c

Q12. True

Q13. False

Q14. False

Q15. True

Q16. a, c

Q17. False

Q18. b, c

Q19. True

Q20. True

Chapter 6, Introduction to C/SIDE and C/AL

Q1. False

Q2. a

Q3. True

Q4. c

Q5. False

Q6. True

Q7. False

Q8. False

Q9. a, b

Q10. False

Q11. a

Q12. True

Q13. a, c

Q14. True

Q15. True

Q16. True

Q17. False

Q18. a, c, e

Q19. False

Q20. a, d

Chapter 7, Intermediate C/AL

Q1. a, b, c

Q2. True

Q3. b, c

Q4. d

Q5. True

Q6. False

Q7. False

Q8. b

Q9. False

Q10. True

Q11. b

Q12. False

Q13.False

Q14. d

Q15. False

Q16. True

Q17.a, c

Q18. False

Q19. False

Q20. True

Chapter 8, Advanced NAV Development Tools

Q1. False

Q2. c

Q3. False

Q4. a, c, d

Q5. False

Q6. b, d

Q7. True

Q8. a, c

Q9. False

Q10. True

Q11. b, d

Q12. True

Q13. False

Q14. True

Q15. False

Q16. True

Q17. False

Q18. a, d

Q19. False

Q20. False

Chapter 9, Successful Conclusions

Q1. d

Q2. False

Q3. a, b, d

Q4. False

Q5. True

Q6. False

Q7. b

Q8. True

Q9. a, b, d

Q10. False

Q11. True

Q12. True

Q13. True

Q14. c

Q15. False

Q16. True

Q17. a, b, c, e

Q18. True

Q19. False

Q20. True

Index

A

Action Icons 121
application tables
  about 23
  simple table, creating 24-26
  simple table, designing 23, 24
Assemble to Order (ATO) 4
Automation data types
  about 132
  Automation Server 133
  DotNet 133
  OCX 132

B

Binary Large OBjects (BLOBs) 116
blank slate approach 231
Block of code 356
bound pages 219
BREAK function 404
Business Intelligence (BI) 6

C

CALCDATE function 391
CALCFIELDS function
  about 396
  versus CALCSUMS function 398
CalcFormula method 143
C/AL code
  about 358
  adding, to report 363
  field validation, adding to table 358-363
  Lookup Related table data 365, 366
  new report heading, layouting 364

report body, laying out 366, 367
  saving 365
  testing 365
CALCSUMS function
  about 398
  versus CALCFIELDS function 398
C/AL Database Functions and Performance
    on SQL Server 353
C/AL Editor 13
C/AL functions
  about 344
  CONFIRM function 347, 348
  ERROR function 345, 346
  FIND function 352, 353
  functions, frequently used 344
  GET function 352
  MESSAGE function 344, 345
  record functions 349
  SETCURRENTKEY function 350
  SETFILTER function 351
  SETRANGE function 351
  STRMENU function 348, 349
  validation functions 384-387
callable functions
  about 513
  codeunit 358 (Date Filter-Calc) 513
  codeunit 359 (Period Form
    Management) 515, 516
  codeunit 365 (Format Address) 516, 517
  codeunit 396 (NoSeriesManagement) 518
  Date Filter-Calc 514
  function models, reviewing 519, 520
C/AL Locals
  about 322
  function local identifiers 323
  trigger local variables 323

C/AL routines
  callable functions 513
  creating 512
  management codeunits 520
C/AL Symbol Menu 378-380
C/AL syntax
  about 337
  assignment 337, 338
  code, indenting 357
  expressions 338, 339
  punctuation 337, 338
card pages
  about 28
  creating 35-39
CASE-ELSE statement 401, 402
changes, NAV 2015
  about 8, 9
  application changes 9
  client enhancements 9
  development tools 9, 10
  other areas 10
charts
  about 187
  Chart Control Add-in 188
  chart part 187
  URL 187
CLEARMARKS function 413
Client Add-ins
  about 544
  comments 561, 562
  constructing 545
  using 545
  WDTU Client Add-in 546-561
Client/Server Integrated Development Environment (C/SIDE) 2
cmdlets 570
Codeunit Designer
  accessing 306
coding considerations, system upgradation
  about 577
  good documentation 578
  low-impact coding 578, 579
Common Language Specification (CLS) 258
complex data types
  about 116
  automation 132, 133
  BigText 141

  Binary Large Object (BLOB) 141
  data structure 132
  DateFormula 133-140
  Date/Time data 131
  FieldRef 140
  Globally Unique Identifier (GUID) 141
  Input/Output data types 133
  KeyRef 140
  objects 132
  RecordID 140
  RecordRef 140
  references 140
  TableFilter 141
  TestPage 141
  Transaction Type 141
  Variant 140
components, reports
  C/SIDE Report properties 263, 264
  Data item properties 269, 270
  DataItem triggers 271
  report triggers 267
  Request Page properties 268
  Request Page triggers 268
  Visual Studio Report properties 265-267
compound statement 356
conditional statements
  about 356
  BEGIN-END compound statement 356
  IF-THEN-ELSE statement 356, 357
ConfirmationDialog page 181
CONFIRM function
  about 347, 348
  used, for debugging 529
constant 116
content modifiable tables
  about 108
  System table 108, 109
COPYFILTER function 411
creative report plagiarism and patterns 297
C/SIDE
  about 302
  Object Designer 302
  text objects 318
C/SIDE integrated development environment 11, 12

C/SIDE programming
  about 327
  custom functions 330
  custom functions, creating 331-337
  modifiable functions 329
  non-modifiable functions 328
C/SIDE Report Dataset Designer
    (C/SIDE RD) 258
C/SIDE Test-driven development
  about 539-541
  advantages 539
  automated mode 540
  regression testing 540
Cues
  URL 176
CURRENTDATETIME function
  about 388
  syntax 388
Customer Relationship
    Management (CRM) 7
custom functions
  about 330
  creating 331-334

D

data conversion functions, NAV 2015
  EVALUATE function 395
  FORMAT function 393, 394
  ROUND function 392, 393
data-focused design
  about 564
  data tables, defining 564
  data validation, defining 565
  required data views, defining 564
  reviewing 565
  revising 565
  user data access interface, defining 565
DataItem 260
data types
  about 116, 127
  complex data types 131
  File 132
  fundamental data types 127
  Record 132
  usage 141
DATE2DMY function 390

DATE2DWY function 390
date and time functions, NAV 2015
  about 387
  CALCDATE 391, 392
  CURRENTDATETIME 388
  DATE2DMY 390
  DATE2DWY 390
  DMY2DATE 390, 391
  TODAY 388
  WORKDATE 388, 389
Date/Time data types
  Date 130
  DateTime 131
  Duration 131
  Time 131
deadlock 568
debugging, NAV 2015
  about 526
  DIALOG functions, techniques 529
  NAV 2015 Debugger 531
  objects, exporting into text files 527, 528
DELETEALL function 409
DELETE function 408
design, for system updation
  about 570
  customization project,
      recommendations 570, 571
  deliverables 575
  project, final steps 576
  testing 571
developer's overview, NAV 2015
  about 10
  C/AL programming language 13
  C/SIDE Integrated Development
      Environment 11
  functional terminology 18
  Object Designer tool icons 12
  object types 11
  terms 14
  user interface 19, 20
development projects
  about 563
  data-focused design 563
  double-check option, using 567
  knowledge source 563
  posting processes, defining 566
  supporting processes, defining 566

DIALOG functions
  about 529
  CONFIRM 529
  debugging, with text output 530
  DIALOG 530
  ERROR 531
  MESSAGE 529
  used, for debugging 530
DMY2DATE function 390
Document page
  about 178
  FastTab 179
DWY2DATE function 390, 391

E

efficient solution, designing
  disk I/O 567
  locking aspect 568
  steps 567
enterprise resource planning (ERP) 1
ERROR function
  about 345, 346
  used, for debugging 531
EVALUATE function 395
EXIT function 405
expressions, C/AL syntax
  about 338
  operators 339, 340
eXtensible Markup Language (XML) 50
ExtractionChoice parameter 390

F

Factbox
  function, creating 431-434
FactBox Area, page part
  about 186
  CardParts 186
  ListParts 186
  page, creating 435-438
FastTabs 36
FieldClass property, options
  about 142
  FlowField 143-146
  FlowField, using 149-154
  FlowFilter 146-148

  FlowFilter, using 149-154
  Normal 143
FIELDERROR function 385, 386
field properties
  about 117-123
  AccessByPermission 118
  caption 117
  CaptionML 118
  Data Type 118
  description 118
  Enabled 118
  Field No 117
  name 117
fields
  about 15, 116
  data structure examples 125
  naming 126, 127
  numbering 125, 126
  properties 117-123
  triggers 124
  variable, naming 126, 127
field triggers
  about 124
  OnLookup() 124
  OnValidate() 124
filter controls
  accessing 162
  Development Environment filter access 162
  Role Tailored Client filter access 163, 164
FILTERGROUP function 412
filtering
  about 154, 155, 410
  experimenting with 155-161
  filter controls, accessing 162
filtering, functions
  CLEARMARKS 413
  COPYFILTER 411
  COPYFILTERS 411
  FILTERGROUP 412
  GETFILTER 411
  GETFILTERS 411
  MARK 413
  MARKEDONLY 413
  RESET 414
  SETFILTER 410
FIND functions 352, 353

FIND options
  SQL Server specific 354, 355
FINDSET function 406
fin.stx file 264
FlowField and SumIndexField functions
  about 395
  CALCFIELDS 396
  CALCSUMS 398
  SETAUTOCALCFIELDS 397
FOR-DOWNTO control 401
FORMAT function 393, 394
FOR-TO control 400
fully modifiable tables
  about 95
  Journal table 97, 98
  Ledger table 99, 101
  Master table 96
  Posted Document type 104, 105
  Reference tables (Supplemental) 101, 102
  Register table 103, 104
  Setup table 106
  Template table 98, 99
  Temporary table 107, 108
functional terminology, NAV 2015
  batch 19
  document 19
  Journal 18
  Ledger 18
  posting 19
  register 19
function local identifiers 323
fundamental data types
  about 116, 127
  Date/Time data 130
  numeric data 128
  String data 129

G

General Ledger Entry table 23
GETFILTER function 411
GETFILTERS function 411
GET function 352
Globally Unique Identifier (GUID) 141

Global symbols 379
Graphical User Interface (GUI) 171

H

Help Activating the Debugger 533
Help Configuring NAS Services 533
Help Server component
  customizing 562
Human Resources (HR) management
  about 8
  functions 8

I

Independent Software Vendor (ISV) 17, 169
INIT function 386, 387
input and output functions
  about 405
  DELETE 408
  DELETEALL 409
  FIND 406
  INSERT 407
  MODIFY 407
  MODIFYALL 408
  NEXT 406
Input/Output data types
  about 133
  Dialog 133
  InStream and Outstream 133
INSERT function 407
interactive report, capabilities
  about 290
  Interactive Sorting 291, 292
  Interactive visible/not visible 292
interfaces
  about 542
  Automation Controller 543
  Linked Data Sources 544
internal documentation 380-383
interobject communication
  about 414
  via data 414
  via function parameters 414
  via object calls 415

L

license 14
list pages
  about 28, 177
  creating 31-35
ListPlus page 180
local currency (LCY) 147
local identifiers 322
locking aspect 568

M

Make to Order (MTO) 4
Make to Stock (MTS) 4
management codeunits 520
MARKEDONLY function 413
MARK function 413
MenuSuite Designer 308-311
Mergetool
  URL 528
MESSAGE function
  about 344, 345
  used, for debugging 529
Method Property 247
MODIFYALL function 408
MODIFY function
  about 407
  Rec variable 408
  xRec variable 408
multi-currency system 522
multi-language system 521, 522

N

NAV 2015
  about 1-3, 443
  application design 22
  application tables 22
  Business Intelligence (BI) 6
  C/AL 301
  Card page, creating 35-39
  C/SIDE 301
  data conversion functions 392, 395
  date and time functions 387-391
  debugging 526
  developer overview 52

developing 21
development backups 51
development exercise scenario 21, 22
development projects 563
documentation 51
ERP system 2
filtering functions 410-413
financial management 4
FlowField and SumIndexField
    functions 395-399
formatting functions 392-394
functional areas 2
Help Server component, customizing 562
Human Resources (HR) management 8
input and output functions 405-409
license limits 15
list page, creating 32-35
List Report, creating 41-48
manufacturing 4, 5
object types 49
pages 27, 169
pages, structure 172
process flow 444
process flow control functions 399-405
project management 8
queries 237
references, URL 579
Relationship Management (RM) 7
reporting 6
reports 237-239
reports, creating 272
report designers 249
report types 252
sample data, creating 40
significant changes 8
Supply Chain Management (SCM) 5, 6
system elements 14
tables 57
URL 518
NAV 2015 Debugger
  about 531
  activating 533
  attaching, to session 534
  Break events, creating 535-537
  code modification, while debugging 539
  window 537-539

NAV 2015 Manufacturing
about 4
capacity and supply requirements
planning 5
Product Design (BOMs and Routings) 5
production scheduling
(infinite and finite) 5
NAV Application Server (NAS) 544
NAV data entry
keyboard shortcuts 311
Navigate
about 523-525
modifying for 525, 526
Navigation Pane, Role Center page
about 463-477
Action Designer 465-468
Departments button 478
Home Button 476, 477
other buttons 478
WDTU Role Center Ribbon,
creating 468, 469
NAV processing
interobject communication 414, 415
NAV report
designers 249-251
types 253-255
URL 298
NAV terminology
complex data type 116
constant 116
data element 116
data type 116
fundamental data type 116
variable 116
negative testing 541
New list pages, WDTU project
keys 88
secondary keys 88, 89
SumIndexFields 88, 89
table relations 88-91
NEXT function 406
non-modifiable functions, examples
DATE2DMY 328
GET 328
INSERT 328
MESSAGE 328
STRPOS 328

numeric data types
action 129
BigInteger 129
Boolean 128
Byte 129
Char 129
decimal 128
executionMode 129
integer 128
option 128

O

Object Designer, C/SIDE
about 12, 302-304
Codeunit Designer, accessing 306
MenuSuite Designer 308-311
navigation 311, 312
new object, starting 304
objects, exporting 312, 313
objects, importing 314-317
Page Designer, accessing 304, 305
Query Designer 306
Report Dataset Designer, accessing 306
Table Designer, accessing 304
tool icons 12
XMLport Designer 307
objects
exporting 312, 313
importing 314-317
Table object changes, importing 316, 317
object types, NAV 2015
about 11
codeunit 11, 49
MenuSuite 11, 50
page 11
queries 50
query 11
report 11
table 11
XMLport 11, 50
operators
about 339, 340
Arithmetic operators 341
Boolean operators 342
precedence 343

Range operator 340
Relational operators 342, 343
Scope operator 340

P

page actions
  about 222, 223
  groups 225
  Navigation Pane Button actions 228
  properties 225-228
  summary 229
  types 224, 225
page components
  about 194
  inheritance 201
  Page Preview tool 199-201
  page properties 196-198
  page triggers 195
page controls
  about 206-208
  bound pages 219
  unbound pages 219
page controls, types
  about 209
  container controls 209
  field controls 209-215
  group controls 209-213
Page Designer
  about 189
  accessing 304
  New Page Wizard 190-194
Page Parts, controls
  about 216-218
  page control triggers 218
Page Parts, Role Center page
  about 460
  charts 461, 462
  for user data 463
  not visible 460
pages
  about 27, 170
  Card pages 28
  components 194
  controls 206
  design, guidelines 171
  document page 29

journal/worksheet pages 31
list pages 28
names 188, 189
NAV 2015 page structure 172-175
page part controls 216
parts 185
properties 196-198
standard elements 27
structure 170, 172
types 175
page structure
  Content Area 175
  FactBox Pane 175
  FilterPane 174
  Global Command Bar 174
  Navigation Pane 174
  Ribbon 174
  Search Field 174
  Status Bar 174
pages, types
  Card page 178
  ConfirmationDialog page 181
  Document page 178
  list page 177
  ListPlus page 180
  NavigatePage 182
  Role Center page 175, 176
  Special pages 183
  StandardDialog page 182
  Worksheet (Journal) page 181
plagiarism 230, 231
plan, system upgradation
  about 576
  benefits 577
Playlist Header
  data fields 420
Playlist Line
  data fields 427-431
Playlist Subform page
  creating 423-426
positive testing 541
process flow control functions
  about 399
  BREAK 404
  CASE-ELSE 401, 402
  EXIT 405
  FOR-DOWNTO 401

FOR-TO 400
QUIT 404
REPEAT-UNTIL 399
SKIP 405
WHILE-DO 400
WITH-DO 403, 404
process flow, NAV 2015
  about 444, 445
  data, maintaining 447, 448
  data preparation 446
  data, utilizing 447
  initial setup 444-446
  Journal batch, posting 447
  Journal batch, testing 447
  maintenance 444
  post 444
  transaction entry 444-446
  utilize 444
  validate 444
processing C/AL code
  completed report, testing 372
  finishing 371
  outputting, to Excel 372, 373
Processing-Only reports 297
project management
  budgeting 8
  cost tracking 8
  project accounting 8
  resource requirements 8
  scheduling 8
  usage tracking 8
Public Service Announcements (PSAs) 22

Q

queries
  about 238
  object, building 239-244
  properties 244
  using 238
query component properties
  about 244
  column properties 246, 247
  DataItem properties 245, 246
  query properties 244, 245
Query Designer 306

Query object
  using, URL 244
QUIT function 404

R

RDLC Report
  about 257
  elements 257
  structure 257
read-only table
  about 109
  Virtual table 110
record 15
Rec variable 408
Relationship Management (RM) 7
REPEAT-UNTIL control 399
report body
  laying out 367
  Request Page, defining 370
  saving 368
  testing 368
  user entered report options,
      handling 368-370
report data
  flow 260-262
  overview 258
Report Dataset Designer
  accessing 305
**Report Definition Language Client-side
    (RDLC) 250**
Report Designer
  used, for modifying existing report 285-289
report designers, NAV
  about 249-252
  Report Designer 249
  Visual Studio Report Designer or SQL
      Server Report Builder 249
Report Layout 259, 260
reports
  about 247, 248
  components 257, 263
  creating, in NAV 2015 272
  creative report plagiarism and
      patterns 297, 298
  existing report, modifying with Report
      Designer 288, 289

existing report, modifying with
    Word 288, 289
interactive report, capabilities 290
naming 256
ProcessingOnly reports 297
Request Page 293, 294
Request Page option, adding 294-296
structure 257
reports, building
existing report, modifying with Report
    Designer 285-287
existing report, modifying
    with Word 285-287
inheritance 290
phase 1 273-276
phase 2 276-280
phase 3 280-285
runtime rendering 290
report types, NAV
about 252
document 252, 256
list 252, 256
posting 255, 256
test 255, 256
transaction 254-256
Request Page
about 293, 294
option, adding 294-296
RESET function 414
ReVision
URL 313
Role Center page
about 175, 176, 448
Action Menus 463
Navigation Pane 463
Page Parts 460
structure 449
System Part 459
URL 176
Role Center, structure
about 449-451
activities page 453
Cue Group Actions 458
Cue Groups 454
Cues 454
Cue source table 455-457

role oriented 19
Role Tailored Client (RTC) 18
ROUND function 393

S

sample application
activity-tracking tables, adding 84, 85
enhancing 75
InitValue property, assigning 83
Standard table, modifying 92, 93
Table Relation Property, assigning 80-82
tables, creating 75-80
tables, modifying 75-80
version list documentation 93, 94
WDTU project, New list pages 88
WDTU project, new tables 85-88
Server Report Builder (SSRB) 249
Service Management (SM) 7
Special pages
about 183
Departments page 184
SQL Joins methods
Cross Join 239
Full Outer 239
Inner 239
Left Outer Join 239
Right Outer Join 239
SQLJoinType Property 246
SQL Server Report Builder (SSRB) 258, 377
StandardDialog page 182
statistical analysis fields, Radio Show
Advertising Revenue (Field 120) 149
Audience Share (Field 110) 149
Average Listeners (Field 100) 149
Date Filter (Field 1090) 149
Royalty Cost (Field 130) 149
storage variables
about 323
arrays 325
initialization 326
system-defined variables 327
temporary tables 323, 324
String data types
Code 129
Text 129

STRMENU function 349
Strong Key Name (SNK) 548
SumIndex Fields 564
Supply Chain Management (SCM)
  about 5
  Inventory Management 5
  purchasing 5
  sales order processing and pricing 5
  warehouse management 5
Symbol table 379
system, upgrading
  about 569
  coding considerations 577
  plan 576
  supporting materials 579

T

table definition 58
Table Designer
  accessing 304
table fields
  modifying 417-419
tables
  about 58, 59
  components 59
  Field Groups 71-75
  field validation, adding 358-363
  keys 67-69
  naming 60
  numbering 61
  properties 61-66
  SumIndexField Technology (SIFT) 70, 71
  types 95
tables, types
  content modifiable tables 108
  fully modifiable tables 95
  read-only table 109
temporary tables, storage variables 323
testability 542
TESTFIELD function
  about 384
  advantages 384
testing
  about 571
  database approaches 572

in production 572, 573
potential problems 573, 574
techniques 574, 575
testing database
  using 573, 574
TestIsolation property 540
text objects, C/SIDE
  about 318
  C/AL naming conventions 320, 321
  compiling 319, 320
  data definitions, changing 319
  practices 318, 319
  saving 319, 320
TIME function
  syntax 388
TODAY function
  syntax 388
trigger
  about 16
  documentation 16
  functions 16
  local variables 323

U

UI Elements Removal Tool 474
unbound pages 219
Uniform Resource Name (URN) 483
Universal Naming Convention (UNC) 132
User Interface (UI) 474

V

VALIDATE function 387
validation functions, C/AL
  about 384
  FIELDERROR 385, 386
  INIT 386, 387
  TESTFIELD 384
  VALIDATE 387
validation logic
  adding, to WDTU application 420-422
variables, C/SIDE
  about 322
  C/AL Globals 322
  C/AL Locals 322
  storage variables, working 323, 324

Visual Studio
    URL 43
Visual Studio Report Designer
        (VSRD) 286, 377

W

W3C
    URL 480
WDTU application, enhancing
    about 416
    FactBox page, creating 435-438
    function, creating for Factbox 431-434
    Playlist Subform page, creating 423-426
    table fields, modifying 417-419
    validation logic, adding 420-422
WDTU page enhancement 202-206, 219-221
WDTU Role Center Ribbon
    Action Groups 472, 473
    configuration/personalization 473-475
    creating 468, 469
    Promoted Actions Categories 470-472
web services
    about 493
    benefits 493, 494
    enabling 497
    exposing 495, 496
    methods 495
    published object, determining 497-499
    publishing 496
    WDTU integration, example 500-506
Which parameter option 354
WHILE-DO control 400
wildcards 127
WITH-DO statement 403, 404
WORKDATE function 388, 389
Working Storage 258
Worksheet (Journal) page 181

X

XMLport components
    attribute 490
    data lines 485
    Element data 490
    line properties 486
    line triggers 491, 492
    properties 481-484
    Request Page 493
    triggers 485
XMLport Designer 307
XMLport line properties
    about 486
    SourceType as Field 490
    SourceType as Table 488, 489
    SourceType as Text 487
XMLport line triggers
    about 491, 492
    DataType as Field 493
    DataType as Table 492
    DataType as Text 492
XMLports
    about 479, 480
    Attribute-specific property 491
    components 480
    Element-specific properties 490
    URL 495
xRec variable 408

Thank you for buying
Programming Microsoft Dynamics™ NAV 2015

About Packt Publishing

Packt, pronounced 'packed', published its first book, *Mastering phpMyAdmin for Effective MySQL Management*, in April 2004, and subsequently continued to specialize in publishing highly focused books on specific technologies and solutions.

Our books and publications share the experiences of your fellow IT professionals in adapting and customizing today's systems, applications, and frameworks. Our solution-based books give you the knowledge and power to customize the software and technologies you're using to get the job done. Packt books are more specific and less general than the IT books you have seen in the past. Our unique business model allows us to bring you more focused information, giving you more of what you need to know, and less of what you don't.

Packt is a modern yet unique publishing company that focuses on producing quality, cutting-edge books for communities of developers, administrators, and newbies alike. For more information, please visit our website at www.packtpub.com.

About Packt Enterprise

In 2010, Packt launched two new brands, Packt Enterprise and Packt Open Source, in order to continue its focus on specialization. This book is part of the Packt Enterprise brand, home to books published on enterprise software – software created by major vendors, including (but not limited to) IBM, Microsoft, and Oracle, often for use in other corporations. Its titles will offer information relevant to a range of users of this software, including administrators, developers, architects, and end users.

Writing for Packt

We welcome all inquiries from people who are interested in authoring. Book proposals should be sent to author@packtpub.com. If your book idea is still at an early stage and you would like to discuss it first before writing a formal book proposal, then please contact us; one of our commissioning editors will get in touch with you.

We're not just looking for published authors; if you have strong technical skills but no writing experience, our experienced editors can help you develop a writing career, or simply get some additional reward for your expertise.

Microsoft Dynamics NAV 2009 Programming Cookbook

ISBN: 978-1-84968-094-3   Paperback: 356 pages

Over 110 simple but incredibly effective recipes for taking control of Microsoft Dynamics NAV 2009

1. Write NAV programs to do everything from finding data in a table to integration with an instant messenger client.

2. Develop your own .NET code to perform tasks that NAV cannot handle on its own.

3. Work with SQL Server to create better integration between NAV and other systems.

4. Learn to use the new features of the NAV 2009 Role Tailored Client.

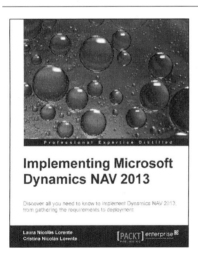

Implementing Microsoft Dynamics NAV 2013

ISBN: 978-1-84968-602-0   Paperback: 554 pages

Discover all you need to know to implement Dynamics NAV 2013, from gathering the requirements to deployment

1. Successfully handle your first Dynamics NAV 2013 implementation.

2. Explore the new features that will help you provide more value to your customers.

3. Full of illustrations and diagrams with clear step-by-step instructions and real-world tips extracted from years of experience.

Please check **www.PacktPub.com** for information on our titles

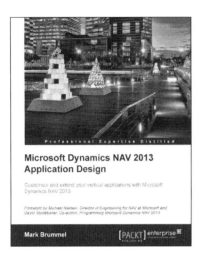

Microsoft Dynamics NAV 2013
Application Design

Customize and extend your vertical applications with Microsoft
Dynamics NAV 2013

Foreword by Michael Nielsen, Director of Engineering for NAV at Microsoft and
David Studebaker, Co-author, Programming Microsoft Dynamics NAV 2013

Mark Brummel   [PACKT] enterprise ✕
PUBLISHING

Microsoft Dynamics NAV 2013 Application Design

ISBN: 978-1-78217-036-5   Paperback: 504 pages

Customize and extend your vertical applications with
Microsoft Dynamics NAV 2013

1. Set up your application for a number of vertical
    industries and scenarios.

2. Get acquainted with Dynamics NAV's data
    model and transaction schema with the help
    of highly efficient design patterns.

3. Consists of two completely designed and
    explained vertical solutions, including
    application objects.

Microsoft Dynamics
AX 2012 R2 Services

Harness the power of Microsoft Dynamics AX 2012 R2 to create
and use your own services effectively

Klaas Deforche   Kenny Saelen   [PACKT] enterprise ✕
PUBLISHING

Microsoft Dynamics AX 2012 R2 Services

ISBN: 978-1-78217-672-5   Paperback: 264 pages

Harness the power of Microsoft Dynamics AX 2012
R2 to create and use your own services effectively

1. Learn about the Dynamics AX 2012 service
    architecture.

2. Create your own services using wizards
    or X++ code.

3. Deploy your services in a variety of ways using
    High Availability.

Please check **www.PacktPub.com** for information on our titles

Printed in Great Britain
by Amazon.co.uk, Ltd.,
Marston Gate.